The
SECRET
of GOLF

The SECRET *of* GOLF

A Century of Groundbreaking, Innovative,
and Occasionally Outlandish Ways to Master
the World's Most Vexing Game

by George Peper
with Mary Tiegreen

An Arran House Press Book
WORKMAN PUBLISHING • NEW YORK

Library of Congress Cataloging-in-Publication Data is available.

ISBN-13: 978-0-7611-3613-2; ISBN-10: 0-7611-3613-4 (paper)
ISBN-13: 978-0-7611-3830-3; ISBN-10: 0-7611-3830-7 (HC)

Cover design by Paul Hanson
Book design by Mary Tiegreen

Workman books are available at special discounts when purchased in bulk for premiums and sales promotions as well as for fund-raising or educational use. Special editions or book excerpts can also be created to specification. For details, contact the Special Sales Director at the address below.

Workman Publishing Company, Inc.
708 Broadway
New York, NY 10003-9555
www.workman.com

Printed in the United States of America

First printing April 2005
10 9 8 7 6 5 4 3 2 1

CONTENTS

INTRODUCTION

I began my golf life as a latchkey child—and forty years later, not much has changed. When I find myself on a practice range with time to kill, I go through the same perverse ritual I observed as a teenager. Having warmed up with a few wedge shots, I move straight to my favorite club, the 6-iron, and start fiddling around. I play the ball way back in my stance—or way up. I lower my right shoulder—or loosen my left-hand grip pressure. I rake the club back to the inside, or pause at the top of my swing, or exhale as I move to impact. Waiting for something to click.

Inevitably, in the course of this pathetic trial and error, I hit a shot of angelic purity. "Hmm," I wonder. "Was that a random occurrence, or could this be it? Could that little hip bump I made at the start of the downswing be the secret?"

I try the move again. If it works, I go into full test mode—five balls. If at least three of the ensuing shots are positive, I stop practicing and head directly to the first tee. I've found my latchkey for the day—the key I will latch onto in the hope it will transform me into a scratch player. Such keys rarely last long—my experience is anywhere from two holes to two weeks. Johnny Miller, a kindred latcher, calls them "wood" keys for their propensity to Work Only One Day. Still I latch, perhaps now

(as a senior golfer) more desperately than ever. At least I'm consoled by the notion that the motto of the town where I now live (St. Andrews, Scotland) is *Dum spiro, spero,* which means "As I breathe, I hope."

Hope springs eternal for all serious golfers—and that's what this book, *The Secret of Golf,* is about. The truth, of course, is that the game of golf cannot be mastered; it can only be wrestled into submission occasionally. The good news, however, is that there are numerous wrestling methods—several secrets, if you will—that will give you a large if limited number of legitimate ways to play the game extremely well.

Interestingly, some of them are diametrically opposed to others. During the twenty-five years I was Editor-in-Chief of *GOLF Magazine,* I received hundreds of letters that went something like this: "How dare you call yourself an editor when, on page 37 of your current issue, you have a tip that says 'keep the left arm straight,' and on page 98 of the same issue, an article says 'let the left elbow bend'? If

> **The truth, of course, is that the game of golf cannot be mastered; it can only be wrestled into submission occasionally.**

you can't make up your mind, I'll get my instruction elsewhere. Cancel my subscription immediately."

I answered each of those readers the same way: "The coexistence of those two tips was not a mistake. Both theories work—one might work for you, the other for me." *GOLF Magazine,* I explained, was a forum for all reasonable ideas on how to play the game. Different strokes for different folks.

What follows, therefore, is a book with forty-seven different strokes, an entire century—from Harry Vardon in 1905 to the present—of innovating, groundbreaking (and occasionally conflicting) advice on how to play the world's most vexing game. All the great teachers are here—Percy Boomer, Ernest Jones, Alex Morrison, John Jacobs, Bob Toski—along with the most insightful of the game's star players, including Tommy Armour, Henry Cotton, and Ben Hogan.

It will come as a surprise to many, however, that neither Bobby Jones nor Jack Nicklaus is represented here, despite the fact that they are two of the most contemplative players (and most prolific authors) the game has produced. The brutal truth is, while each of them gave us a substantial amount of solid advice, neither had anything earthshakingly new to say. This may be because they both came from privileged families and had the benefit of private instruction. They were taught just about everything they knew—Jones by Stewart Maiden, Nicklaus by Jack Grout—while scrappers like Hogan dug it out of the dirt.

But the true heroes of this book are the dozens of unsung innovators—the pioneers, inventors, evangelists, scientists, and savants—who spent their lifetimes thinking about and working toward a better way to play, then on one glorious day experienced a genuine eureka moment. I'm referring to the likes of Paul Bertholy and his swing pipe, J. Douglas Edgar and his gate to golf, John Novosel and his discovery of tour tempo, David Lee's gravity golf, and the inscrutable Count Yogi, exhorting us to hit up on the ball with elegance and grace.

You can't have the secret of golf—you can only borrow it. But forty seven of the finest lenders are on the pages that follow.

George Peper
St. Andrews, Scotland

*To all those who have found—
and shared—their secrets of
golf, and all those who
continue the quest*

CHAPTER 1

A PUGILISTIC APPROACH

"There are at least six people who want to be taught golf for every one who wants to learn."

When you took a lesson from Tommy Armour, you did things his way. One morning his pupil was a rampantly incompetent matron from Chicago's Medinah Country Club, where Armour summered during the 1930s. It was just the two of them on the practice tee. Armour, as was his custom, sat in a lawn chair beside his student.

She had a 5-iron in her hands and he had a shotgun in his. As she flailed fruitlessly at ball after ball, Armour remained impassive, amusing himself by taking occasional pot shots at the squirrels scurrying amid a stand of oaks at the end of the range. At length the lady became as frustrated by the pedagogical neglect as by her own ineptitude.

"I think you should be concentrating more on me," she said.

Armour gave her a long appraising look, then slowly turned so that the gun barrel pointed straight at her sternum. "Don't tempt me," he said.

A Scotsman by birth, Tommy Armour embodied the greatest combination of playing and teaching talent the game has ever seen. He was a fine all-around athlete while at Edinburgh University but did not make his mark as a golfer until after World War I, when he served first as a machine gunner and later as an officer with the Tank Corps. During one battle, a mustard gas explosion left him blinded and with metal plates in his head and left

THE SECRET:

Hit the heck out of the ball with your right hand.

arm. After a six-month convalescence he regained the sight in his right eye, and took up golf as a form of extended therapy.

The recreation became an addiction. With the benefit of lessons from Harry Vardon, James Braid, and J. H. Taylor, among others, Armour rose to become one of the finest amateurs on either side of the Atlantic. In 1924 he turned professional, and three years later won the U.S. Open, defeating Harry Cooper in an eighteen-hole playoff at Oakmont.

Armour (center) with two of his contemporaries on tour, Gene Sarazen and Walter Hagen.

He went on to win every important title of the day, including the 1930 PGA Championship and the 1931 British Open.

Armour was a slender man, not powerfully built, but he had enormous hands, described by sportswriter Grantland Rice as "two stalks of bananas." He once bested prizefighter Jack Dempsey in a test of hand strength that involved holding billiard cues out from the body by grasping them at the tip. Dempsey was in his prime and considered to have the strongest hands on the planet, but Armour's proved almost twice as powerful.

His whipcord wrist action, combined with superb natural timing, gave Armour a long, raking draw with phenomenal accuracy.

He remains one of the most accurate iron players the game has ever seen. Ironically, however, it was also his hands that ended his career. Armour is credited with coining the term "yips." "Once you've had 'em, you've got 'em," he said of that insidious crisis of confidence that converts a smooth putting stroke into a convulsive flinch. At one point he threw his entire stash of putters into Scotland's Firth of Forth.

So as Armour's playing career ended—barely ten years after it had begun—he became a full-time teacher of the game. He'd always been a keen student of the swing and had arrived at a set of principles that he could communicate with equal clarity to the hapless duffer and the superstar. As early as 1926, Bobby Jones had sought Armour's advice and had gone on to win the U.S. and British Opens that year.

Armour taught at some of America's most prestigious clubs. In addition to Medinah, he spent time at Congressional (MD), Tam O'Shanter (MI), and Winged Foot (NY). But he is best known for his winter gig at the posh Boca Raton Club near Palm Beach. It was there that he established himself as golf's first teaching guru. A half-hour lesson with Tommy Armour—that's as long as he would teach anyone—went for $50 (a sizable sum during the Depression) and he was typically booked solid for six months in advance, his list of pupils ranging from Lawson Little to Babe Zaharias to Richard Nixon.

> He said little to his students and allowed them to hit no more than 20 balls.

He worked only mornings, sitting under a large flowered umbrella. Beside him was a table and on that table was always an adult beverage, or several. He did his drinking as a sort of three-part ritual, beginning with a concoction called a gin buck—a stiff shot of gin topped with ginger ale and a slice of lime or lemon. After a couple of those, he went to a tall scotch and soda, and finally, to clear things out a bit, a Bromo-Seltzer. At the end of a lesson, the table was so crowded with tall glasses that, in the words of golf writer Herb Graffis, "it looked as if at any moment Armour might launch into a pipe-organ recital."

He said little to his students, and allowed them to hit no more than 20 balls. "I won't tell you what you're doing wrong," he said, "because that would take all day. Instead, I'll show you the right things to do."

Armour wrote three books. The first of them—*How to Play Your Best Golf All the Time*—was an instant success when it appeared in 1953, rocketing all the way to the number-one spot on the nonfiction bestseller list, the first sports book to do so. It sold more than 400,000 copies that year alone and remains in print more than half a century later. Like Armour, the book is terse, with an in-your-face directness—160 pages of large type, with numerous illustrations and the key passages helpfully highlighted in red ink.

Perhaps because of his own physical assets, Armour emphasized the role of the hands, hammering at the importance of a sound grip. However, in a move that at the time was deemed heterodoxy, he advocated whacking the ball as hard as possible with the right hand. Until then, golf in America had been taught and played as a two-handed game, with the Hogan/Nelson/Snead triumvirate leading the way. Armour showed the world how to slug a ball like Dempsey—but more powerfully.

ARMOUR'S SECRET

Innumerable times I've had golfers come to me complaining about some fault that is ruining their swings.

Generally, in such cases I find that the cause of the trouble is an incorrect grip which makes it utterly impossible to get any element of the swing correct. The situations have a parallel in your own automobile. If the transmission isn't right, everything else can be O.K., but the car won't go. When you haven't got the connection (the hands) functioning properly, your arms, elbows, shoulders, body, legs, and feet can't work in the correct manner. **The basic factor in all good golf is the grip. Get it right, and all other progress follows.** To hold the club properly,

let the shaft lie where the fingers join the palm of the left hand. The last three fingers of the left hand are closed snugly to the grip.

A good tip is to keep the little finger of the left hand from being loosened; then the next two fingers will stay firm.

The left thumb is placed down the right side of the grip. Where a mistake in the left-hand grip frequently is made is in having the shaft lie from the root of the forefinger diagonally across the palm, about to the heel of the hand. After the club is placed at the roots of the fingers of the left hand, and the fingers closed snugly against the

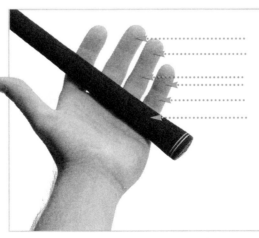

When the fingers of left hand are closed properly to the grip, these are the firm points of pressure you feel.

grip, the grip is pressed up slightly toward the heel of the hand, although it continues to lie in its original position against the left forefinger. Therefore, some make the mistake of believing that the proper placement at the beginning is diagonally across the palm. What you always should do with the left hand grip is to keep it just as near to the roots of the fingers as possible.

The position of the left hand on the shaft definitely must be slightly over to the right of the shaft so the V of the thumb and forefinger points to the right shoulder. That's old advice, but still the best.

Your right hand should be put on the grip with the club lying in the channel formed when the fingers are bent, and with your left thumb fitting snugly under your right thumb.

The right little finger goes over the forefinger of your left hand, or curls around the exposed knuckle of the left forefinger. It doesn't make any difference which of these two positions the right little finger takes— whichever one you like.

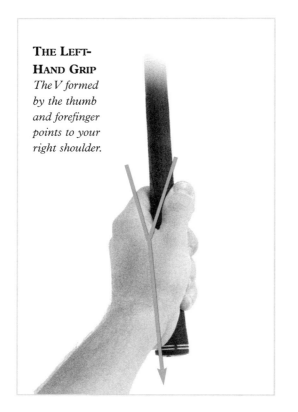

THE LEFT-HAND GRIP
The V formed by the thumb and forefinger points to your right shoulder.

THE GRIP WITH BOTH HANDS
The right-hand V also points to your right shoulder. The right forefinger is against the side of the shaft, in the strongest position for the hit.

The right hand is placed slightly to the right of the top of the shaft. The right thumb is in a natural position to the left of the shaft. It is important that the right thumb and forefinger be as close as comfortably possible because these two parts of the right hand are a vital combination in a grip for power. The right thumb-forefinger combination enables you to whip the club through with all possible speed. The club is held in the right hand with about half the pressure of the left-hand grip.

Keep both hands fitted compactly together. They must coordinate the essential factors of left-hand control and right-hand power, and unless they're working closely, your hand action will be faulty.

What you are seeking and must have in your grip is the utmost effectiveness in power and control. You need to keep the face of the club in correct alignment with the path of the swing at all times, until the ball has left the clubhead.

The most serious and most frequent deviation of the clubface from its proper position occurs at the top of

The correct left-hand grip at the top of the swing. Note how last three fingers make the firm coupling with the club. This is absolutely essential and must not be relaxed.

Here is the most serious frequent error at the top of the swing—loosening the left-hand grip. That compels you to make the mistake of starting to hit from the top of the swing, and to hit with the body instead of the hands. Then anything can happen—slicing, hooking, topping, hitting under the ball, or missing it altogether.

the swing. What very few golfers—outside of the experts—understand is the difference between holding the club tight and not letting it get loose at the top of the swing. When I see a player hold the club tightly at address, I know that the odds are about ninety to one that the firm grip of the last three fingers of his left hand is going to open at the top of the swing, and he'll never be able to regain control of the club for his downswing.

The big idea—the essential one— is to hold the club at address with easy security rather than grim, tightening intensity. You can keep that kind of hold on the club throughout the swing. The last three fingers of the left hand hold the club firmly.

> **The correct grip is the greatest single detail towards achieving direction and distance of the shot.**

The right-hand grip is relaxed, and not at all tight throughout the backswing and the early stage of the downswing. When your right-hand grip does get firmer, just before and at the moment of impact, the tightening action will be spontaneous and precisely timed without conscious effort. The action must take place with such lighting speed that there is no possibility of deliberate application of the muscular strength that's available in the hands.

Golf is a game to be played with two hands. Your left guides the club and keeps the face in the desired posi-tion for the hit, and the power pours through the coupling of the right hand and the club. Your hands must be together and work together to get the utmost leverage, balance, precision, and speed that can be applied.

Always have your mind made up that you are going to whip your right hand into the shot. That is a "must." Anytime you hear an argument advanced against the right hand whipping into the shot, you may be sure that the objection is fallacious.

Something about the right hand that must have your thought and practice is having that part of the right forefinger, which is nearest the palm, functioning positively in the hitting action. When the right-hand grip lies firmly between the forefinger and the thumb, it is in perfect position for a fast, firm, lashing action. The lashing action springs from the joint functioning of the forefinger and thumb.

When your left hand retains control of the club as it should, you will not suffer the usual error of the higher handicap player. This is the mistake of wasting the hand action too soon. Usually this mistake is made by straightening the wrists almost immediately after the downswing starts. Then, the ball is contacted by a stiff-arm push instead of with a vigorous whipping action.

You probably won't be able to observe in the fast action of the experts' play how their hands are over the ball or slightly past

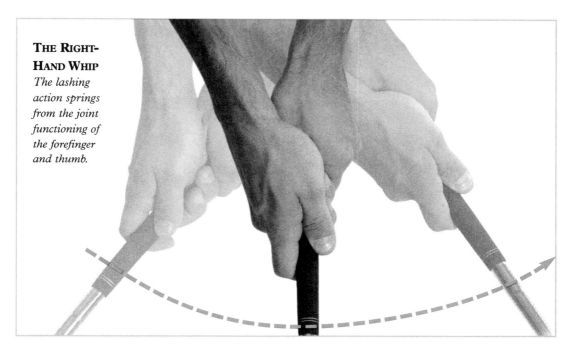

THE RIGHT-HAND WHIP
The lashing action springs from the joint functioning of the forefinger and thumb.

it before their wrists start to uncock. But, when you look at photographs of the stars in action, you will see how they get the right-hand whip precisely at the most effective time—and much later than the average player does.

When the grip is correct, there isn't an inclination to let the right hand whip in too soon. What causes the right hand to throw from the top of the swing is that the left hand is loose, and the right hand tries to take over the function of control as well as power. Therefore, the right hand is in frantic action in a spontaneous effort to do the whole job.

By becoming acutely conscious of the necessity of a right-hand whip when the club

is getting close to the ball, you will be pleasantly surprised at how your shoulders, hips, and footwork are naturally disposed to coordinate with the hand action.

The correct grip, which is the governing component of hand action, is certainly the greatest single detail towards achieving direction and distance of the golf shot. When you get your grip right, you have automatically eliminated many of the bothersome details which may confuse you and prevent proper execution of shots.

FROM *HOW TO PLAY YOUR BEST GOLF ALL THE TIME* BY TOMMY ARMOUR

CHAPTER 2

DICK AULTMAN

1960s RADICALISM

"Eventually, most serious golfers discover The Secret—
at least a half-dozen times each summer."

The 1960s were a time of upheaval in America, an era marked by widespread racial unrest, an unpopular war in Vietnam, and the assassinations of John F. Kennedy, Robert Kennedy, and Martin Luther King, Jr. The Woodstock Generation led a counterculture revolution in music, art, and fashion while a tide of rebellion swept through the nation's universities.

It was the most turbulent decade of the twentieth century, a time when everything was questioned and challenged, from religion to politics to sexual orientation. Nothing was sacred—not even golf instruction. In fact, it was the game's leading publication, *Golf Digest*—long a bastion of traditionalism—that led the insurgency, by endorsing something called the square-to-square golf swing.

For decades, conventional wisdom had held that golf was a right-sided game, that the proper swing was a sort of throwing action of the club through the ball. This was essentially the way the first golfers played, using their hands, arms, and wrists to wield flexible-shafted hickory clubs for the low-trajectory wind-boring shots that the early British links demanded.

The square-to-square merchants, led by noted instructor Jim Flick, claimed that the major advancements in golf equipment—chiefly the advent of the steel shaft—demanded a new and better method, namely a pulling action of the left side, led by the muscles of the legs and back, that produced the longer and higher-flying shots required by the hefty, hazard-strewn courses of modern America.

The older method may have seemed more natural, especially to those who had played throwing games as youths, but the square-to-squarers argued that "the idea of pulling 10–15 pounds of hand and arm with 150 pounds of body is more logical than pushing 150 pounds of body with 10–15 pounds of hand and arm."

At the 1968 Masters, Flick met with *Golf Digest*'s editors and put together an article that became the first of a lengthy series on the square-to-square method. The new swing captured the attention of not only readers but of PGA professionals across America who began teaching its principles. Virtually overnight, square-to-square inveigled thousands of golfers. Dick Aultman, a left-handed three-handicapper who was then the Editor of *Golf Digest,* spent an entire summer revamping his own game—without much success—until a three-hour session with Jim Flick brought him to full enlightenment. "I discovered more about the golf swing in that period than at any other session in my life," he said. "But, what's more, I saw how the square-to-square swing could be put on paper in a way that would be applicable to the average golfer and easy for him to grasp. It was one of the most exciting things that had happened to me in my golf-writing life."

The Square-to-Square Golf Swing: The Model Method for the Modern Player appeared under Aultman's byline in 1971 and swiftly became one of the largest-selling instruction books in history while also establishing *Golf Digest* as a leading force in the teaching of the game. The Golf Digest Golf Schools appeared soon thereafter, with Flick as their leader and square-to-square as their foundation.

THE SECRET:

Keep your left hand, wrist, and forearm in a straight line throughout the swing.

Over time, however, the evidence showed that square-to-square hampered more people than it helped. The reason: It was a highly unnatural method that called for radical change—actually retraining the weaker muscles of the left side to dominate the stronger muscles of the right. As such, it required hours of practice and months of patience. Students usually got worse before they got better, and some never made it back to square one. Still, even today the method retains its dedicated devotees, and the logic of its teachings cannot be denied.

In putting together *The Square-to-Square Golf Swing,* Aultman showed a fine editor's sensitivity, using simple, straightforward language—aided by illustrations by the incomparable Anthony Ravielli—to make a convincing case for an ill-fated idea. The excerpt is from the book's most important chapter, on the backswing.

A U L T M A N ' S   S E C R E T

Those who teach the Square-to-Square Method stress over and over to their pupils that the proper backswing will not feel natural while they are learning the Method. The reason why this correct backswing feels unnatural is simply because the normally weaker left side must dominate the normally stronger right side from waggle through impact.

Bear in mind, however, that as the Square-to-Square Method becomes more natural through practice—and as you begin to strengthen the "new" muscles of your left side (or the right side for left-handers)—you will gradually regain your old rhythm as well as new, and far superior, shot-making skill. The more you strengthen your left side and "teach" it to dominate your right side, the more you will improve.

A very important move of the swing, according to those who teach the Square-to-Square Method, occurs at the very start of the backswing. This is the move that establishes the straight-line, "square" relationship between the back of the left hand, wrist, and lower forearm.

The more you strengthen your left side and "teach" it to dominate your right side, the more you will improve.

Those who teach the Method describe this vital, first move of the backswing as a *slight* "curling under" of the last three fingers of the left hand. Nothing more. There is no turning of the whole arm involved in this initial move. Only the last three fingers "curl under." This curling under occurs at the very start of the backswing, just as the clubhead moves back from the ball.

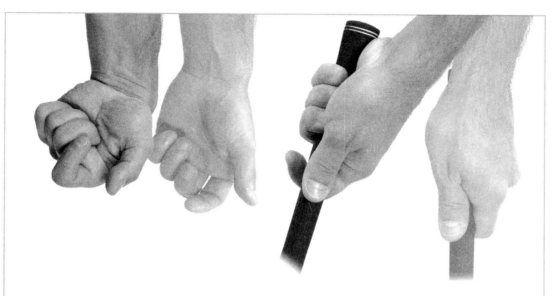

CURLING UNDER

A slight "curling under" with the last three fingers of the left hand while the clubhead moves straight back from the ball not only helps establish left-side dominance, but also puts the back of the left hand, wrist, and lower forearm into the vital straight-line, "square" impact position at a time when the golfer has maximum control of his or her swing. Once this square position is established, the player must merely maintain it through impact to assure that the clubface will be square to the target line when it strikes the ball. The curling-under, accentuated here and shown from two different perspectives, should be slight—merely enough to establish straight-line position.

To get an idea of how this move looks and feels, merely put your left hand out in front of you in the same position it would be in if you were gripping a golf club. Hold this imaginary club very gently.

Now squeeze the "club" with the last three fingers. As you squeeze you will notice that these fingers want to "curl under." Let them. As you squeeze and as these fingers curl under, you will gradually see less and less of the back of your hand. *Continue the curling under only until the back of your hand and the back of your forearm form a straight line.*

Practice this move a few times until the curling under and squeezing of the last three fingers feels natural. You should feel a bunching of muscles of the *underside* of your forearm.

SQUARE-TO-SQUARE TAKEAWAY

As you "curl under" with the last three fingers of your left hand, you should push the clubhead straight back from the ball with left arm extending fully.

Taking the clubhead straight back forces your left shoulder to start turning under on a plane that will help give you a sufficiently upright swing. If clubhead moves inside target line too soon, swing plane probably will become too flat. If you curl under properly, and just enough to establish a straight-line relationship between the back of your left hand, wrist, and lower forearm, your clubface will continue to look down the target line, with no indication that its toe is moving back ahead of its heel.

"Working" the Club Up

If you have worked the club up by turning your shoulders on a tilted plane, the clubshaft should be about vertical and your left arm should be straight at the moment when your hands have reached shoulder height. Working the club up in this manner helps assure that your left side remains in control and that you are fully stretching the big muscles of your back and legs. If you raise the club by merely lifting your hands, without much shoulder-turning, your left arm will bend and your clubshaft will move past vertical by the time your hands reach shoulder height. You will fail to create sufficient tension in your back and leg muscles.

Incorrect

A U L T M A N ' S   S E C R E T

SQUARE POSITION AT TOP OF SWING

If the golfer has worked the club up on a sufficiently upright plane, the straight-line relationship between the back of the left hand, wrist, and lower forearm indicates that he is in the "square position" at the top of his swing. No further manipulation of the club will be needed to return it to a square impact position so long as the left side remains in control. When the back of the left wrist bends outward (convex) or cups inward (concave), the golfer must compensate on the downswing to avoid striking the ball with closed or open clubface.

At the beginning of your actual swing, as you curl under on your takeaway, you should move the clubhead along a path straight back from the ball. Your left arm should be extending fully. If your right hand and right side are sufficiently subordinate and relaxed, you will feel that your left hand and arm are pushing the clubhead back and out along that portion of the target line that continues behind the ball.

If you have curled under properly, your clubface should continue to look at the target—square to the target line—as long as it is moving along that line. There should be no indication that the toe of the clubhead is moving back before the heel. If the toe leads the way back, you have fanned open the clubface. If you find that this is occurring, you must further emphasize curling under, until it seems that the heel of the club is

It is the turning of the shoulders on a *tilted* plane that forces the clubhead to begin moving inside the line *and* upward. The club must not be lifted by the hands and arms independently of the shoulder turn.

leading the toe going back.

The clubhead should move straight back from the ball until it passes the right foot, and then gradually begin to move inside the target line. Taking the club straight back for this distance serves two vital purposes. First, it assures that you achieve full extension of your left arm. This extension is vital if the left side is to dominate the swing. Should the left arm bend, the right hand will take over control of the club. Second, moving the clubhead straight back for a goodly distance encourages the shoulders to tilt on a sufficiently upright plane. If the clubhead is allowed to move inside the target line and around the body at this stage, the shoulders will turn on too level a plane.

It is the turning of the shoulders on a *tilted* plane that forces the clubhead to begin moving inside the line *and* upward. If the shoulders turned on a level plane, one with no tilt, the clubhead would move inside, around the body, but it would not move upward. It is the *tilting* of the shoulders—lowering of the left shoulder and the resultant raising of the right—that causes the clubhead to move upward. Those instructors who teach the Square-to-Square Method insist that during the backswing the club must be "worked" up by the left shoulder's moving down and under the golfer's chin. The club must not, they stress, be lifted by the hands and arms independently of the shoulder turn. When the club is lifted, the right hand and arm will automatically do much of the lifting. This puts the normally stronger right hand and arm back in control and forces the club to move out of proper plane.

At the top of your backswing your left wrist should be firm and straight, forming the continuous line between the back of your left hand and lower forearm. Again, this is the "square" position that you must maintain throughout your swing until the ball is well on its way. Check yourself in the mirror to see that you have maintained this relationship.

FROM *THE SQUARE-TO-SQUARE GOLF SWING: THE MODEL METHOD FOR THE MODERN PLAYER* BY DICK AULTMAN

AULTMAN'S SECRET

CHAPTER 3

JIMMY BALLARD

THE KING OF CONNECTION

*"I won't guarantee you'll win the club championship
in two years, but I will give you four to one that,
in the near future, your opponents will get tired
of paying your green fees and bar bills."*

It all started with Babe Ruth and a hankie. During batting practice, the New York Yankees' famed Sultan of Swat used to place a handkerchief under his left arm as a way of insuring he kept the arm tight to his body, a move he felt contributed to his prodigious power. If the handkerchief fell to the ground, it meant he'd lost connection with this body, and thereby diminished the thrust of his swing.

Ruth's road-trip roommate during much of his heyday was a fellow named Sam Byrd, an outstanding athlete who played six years as a Yankee outfielder and two with the Cincinnati Reds before an injury forced him to leave professional baseball. Byrd turned to professional golf and found his true success, winning four tournaments, finishing third in two Masters, and coming in second to Byron Nelson in the 1945 PGA.

After his Tour years, Byrd owned and operated a par-three course and driving range in Birmingham, Alabama, where he began to teach the golf swing as nothing more than a baseball swing on a more upright plane. A good golfer, said Byrd, kept that left arm connected to his body, just as the Babe did. He also braced his right leg on the backswing, allowed his head to shift a bit as the body coiled, and then "fired" his right side into the ball, in the same manner as every major leaguer.

In 1960 Byrd hired Jimmy Ballard, then seventeen and a state amateur junior champ, as his teaching assistant. Byrd and Ballard would spend nearly two decades together and in the process turn out a stream of national, state, and local women's and junior champions. Ballard was brash and outspoken, and more than once he clashed with the "swing the arms" establishment of the time, but he had a way of communicating to his students with precision and simplicity, and his reputation spread quickly.

Eventually, he set up his own shop at the Pine Harbor Golf and Country Club, close to Pell City, Alabama. By the late 1970s, the who's who of professional golf had begun to find their way to that rural corner of Alabama. Ballard worked on the swings of Mac McLendon, J. C. Snead, Leonard Thompson, Dewitt Weaver, and Jim Colbert, helping all five of them to their breakthrough victories on the PGA Tour. Gary Player and Johnny Miller became ardent supporters of Ballard's teachings, as did Jerry Pate, Frank Beard, and Hubert Green.

In the early eighties, when Ballard transferred to the Doral Golf and Country Club in Miami, a promising Louisiana golfer named Hal Sutton came to him. Soon thereafter Sutton captured the 1984 PGA Championship and vowed never to work with anyone else again. "If I do, I hope somebody shoots me," he said.

Sutton was followed by Sandy Lyle, a gifted Englishman who had gone into a slump. After working with Ballard, Lyle won the 1987 Players Championship and the 1988 Masters.

Jimmy Ballard is brash and outspoken, but he gets results.

But Ballard's most notable product was surely Curtis Strange, who used a Ballardized swing to win back-to-back U.S. Opens in 1988 and 1989 and lead the tour's money list. It was no wonder *GOLF Magazine* named Jimmy Ballard the "Teacher of the Decade."

"What I teach is nothing new," said Ballard. "It's the same swing Ben Hogan won with—a swing Hogan learned with help from Sam Byrd, although Hogan never gave Sam the credit he was due." Whether original or not, Ballard had a way of getting his points across to people, and getting results. His fullest expression came with the 1981 publication of *How to Perfect Your Golf Swing*. In it, he delineated the "seven common denominators" of good players and debunked a host of misleading terms. Most importantly, he set forth "connection" as the indispensable key to a sound swing.

THE SECRET:

Plug your left upper arm against your body, let your head shift a bit as you coil, and then fire your lower right side into the ball.

BALLARD'S SECRET

As a young teacher, I spent countless hours trying to find a way to communicate to my students the natural, sequential wholeness or the unified efficiency of the actions that I could plainly see in the swings of all of the great ball strikers. In fact, my observations were not limited to golf. I could see the same unified quality of movement exhibited in the performances of top-level athletes in all sports.

It became obvious that these individuals had learned to use the entire anatomy in a manner that produced the most effective and visually pleasing combination of power, accuracy, and grace. Such a sight once prompted a spectator to observe: "Watching Sam Snead practice short irons is like watching a fish practicing swimming!" A spectator could satisfy his compulsion to share an experience with a friend by talking of ease, timing, smoothness, rhythm, or tempo. But these are fiendish words to the serious teacher. How can I teach you rhythm in an hour with any assurance that what I provide will be retained? I probably can't! It's like the little boy who, fascinated by the wind, runs outside and traps some in a shoe box, only to return to his room, open the box, and find nothing but stillness.

Obviously, trying to constantly redefine these same old "airy" golf terms was not the answer. How then could I reduce this visual wholeness to something that would capture the essence, and also provide me with a tool to communicate and build this efficiency of motion into the swing of a student?

The word I found was "connection." The physical activity of any top level athlete was connected, as opposed to being a disjointed or disconnected action. And it seemed to me to be particularly apparent in any of the striking or stick-and-ball sports. Whether the athlete was swinging a club, racquet, bat, or paddle, the very best players controlled the hands and arms with the big muscles of the body—the large muscles of the legs, torso, and shoulders—rather than with the smaller muscles of the arms and hands. Proper utilization of the body initially produced the power, which was then transmitted through the arms and hands. Never the reverse! It was particularly noticeable in golf, and the evidence was quite simple. All poor golfers were arm- and hand-dominant, and all great ball strikers were not. The average player was allowing the tail to wag the dog. The great ball strikers all had the dog wagging the tail!

In my teaching, the idea of connection became the master fundamental. It was not at all complicated, and I didn't really consider it as either theory or concept. It was an observable physical reality—what was actually happening in the best golf swings. Initially, connection was made up of grip, position, and balance, and a connected golf swing possessed all of the common denominators—the essential fundamentals. In other words, connection was introduced into the player's set-up and maintained throughout the swing by the presence and sequential continuance of the fundamentals. Any fundamental departure was a disconnection which interrupted the correct interrelationships. This made it possible to view the whole swing as connected and the parts as elements of connection. The process begins by teaching a student the braced connected address position. From there, we proceed to each of the fundamentals (the common denominators) as they appear from the time the player swings the club away from the ball, until he reaches the straight balanced finish. At this point, the golfer should understand the essential elements of the connected golf swing. Then, with some application, the player can train his golfing dog to wag his golfing tail and perhaps enjoy one of man's best pastimes for the first time in his life.

Suppose I ask you to assume your normal address position, standing sideways to an open door or window some 15 feet away, holding a shag bag full of practice balls in front of you. Now I ask you to hurl the shag bag through the window with some authority.

How would you naturally perform this action? Let me answer that for you, describing what you would do in some detail, not because I expect you to be consciously aware of these details during such an action—quite the contrary—but simply to familiarize you with golf's master fundamental a little better.

> **The word I found was "connection." The physical activity of any top level athlete was connected, as opposed to being a disjointed or disconnected action.**

BALLARD'S SECRET

With the weight equally distributed on the insides of your feet and legs, you could coil the entire upper body, the hands, arms, shoulders, and torso together, against what I call a brace or set of the right leg. In the process, the head moves marginally to the right, simply following the spine.

As the bag reaches a point just above waist level going back, your weight moves onto the inside of the right foot and right leg, and your point of balance is six to eight inches behind the mid-line of your body.

From here, you reverse the thrust of the legs from the ground up. Since the weight is predominantly "loaded" on the inside of the right foot, leg, and hip joint, you must start the weight transfer from there with a thrust of the right foot and right knee combined, followed immediately by a thrust of the whole right side, upper body, arms, and hands.

The golfer must first connect the left arm to the shoulder area. We are teaching this because in the swings of all the great ball strikers, the shoulders swing the arms.

With this thrust or kick of the right foot and knee, your point of balance shifts to the left foot some 6 to 8 inches in front of the mid-line of your body. Having accomplished this, your left side clears to accommodate the weight transfer and your arms are now swinging directly toward your target.

As you release the shag bag, your hands are pointing at the open window, your weight is almost totally on the left foot, your hips and shoulders are level, and the head and eyes are up, tracking the bag to its destination.

In this way, you have thrown the shag bag properly, using natural rhythm and coordination in a totally connected tossing action. It is precisely the action present in the swing of every great striker of the ball, past, present, and future.

Connecting the Arms to the Body

In learning to grip the club correctly, the left hand heel pad and index finger exercise introduced you to an awareness of the fact that gripping the club involves more than wrapping the hands around the shaft. We noticed that there was a natural tendency for the left arm to seek connection with the left shoulder. In lesson situations, I'll often ask a golfer to point to his or her shoulder. Usually, the player will point toward the top of the shoulder, approximately where the shirt stops and the sleeve begins—designating the shoulder *joint*. This is understandable, as in our daily lives we see our shoulder as something that helps us reach away from the body, to pick up coffee cups and telephones, take clothing

LEFT-ARM CONNECTION

Golfers mistakenly think of their left shoulder in terms of the shoulder joint instead of the entire shoulder area including the surrounding large muscles in the back and chest. If you take the club back with the shoulder area, you deprive yourself of the strength resident in those larger muscles, the "pecs" and the "lats" in

weightlifter lingo. Notice how our imaginary electrical plug rips out of the socket when the golfer uses only his arms to swing back. The swing remains connected and will yield much more power when the left arm and left shoulder area operate as a unit in taking the club back.

off hangers, or change lightbulbs. However, if we use the shoulder joints in this manner while swinging a golf club, we'll end up wishing we had stayed at the office or attended to some household chores. We never want to swing a golf club from the shoulder joints.

From this point on, when we mention the shoulder, understand that we are referring to the shoulder area. Your golfing shoulders include the upper arms and the "lats" and "pecs," the large back and chest muscles. The golfer must first connect the left arm to the shoulder area. We are

teaching this because in the swings of all the great ball strikers, the shoulders swing the arms. The arms never move independently, operating from the shoulder joints. Many fine players may feel that the arms pull the shoulders or express various individual feelings. However, a look at their swings indicates what really happens. They operate as a unit. To give you a visual appreciation of this, study the swing sequence of any great player, directing your attention to the shoulder area. You will notice that the connection created at address is maintained throughout the swing. The upper portion of the left arm never separates from the left side until late in the follow-through.

I've found that a good way to get this idea across to players is to use the analogy of a standard two-prong household plug and wall socket. At address, when the left arm comes straight out from the side—as if you were shaking hands left-handed—you can feel the upper portion of the bicep and the pec muscle touching a fraction beneath the upper arm. Suppose you had two prongs in the side of the chest, and you plugged the two together? This doesn't mean to contract the muscles of the bicep or pec. Don't ram

the plug into the wall; simply complete the contact so the two are touching. Now you have connected the left arm to the body. And this next statement is of paramount importance: wherever it starts, it never changes. (It will unplug naturally, late in the follow-through. If it didn't, you'd screw yourself into the ground.)

Another way to get a feel for this is to hit some medium or short irons with a handkerchief under your left shoulder. If you drop the handkerchief, you've unplugged, or disconnected, allowing the arms to work independently of the body.

RIGHT-ARM CONNECTION
The most natural position of the right arm at the top of the back swing—akin to a throwing motion—is also the most effective because it permits the arm to work in tandem with the large muscles in the right shoulder area. Keeping the elbow tucked into the ribcage (near right), or lifting it unnaturally high (far right), are forms of disconnection because effective contact with the right shoulder area is lost.

The connected left arm creates the consistent radius of the golf swing. You never want to allow the left arm to get "longer" or "shorter" from the point of connection. One of the most common faults in the golf swing takes place here, and I refer to it as "run-off." When a player swings the club from the shoulder joints, working the arms independently and unplugging his connection, the arms get longer but the body has not gone with them. The result is longer arms and a shorter swing arc. Since the arms have "grown" on the backswing, they will have to be pulled or sucked back in on the downswing if the player is going to make contact with the back of the ball. There is no chance of doing this consistently.

With the legs braced, spine erect, and the left shoulder connected, arm run-off can be prevented when the player measures to the ball. Measuring creates the uniform radius of the swing at the outset, and maintaining connection preserves it. A player should place the club behind the ball by employing a semi-sitting position, by lowering the body without changing body posture. Thus, the low point of the arc is established with connection. In this regard,

Ben Hogan's compact swing exemplified connection.

butt of the club is out of plane immediately and the backswing can't begin without hand-arm manipulation.

When a player measures to the bottom of the ball on an iron shot (lightly soling the club to the ground), he has created the connected relationships necessary to deliver a crisp descending blow down and through in the impact area.

When the ball is set up, on a tee, measuring to the bottom of the ball insures that the player will contact the ball at the bottom of the arc where the club is traveling level. In this way, the 12-degree loft of your driver face will provide the correct shot shape—that is, the desired combination of length, accuracy, and trajectory.

When a player measures with connection, he extends the club from the lat muscle because he coils the hands, arms, shoulders and body away together. Swinging from the shoulder joints creates an immediate disconnection in that you

You will notice that connection is maintained throughout the swing. The upper part of the left arm never separates from the left side until late in the follow-through.

Hogan's analogy of a golfer lowering as if to sit on a spectator sports stick was excellent.

The most common error at this stage is a player beginning the process of connecting, only to destroy it by bending the spine, which drops the chest forward and down, threatening balance and erasing the proper levels at address. If the back is humped over, the center is dropped down and the player can only begin the swing from the shoulder joints. Also, when the center is down, the

are not using your newly defined golfing shoulder and thus your body. You'll often hear a player observe that another player's swing is "all arms." The player has swung the club from the shoulder joints. Usually, severe run-off is created by the golfer trying to attain what he mistakenly perceives to be greater extension. But by disconnecting—making the arms longer, he has actually shortened his arc.

Once you've placed the left hand on the club and connected the left arm to the shoulder area, swing your right arm by the right hip pocket as if you were going to shake hands with the club. Once you set your right hand grip as explained previously, the right arm and shoulder are in a natural position, and from here with both arms connected, the arms and shoulders go away together.

As to connecting the right arm, we come to another area replete with instructional contradiction. A lot of players and teachers have advocated that golfers keep the right arm and elbow down and in toward the body at address, and against the right side of the backswing.

All of this comes from a phobia about a flying right elbow. The right elbow has to come away from the side when the player moves into the strong backswing position. Anything else is unnatural. The next time you go down to hit a bucket of balls, prove this to yourself with a simple exercise. Without the club, but with a golf ball held in your right hand, assume the braced, connected address position. Now throw the ball vigorously out onto the range. How did your right arm react to throwing the ball? If you tried to freeze your right elbow against your right side, you'd throw some kind of a wild blooper, and the feeling would be totally unnatural. So also, if you swept the right arm out away from your body, so that the elbow shot semi-skyward (this would be a genuine flying right elbow), the feeling and results would be equally as discomforting. However, if you threw the ball naturally, without giving it a second thought, your right arm motion would very nearly approximate the motion of the great ball strikers during the backswing.

FROM *How to Perfect Your Golf Swing Using "Connection" and the Seven Common Denominators* by Jimmy Ballard

BALLARD'S SECRET

CHAPTER 4

PETER BEAMES

A BOLD STEP FORWARD

"I believe, and my thousands of students will attest, that this swing will, with a little practice, change one's game beyond recognition."

In the middle of his career—a career that produced more than one hundred victories around the world, including seven major championships—Gary Player suddenly changed his golf swing. Seemingly out of nowhere, he began hurling himself through the ball with such force that, after impact, he actually stepped forward toward the target, finishing with his right foot in front of his left.

He had developed the technique during the off-season at his home in South Africa, but the idea had come to him from one of his rivals, Billy Casper. During a series of exhibition matches with Casper, Player noticed him sliding his right leg through impact. Battling lower back problems at the time, Player reasoned that Casper's move would be far less stressful than his own twisting, bent-over-backwards finish.

Not only was it less stressful, it also produced better shots. In 1974 Player won both the Masters and the British Open, rifling shot after shot while "walking through" impact. Most observers dismissed it as a swing flaw.

Peter Beames knew better. A young English professional who had struggled with a bad back of his own, Beames had analyzed a century's worth of world-class players and had reached the conclusion that the best step a golfer can make is the one he takes towards the hole after impact. As far back as Willie Park, Sr., and the first British Open in 1860, champions had been walking through the

Beames demonstrates his walk-thru swing, using a super-sized club to show clubface positions and wearing two-tone trousers for clarity.

ball. Jones, Hagen, Sarazen, Hogan—all of them understood, and to some extent, implemented, this exaggerated release of the body.

Early in his career on the international circuit, Beames had met Player, but in the wake of Player's spectacular 1974 season, they met again and became instant allies. Together they began to spread the gospel of walk-through golf, a swing that they argued was both easier to learn and easier on the body than the shut-faced and square-to-square methods then in vogue.

Truth be told, they did not get very far. In his senior years, Gary Player continued to walk through, but not as markedly as earlier, while Beames attracted a loyal but small group of devotees. He did, however, produce both a book and a video, both entitled *Walk-Thru to Par,* and today he still teaches his method actively.

The book, as one might expect, is not a long one and it's written more or less as an interview between Beames and his co-author, Frederic Swan. However, for the player whose aching back has all but driven him from the game, this may be a step in the right direction.

> He had analyzed world-class players and reached the conclusion that the best step a golfer can make is the one he takes towards the hole after impact.

THE SECRET:

Walk through the ball. As you move into impact, allow your right foot to step over your left.

BEAMES'S SECRET

"Now I can finally ask you the question, Peter: Why do you and Gary Player and others so often walk through the hitting zone after ball impact? I mean, actually stepping over the left foot?"

"Very simple answer. To prevent permanent injury to our backs—and, to consistently hit the ball straight at the target. If we did not permit the body to become erect to dissipate the momentum developed from the swing, we would have to go through the Reverse-C contortion. That would mean keeping the head down, behind where the ball was, while the curved back puts a check to the kinetic energy developed."

"I see. But, just why have the professionals developed and recommended the Reverse-C in recent decades?"

"The body position at impact and its follow-through is dictated by the techniques used to get to the top and come down. No matter what you do going up, you must compensate coming down so as to hit the ball squarely. As the idea developed in golf lore that the left wrist must be kept stiff and straight going back and on top, the solution to hitting the ball straight at impact became the Reverse-C fashion. That straight wrist tended to close the club face at the top. Then it had to be opened on the way down by holding the top of the body back, behind the ball, through impact and follow-through.

"In *Walk-Thru* golf, we purposely open the face of the club going up and use the body to help close it coming down. This permits the walk-through after impact. Voila! New freedom for the back."

"Do I always have to bring my right foot over the left one in every shot, Peter?"

> Willie Park, Sr., walked through his swing when he won the first British Open at Prestwick in 1860, and three more times after that.

"No. Of course not. That trademark of this swing is used only when needed to most easily dissipate great momentum when it is developed, as in a full swing. Frequently, with mid-iron finesse shots, the right foot will just end up on its toe, perhaps dragging toward the left foot.

"In any case, though, you will bring your body erect as part of the energy-absorbing process, as many current champions are now doing, like Leonard Thompson and Curtis Strange. They have both been Jimmy Ballard disci-ples for many years. Ballard also stresses having the body erect at the finish, a step away from walking.

"Do you remember Gary Player's win at the first Skins Game, in late 1983? He hit a wedge stiff to the pin and walked before the ball landed. Nicklaus said he looked like he came out of the 'start-ing blocks.' And Seve Ballesteros on the 18th hole at Lytham, when he won the British Open? He straightened up and walked.

"Champions have, in fact, been walking through since the beginning of the game. Willie Park, Sr. walked through his swing when he won the first British Open at Prestwick in 1860, and three more times after that. We know of this from the book published in 1896 by William Park, Jr., after he, too, had won that Open, in 1887 and '89. He wrote that 'My father, who it is well known, was one of the straightest and longest drivers of his day, carried out the principle of the follow-through to such an extent that he used fre-quently to run a yard or two after his drive.'"

"That's fascinating, Peter. Does it matter, though, where I place my foot when I walk through?"

"Definitely. But let's keep the horse in front of the cart. It is what you did before you hit the ball that will determine the direction you walk. If you do everything right, you automatically will place your right foot over the left along a line to the target. If you overturn, you will step left. If you lack hand action and push the ball, you will step right."

These Are your Objectives:

1. To let your body absorb in a natural way the kinetic energy remaining after ball impact.
2. To do so with the least strain on the back.
3. To consciously set a pattern of following through that will consistently cause you to move your weight through the ball every swing.

If you do everything right, your right foot will automatically step over your left along a line to the target. Note: For most players, this full release occurs only on the longer shots. On middle and short irons and finesse shots, the right foot may only end up on its toe, dragging a bit toward the left.

Your head and shoulders will rise after impact and you'll stand erect to watch your shot with the club over your shoulder. If you suffer from a bad back, you'll find this a much more comfortable way to swing, with none of the twisting and torsion inherent in the Reverse-C type of finish.

How To Achieve your Goals:

1. After impact, let the club continue toward the target as long as possible, while rolling your hands.
2. Let the right side of the body continue on through, as all of your weight settles onto your left foot while your head and shoulders rise.
3. Let the right foot walk over the left foot, if you hit hard enough, and stand erect to watch your shot in comfort.

These Are Your Rewards:

1. You will hit the ball farther, because you will have no tendency to slow acceleration of the downswing due to a false sense of need to stay behind the ball in the follow-through.
2. You will discover a new feeling of body freedom in your swing.

3. You will not put a severe strain on your back.
4. Your head will be in a perfect position to watch the ball land on target.

Ask Yourself these Questions:

1. Did I let my weight go through the ball, ending on my left foot?
2. Did I let the club continue toward the target as I rolled my hands?
3. Did I release the pressures on my back after impact by letting my head and upper torso rise to an erect, or forward-leaning position?
4. Did I walk through straight ahead?
5. Was my belt buckle left of target and my right shoulder pointing to it, with the club over my shoulder?

FROM *WALK-THRU TO PAR* BY PETER BEAMES

CHAPTER 5

LET YOUR BODY MEMORIZE THE SWING

"The human body is a remarkable computer. By feeding into it the type of swing desired, with correct positions, over time that is the swing that will be built."

The pivotal moment in Paul Bertholy's education as a golf instructor came when he was six years old and helped his grandmother chop off the head of a chicken. Young Paul had been holding the chicken's legs, but once granny's axe hit the block, the decapitated hen broke loose, hit the ground, and began running all around her Sandusky, Ohio, kitchen.

Years later, after giving a particularly difficult golf lesson, that moment came back to Bertholy. His pupil had not been able to do a single thing he'd asked him to do.

"Somehow his mind and body weren't communicating," Bertholy recalled. "Thinking back to the chicken, I realized that if its head wasn't connected to its body then the head couldn't tell the body to run. If that much were true, there must be a separate memory—and it must be true for humans as well."

With that hypothesis, Bertholy began to educate himself in the details of the human neuromuscular system. What he found was that we do indeed have a sort of kinesthetic memory vault—our muscles can remember. And so over the

THE SECRET:

Teach your muscles to memorize the seven key positions in the swing.

next forty years, Paul Bertholy devoted himself to the creation of a method by which the body could memorize the swing, a way to train the muscles so that the act of hitting a golf ball becomes virtually automatic—in a sense, mindless.

During much of that process, he was dismissed as an eccentric. Bertholy's modus operandi—a series of tedious drills in which pupils were asked to take a heavy "swing pipe" and hold it in various positions for ten seconds at a time—was anathema to everything the teaching fraternity had long embraced. There were no sessions on the range, no back-and-forth chats between teacher and student, and very few actual golf swings. Indeed, the entire Bertholy method could be learned indoors, without ever striking a ball. It nonetheless required enormous commitment—drilling one's body five days a week, thirty minutes a day, for up to two years.

But it got results. A local Ohio boy taught by Bertholy won thirty-two junior events by the age of nine. A businessman dropped his handicap from 15 to 2 and, after eighteen months on the system, shot a 68. When Bertholy's methods were published in a nine-part series in *Golf World* in 1966, the

Paul Bertholy in 1955

magazine's mailbag overflowed with praising letters. A few years later, when he joined the teaching staff at *GOLF Magazine,* the same thing happened. "Every now and then we're able to corral one theory or method that meets with overwhelming acceptance from our golfers," said the magazine's editor. "Such was the case with Paul Bertholy's series. We have been pleasantly inundated with a stream of letters from grateful golfers telling us about their success with the Bertholy system. Some indicated it has opened up a whole new approach to the game for them."

Suddenly, leading teachers like Bob Toski and Gary Wiren began to recognize Bertholy's methods, praising his use of practice drills to reinforce his teaching. Fifty years ago, almost no instructor asked his pupils to do drills. Today, almost no instructor does *not* include drills as a cornerstone to his method.

Bertholy died in 1998, but four years later, his chief assistant, Doug Ferreri, assembled the master's nearly five decades of teaching wisdom. The excerpt that follows describes just one of the dozens of Bertholian exercises, but it is the most important.

BERTHOLY'S SECRET

To feel the correct centrifugal force golf swing, take a driver and grasp the hosel with the left hand. Hold the shaft with the right hand about 10 inches away from the left hand. Straighten the left arm and fold the right elbow in to the navel while cocking the left wrist in radial deviation. Now swing the club to the top of the backswing. Start down with the lower body moving first, followed by the **Vertical Drop.** Once the left hand has passed the ball position, release the shaft with the right hand, generating a whistling sound past the ball position.

Practice this until you can recreate the whistling past the ball position. The louder the whistle, the better the technique. For mental identification it is important to feel the incorrect premature release. Take the club in the same fashion to the top of the backswing. Now, instead of starting with the lower body, first push the club shaft from the top of the backswing. Do this with the upper right quadrant, first with the **right hand cast, right arm thrust, and right shoulder roll.** Do this until you create the whistling sound of the club shaft prior to the ball position. Become totally aware of how you created this faulty distance-destroying action. Identifying the exact moment and cause of this action is essential to eliminate this cancerous action. Once the culprit has been isolated, we can readily deal with it. This is the number one enemy of all golf swings, hacker and superstar alike.

This maximum-speed sensation must be cultivated to the extent that there is total kinesthetic identification. Make certain that at the end of the swing motion, the finish has the weight resting on the left foot with the right foot in an upright position.

This drill—in which you release the shaft with the right hand just as the left hand passes impact—instills the feel of centrifugal force.

Part A of the Golden Exercise

Now you are ready for the ***Golden Exercise.*** You will now attempt to adapt a golf club to a specific object to make this embryonic golf swing we have been building practical. A golf club and a specific target to be aimed at and struck will be used. This program is done outdoors. An old 2, 3, 4, or 5 iron should be used so that if the shaft becomes bent, no harm is done to your regular set. Three tees, preferably of different colors, will be used. A white tee is used to represent the ball position or a half-buried golf ball can be substituted. A blue tee rests 6 inches beyond the ball position on the line of flight representing the release position. Still on the line of flight 8 to 12 inches beyond the blue release tee is a red tee, which will represent the true target for this conditioning program. If available, substitute a pinecone for the red tee. The distance the pinecone will travel with a correctly done ***Golden Exercise*** is amazing.

Holding the club only in the left hand, the right arm assumes the **claw** position. Start the club back with an all-inclusive action from above the belt with the shoulders. After the left hand has passed the stabilized right thigh, grab the shaft of the club about 12 inches from the left hand on the steel portion of the shaft. Proceed to the top of the backswing, making sure the upper body turns against the lower body. Once

Golden Exercise Part A

The number-one fault of golfers is the hit impulse, starting the downswing with the upper body instead of from below the belt. This exercise, when performed repeatedly at about one tenth the speed of a normal swing, will combat the "hit at" tendency.

Hold the club in the left hand only. The right hand assumes a claw position.

1

As the lower body buckles, drop the arms and hands vertically toward the ball.

4

At this point, release the retaining right hand.

5

As the left hand passes the right thigh, grab the shaft of the club with the right hand.

2

Continue to the top of the swing, being sure to turn the upper body against the lower body.

3

Maintain the claw position of the right hand as the club whips through impact.

6

Point the club like a rifle barrel and hold this position for at least ten seconds.

7

maximum torsion of the upper body has been achieved and the high hands attained, creating a big swing arc, it is time to start the downswing.

The golf swing should become a pure swinging motion of centrifugal force, not a pushing, striking motion that most golfers are inclined to do.

Starting from below the belt, the left knee buckles toward the target, allowing a slight sitting action in the knees, as weight is transferred, developing the Sam Snead bow-legged appearance. This is followed by the **Vertical Drop** of the keystone, that is the fixed left arm, flat left wrist, bent right arm, the cocked right wrist, or preferably even more cocking of the wrists. When the **Master Movement** is done correctly the clubhead will still be to the left of the golfer's head. This action will purge the **Hit Impulse** and help create the first stage of the delayed hit of magnificent control and sneaky long distance. Ben Hogan and Sergio Garcia, both with slight builds, used/use this action to the utmost. It is not surprising the length these two competitors produced/produce. After this difficult move is accomplished the lower body continues the **buckle, sit, slide, and bump action.** The right arm and hand retain, as the right elbow immediately seeks the navel. The grip end of the club will point at the ball/target line but never outside the line the ball rests on. Continue the forward swing until the left hand is beyond the ball position opposite the blue tee. At this point, release the retaining right hand completely, allowing the club to miss the first tee (representing the ball), and the second tee (the release point), and making contact with the third tee (pinecone), which had been placed 8–12 inches beyond the release point. The golf ball must become incidental to the whole process, while the second impact object, the tee (pinecone) and the divot must become primary. The mind and body must be conditioned to allow the ball to be secondary to the whole process. The body should be conditioned to anticipate a secondary resistance, a need or appetite for a divot after the ball.

Allow the club to continue to the rifle barrel position with the left palm facing the sky. The right arm maintains the "claw" while the eyes view the divot for at least ten seconds. This is a program of adaptation, i.e., adapting the club to an actual object. We are making the swing practical while conditioning the mind and body to dig soil or turf, the secondary impact. This also develops the all-important **P.S.M.,** proper sequential motion. Remember **P.T.** and **P.S.M.** are the glues that hold the swing together.

Do this full sequence at about ¹⁄₁₀ of normal swing speed. It is much more important to have exact positioning than to have imprecise positioning at a faster speed. As proficiency is obtained, gradually increase the speed of this exercise to about 25 percent of normal speed, but never faster. Master the program to such an extent that you can have a strong, neutral, or weak left palm position in the extension at will.

It is absolutely vital to the player's development toward his potential that he be conditioned to take a divot. **To keep the golf swing healthy, feed it post-hit divots with an iron.** Over time dig several bushes of soil in this fashion. Most golfers are ground or turf shy. This shyness must be overcome to the point where a swing that has not cut a nice long thin divot with an iron is unfulfilled. **The divot taken while playing an iron should resemble a bacon strip, not a pork chop.** The number one fault of all golfers, hacker and superstar alike, is the *Hit-Impulse,* starting the downswing with the upper body instead from below the belt. The Bertholy Method *Golden Exercise* may very well be the most effective system ever devised to minimize this dreadful fault.

Part B of the *Golden Exercise*

Part B is identical to Part A but should not be done until total proficiency is gained at Part A. The only difference between the two is instead of finishing in the rifle barrel, we will continue to the follow-through, making sure of keeping the claw position.

Develop a full turn at the top of the backswing and a full turn at the finish of the swing. The golf swing should become a pure swinging motion of centrifugal force, not a pushing, striking motion that most golfers are wrongfully inclined to do.

Part C of the *Golden Exercise*

Part C of the *Golden Exercise* is exactly like Part A with one exception. For the first time, the conventional golf grip will be used. Our object is still to miss the half-buried golf ball while cutting post-hit divots. Although this might appear to be an easy task, adapting the program to a functional golf grip while remembering the retaining quality of the upper-right quadrant and the right hand will take some time. Again, address the playing ball, which is half buried, taking a slow $1/10$ speed golf swing missing the playing ball and cutting the secondary target divot about 3 to 12 inches beyond the half-buried playing ball. Put a pinecone or golf tee in front of the ball to give a visual cue to the actual objective. This will purge the early hit and further develop the feel of the late release with the post-hit divot, which

> The golf ball must become incidental to the whole process while the secondary object—the divot—must become primary.

This time address the ball with a conventional grip.

1

Take the club back with the shoulders, at $\frac{1}{10}$ normal speed.

2

The vertical drop. This time maintain the grip with both hands.

4

The hit. Bypass the real ball and concentrate on the secondary target.

5

Turn the upper body fully against the resisting lower body.

3

Once again, hold the rifle-barrel position for ten seconds.

6

Golden Exercise Part C

This exercise is exactly like Part A except for the grip. Adopt a conventional grip and repeat the exercise, remembering to cut post-hit divots.

all fine players experience. **Any golf swing that does not cut a post-hit divot with an iron is a fake.** *Since there is latitude in the golf swing, there are variations of this theme.* Some great players just slightly scratch the turf past the ball, while others take large divots. On normal lies on the fairway I prefer the divot to be long and thin, resembling bacon strips rather than pork chops. This time spent will well be worth the effort as pure ball contact is achieved. This action will never fear tight lies or lies from divots. Have patience! Become an expert at these programs. **Remember, only the lazy ones fail!**

FROM *GOLF SWING CONSTRUCTION 101-THE BERTHOLY METHOD REVISITED* BY DOUG FERRERI

BERTHOLY'S SECRET

CHAPTER 6

MINDY BLAKE

LEAD WITH THE LEGS

"I am quite certain that the method I've developed is not merely right for me. I believe that, with practice, preferably a little every day, it can help anyone to play better golf."

Ed Sullivan, the host of America's most popular TV show during the 1960s, is well known for having introduced the Beatles to the United States. What almost no one knows is that Sullivan also launched the career of one of golf's most innovative teachers.

An avid but average golfer, Sullivan was playing the Wentworth course near London in 1967 and having a career-worst day. Midway through the round, as his frustration reached a peak, he vowed it would be the last eighteen holes of his life—he would never set foot on a golf course again. "I wonder," said one of his playing companions, "if you'd like to try a different method."

The desperate Sullivan listened as the gentleman briefly explained a new way to address and hit the ball. Then he teed one up and hit it out of sight. Sullivan used the new method for the remainder of the round and played brilliantly. So delighted was he with this instant revival of his game that he walked into the Wentworth pro shop, bought out its entire stock of golf balls, and presented them to his new best friend.

The fellow's name was Mindy Blake, and at the unlikely age of fifty-four, he was about to become a famous golf teacher.

But everything about Mindy Blake was a bit unlikely. He was born and raised in New Zealand, the son of a schoolteacher who mortgaged his insurance policy to buy a chicken farm where Mindy could live and work while also attending university. For four years the boy plucked chickens and milked cows, while earning an honors degree in mathematics and narrowly missing out on a Rhodes Scholarship. At the same time Mindy established himself as a talented pole vaulter. Just two months after taking it up he set a New Zealand record and became the national champion. He briefly trained for the Olympics, but war was brewing and in 1936 he joined the Royal Air Force.

Again he excelled, rising to Wing Commander and winning the Distinguished Flying Cross and Distinguished Service Order. He flew in the Battle of Britain, among others, and shot down ten enemy aircraft, while being shot down himself, not once but twice. Blake was the first man to bail out of a Spitfire and survive, thanks to his knowledge of math and physics. He had seen comrades losing their lives through the sheer speed of impact of the new aircraft landing on water, so he had decided that if he had to crash land, he would turn the aircraft side-on so that the wing would strike the water first. The effect would be, he hypothesized, to cartwheel the aircraft until it lost momentum and dropped onto the surface of the sea. When it did happen, he applied his theory, which happily was a complete success. He was able to climb into his rubber dinghy and row toward the English coast.

Blake, above all, was an inventor. When egg grading became compulsory in New Zealand, he invented an egg-weighing machine. When he was captured by the Germans, he spent his time in prison camp designing a rotary engine, a superior fighter plane, and a car seatbelt.

Mindy Blake did not take up golf until after the war, at the age of thirty-four. Good athlete that he was, he got to a 9 handicap in his first year, 6 in his second, and eventually to a 2. But ultimately he was frustrated. "Even when I actually played to my handicap, I was aware that I struck the ball indifferently," he said. And so he focused his resourceful mind on a quest for a better way to swing.

For inspiration he turned to the athletic movements he knew best—pole vault, shot put, javelin, and discus, all of which relied heavily on the lower body. "The legs are the powerhouse," he said. "Everything else simply responds." With that as his thesis, Blake developed a unique method—incorporating a strong grip, an abbreviated backswing, and a prolonged drag of the club through the ball, keeping it on the target line as long as possible. His own accuracy and distance improved greatly. Only 5'8" tall, he began hitting the ball an average of 280 yards and continued to do so into his sixties.

But he never shared his thoughts until a man named Harry Weaver knocked on his door. A columnist for the *London Observer*, Weaver had heard about Blake from Ed Sullivan. Blake and the writer sat down, and the result became *The Golf Swing of the Future*.

> ## THE SECRET:
> Open up your stance, make a limited hip turn, and start your downswing by driving forward with your legs.

BLAKE'S SECRET

From the start of my quest for an athletic and scientific swing, I realized that progress could be made only by developing a swing in which the position of the right elbow at the hit was at least six inches farther forward—towards the center of the body—than the present accepted position. This corresponds to the extended right-arm position of the modern javelin thrower and enables the power to be poured directly from the legs to the clubhead.

Over the years I have built in swings and modified them to achieve this aim. The recurrent problem I encountered was the question of opening and closing the clubface during the swing. The reason why the club opens on the backswing—even in the so-called square-to-square method it opens 90 degrees—is that, when the club is held in two hands with a conventional grip, the wrists would have to dislocate if the face was to remain square to the direction of travel as with, say, a tennis racquet.

This opening and closing of the clubface means that you are trying to hit the ball with the face of a club which is rotating in two planes. Golf must therefore be a difficult game.

An even more vital point is that you cannot develop a swing in which the legs are the source of power and the rest of the body is used in reflex if you have rolling of the wrists.

Think of the movement you use when hammering a nail. There is no rolling of the wrist and the head of the hammer remains square to the direction of travel. I wondered, could a golf club be used in the same way? My breakthrough came when I found a grip which enabled my left hand to swing the club like a hammer while the right hand

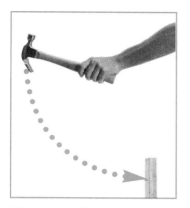 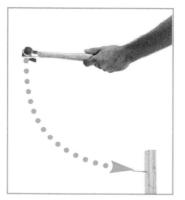 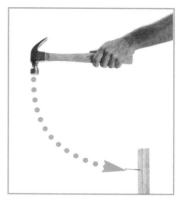

These photos show a hammer being used similarly to a golf club hitting a ball. At left, the old-fashioned swing, where the clubface was rotated open during the backswing. In the center, the square-to-square method, where the clubface is manipulated into alignment with the back of the left hand. At right, the way a hammer would be used naturally.

moved relative to the left so that it locked in a powerful hitting grip, like a two-handed tennis backhand, at the top of the swing. I realize that quizzical eyebrows will be raised at the notion of a deliberate grip change during the swing. Yet, in any other two-handed action, whether it is baseball, cricket, or chopping with an axe, there is always a change of grip on the backswing.

Before enlarging on this subject, we should consider the foundation on which all else depends—posture. Assuming a good hip–shoulder relationship at the address is by far the most difficult part of the swing. The ideal in the old swing was for the shoulders to turn through 90 degrees and the hips through 70 degrees. In the modern swing, while the shoulders still turn 90 degrees, the hips turn 45 degrees or less. With practically all bad golfers the hips turn as much as the

shoulders. There is then no tension in the body because the back muscles have not been stretched, and the only way back to the ball is by pulling round with the shoulders. The outcome is loss of distance and a hook or slice of varying degrees of violence.

The ideal at address is to have the hips slightly open relative to the shoulders. The shoulders will then turn more than the hips on the backswing, the shoulder and back muscles will be fully extended, and, at the top of the swing, there is a substantial increase in stored power for the shot.

It is not a question of being supple. Once the right foot is turned 10 degrees toward the hole and the knees pressed to the left, a good hip–shoulder relationship can be assumed by practically everybody, and it is easy, even for the stiffest person, to make an adequate turn with the shoulders

There are very few people who cannot turn their shoulders 90 degrees without turning the hips, providing the hips are anchored. There is therefore no reason to complicate the backswing by letting the hips turn. It detracts from the power of the shot and makes it more difficult to maintain balance.

accompanied by a relatively small amount of give in the hips.

The address position I have suggested is an athletic position. At the top of the backswing, it produces a position in which it is instinctive to start the downswing with the legs, and there is no inclination to pull around with the shoulders. It is not necessary to worry about bad backs. Bad backs are far more likely to be caused by trying to hit with a faulty posture in which your joints are at a mechanical disadvantage. A weak back will be strengthened, and a bad one possibly improved, by using it in conjunction with a good posture, exercising it as it should be exercised.

To summarize:

The knees must be flexed and pushed towards the target just slightly.

The weight must be on the heels.

The head and shoulders must be absolutely square to the direction of the shot and behind the club. The position of *the head* should be such that, after the stroke, the eyes come up in a vertical, not horizontal, plane with the right eye turning under the left eye. If the eyes turn in a horizontal plane, it means you have swung round with the shoulders.

The right arm, to be used in reflex, must be placed across the body at the address so that the right elbow is inside a vertical line through the ball joint of the right hip. This elbow position hardly moves, relative to the shoulders, throughout the swing. The arm is turned so that the inside of the elbow joint faces away from the body.

The left arm hangs as near vertically as possible.

The grip I am advocating is unorthodox.

The Grip

The left hand has a strong, four-knuckle grip with the left thumb down the back of the shaft. The right hand is placed on the club by taking the shaft in the middle and third fingers and "screwing" the hand to the left. The feeling then is that the club is being held by the tips of the third, middle, and index fingers of the right hand and that these fingers are under tension. The pad of the right hand just touches the "V" formed by the left thumb and forefinger. The arms are pressed together. This grip is my solution to the twin problems of being able to swing the club straight back with the clubface remaining square to the direction of travel and, at the same time, getting the right elbow into a position in which the power of the legs can be transmitted directly to the club. The left hand will take the club back and, as it is turned under, the left thumb will slip into the palm of the right hand, forming a very strong grip. This unorthodox grip, however, is advocated only for those who have already mastered the rest of the swing. You should be playing well into single figures before attempting it.

The Backswing

The swing is started with a forward press of the legs. Both knees are pushed toward the

At the start of the swing, both knees push forward, toward the target, and they remain in that position throughout the backswing.

The club is taken straight back and steeply up, the hips feel as if they have not moved, and the feet stay firmly planted.

The top of the swing—a position from which it is instinctive to drive with the legs.

forward movement of the legs to counter the backswing. With the clubhead resting on the ground, the press forward with the legs increases the tension on the hands. As this tension relaxes with completion of the forward press, the club is swung back very slowly, the left hand turned under the right in a reflex action from the press. The feeling is that the left arm is going under the right arm, that they are turning in the opposite direction from that in the old-type swing. In modern terms it would be said that the clubface is being shut, although, in fact, it is merely being kept square to the direction of travel. At the halfway stage the left thumb has slipped into the palm of the right hand. The inertia of the swinging club is producing an anti-clockwise turning force on the right hand, which is tensing the right elbow, forcing the elbows together. The club has been taken straight back from the ball in a steep arc. The hips feel as if they have not moved. The feet are firmly on the ground.

target slightly (about an inch), taking care the head is kept back. This position of the legs and hips is held and the takeaway is with the top part of the body alone. The rhythm is for the knees to move forward on the press, hold their position on the backswing, and move forward again from the top. I am trying to stop any transference of weight and to get a counter-movement—that is, the slight

The Top of the Swing

There has been a full shoulder turn. The right leg has remained as at the takeaway.

The left hip has moved slightly to accommo-date the shoulder turn, but it feels as if there has been no hip movement at all. Both feet are firmly on the ground. The clubface is in what, in modern parlance, would be called a tightly shut position. The left wrist is flat, or convex. The left thumb is still behind the shaft and the pressure of the club on the right fingers is keeping the right elbow

under tension and pressed towards the left arm. The left arm has gone round the body hardly at all and feels as if it is in line with the target. The back and shoulder muscles have been fully stretched and the arms and hands are an extension of this tension. It is a position from which it is instinctive to drive with the legs. The position of the right elbow is all-important. If it were slightly farther around the body, the pressure on the right hand would not force the right elbow forward and the firm and flexed connection between the hands and body would be lost. In effect, it has been necessary to introduce a radical change in grip and stance, as well as in the takeaway, to get the right elbow in a position at the top of the swing which enables the right arm to be used in reflex like that of the javelin thrower.

The first movement down—both knees shift toward the target, pulling the shoulders, arms, hands, and club downward in one piece.

The First Movement Down

It is instinctive for the legs to start the downswing. Both knees move toward the target. The pressure is felt on the left thumb and the left hand feels as if it is being twisted anti-clockwise. As the pressure increases and the right hand is bent backwards, the right elbow will come well forward of the right hip. The legs are making the shoulders, arms, hands, and club move in one piece,

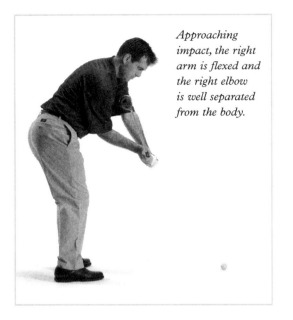

Approaching impact, the right arm is flexed and the right elbow is well separated from the body.

The legs continue to lead and clubhead speed increases as you prepare to release power into the ball.

and increasing the tension in the muscles of the back, shoulders, arms, and hands as the clubhead is being dragged down. The mental impression is that the hit is with the left thumb, which drags the club through the ball. If the right foot is turned insufficiently (less than 10 degrees) to the left at the address, only the right leg, instead of both, will drive and much of the rhythm will be lost.

The Hitting Area

The club is dragged into the hitting area by the legs. It is the position of the right arm, with the elbow well forward, that makes it possible for the pressure of the legs to be transferred to the club. The right arm is flexed and a considerable amount of energy is being stored up in the extended muscles not only of the arm but of the back and shoulders. As the leg drive continues, the speed of the clubhead is increasing and the muscles of the back, shoulders, arms, and hands are being further tensed. The energy is being stored up to be released at impact. It can be seen that the pressure of the legs must build up progressively if the maximum energy is to be stored up in the swing for release during impact. The position of the right elbow is six inches forward of the present accepted position, and to achieve this position in the hitting area, it has to be well away from the body.

At impact the clubface does not turn over—there is no fade or draw—and it stays on the line of flight for the maximum distance.

The Impact Position

There is no actual hit. The club is dragged through the ball. As the clubhead meets the ball, the shock of impact bends the clubshaft and further extends the muscles of the hands, arms, shoulders, and back. The legs are still keeping up the pressure. It is the reflex action of the muscles, especially those of the right arm, that keeps up the pressure on the ball that bit longer at impact, giving extra length and control. With a pure reflex hit such as I have described here, the ball is on the clubface for the maximum length of time. This gives "feel," control, and good flighting. The clubface is not rolling over. The shot is straight. There is no draw or fade, no hitting from inside to out to counter rolling of the wrists, and the clubface is on the line of flight through the hitting area for the maximum distance. The position of the right elbow, well forward of the right hip, is what this book is all about. It is the only position in which it is possible to make full use of the power of the legs and so hit the ball farther, straighter, and with more control.

After Impact

The clubface is still square to the direction of travel and has only just come off the line of flight. The clubhead has not passed the hands and there is no rolling over of the wrists. The feet are still firmly on the ground although the outside of the right foot has begun to lift slightly. The head is well back with the right eye coming up under the left. The knees are still bent.

The Finish

The hands finish high and the grip has gone back to the address grip. The knees have not straightened and the weight has not shifted. Although the head has turned, with the right eye coming up under the left, its position has not altered.

FROM *THE GOLF SWING OF THE FUTURE* BY MINDY BLAKE

CHAPTER 7

PERCY BOOMER

BORN TO TEACH

*"The golf swing is a connected series of feels,
and when you get these feels right and rightly connected,
you will swing perfectly."*

Teaching was in Percy Boomer's blood. His father was the schoolmaster in Grouville, a remote village on the Channel Island of Jersey, where, remarkably, Percy's schoolmates included a pair of lads who would rise to dominate the game of golf—Harry Vardon and Ted Ray. With those two as his inspiration, Percy became a fair player himself.

But he was no Vardon. "I am not a natural golfer," he admitted late in his career. "There is nothing instinctive about my game. Everything I have ever done in golf I had to learn to do." Happily, Percy enjoyed the learning—and the teaching as well. For a couple of years he followed in his father's footsteps, but in his heart he knew it was not history or mathematics he wanted to teach, but golf. So he left the schoolhouse for the clubhouse, joining the Bournemouth Golf Club as assistant professional.

His opening drive at Bournemouth was less than auspicious. In front of his brand-new bosses, he topped the ball off the first tee. It was a shot he would never have hit, had he not been a bundle of nerves. But the embarrassment of that moment gave way to a fascination with what had caused it—that insidious golf linkage between the mind and the mus-

THE SECRET:

Get the feel of three key moves. Once you do that, your mind will free up and your swing will flow.

cles. Boomer would become the first major teacher to explore the psychological challenges inherent in the game.

After a series of jobs in southern England, he landed the head professional position at St. Cloud near Paris. It was there that he came into his own as both a player and a teacher, winning the Belgian, Dutch, and Swiss Opens while developing a new way of learning the game.

"My father had always taught me that one of the greatest virtues in the world is simplicity," he said, "and so I sought a simple way of making a swing. Then I sought a simple way of teaching that swing to others."

Among the concepts he advanced was the notion of muscle memory, of ingraining positions and movements so that they could be repeated naturally, without attention to mechanics. In fact, he urged his students to view the swing not as a motion but as a "feel"—actually a series of feels and images— that when properly executed become one smooth, seamless continuum. He also believed that every shot in golf was the same, often repeating the mantra "you drive as you putt, you putt as you drive."

Boomer claims he tried twenty times to write his opus, *On Learning Golf*, never thinking he could quite bring it off, but on the twenty-first attempt in 1942, he did. For a man bent on simplicity, he produced an oddly chatty book—full of gossipy anecdotes and meandering asides, with instructional "interludes" as he calls them. He may have

Boomer won the Belgian, Dutch, and Swiss Opens, but was always a teacher at heart.

formatted the book in this way because his musings on the golf swing tend to be very detailed and require the reader's complete attention. But Boomer's inquisitive, inventive mind is there on every page—part player, part teacher, part psychiatrist—ever seeking ways to simplify the game. A classic example is his image for the proper backswing: Turn in a barrel. It's as apt today as the day he came up with it. Indeed, nearly every top teacher of the last fifty years will tell you he owes something to Percy Boomer.

BOOMER'S SECRET

The most difficult thing about learning golf is to learn to distract your mind from everything except the feeling of what you are about to perform.

Now no teacher can *tell* you in exact words how it feels when you make a certain movement correctly. You will have to use your imagination to interpret what he says, and if he is wise he will encourage you to use it.

Let me give you an example. I want to teach you to pivot from the hips. Now I can show you how it is done and issue the usual mass of detailed instruction, but that does not call up your imagination and it gives you no conception of how it *feels* to pivot correctly.

So, instead of explaining all the mechanical and anatomical details of the pivot to you, I show you how to pivot and then tell you to do it yourself *imagining that you are standing in a barrel hip high and big enough to be just free at each hip but with a close enough fit to allow no movement except the pivot.* At once you get the *feeling* of the pivot. Incidentally, nine out of ten golfers would improve their games if they would use this image to the fullest degree in practice.

So far so good; we can learn to feel the body turn to the right and round to the left, beautifully fixed in space by the hips. Now carry the image a stage further: First, as you pivot, *sink down from the knee*—you will feel that if you sink down, even ever so little, you will

Any excess of upness (that is, actual shoulder lift) will result in the ball being lost sight of. In short, the fixed head determines the limit of lift and dip of the shoulders.

become stuck in the barrel. *This will not do,* so you must feel that you keep your hips up on a level with the top of the barrel. Do this and you will develop the feel of keeping your hips *up* as you pivot—a thing which, unfortunately for our golf, very few of us do.

We have laid our foundation by getting the *feel* of the pivot from the hips. This movement goes up through the body to the next control point—the shoulders. And here I believe that wrong imagination does a great deal of damage to many people's swings.

We think that in the fine swing, we see the left shoulder come down as we come back and the right shoulder come down as we come forward; so we feel that this shoulder movement is *right* and tend to encourage it—to the detriment of our swings, because it is *wrong*. And I say it is wrong, cheerfully certain that it *is* wrong in spite of its almost universal acceptance. How much the shoulders actually dip depends upon how erect we stand when addressing the ball. We should stand as erect as possible and I contend that we should *not* feel our shoulders go down but should feel that we are keeping them fully up.

As we address the ball, we look at it a little sideways—we *peep* at it. The head is fixed (because you "keep your eye on the ball"), and the movement of the shoulders is not an independent movement of the shoulders at all, but is due to the shoulders *being moved around from the pivot.* We can only keep the shoulder movement in a fixed groove and make it *repeatable* time after time, by keeping the shoulders at the limit of *upness* in whatever position the turn from the hips may have placed them. Any *excess* of upness (that is, actual shoulder lift) will result in the ball being lost sight of. In short, the fixed head

determines the limit of lift and dip of the shoulders.

You will see that this is why you must feel you keep the shoulders up to the same degree with, say, a driver and a full swing and a mashie niblick (a more upright club) and a half swing. The closer you stand to your ball, the more upright the swing and the more directly downward your sight of the ball. Also, the less extensive the swing you can make without losing sight of the ball.

Now try this conception of the shoulder action without a club, and *link it to your feel of the pivot from the hips.* Feel how the two

Among Boomer's swing keys: A passive upper body, active lower body.

A controlled swing rests on three "feels":
1) lower-body pivot, 2) the shoulders
moving in response to the pivot, and
3) the arms moving in response to the
shoulders.

become connected. This is the first connection in our building up of a controlled swing—and a very important one. You cannot take too much trouble in understanding it and building it up.

From the shoulders our power travels down through the arms, and as to arm action, also I believe the common conception to be erroneous. Most people think they lift their arms to get them to the top of the backswing. With a modern controlled swing they do not lift them. The arms work absolutely subjectively to the shoulders, that is why they *are* controlled.

But, you may say, if I do not lift my arms, how do I get them up to the top of my swing? To find the answer, think this

out. As you stand to the ball with the wrists slightly up, there is a straight line practically from the clubhead up the shaft and along your arm to the left shoulder, and as your hands are already waist high, it needs only the inclining of the shoulders as we turn (on the pivot) to bring them *shoulder high,* without having altered their relative positions at all. They have not been *lifted;* they have gone up in response to the shoulder movement. This accounts for the curtailment *and* the control of the modern swing.

Naturally, the more flexible we are, the more we can get our hands *up* without breaking up this connection, that is, without moving the arms independently. The triangle formed by our arms and a line between the shoulders should never lose its shape. It should be possible to push a wooden snooker triangle in between the arms and to leave it there without impeding the swing back or through.

Now to my mind the foregoing are the three basic *feels* of the golf swing—the pivot, the shoulders moving in response to the pivot, and the arms moving in response to the shoulders. These are the basic movements of a connected and therefore *controlled* swing, and they must all be built into the framework of your *feel* of the swing.

FROM *ON LEARNING GOLF* BY PERCY BOOMER

Mr. Unflappable's Effortless Power

"People often ask me,
'How do you hit the ball so far when you swing so easy?'
The answer is simple. I hit hard."

Today we have Ernie Els. Half a century ago, the man with the unflappable demeanor and effortless swing was Julius Boros. No one made the game look easier.

The fourth of six children born to Hungarian immigrants, Boros caddied as a youngster, played on his high school golf team, and after four years of playing at Biloxi Air Force Base while with the Army Air Corps, returned home to Connecticut as one of the finest players in the state. At that point, many men would have jumped onto the pro tour, but Julie liked to do things at his own pace. Instead, he became an accountant.

It wasn't until four years later that he made his move, and then only after encouragement from no less than Sam Snead. The Slammer, after one look at Boros's syrupy smooth swing, urged him to begin playing for pay. So in 1950, Boros and his young wife took the big step.

In his first tournament, he finished ninth. More than a year later, however, Boros had not made his mark, and he was about to face the darkest moment of his life. It was just days after the arrival of their first child, but a big tournament—the Empire State Open in Albany, New York—was on the schedule.

"I'll be alright," said his wife, nicknamed Buttons. "You just go ahead and win."

A few days later, Ann Cosgrove Boros was dead of a cerebral hemorrhage. She was twenty-three. Boros was devastated and considered giving up the game, but after a four-month layoff returned to the Tour in

In 1963 at Brookline, Boros received the U.S. Open trophy from Francis Ouimet, who won there in 1913.

the Country Club in Brookline, Massachusetts (he birdied the last three holes to reach an eighteen-hole playoff in which he beat Jackie Cupit and Arnold Palmer). At age forty-eight, Boros won the PGA Championship in 1968, making him the oldest man ever to win one of the game's four major titles. Boros competed in four Ryder Cups, and lost only three of the sixteen matches he played.

THE SECRET:

*S*wing back with your shoulders—that way, you can't swing too fast—but release powerfully with your hands.

Surely both his match-play mettle and the longevity of his competitive career were reflections of his placid, almost phlegmatic personality. He never agonized over a shot and took little time pulling a club from his bag. His credo was "By the time you get to your ball, if you don't know what to do with it, try another sport."

But if Boros's pace of play was swift, his swing was anything but—an almost listless pass through the ball that seemed to be delivered at about sixty percent of his power but nonetheless produced prodigious drives. There was a time in America when everyone wanted to swing not like Palmer or Nicklaus, but just like Julius Boros. In 1965, with his book *Swing Easy, Hit Hard,* he told them how.

1952, determined to fulfill his wife's wish for a victory. That June, it happened. At the Northwood Club in Dallas, Texas, he outplayed Ben Hogan to win the biggest prize of all, the U.S. Open. Boros finished as the Tour's leading money winner that year.

He would remarry and go on to produce six children and eighteen professional victories, including a second U.S. Open in 1963 at

BOROS'S SECRET

The Dependable Backswing

The proper backswing is the most crucial part of the repeating swing. The very first move of the backswing—the first few inches—determines everything which will come later. If something is wrong in the beginning, some compensation will have to be made to bring about correct contact at impact. (In most cases this leads to further disaster.)

The term "one-piece swing" has been so abused and misinterpreted that I hesitate to use it—but here it is: If you can visualize yourself, at address, as cast in solid concrete from the hips up, with movement only in your wrists and neck, it might help you to understand how important this starting spot is. Although concrete would be rigid, you must not feel rigid or tense.

Start back by turning your shoulders and everything else will move smoothly and slowly. This will

A fast backswing doesn't contribute any extra power but it will upset control.

help prevent jerking, lifting, and swaying. It's worth repeating. *Turn with your shoulders.* Swing back as far as you comfortably can and if you have kept undue tension out of your arms, your wrists will cock or break naturally. You would have to act deliberately to stop them from cocking.

Throughout the entire swing your left arm should remain comfortably straight and in complete and constant control. Your right hand retains a firm but inactive grip. When

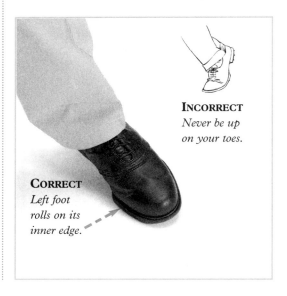

INCORRECT
Never be up on your toes.

CORRECT
Left foot rolls on its inner edge.

fully turned, you will be looking at your ball over your left shoulder. Your left foot has rolled onto its inner edge and your left knee will be bent toward your right foot. The left heel remains on the ground or it may lift off slightly, never very much. Pressure should be felt on the inner edges of both feet.

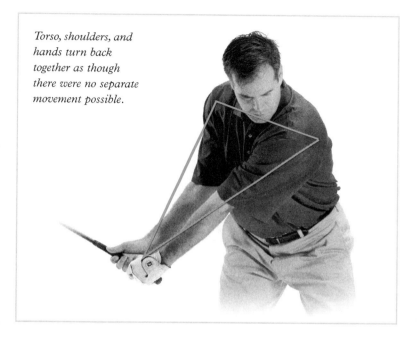

Torso, shoulders, and hands turn back together as though there were no separate movement possible.

The backswing should be smooth and easy as all it is doing is pulling the left side muscles taut, like pulling back a bowstring. A fast backswing doesn't contribute any extra power but it will upset control. The fallacy that you have to swing hard and fast is one that everyone should get over now. It is impossible to hit the ball well consistently if you're swinging too fast.

The Power-Producing Forward Swing

As your forward swing or downswing starts, your left side muscles start to contract in proper sequence. They start contracting gently just before your backswing has been completed, which is the reason for being able to stop your backswing under control.

This is like gently applying your brakes so that you can glide smoothly into your forward swing without a jerk. (Practice this in slow motion and study each part in the sequence.)

Chain Action

First your left heel goes down to the ground, which causes your left knee to straighten some. Your hips slide laterally around and toward the left as your leg and hip muscles pull. Your left leg now becomes the strong anchor point of resistance, around or against which the rest of the action takes place. The chain action now pulls your shoulders

Begin with your weight a little heavier on your right foot—ball about two inches back of your left heel. Right knee bent left a little— all parts firm but relaxed.

just as they did on the backswing. Let your shoulders lead your hands down. Your forward swing starts smoothly and slowly, and as your powerful shoulder and back muscles come into full play, the entire action picks up momentum.

At the point where your left arm has pulled your hands down to about waist height, which is the start of the hitting zone, your right elbow is still bent at almost a right angle and your wrists are still in a fully cocked position. At this point your weight is pretty evenly balanced on both feet. Your right knee is pulling in toward the ball, forcing your weight against your left leg, which is straightening and providing the necessary resistance for hitting power. The straightening of your left knee at this point pushes your body up from the "sitting down" position. Your left shoulder goes up and your right shoulder comes in under, square to the intended line of flight. Your shoulders turn fast enough to bring them square to the line in good

around and your left shoulder and back muscles start slowly pulling your left arm down. The strong muscles of your right chest are pulling your right arm down. Your shoulders and hands are moving as a unit

timing and you hit with your hands. It is an easy mistake to turn your shoulders too fast at this point, as if you were hitting with your shoulders, thus losing the feeling of control in your hands.

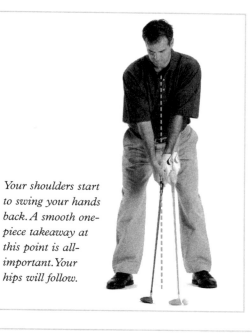

Your shoulders start
to swing your hands
back. A smooth one-
piece takeaway at
this point is all-
important. Your
hips will follow.

This is as far back
as you can go on
the backswing
without a full
shoulder turn.

The top of the swing. Shoulders
are turned further than the
hips, left arm is straight, wrists
are fully cocked. Club is almost
horizontal in closed position.
Right knee is slightly flexed;
left knee is bent to the right.
Left foot has rolled onto its
inner edge. You are "set" to
start your forward swing.

BOROS'S SECRET

Forward-swing sequence: the hips have shifted laterally and turned. Push is against the left leg. Balance is centered.

Shoulders are turning, pulling the arms down. Right elbow has dropped into the side. Wrists are fully cocked as they approach the hitting zone.

The Explosive Blast-off

Now comes the explosive blast-off. The unwinding body pivot continues smoothly. Your right elbow straightens forcefully, and because of the great speed your clubhead is already traveling, your cocked wrists will be forced to release your hands. The speed you choose to use is determined by you beforehand. The faster your clubhead speed, the farther your ball should go if contacted solidly. Your right side has taken positive action. Your left hip has turned past the line a little as it must be in the lead and out of the way of your hands. After impact your

body weight moves onto and beyond your left foot in a continuous motion to a complete follow-through, which causes you to roll onto the outer edge of your left foot.

Although each of these movements do take place as I have described them, they follow each other so rapidly that it feels like everything is moving in "one piece." You shouldn't be conscious of any separate actions.

Swing Easy, Hit Hard

Probably the heart of the action which makes my swing look easy, and which

The hips have shifted fully and turned out of the way of the hands. Right shoulder has come in under, square to the line. Right forearm has straightened, wrists have released, lashing the clubhead into the ball. The upper body weight has remained behind the ball.

Wrists releasing after your hands have reached the hitting zone, contributing to a greater hitting force.

brings about the title of this book, *Swing Easy, Hit Hard,* lies in this chapter. I never feel that I am in danger of being too fast on my backswing simply because my shoulders just won't start too fast. As my hands reach the hitting zone, I can increase their speed

to anything I choose within my capabilities. So here you have the secret. *Turn with your shoulders; hit with your hands.*

FROM *SWING EASY, HIT HARD* BY JULIUS BOROS

BOROS'S SECRET

HENRY COTTON

HELPING HANDS

"All that counts in golf is to find the back of the ball squarely with the middle of the clubface. Any style or method will do, and if it enables a player to strike the ball hard, squarely, and consistently, then it is a good swing, no matter how it may depart from the classical."

Thomas Henry Cotton was the greatest British golfer of his time. In an age when no other Briton won the Open Championship more than once, Sir Henry won it three times while also bringing a large measure of style and dignity to his profession.

From the mid-1930s through the early 1950s, he dominated the game in Europe as no one had since Vardon. Then he retired to become golf's first renaissance man, a successful teacher, author, broadcaster, and golf-course architect.

Cotton lacked the natural talent of most top players but compensated with a world-class work ethic, pursuing technical perfection with an intensity equaled perhaps only by Ben Hogan. Like Hogan , Cotton was a supremely analytical man who spent as much time thinking about the game as playing it.

One of the first things he came to realize was that he lacked the raw strength of most of his rivals. Among them was Abe Mitchell, a man whose flashing, powerful swing allowed him to drive a ball 300 yards and more, even with hickory shafts.

"I dreamed of one day having hands and wrists that would enable me to do what he did

> **THE SECRET:** "Educate" and strengthen your hands by hitting repeatedly against the side of an automobile tire.

Style and substance: Cotton was the finest British player of his time.

until I realized that just swinging a golf club and hitting golf balls wasn't enough. I was getting better, but too slowly. Abe had been a gardener as a young man and hard manual work had given him tremendously strong arms and hands and a tough yet supple back. I decided that I too needed a stronger drill."

Sadly for Cotton, he did not find that drill until relatively late in his career, but he embraced it with fervor and was able to win tournaments well into his forties. Even at age fifty, he finished tied for sixth in the Open Championship, beating every Briton in the field but one.

The drill came to him serendipitously as he was walking from his car to the pro shop of his golf club in England. He would describe the

with the clubhead: swish it through the ball with a piercing whistle," said Cotton. "So I tried and tried, and practiced day and night

moment in *Thanks for the Game,* one of several chatty, anecdote-filled instruction books he wrote after his playing days had ended.

COTTON'S SECRET

I had concentrated on playing and practicing golf seriously since I was about sixteen, and looking back I realized I should have done other exercises. I ought to have carried on playing football and cricket, and gone on building my body in the gym, and done more running. So I began thinking of what I could do to drive the ball farther and develop a faster impact. I finally hit on the idea of swinging in long grass as a way of offering greater resistance to the clubhead.

I used to go to a quiet spot on the golf course and swing away for hours in the deepest rough I could find, using the clubhead like a scythe. It took some doing, and was extremely hard work, but it worked: I began to win tournaments.

Then golf courses became more manicured. There was less long grass and I couldn't find enough "hay" to mow. When I had practiced for years hitting the ball one-handed using each hand in turn, my left hand became so "well educated" that I could use it alone to hit a 4-wood "off the deck" almost 200 yards every time.

But with the long grass needed for practice becoming more and more difficult to find, I had to discover a suitable substitute. Then one day at Temple, near Maidenhead, my home club at the time, I parked my car right behind the professional's shop and saw an old motor tire lying abandoned on the ground. Whoever dumped it there had no idea of the contribution he was unwittingly to make to the game of golf! I gave the tire a good kick to move it out of the way and it suddenly occurred to me that this was the thing to hit with a golf club to strengthen

Hitting against a tire will "educate" your hands, giving them added strength and flexibility.

and educate the hands. I popped into my shop, selected an old iron, and set about striking the tire. It worked so well that I had mixed feelings: I was delighted to have made the discovery, but regretted it had come so late, for by this time I had practically retired from competitive golf.

In 1968 I finally moved to live and work in Penina, Portugal, where two years earlier I had completed building the new course. Pupils and promising amateurs wanting to turn pro took to the new exercise with enthusiasm, and news of its value quickly spread through the golfing world. The "tire drill" certainly developed strength and flexibility but I also wanted to achieve greater *speed* through the impact area. So, using a steel golf shaft without a head, but with a grip, I devised a set of exercises involving a fast to-and-fro whipping action inside the tire. As the headless club could be moved to and fro so much faster than a real club, overall speed of action was improved, but perhaps more important, the pupil could concentrate on taking the full shock of impact on the hands, while maintaining a tight grip on the club, but *without* slowing down the speed of the clubhead.

Many players seem to relax the hands at impact because if they grip too tightly they slow the action. But if they hold the club loosely, it tends to slip. It is all a question of finding the optimum grip required to keep the clubhead moving fast while retaining strength enough to avoid mis-hitting if you do fail to make contact with the dead center of the clubface.

The tire drill is now a ritual for me. A few blows at a time are enough and then it is a matter of recognizing any weak points and working on them—educating the hands to complement each other so that they work in harmony. Some people will whack the tire too often or for too long, not realizing how tired they are becoming—and then immediately go out to play a game only to find they are not striking the ball well. Muscles need hard exercise, but they also need a period of rest before being asked to perform at peak. Working out a practice routine to suit your individual game is one of the secrets of success.

FROM *THANKS FOR THE GAME* BY HENRY COTTON

J O E   D A N T E

A DOCTOR AFTER ALL

*"The golf swing is heavily overlaid
with a sludge of fallacy, misunderstanding,
faulty theory, myth, and just plain ignorance.
It is this sludge that we will cut away."*

Joe Dante didn't want to become a golf professional. Oh, he had the requisite talent. He'd compiled quite a playing record as a kid in his home state of New Jersey, even made it to the U.S. Open one year. But he didn't want to be a golf pro—he wanted to be a doctor.

Some things, however, simply are preordained. The first thing that compelled Joe's path was World War II. Like just about every able-bodied male of the time, he enlisted and was shipped off to Europe. In December of 1944, he helped defeat an army of 600,000 Germans in the Battle of the Bulge. By the time he came home, however, he was twenty-five years old, and a medical education seemed just too long a haul. Meanwhile, golf—specifically the teaching of golf—was in Joe Dante's blood. His father, Jim, was one of the most highly regarded teaching professionals in the New York area, a founder and president of the New Jersey State Professional Golfers Association. From his dad, Joe had learned not only how to play the game but how to teach it. And so, in the summer of 1945, Joe Dante joined the staff at the Braidburn Country Club, in Florham Park, New Jersey, as assistant professional to Jim Dante. A few years later, he moved to the foot of the Pocono Mountains and became the head professional at Rockaway

> **THE SECRET:**
>
> Start your downswing with a slide of the hips.

River, the club where his father had begun—in 1920—the year of Joe's birth. Yes, some things are pre-ordained.

Joe would become an institution at Rockaway River, running the golf operation for thirty-six years and becoming a highly sought-after teacher. Like his father, who once had the temerity to suggest that Harry Vardon did not swing the way he said he did, Joe had a keen eye for swing faults and an ability to communicate his points clearly to his students.

In 1947 Jim Dante wrote a manuscript for an instruction book, *The Nine Bad Shots in Golf and What to Do About Them,* but since he had no national reputation, Leo Diegel, a two-time PGA Championship winner, was paid to put his name on the cover as co-author. The book became a best-seller.

Dante believed the first move of the downswing was the most important area of golf.

Joe Dante would outdo his father, writing not one best-seller but three of them, in the process proving to be every inch the healer he'd aspired to become. He begins *The Four Magic Moves to Winning Golf* by "sweeping out the rubbish," debunking the myriad myths that cloud most golfers' minds. Then he sets forth his keys, among them the notion of an early wrist break on the backswing, a con- cept that Dante was among the first to sug- gest. He is also acknowledged as the first teacher to relate the physics theory of "con- servation of angular momentum" to golf, as applied to the delayed release of the wrists. What follows is his discussion of the faults and cures in "the most important and critical area of golf," the first move of the downswing.

DANTE'S SECRET

We have now reached the most important and critical area of golf—the first movement of the downswing. With it we uncover the most common and at the same time most devastating flaws.

Fatal flaw   Sunday duffer spin.
Awful results   Pull, slice, hook, smother, or shank.
Magic move   Lateral hip slide, with head back.
Check points   One knuckle of left hand visible, two of right hand; right arm touching side.

The golf swing itself is probably the most difficult and certainly the most elusive action in all athletics. Beyond question it is the most frustrating, and nowhere more so than at this very point, where the club and the body make their first moves down toward the ball.

The peak of frustration is reached here because, no matter what has gone before it, this one move can make a greater difference in the result of the swing and the shot than any other. We can have a perfect grip, start back from the ball properly, reach the top in faultless position—and then ruin it all by the next move we make. Not only *can* the swing be ruined by this move, it *is* ruined about 95 percent of the time.

The Fatal Flaws

The deadly moves, the most fatal flaws, are these:

(1) Spinning the hips without moving the weight laterally, (2) with this spinning motion turning the right shoulder high toward the ball, and (3) trying to move the clubhead or slowing down the hands.

These moves bring quick disaster by causing two things. They make us hit too soon and they make us hit from the outside in. The first robs us of distance, the second

To counteract spinning-out, and the many poor shots it leads to, the master move is a slide of the hips at the start of the downswing. The weight moves left as the hips shift laterally rather than spinning around. As a result, the right elbow returns to the right hip and the wrist cock is retained in preparation for a powerful hit.

of direction—and what else do we want from a full shot?

Because we hit too soon, the drive that might have gone 220 yards goes only 190, and into that trap that juts out into the fairway.

Because we hit from the outside instead of from the inside, the ball is pulled, and, if the face of the club is not square, it will be hooked or sliced, or perhaps smothered or even shanked. The best we can hope for is that we will slice it only a little and that, after starting to the left, it will curve back into the fairway. Even if we are that lucky, we will know we have hit a weak and sloppy shot.

These are the actions and these are the shots that we see on every private course in the country, every public course, and in stall after stall of every driving range. It can truthfully be said that this is the natural way to hit a golf ball—with the Sunday duffer spin.

The golf swing itself is probably the most difficult and certainly the most elusive action in all athletics.

It is also the principal reason that the scores of our millions of players remain so high.

The Magic Moves

So what are the right moves, the magic moves? They are, simply: (1) Move the hips *laterally* to the left, while (2) keeping the head back and (3) making no effort whatever to move the club.

The hips will turn if they are moved laterally, but they are very liable not to move laterally if they are merely turned.

We cannot emphasize too strongly that the movement of the hips must be *lateral* and not a turning motion. When the hips are moved laterally to the left from the top of the swing, they carry the weight (which has been mostly on the right leg) along. They move it toward the approximately equal distribution, at least, which we must have at impact.

That is the first reason we must move the hips laterally. The second reason is that, since we are twisted and wound up tightly at the top, any turning movement of our hips turns our shoulders too. It turns our right shoulder around high and toward the ball. Hence, when we bring the club down, we have to bring it from the outside in.

The hips will turn if they are moved laterally, but they are very liable not to move laterally if they are merely turned. You can prove this to yourself by standing up and moving your hips to the left as far as they

will go. As they near the limit of extension, they will turn and you cannot stop them. At the top of the swing, of course, the hips are turned somewhat to the right, maybe 45 degrees, and as you move them laterally, they will quickly begin to turn back to the left. The trick is to get them going to the left, laterally, before they turn too much. If you ask how much is too much, you become hopelessly involved. You might as well ask how many angels can dance on the head of a pin. You don't have to worry about that. Just be sure you get the hips going laterally and that you don't *try* to turn them.

A third reason for the lateral slide of the hips is that this is the movement which *starts the club down toward the ball*, by causing the shoulders to rock slightly as they turn. That movement of the hips—and nothing else—provides the first impetus for the downswing.

It might help you to visualize this action if you think of the spine as being the axis of the swing. Now think of the axis as being a T-square, with the shank as the spine and the crosspiece the shoulders. The end of the shank reaches down to the pelvis or hips. As we address the ball this T-square is, for purposes of the comparison, vertical. On the backswing the hips

That movement of the hips—and nothing else—provides the first impetus for the downswing.

move slightly to the right, causing the cross-piece to tilt slightly to the left, as it turns, of course, with the turning shoulders. On the downswing (and here is the critical point), the low end of the shank (the hips) is moved sharply to the left. This causes an immediate and definite tilting of the crosspiece to the right—and that is what starts the shoulders, arms, and club moving down toward the ball. This will be true so long as the whole swinging system
is twisted tight, so that a movement against the twist in any one part moves all the other parts. Make no mistake about it, the hips are what move the shoulders and club and start the downswing.

Our second injunction was to *keep the head back*. The head, at this stage, plays a vital role. You have often heard and read that the head is the anchor of the swing. Right here it is. If we keep the head back as we move the hips laterally, it keeps the upper part of our body from going with the hips and thus loosening or relaxing the tension we have been at such pains to build up with the backswing.

This tension that we had at the top of the swing must be kept as long as possible as the swing comes down to the ball. This is one of the chief factors that give power to the swing and speed to the club. If the head comes forward at this point, we lose the tension and get ourselves, in a manner of speaking, "over the ball" as we hit it.

If we keep the head back we do in truth

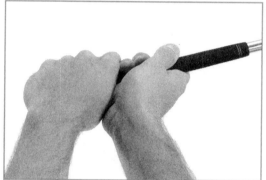

To check your hand-wrist position, stop your down-swing at the so-called hitting position. You should see only one knuckle of the left hand and two knuckles of the right, as above. If you see two or three knuckles of the left and only one of the right, as below, you have lost the position gained by the backward break.

stay back of the ball where we should be. That is what is meant by the advice to "stay back of the ball."

The head, as a matter of fact, has a strange little action of its own during the first movement of the downswing. Contrary

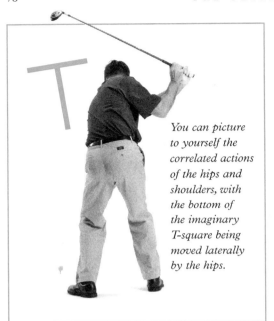

You can picture
to yourself the
correlated actions
of the hips and
shoulders, with
the bottom of
the imaginary
T-square being
moved laterally
by the hips.

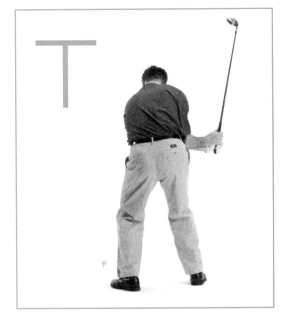

This causes the
cross-piece of
the square
(the shoulders)
to tip somewhat
and bring the
hands down
inside instead of
outside.

to the old principle that the head must be kept still at all costs, it moves. Pictures of our best modem golfers show that the head not only stays back but that it drops somewhat and, with most, even moves backward a couple of inches.

Almost sacrilegious, this seems. Yet there is a logical reason for it. As the hips move as far as they can to the left, and turn when they can move laterally no farther, and as the shoulders tilt, elevating the left and depressing the right, the body bows out toward the target. If the head doesn't go forward with the body, it has to come down—unless we suddenly grow a few inches during the downswing. An archer's bow may be used as an example of what we mean. The bow may measure five feet from tip to tip before it is strung. When it is strung it curves outward and the distance from tip to tip is less than five feet. When the archer draws it to shoot an arrow, the tip-to-tip distance is still less. When a golfer hits the ball as he should hit it, his body takes the place of the bow: It curves out toward the target and the distance from head to feet is less than when he stands up to the ball.

Another reason the head drops slightly as the ball is hit is that most of the better players develop a rather definite knee bend as they come into the hitting area. They make it a practice to keep both knees bent all through the swing, as they should be, and when they bring the club down to the ball with great speed, the centrifugal force exerted by the flying club head seems almost to pull them down just slightly and hence bend their knees ever so little more.

Our third injunction in this first move from the top was *Make no effort to move the club.*

The club, of course, will move. It will be moved by the shoulders. What we mean is that no effort should be made with the wrists, hands, or arms to make the club move. That is the important point. If we could turn the arms, hands, and wrists into wood for a fraction of a second as the downswing begins, it would be perfect. Then they and the club would be "frozen" into one solid unit and they would all start down together in one piece, motivated by the rocking, turning shoulders. Then if, with some electronic impulse, we could switch them back to life again as the hands got down to about the hip position, we would have the perfect movement.

When a golfer hits the ball as he should, his body bends like an archer's bow. It curves out toward the target and the distance from head to feet is less than when he stands up.

The whole downward action is initiated by the lateral movement of the hips to the left. Since at the top we are in a tightly coiled position, this hip action causes the shoulders to rock to the right and turn. The rocking action, with the left shoulder coming up and the right going down, is what moves the arms and the club. If the right shoulder comes down (rocks slightly) as it begins to turn, it brings the upper right arm against the right side and the swing starts down on an inside line. It is when the shoulders turn, throwing the right shoulder high and out toward the ball, that the swing goes outside. Keeping the head back helps the slight rocking action which brings the right shoulder down.

> **One of the most important things in golf is making the first move from the top without letting the angle between the shaft and the left arm open.**

One of the most important things in golf is making this first movement from the top without letting the angle between the shaft and the left arm open. The peculiar thing about it is that if the hip, shoulder, and hand actions are correct, the angle will not open. If they are wrong, it will.

The instant the right shoulder starts to move out high toward the ball, the arm-shaft angle begins to open, even if no effort is made by the hands to swing the club. Most of the time the angle is opened up because the hands are trying to do something with the club. But even without the hands doing anything, the angle will still open if the wrong shoulder action is made.

We have said several times that the arm-club angle should be held as long as possible. From our use of the words *keep, hold,* and *retain,* you may have gotten the idea that a conscious physical effort must be made to hold this angle. This is not true. What we mean is, if the swing is right, the angle will automatically be preserved until late in the downswing. So, when we say the angle must be held, we mean that you must work on attaining the correct hip, shoulder, and hand motion which will permit the wrists to remain cocked and the angle preserved. Do nothing, in any event, to get rid of the wrist cock.

The motion is essentially that of the hips. If you have read much about the technique of the swing, you have read that the left hip should lead the downswing. You have read in this chapter that the first movement from the top is a lateral thrust of the hips to the left, eventually followed by an automatic turning of the hips. This is true. But there is more than that.

The hips must not only move to the left and turn, *their movement must be so closely tied to the left arm that it pulls the arm and the club down and whips them through the ball.*

There must be a definite, conscious feeling that this is happening. It is the single most important movement that a good golfer makes.

THE ETERNAL TRIANGLE

Here we see how the wrist cock is retained through the first part of the downswing, finally breaking open only after the hands get down to waist height or even a little below. The average player breaks the triangle much too early.

*Fully coiled
at the top.*

*The lateral
hip slide
begins.*

*This sequence shows how the left hip and left
side lead the hands and the club all the way
down and through the ball. It also shows how
the hips must go through all the way, to bring
the weight far over to the left leg while the head
and upper part of the body stay back. Finally,
it reveals how the hips turn toward the target
as they reach the extension of their lateral
movement. Are your hips ever in this position
when you hit the ball?*

This is not to be confused with the mistaken advice to start down with a pull of the
left arm. What happens, actually, is that the
left arm itself is *being pulled* by the hips. The
arm is merely the connecting rod between
the hips and the club.

When the hips exert this pulling action,
they cause the shoulders and the left arm to
revolve so fast around the axis of the upper
spine that the hands have little or no time to
manipulate or do anything whatever with the
club except hang onto it.

If there is one single secret to the golf
swing, this is it. Moving the hips in this fashion would seem a simple thing to do. It is

The left arm and club are pulled into impact.

The hips, having shifted fully, rotate toward the target.

easy to say and easy to understand. Yet nearly all of the vast army of golfers fails to do it.

They fail for two reasons. The first is that this is a *big* movement and they are afraid to make it. The second is that, preoccupied with what they think they must make the club head do, they completely forget the fundamental hip action and let it die.

The tight connection between the hips and the club, and the consequent pull the club gets from the hip action, is the single greatest source of power in the golf swing. The big muscles of the upper legs and of the torso are giving the club a flying start before the hands do anything.

How do we know when to start the hip movement? We start it the instant we feel the backward momentum of the club start to pull against our hands at the top. This is a reflex action with most of us, but for those who want the moment pinpointed, there it is. And once you start to move the hips, keep them flying—all the way through until they turn toward the target. This action alone will cure a great number of golfing ills.

FROM *THE FOUR MAGIC MOVES TO WINNING GOLF* BY JOE DANTE

J. DOUGLAS EDGAR

THE INSIDE WORD

"I have not discovered any wonderful new secret that has made golf easy for myself or is going to do so for you; what I have discovered, however, is the underlying secret of success of all the greatest players, and even of the worst players when they have unexpectedly made a good shot."

James Douglas Edgar had three first names and one first-rate idea.

Born in 1895 in Newcastle-on-Tyne, England, Edgar took to the game at an early age, combining natural athletic ability with an intuitive grasp of swing mechanics, and quickly became one the top players in the British Isles. Six-time British Open Champion Harry Vardon hailed him as "the man who one day will be the greatest of us all." By age nineteen, Edgar had won the French Open, landed the professional's job at Northumberland Golf Club, and begun to gain a reputation as a top-notch teacher.

It was only a short time before that reputation spread to America, and in 1918 he was offered a job as professional at the Druid Hills Golf Club in Atlanta. Leaving his wife and two children behind in Newcastle, Edgar moved to Georgia and became an immediate sensation, both with Atlanta's gentlemen golfers and with their wives.

"He is an artist in golf in the same way Caruso is in music. When the mood is on him, he could tear apart any golf course," wrote a local journalist, while a member of the fairer sex described Edgar as "the most fascinating man that ever hit this town."

Edgar took enough time off from teaching and partying to win the 1919 Canadian Open by 16 strokes, a margin of victory that has been equaled but never bettered in any professional event. A year later he successfully defended his title and finished second in the PGA Championship.

Men were impressed by Edgar's golf. Women were impressed by Edgar.

A year after that, J. Douglas Edgar was dead—murdered. The details of the incident were never learned, but Edgar was found unconscious outside his boarding house, with blood gushing from his severed femoral artery.

"He was still alive when I got to him," his roommate and lifelong friend Tommy Wilson told the police. "He tried to tell me something but I couldn't understand. He died before we reached the hospital."

Initially, Edgar was deemed the victim of a hit and run. Several neighbors reported hearing a car hit something, and one saw a vehicle speeding away from the scene. But Edgar's body wasn't bruised, and the wound that killed him was half an inch wide and three inches deep—more consistent with a stab by a knife than a ram by a Model T.

Given Edgar's knack with the ladies, there were rumors and suspicions, but the police investigation turned up nothing and his death was recorded in Georgia's Bureau of Vital Statistics as "possibly caused by an automobile accident."

J. Douglas Edgar's life ended just as he'd reached the height of his powers as both player and teacher. However, in the year prior to his death, he'd recorded his thoughts on how a golf ball should be struck. His sixty-page book, *The Gate to Golf,* was built around one notion—the proper path for the clubhead to follow in the impact zone. Those who bought the book actually received their own gate—a rubber contraption through which to swing the club—but the truth is, the gate could be simulated with any two objects.

With his gate, Edgar became the first instructor to show that the club must approach the ball on an in-to-out path, thereby helping legions of beginning American golfers banish their out-to-in, slice-causing swings. No less an instructor than Tommy Armour hailed this as a monumental contribution to the game, and nearly a century later, Edgar's inside path remains an integral part of golf teaching philosophy.

> **THE SECRET:**
>
> **M**ake your club approach the ball on an inside-to-out path.

E D G A R ' S   S E C R E T

The Movement

What is the movement? The *movement* consists of making the clubhead meet the ball in a certain manner, which will be made clear to the reader by a careful study of the photographs showing how the clubhead passes through The Gate.

For a straight shot with wood off the tee or from a good lie, the clubhead does not travel in a straight line along the line of direction, but crosses it in a curved arc. This statement may seem rather startling to some players and quite different from the principle they have hitherto acted upon. Precisely! That is my chief reason for designing this Gate and publishing this book, as there are so many golfers at the present time who are, so to speak, groping in the dark. They may have worked hard at the game, and know a certain amount about it, but while they can probably play other games, such as lawn tennis, well, they have never "got away" with golf as they feel they should.

The manner in which the clubhead meets the ball is the essential part of the

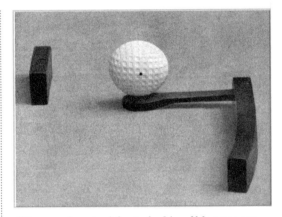

Edgar made a special gate for himself, but two tees work just as well.

golf swing. It is in the two or three feet immediately before and after impact where the real business takes place; it is *there* that the master-stroke is made and the duffer's shot is marred, and it is to this part of the swing that I am referring when I speak of *the movement.*

It is not the position of the hands, wrists, elbows, body, etc., at the top of the swing that makes the shot, nor is it a wonderful follow-through. It must not be concluded, however, that the position of body and hands at the top of the swing

J. Douglas Edgar stands at his Gate.

is of no account. On the contrary, it is a matter of considerable importance, for only an artist can be hopelessly wrong at the top and yet be able to adjust himself in time. But what I do want the reader to remember is that though the position at the top is important, far, far more essential is the movement.

However fine golf may be for the few lucky natural golfers, I think that for those who have acquired *the movement*—and all can certainly do so by exercising self-control and by practice—golf is intoxicating. It has the exhilarating effect of Champagne, without the after-effects.

How to Cultivate the Movement

The movement is not a natural movement, and it will not come to the ordinary golfer either naturally or easily; it will have to be cultivated and practiced. While addressing the ball, the player should have the feeling of being about *to throw* the ball to its destination, and not to lift it there. In his backward swing he should get the feeling of throwing the club round the right hip; also, he should not be afraid of letting his body go well round also. This will give him a feeling of immense power at the top, which, if followed by *the movement,*

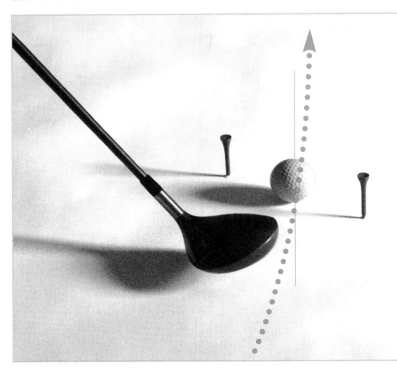

Edgar's gate can be simulated by positioning two tees as shown here—one just forward of the ball and inside the target line, the other just in back of the ball and outside the line.

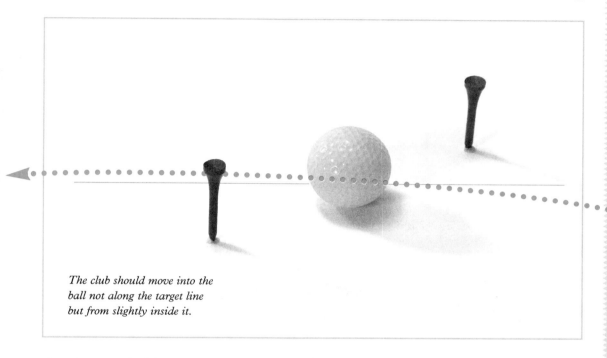

*The club should move into the
ball not along the target line
but from slightly inside it.*

also gives wonderful control over the ball.
Many players hold themselves in a very
cramped position on the backward swing,
the idea probably being that this adds steadi-
ness to their game. If, however, they were to
let a little more abandonment and "joie de
vivre" creep in, they would drive better and
farther, and at the same time get more of the
glorious exhilaration that this game holds in
store for them.

If, then, the player has thrown his club
and body well round on the backward swing,
he is now in the easiest and most natural
position to swing the clubhead through
The Gate, and so get *the movement.* During
the whole of the downward swing, his mind

should be concentrated on swinging the
clubhead through The Gate, thus getting
the movement, and for this purpose the
player should have a mental picture of the
path or sweep the clubhead has to take. Just
as in order to turn a four-in-hand through
a gate from off a road it is necessary to
have complete control of your team with
your hands, and at the same time to make
a mental picture of the sweep you are going
to take to guide your team safely through;
so in golf, complete control of the club
with the hands, and a mental picture of the
sweep, are necessary to guide the clubhead
through The Gate.

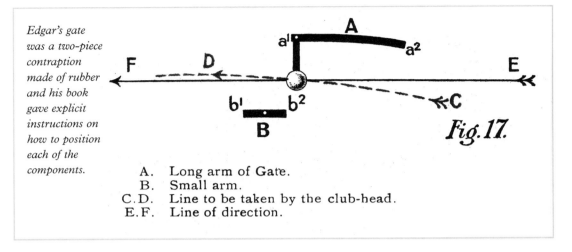

Edgar's gate was a two-piece contraption made of rubber and his book gave explicit instructions on how to position each of the components.

A.   Long arm of Gate.
B.   Small arm.
C.D.   Line to be taken by the club-head.
E.F.   Line of direction.

The Swing through The Gate

For the good player, the width between the points a₁ and b₂ will be 5½ to 6 inches. Now we come to the method of swinging through it, taking the wooden clubs first.

The important point to note is that the line taken by the clubhead is curved; that it crosses the line of direction from left to right and continues on the outward arc for a foot or so after impact, and then turns over to complete a natural finish. This gives the swing through The Gate without touching either side. Should the sides be touched or knocked over the swing is incorrect. Take up the position most suitable, easy, and comfortable to swing through on the correct line.

Some players prefer the open, others the square stance. The latter will no doubt be the easier for the majority, because when using the open stance it is much more diffi-

cult to bring the clubhead down behind to get *the movement.*

The Raison d'Etre of The Gate

Now I want most particularly to impress upon my readers that the whole idea of my Gate is to make the player concentrate on swinging the clubhead through The Gate, and that answers a two-fold purpose:

1. It compels the player to concentrate his attention on swinging the clubhead in a special way to get through The Gate, so that he has neither time nor inclination to think about trying to hit the ball. The Gate should be a strong and potent attraction to completely fill his mind, and all the cells of his brain.

2. It makes him swing the club in the correct manner, which gives him the movement.

EDGAR'S SECRET

Edgar based his teaching on just one key—swinging from in to out.

As he gets proficient from practice, the player will be able to narrow The Gate until he has such perfect control over his clubhead that he can adjust The Gate for a pull or a slice, and still swing safely through and get the required flight with comparative ease.

Practice Makes Perfect

My strongest advice to those who mean to improve in the shortest time possible is as follows: If indoors, place the Gate on a piece of oilcloth, and test yourself to see if you can swing through it confidently without hitting it; then gradually narrow it, and adjust it for different flights of the ball, until you really begin to get complete control over your club. The player with control of his club and therefore of the ball, and so necessarily control of himself, is a golfer in the true sense of the word. Some may say "I could never bother"; those who "don't bother" will never be golfers.

Finale

To you and your Gate I wish the best of luck, and remember that golf after all is a simple game, but never easy.

FROM *THE GATE TO GOLF*
BY J. DOUGLAS EDGAR

EDGAR'S SECRET

CHAPTER 12

W. TIMOTHY GALLWEY

SET YOURSELF FREE

*"I was surprised to discover that there seemed
to be at least two identities within me.
One was playing tennis; the other was telling him how."*

Some of the most insightful advice on how to improve at golf has come from the mind of a tennis player. Tim Gallwey didn't take golf seriously until he was well into his thirties, but by that time he'd already learned a great deal about how to play the game.

As a youngster growing up in California just after World War II, Gallwey gravitated toward tennis and became one of the better high school players in the state. At age fifteen, he reached match point in the National Junior Tennis Championship before missing a heartbreakingly easy volley that led to his defeat. From that moment, Gallwey became fasci-

nated with the problem of how human beings interfere with their own ability to perform.

Gallwey attended Harvard, where he majored in English and captained the tennis team. More importantly, he enrolled in a sophomore seminar taught by Dr. B. F. Skinner, "the father of human behaviorism," whose research using lab animals and a "Skinner Box" introduced the concepts of positive and negative reinforcement. The class had a profound impact on Gallwey, who reasoned that his own actions and choices had been far too influenced by outside forces—social conditioning that reinforced culturally desired behavior. He also recognized a natural human desire to be free of those forces.

After Harvard, Gallwey served in the Navy, and later became one of the founders of a liberal arts college in the Midwest, but throughout that time he continued to ponder the notions of teaching and learning. The result of all that thinking was a groundbreaking 1974 book called *The Inner Game of Tennis*. Its detractors dismissed it as Zen with a racket, but Gallwey had raised a cogent point—that traditional tennis teaching was far too judgmental—and he'd also offered an alternative, a way for people to improve by finding their own best game. For thousands of tennis addicts, it clicked. Today the book is regarded as a classic not only in the literature of sports but in psychology as well.

> **Ninety-nine percent of a round of golf is "down time" between shots— time when the average player feels anger, embarrassment, disappointment, anxiety, and doubt.**

The Inner Game of Tennis launched a mini-industry for Tim Gallwey. He followed with *Inner Skiing, The Inner Game of Music,* and *The Inner Game of Work;* he also became a sought-after lecturer and consultant to the corporate world, helping companies create environments for learning and peak performance.

For years, Gallwey was urged to produce an Inner Game book for golfers, but he resisted, initially because he was not an avid golfer, and later, after he'd come to the game, because he realized that his methods would be more difficult to apply to golf. In contrast to other games that are largely reactive, in golf there is just the player and the stationary ball, and the actual time of physical action is minimal. Ninety-nine percent of a round of golf is "down time" between shots—time when the average player feels anger, embarrassment, disappointment, anxiety, and doubt.

But eventually Gallwey found a way and in 1981, *The Inner Game of Golf* appeared. Not since Arnold Haultain's *The Mystery of Golf* had the game's mental side been explored so intriguingly. In the thirty years since, dozens of mental-game books have followed, but none is more original or more compelling.

> **THE SECRET:**
>
> **B**eat the bad guy inside your head. Occupy your judgmental alter ego with a trivial task, and the natural athlete within you will emerge.

GALLWEY'S SECRET

Self 1 and Self 2

A major breakthrough in my understanding of the problem of control of mind and body came when, as a tennis instructor, I became aware of a constant commentary going on inside my head as I played. I realized that my students were subjected to a similar flow of self-instructional thoughts while taking lessons: Come on, get your racket back earlier . . .

You hit that one too late again . . . Bend your knee on those volleys . . . Uh-oh, here comes another high backhand like the one you missed last time . . . Make sure you don't miss it again . . . Damn it! You missed it again . . . When are you ever going to hit those things? . . . Watch the ball, watch the ball . . . What am I going to say to my doubles partner if I lose this match?

As I began to take a closer look at the thoughts going through my mind during a tennis match, I found myself asking, Whom am I talking to, and who is doing the talking? I was surprised to discover that there seemed to be at least two identities within me. One was playing tennis; the other was

telling him how. I observed that the one doing the talking, whom I named Self 1, thought he knew all about how to play and was supervising Self 2, the one who had to hit the ball. In fact, Self 1 not only gave Self 2 instructions, but criticized him for past errors, warned him of probable future ones, and harangued him whenever he made a mistake. It was easy to see that the primary feeling in the relationship between these two selves was mistrust. Self 1 didn't trust Self 2 to hit the ball, and precisely to the extent that he lacked trust, he would try to force Self 2 to conform to his verbal instructions. I noticed that when I had more confidence in my ability to hit a shot, there was a corresponding decrease in instructions from Self 1, and that Self 2 would perform amazingly well without him. When I was on a streak, there was no talk in my head at all.

Once I became aware of Self 1, it grew increasingly obvious that this judgmental little voice barking away like a drill sergeant inside my head was not the best thing for my tennis game. Self 1 was more of a hindrance than the great help he wanted me to think he was. Thereafter I began looking for ways to decrease the interference of Self 1, and to see what happened if I trusted the potential of Self 2. I found that when I could quiet Self 1 and let Self 2 learn and play without interference, my performance and learning rate improved significantly. My Self 2 was a great deal more competent than Self 1 gave him credit for. Likewise, I found that when, as a teacher, I didn't feed the instruction-hungry Self 1 of a student with a lot of technical information but, instead, trusted in the capacity of *his* Self 2 to learn, the progress of my students was three or four times faster than average, and they learned with much less frustration.

In short, I found that Self 1—the verbalizing, thought-producing self—is a lousy boss when it comes to control of the body's muscle system. When Self 2—the body itself—is allowed control, the quality of performance, the level of enjoyment, and the rate of learning are all improved.

When Self 1 and Self 2 are clearly defined in this way, the basic premise of the Inner Game can be expressed in a simple equation. The quality of our performance relative to our actual potential is equal to our potential (Self 2) minus the interference with the expression of that potential (Self 1). Or: Performance = Self 2 (potential) minus Self 1 (interference).

Thus, the aim of the Inner Game is not so much to try harder to persuade Self 2 to do what he is capable of doing, but to decrease the Self 1 interferences that prevent Self 2 from expressing himself fully.

Still, I found that like most tyrants, Self 1 didn't like losing control and resisted efforts to minimize his influence. The process of decreasing his control in favor of Self 2 proved to be a challenging one, which required the development of concentration techniques designed to keep Self 1 occupied in noninterfering activity and to consciously allow Self 2 to hit the ball. Once Self 1 was focused in a concentration exercise, his interference with Self 2 decreased significantly, and performance instantly improved.

> As I began to take a closer look at the thoughts going through my mind during a tennis match, I found myself asking, Whom am I talking to and who is doing the talking? I was surprised to discover there seemed to be two identities within me.

The Magic of Bounce-Hit

One exercise that found considerable success among tennis players at all levels of proficiency was the bounce-hit technique. In explaining it to a student, I would emphasize at the outset that this technique was primarily for increasing concentration and not for improving results, although improved concentration could only help performance. Then I would ask the student to say the word *bounce* when the ball bounced on the court and to say *hit* when it made contact with the racket. The object was simply to keep in visual contact with the ball and to say "Bounce—hit, bounce—hit" aloud with as much accuracy as possible.

After letting go of their concern about results, most students would find even at the beginning stages of this exercise that their concentration was stronger, that they returned many more balls than usual, that they hit balls they normally could not reach, and that in general their tennis was more effortless.

I realized that there were two basic reasons for the success of the bounce-hit exercise. First, it is interesting enough to absorb the attention of Self 1, distracting him from his normal

> **I found that Self 1—the verbalizing, thought-producing self—is a lousy boss when it comes to control of the body's muscle system. When Self 2—the body itself—is allowed control, the quality of performance, the level of enjoyment, and the rate of learning are all improved.**

interference patterns with Self 2. Secondly, the added concentration on the ball gave Self 2 better feedback, enabling him to perform his eye-body-coordination task better. Students who practiced the exercise conscientiously attained a state of mind that improved their technique automatically and made their tennis seem effortless. I called this state "relaxed concentration" because the mind was alert and focused, yet not tense, and the body moved with an economy of effort that gave the impression of ease. In this state, tennis players would say that they were playing "out of their minds"—and never "better."

Back-Hit: The Bounce-Hit of Golf

Of course many golfers who were familiar with the Inner Game of tennis were asking me the very question I was asking myself: What is the bounce-hit of golf? What single concentration exercise could keep Self 1 so occupied that he wouldn't interfere with the golf swing? It needed to be interesting enough to absorb Self 1, and at the same time assist Self 2 by giving him increased feedback.

Although I experimented with a number of exercises for focusing attention on the golf ball—such as watching a dimple, the label, or a speck of dust—none of these seemed to keep Self 1 quiet for long. The problem was that the darn ball just sat there.

My mind would grow easily bored looking at it, and if I forced the exercise, my mind became strained and my swing stiff. The bounce-hit magic seemed to have something to do with the mind's fascination with the movement and rhythm of the tennis ball, and this simply didn't apply to the golf ball. Also, in order to hit the golf ball, Self 2 didn't need moment-to-moment visual feedback; the ball wasn't going to go anywhere until I hit it. The very lack of motion of the golf ball, which gave one so much time to think and grow tense, was exactly what was impeding concentration.

Finally I came to the conclusion that the primary focus of attention in golf should be *not* the ball but the clubhead, the critical moving object. The movement was *there,* the feedback needed was *there,* the rhythm that fascinates the mind was *there*—not in the ball. But I couldn't follow the clubhead with my eyes; if I wished to focus attention on it, I would have to use my sense of feel, and I didn't know how difficult this would be. How much could I actually *feel* the clubhead moving during my swing? I decided to go out to the driving range to experiment with clubhead awareness.

At first I had relatively little sense of where my club was. I found that only if I didn't worry about whether I hit the ball or not, I could feel it better. I tried shutting my eyes and swinging, and found that my awareness of feel increased even more. The movement of the clubhead was becoming interesting enough to hold my attention throughout the arc of the swing. Whenever I would try simply to *feel* the clubhead and not to *control* it, the club seemed to swing itself, and I got excellent results—the same kind I had in tennis when my mind became concentrated. But when I split my attention—half to the feel of the clubhead and the other half to trying to swing—the results weren't so good.

To keep Self 1 focused on the club and away from the process of controlling it, I conceived the following concentration exercise. Keeping my attention on the feel of the clubhead, I would say the word *back* the instant I felt the clubhead reach its furthest extension at the completion of the backswing. I would simply sense its position, without worrying at all whether it was accurate. Then I would say the word *hit* the instant the clubface met the ball. "Back—hit, back—hit." This exercise kept me in touch with the clubhead throughout the arc, and was exacting enough that Self 1 couldn't easily do the exercise while issuing commands at the same time. Actually, this drill requires somewhat more concentration than the "bounce-hit" in tennis, and, though it's a little harder to do, it is even more effective.

> **Finally I came to the conclusion that the primary focus of attention in golf should be not the ball but the clubhead.**

BACK

It was surprising to many golfers to whom I showed this exercise how unaware they actually had been of their clubhead. Although most had interesting theories about where it should be at the back of the swing, they were often 6 to 18 inches off in their estimate of where it *actually* was. One thing I had learned in tennis was that it is more important to know where your racket *is* than to know where it *should* be. The tennis ball is hardly ever where it should be, but always where it is. I told my students, "*Should* and *is* usually miss each other."

After only a few minutes' work with this exercise, there were often dramatic improvements in swing technique and results. The only real difficulty was in the tendency to want to control the swing instead of simply doing the exercise. It is natural not to want to give up all of Self 1's control at once. But even with 50 percent of Self 1 occupied in "back-hit," there was significantly less interference with the swing. Then, as confidence grew in Self 2, it was easier to risk focusing more of Self 1 on the exercise and leaving the hitting to Self 2.

HIT

The same is true in golf. What the body needs to control the path of the clubhead is not a lot of instructions, but accurate, moment-by-moment feedback about the position of the clubhead. Back-hit was effective in increasing this input, as well as in quieting Self 1. It took practice and trust, but it paid off in results.

Of course there is nothing magical about the words themselves. One can just as effectively attain the same concentration by saying "One-two" at these moments. I also realized that it was helpful for most players to carry through their awareness of the club head to the completion of the swing, so I began experimenting with "Da, da, da"— the first at the back of the swing, the second at contact, and the third at the end of the follow-through. This three-beat cadence captures the crucial moments in the golf swing and is preferable because it doesn't overemphasize the moment of contact. Some prefer leaving out the contact beat altogether and simply say "Back—stop."

The principle behind all the variations of this exercise is the same, and individual preferences will emerge if you choose to experiment with them. The only important thing is to make a commitment to doing purely the concentration exercise. Don't try to add it to another tip or to other forms of swing control. Put your mind totally into the clubhead and *let Self 2 swing the club.* Then you can find out for yourself what Self 2 can do with less interference from Self-1 thinking and control.

My recommendation is that the exercises be practiced for at least a short time on the driving range and putting green before attempting them on the course. It is difficult enough to let go of conscious control over your swing when in practice; it is almost too much to ask under playing conditions. Once he has found the exercise that works best for quieting his mind, the player should stick with it and give it a chance to work. Eventually it will be difficult not to want to use it in the pressure situations. One can expect, however, that the greater the pressure, the harder it will be to quiet Self 1 and attain the same level of concentration as in practice. But then, that's just when you need it, so persevere.

FROM *THE INNER GAME OF GOLF* BY W. TIMOTHY GALLWEY

CHAPTER 13

PHIL GALVANO

ADVICE FROM A SELF-MADE MAN

"Great putters are not born, they are made."

Phil Galvano is a classic American success story. Born in Brooklyn in 1915, the youngest of nine offspring of struggling immigrant parents, he was never able to attend school. Instead, he worked his entire life, beginning at age six. His first job was in a belt factory, and it lasted a year. His next job was in golf—as a caddie—and golf would remain his occupation for three quarters of a century.

At that time—the Roaring Twenties—golf was still a fledgling sport in America. Francis Ouimet's victory in the U.S. Open at Brookline (1913) had brought the game to the attention of the masses, and the exploits of young Bobby Jones had captured the public's imagination, but the teaching of the game was still a bit haphazard, left largely to a band of immigrant Scots and a handful of enterprising caddies like Phil.

A natural athlete, he taught himself to swing by watching the better players for whom he caddied. Then he taught himself to read. And then he read everything he could about how to play—and teach—the game. Not just the ABC's from Harry Vardon and Ernest Jones, but a much broader spectrum including the four P's—physics, physiology, psychology, and

THE SECRET:

Jut your left elbow down the target line, and hit your short and mid-length putts with an abbreviated, popping stroke.

philosophy—from Newton's laws to Gray's *Anatomy*, Pavlov to Zen. For ten years Phil Galvano became a full professor of golf while simultaneously teaching himself and others to play it.

In 1941, having become a PGA professional, Galvano rented space in Manhattan and set up shop. His quarters were a bit modest at first—a small loft with a ceiling so low that only short players or those with flat swings could be accommodated—but before long both his business and his office enlarged. Bob Hope became one of his regular students, calling Galvano "the miracle teacher." Other celebrity pupils included Milton Berle, Ed Sullivan, Joe Dimaggio, Carol Burnett, Perry Como, and Nelson Rockefeller. Willie Mosconi sought Galvano out for snooker matches, and Arthur Murray was so impressed by his teaching system that he hired Galvano to design the teaching methods for his dance studios.

Bob Hope called Galvano "the miracle teacher."

Galvano mixed easily with the luminaries. A talented musician, he played nine instruments, all by ear, and occasionally sat in with pupils Billy Eckstein, Frankie Laine, and Robert Merrill. He also had an Erroll Flynn look, complete with a thin, waxed mustache (his alignment aid, he said) that may have helped him land a gig as host of the first sponsored golf show on network television.

But fundamentally Phil Galvano was always a teacher. Following three decades in Manhattan, he became Director of Golf at the famed Grossinger's Resort in New York's Catskill Mountains. In 1969 he moved his family to Bradenton, Florida, where he founded the Galvano Golf Academy, teaching there virtually every day until he died in 1996 at the age of eighty-one. Today the academy continues, run by his son Phil, Jr., one of five Galvano offspring who became golf professionals.

Galvano is credited with coining several teaching images, including the "railroad tracks" for proper alignment, and the notion of gripping a club as if you're holding a little bird, an idea he got from actor Basil Rathbone, who had taught him to fence and had instructed him to hold the foil in that way.

Galvano wrote four books, two of which became *New York Times* best-sellers, and it is in his *Secrets of Accurate Putting and Chipping* that he left his most important mark. The cover of that book shows Phil stroking a putt, his left elbow jutting straight out so it points down the target line. Through this position he taught his students to eliminate wrist action in putting. Published in 1957, this was one of the first expressions of the arm-and-shoulder stroke that is now embraced by nearly every top teacher and player.

GALVANO'S SECRET

T here is nothing mysterious or complicated about building a proper putting stance. It is simply a matter of placing your feet and body in the proper position in relation to the ball and target.

In order to build a proper putting stance, you need a target. Let's not use a putting cup. Let's use a very difficult target: an ordinary straight pin, stuck through a small piece of paper so that it can be seen from a distance. Now place your ball approximately 6 feet from the target. (Do not worry about your putting grip; we will get to that a little later on.)

Using your master eye, form an imaginary line from the pin through the center of the ball. Then place the toe of your putter in back of the ball, cutting the ball in half at a perfect right angle to the imaginary line.

This will give you a finer line to work with, rather than one the thickness of the diameter of the ball.

By aiming with the toe of the putter, you can also see how far away your left toe should be from the ball. Place your left foot so that your left toe is behind the ball at a perfect right angle to the imaginary line and close enough so that your eyes are directly over the ball.

Place your right foot parallel to your left. Both toes and heels should be parallel and far enough apart so that the outer edge of your feet are the same distance apart as the width of your hips.

Bend both knees slightly and equally, so that you are in a squatting position. Bending your knees will relieve nerve tension. The weight of your body should be on the left foot and toward the heels. This weight position will reduce body motion to a minimum. If your weight is equally divided, your heartbeat will make your body move. That is why the expert rifleman keeps his weight wholly on one foot. Keep yours on your left foot.

Hold your breath during the putting stroke. This will further eliminate body

The toes are parallel with the intended line of putt. Eyes are directly over the ball. The right forearm is resting lightly against the right thigh and the left elbow is pointing in line with the toes. Body weight is slightly back and toward the left foot.

upswing, rather than on the downswing.

Just before stroking the ball, pick your putter blade off the ground very slightly and slide it forward gently and carefully while the blade is still in the air. Slide it forward until the "sweet spot" on your putter is directly in back of the ball. Do not train yourself to slide the blade forward while it is resting on the ground; for, when you are on the green, the grass will make the clubhead stick. This sliding forward will eliminate the nervous tension that is caused by jumping the blade back and forth over the ball as you address it.

Now, let's get to the all-

vibration. Of course, don't forget to resume breathing after you finish the stroke.

The distance of the ball from the left toe depends on the type of build you have. Your eyes should look down at the ball in a perfectly straight line. That will bring the ball approximately four inches away from your left toe. Very rarely is it ever farther than five inches away.

Remember, overspin is desirable. By placing the ball off the toe of your left foot, you automatically get the desired overspin. The club will be stroking the ball on the

important putting grip so that we can continue to that magic basic putting stroke.

The Basic Putting Stroke

In the basic putting stroke, the clubhead travels straight back about four inches and follows through approximately twelve inches. The actual stroking is done with the arms, not with the wrists.

Why should you use the arm rather than the wrist? For this reason: The object of developing a good basic putting stroke is to create

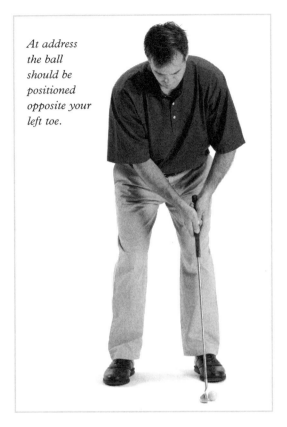

*At address
the ball
should be
positioned
opposite your
left toe.*

*Take the club
back with your
right elbow,
keeping the left
elbow pointed
down the line.*

straight strokes of various lengths with the putter. Let's find out how we best can do this.

Try to draw a straight line with a pencil without moving your forearm, using only your fingers and wrist. You will find that you cannot draw a straight line more than a few inches long. Now try drawing a straight line, not using your wrist but only your arm. You will have no difficulty in drawing a straight line several feet long.

I repeat, the actual stroking is done not with the wrists, but with the arms. The right elbow stays close to the body throughout the stroke, brushing the right side gently as it goes back. If you start your putt back with your fingers or wrists, you may, under tension, close the clubface sharply as you stroke the ball, causing a pull to the left. Only when using your arms is it possible to keep the clubface square from the start to the finish of your putting stroke. *The point of energy comes from the right elbow.*

In short, take the club back with your right elbow. *The force that strokes the ball*

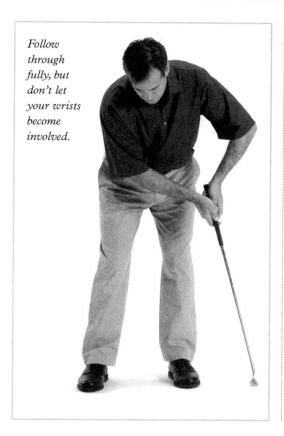

Follow through fully, but don't let your wrists become involved.

comes from the length of the stroke rather than from the strength applied.

Practice your basic putting stroke by drawing a diagram similar to the one shown. Start at the point where the solid and dotted lines meet. Take a backswing to the end of the 4-inch line and then follow through to the end of the 12-inch line.

Practice this without a ball until you can follow the diagram quite easily. Then practice your basic putting stroke with a ball. Place the ball where the solid and dotted lines meet in the diagram. (If you put the diagram near a wall or any other solid object, the ball will bounce back to you without your having to retrieve it.) A few minutes of practice each evening for a few evenings will pay big dividends on the putting green.

FROM *SECRETS OF ACCURATE PUTTING AND CHIPPING* BY PHIL GALVANO

GALVANO'S SECRET

THE BASIC PUTTING STROKE

A diagram of this type can be laid out on the floor of your living room for practicing the basic putting stroke.

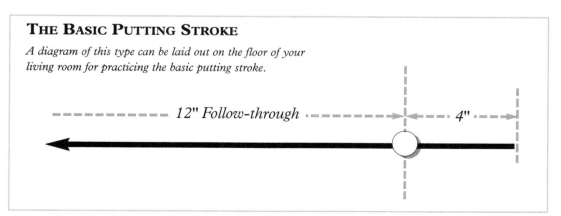

12" Follow-through   *4"*

CHAPTER 14

DARRIN GEE

HOLISTIC HEALING

*"Golf has a magnetic, almost spiritual quality to it.
For every eighty to one hundred 'terrible' strokes in a round,
there may be only one great shot. If you played any other sport
and experienced that ratio of failure to success, you'd quit."*

"Never hurry, never worry, and always remember to smell the flowers along the way." That was Walter Hagen's mantra, and it served him well. The Haig won forty-four tournaments, an impressive nine of them major championships. Only Jack Nicklaus (twenty) and Bobby Jones (thirteen) have won more majors.

The difference is that Nicklaus, Jones, and just about every other champion golfer of the last century brought to the game a seriousness and intensity of focus that allowed for precious little flower-sniffing. And sadly, several million weekend golfers have followed their lead.

One of them was a young fellow named Darrin Gee, who took up the game in his freshman year at UCLA. A good athlete who had played basketball and tennis as a youth, he got his handicap down to 5 within a few years, but then stopped improving.

"It really got to me, the frustration of hitting two good shots followed by a bad one," he said. "Finally, I just quit the game for a while." At the same time, he was feeling less than satisfied with his career. After graduating from UCLA, he'd earned a masters degree in business administration from Northwestern, and was working as a management consultant.

> THE SECRET:
>
> Get your swing— and your life— in balance.

Gee's school, based in Hawaii, helps students find balance and rhythm in life as well as golf.

When Gee returned to golf, he realized that his best shots were those in which he didn't overthink, didn't put pressure on himself, "when my mind was quiet, when I was allowing it to do what it already knew how to do." So Gee began to teach himself to quiet the chatter in his brain, to visualize the shots he wanted to play and focus on one shot at a time. At the same time, he quit his job and made time for some introspection. "I asked myself, What do I want to do?," he said. He found his true calling in golf instruction.

But Darrin Gee did not join the PGA of America, and the things he teaches have little to do with swing planes and pronation.

Instead, he incorporates Eastern and Western techniques of relaxation and concentration in a program that helps each individual to find his or her own rhythm not just in golf but in life. The core of his teaching is what Gee calls the Seven Spiritual Principles of Golf, the first of which—balance—is presented here.

Gee's one-day school includes everything from tai chi to meditation, yoga to spa treatments. It's not for everyone, but for those whose inconsistent golf has driven to them to near hysteria, it may be the answer, particularly since the school is based on the Big Island of Hawaii, a fine place to stop and smell the flowers.

GEE'S SECRET

*"**Y**ou can will something to happen, with your body, with your mind. The mind is that strong. You can say, 'I want to get this close to the hole.' That's where the mind comes in. The mind has to produce positive thinking. All the great players do that."*
—Byron Nelson

Most people think that if they are standing still, they are balanced. However, this theory quickly erodes during the golf swing. If a golfer has not established a strong, well-balanced stance prior to swinging the golf club, he or she will surely have a difficult time striking the ball crisply in the sweet spot.

In most other sports, a balanced, athletic stance is required. Whether it be volleyball, tennis, basketball, football, or martial arts, you must be prepared to move in any and all directions, almost reflexively. Not knowing where your opponent or the ball is going, you must have perfect balance at all times to respond accordingly. We can use that same mentality when golfing.

I had one student who was an accomplished athlete in many sports, including basketball, football, and baseball. He was strong, quick, and had outstanding hand-eye coordination. He demonstrated outstanding balance in every sport he participated in, except for golf. When he addressed the ball, he was off-center, often leaning back on his heels. When he swung the club, he often finished out of balance, wobbling around trying to remain standing.

With golf being a "still" sport, where you are primarily stationary, balance is even more important than in other sports. In most other sports, if you lose your balance, you can move your feet to regain it and resume play. In the game of golf, the swing takes less than two seconds. In such a short period of time, you don't have time to move your feet and adjust. Shifting your entire weight from one side of your body to the other, without moving your feet, while swinging a golf club and trying to hit a tiny ball, is probably one of the most difficult motions to master in sports.

I believe that balance, or getting grounded, is the core and foundation of the golf swing. A golfer may have a beautiful, fluid swing, but if coupled with poor balance, the result is often an off-center shot. You must first establish a grounded, balanced stance as the basis for a solid golf swing.

You often see professional golfers shuffling their feet around, rocking back and forth, and adjusting their stance, in preparation for a shot. Often misunderstood as a nervous habit, more often than not, they are just trying to find their balance and establish solid grounding before making their swing.

A student of mine named Don visited me at our golf school on the Big Island of Hawaii, desperately wanting help with his golf game. He and his buddies had all started playing golf at about the same time. His friends seemed to improve, while he did not. He often felt embarrassed by his poor play and worried what others thought about him and his game. Compounding the situation, he doubted his golf swing and often found himself thinking a million different swing thoughts before, during, and after a shot. As a result, he often tightened up during his swing, hitting more dirt than ball.

Don had taken lessons, read golf instruction books and magazines, and tried several swing aids and gimmicks. He improved a little each time, but always regressed back to his original ability, sometimes getting even worse. Because of his struggles with the game, he nearly quit, until I shared with him a few things about quieting the mind, finding his balance, and trusting his body.

Don had so much on his mind, including golf and non-golf related thoughts. He often rushed his shots as an attempt to "get it over with." He rarely took the time to establish a sound foundation. As a result, he often lost his balance during his swing and rarely made solid contact with the ball.

I asked him to get as balanced as possible as he set up to the golf ball. Once he said he felt balanced, I gave him a gentle, two-finger nudge on his shoulder. He nearly toppled over. Don needed to improve his balance and learn how to ground his body.

I believe that balance, or getting grounded, is the core and foundation of the golf swing.

First, I had him stand on his toes and lean forward, while maintaining his balance throughout. Then I had him lift up his toes and stand on his heels. This proved to be very challenging to him. I then asked him to rock back and forth, heel-to-toe, toe-to-heel, imagining that he was a rocking chair. This exercise helped him gain a better sense of balance and rhythm. I told him to slow down and shorten the rocking motion until he reached an equilibrium point between his toes and heels.

He then repeated the same exercise laterally, or sideways. Finally, I had him make small circles with his hips. As he was doing this, I told him to imagine circling around the center of his body. I told him to make smaller and smaller circles, spiraling until he reached the center point.

At this point, he had essentially found his center. However, this was not enough. In order to lock in this feeling of total balance, I told Don to imagine the spikes in his shoes growing into the ground like the roots of a tree. Using the imagery of roots growing down and spreading in all directions helped him establish a solid foundation. I had him put particular emphasis on the balls of his feet, which gave him a solid, grounded feeling.

Standing on one foot with your eyes closed will give you feedback on your balance. Notice how you must adjust to find the perfect balancing point.

I asked him to swing his arms back and forth around his body, while keeping his feet firmly planted. He built a strong foundation, and yet he was completely loose and flexible on top. Using the imagery of a palm tree or willow tree, Don was able to achieve balance of strength and flexibility, exactly what is needed for the golf swing.

A good swing, like a palm tree, has strength and flexibility.

With his eyes closed, Don learned to maintain his balance and notice the difference between "thinking" he was balanced and actually "being" balanced. By focusing on his feet and legs being firmly rooted into the ground, his swing improved dramatically. He didn't change his swing necessarily. In fact, his swing was essentially the same. What changed was his balance. What was a swaying, imbalanced, and off-centered swing before became a solid, flowing, and effortless motion.

I told him to close his eyes and practice his swing. He could immediately discern the difference between good and poor balance. When he concentrated on his feet and legs being rooted into the ground, he had better balance. If he thought of anything else, he lost his balance.

When Don started hitting golf balls after this exercise, he hit them with precision and accuracy. His shots lofted in the air like he had never seen before. He was amazed. The First Principle of "Getting Grounded" helped Don focus on establishing a strong connection between his body and the ground, which led to solid swings.

There are a few simple ways to test the quality of your balance. Standing on one foot with your eyes closed is an exercise that will give you feedback on your balance. Notice how you must adjust to find the perfect balancing point. You may wobble a bit, but the exercise will help you establish better balance for future golf swings. Remember to do this with each foot, as we often favor our stronger leg first. You want to feel so grounded, that you would be able to maintain your balance on uneven lies and in gusty and windy conditions.

Making practice swings with your eyes closed will also help you find your balance. Notice how your feet and legs must work diligently to maintain your balance throughout the swing. This is no different when your eyes are open. Keep swinging with your eyes closed, until it feels smooth, rhythmic, and flowing. Then take a few swings with your eyes open and notice how your balance has improved.

Another way to achieve better balance is with an exercise called the two-foot jump stop. Used in almost all sports, including basketball, baseball, tennis, and volleyball, this exercise teaches you how to achieve a solid, balanced stance without trying or thinking. Take a few steps in succession followed by a short hop, landing with both feet on the ground simultaneously. Allow your knees to bend and flex naturally. You may find that when you land, you have the majority of your weight on the balls of your feet or slightly forward. This is a very natural stance and perfect for the golf swing. Let your arms dangle and this is usually a very sound stance.

If you lean too far forward during this exercise, you'll fall over; if you lean too far backwards, you'll get jolted back. With a few repetitions, this exercise will help you find perfect balance.

Applying the First Spiritual Principle of Golf: Get Grounded On the Golf Course

1. Finding a comfortable stance, stand tall on your toes. Gently lean forward as far you can while maintaining your balance, and hold for ten seconds.

2. Reverse your weight to your heels and raise your toes up, using your arms as

necessary to maintain your balance, and hold for ten seconds.

3. Rock back and forth from heel to toe, toe to heel. Imagine you are a rocking chair as you are rocking back and forth. Just like a rocking chair, your rocking motion will shorten and slow down, eventually stopping at the equilibrium point, where there is equal weight distributed between the toe and heel.

4. Rotate your hips round and round, making small circles. Switch directions and with each successive circle getting smaller and smaller, you are going to spiral until you reach the center. Settle and sink into this position.

5. Imagine the spikes in your golf shoes growing deep into the ground, as if you are a tree with roots spreading underground. Put particular emphasis and awareness on the balls of your feet, imagining those two roots anchoring and connecting deeply to the core of the earth. Feel the energy and power in your feet, calves, thighs, hips, and lower abdomen. Notice how strong a foundation you have created.

6. Swing your arms freely around your body, while maintaining this strong foundation. Imagine a palm tree, willow tree, or bamboo reed, having a solid and strong foundation, yet extremely flexible on top, able to bend and twist easily. This is exactly what you want for the golf swing.

Applying the First Spiritual Principle of Golf: Get Grounded Off the Golf Course

Overwhelmed by life and your responsibilities? Trying to balance your career with family? Never seem to have any time for just you? If you answered "yes" to any or all of these questions then, more than likely, you are a normal person.

As you attempt to organize and re-organize every part of your life, your mind constantly works to establish some sort of order. However, as you try to get ahead, you only find yourself just barely keeping up. Job, family, relationships, money, lack of free time—it never ceases. All you can do is to try and organize it into an acceptable, livable existence.

At delicate times like these, you could topple over with just a slight nudge. The mind fills with so many thoughts of what to do, you tend to float from one task to another, with very little awareness. The best way to establish balance in your life is to quiet your mind and establish a strong feeling of connection.

In a recent magazine interview, Tiger said, "To me, it's all about balance . . . If I feel something is out of balance, I try to get it back in balance somehow. Your entire life, you're always working to keep everything in balance, because the more harmony there is, the smoother life goes."

1. **Quiet the mind.** Muddled with so many thoughts, most people in Western culture lose their sense of being or existence. Practice quiet moments. Notice and appreciate silence and simplicity. Sitting quietly with your eyes closed, meditating, going for a walk, exercising without reading or watching TV, practicing tai chi or yoga are all effective ways to achieve a sense of calm and relaxation. Even when you are in the midst of activity, be it mental or physical, take a breath and find the quiet within. You will sense and feel a calming sensation.

2. **Ground your body.** Notice how your body physically connects you to the ground. Wherever you are, whether at home, in the car, on an airplane, on the golf cart, or in the office, plant your feet firmly to the ground. Notice the weight and mass of your body molding into your seat. Secure your feet on the floor and imagine them rooting into the ground.

This practice will give you a sense of being grounded, and building a solid foundation. You can practice this anywhere, at any time.

3. **Establish a strong connection with your body**. As you ground yourself, notice where your energy is centered. Is it in your head, or your chest or your legs? Begin to focus your energy towards the spot two inches below your navel, in between the front and back of your body. This is called the *hara* in Japanese or *dantien* in Chinese. This is considered in martial arts as the center of your body. With each breath continue to focus on the *hara,* inhaling and exhaling from your center. Feel the energy or *chi* emanating from this center, creating a strong connection with your body.

FROM *ONE SHOT AT A TIME: SEVEN PRINCIPLES FOR TRANSFORMING YOUR GOLF GAME AND YOUR LIFE* BY DARRIN GEE

GEE'S SECRET

CHAPTER 15

BEN HOGAN

THE HAWK TALKS

"I do genuinely believe this: The average golfer is entirely capable of building a repeating swing and breaking 80, if he learns to perform a small number of correct movements and conversely, it follows, eliminates a lot of movements which tend to keep the swing from repeating."

By the spring of 1956, Ben Hogan's career as a professional golfer had effectively ended. He'd recorded sixty-two of his sixty-three career victories, all nine of his major championships, and although he would continue to play the tour actively, he'd begun to turn his mind to other, less physical aspects of the game, most notably the equipment-manufacturing company that bore his name.

At the same time, Hogan had started to crystallize his three decades of thinking on the golf swing. While in Florida preparing for the Masters, Hogan reached a sort of epiphany—namely, that a sound, repeating swing depended on just a few simple movements. He called Sydney James, editor of a fledgling magazine named *Sports Illustrated*, and offered him the first chance at an article describing those keys to the swing.

James jumped at the opportunity, dispatching his chief golf editor, Herbert Warren Wind, along with illustrator Anthony Ravielli to Hogan's home in Fort Worth. It would be

> **THE SECRET:**
>
> Start your downswing with a turn of the hips—then think of just one thing: hitting the ball.

the first of two visits during which Hogan talked, Wind scribbled copious notes, and Ravielli snapped photos and made quick, incisive sketches of the positions that Hogan wanted to emphasize. The result was not just one article but a five-part series that grew into what is probably the most widely read instruction book in the history of the game: *Five Lessons: The Modern Fundamentals of Golf.*

The genius of the book derives chiefly from Hogan, of course, but the contributions of his two collaborators cannot be understated. Wind distilled Hogan's thoughts with simplicity and clarity—every word of the text has meaning—and Ravielli's distinctive scratchboard drawings were the most captivating instructional illustrations the game has ever produced.

Like any resounding success, the book has had its detractors, who claim it is useful only to those who are fighting an insidious hook, as Hogan did for the first half of his career, and that his advocacy of a neutral grip (the "V" formed between the thumb and forefinger of each hand pointing toward the chin) is no longer valid (most modern teachers advocate a stronger grip, with the "V" pointing to the right shoulder). Others say it is useful only to those select few with the combined time, talent, and temperament to absorb and apply its teachings. But

Ben Hogan won the British Open the only time he played it, in 1953.

none of those critics seems to have had much effect. Nearly half a century after its publication, *Five Fundamentals* remains a perennial best-seller on the golf book list, and literally hundreds of thousands of golfers have incorporated its teachings. This excerpt details Hogan's thoughts on the downswing.

BEN HOGAN'S SECRET

BEN HOGAN'S SECRET

In this chapter we will be taking up the phase of the swing in which the player actually hits the ball. This second section of the swing—from the start of the downswing to the finish of the follow-through—is the most crucial part, necessarily.

Since, in the method we are teaching, each action is the direct result of preceding actions in the chain-action sequence of the swing, it strikes me that it would be extremely profitable, before tackling the downswing, to review briefly the plane of the backswing.

As he addresses the ball, the golfer creates the angle of the plane of his backswing:

The plane inclines along this imaginary line running from the ball to the top of his shoulders and on upward at that established angle of inclination.

Learning to think in terms of this plane has helped tremendously to improve and stabilize the swings of many friends of mine. Like no other visual suggestion, it seems to induce a golfer to make the correct back-swing movements **time after time.** He folds the right elbow in, just as he should; his left arm is fully extended but not rigid, just as it should be; he completes his full shoulder turn; his hands cock themselves

The backswing plane, as seen from a top-view position. At the top of the backswing, the left arm should incline at the exact angle of the plane. The arm brushes against the glass pane.

naturally, without any conscious effort, and the back of his left hand is an unbroken extension of the line of his left wrist and forearm. Not only are his arms and the upper part of his body correctly aligned throughout the back-swing, but these various component parts tend to be poised **time after time** with the proper degree of live, stretched muscular tension ready to be released on the downswing.

On the downswing, a golfer swings on a slightly different plane than on the backswing. **The plane for the downswing is less steeply inclined and is oriented with the ball quite differently from the backswing plane.** The golfer gets on this second plane—without thinking he is changing planes—when he turns his hips back to the left at the start of the downswing. This moves his body to the left and automatically lowers the right shoulder. You will remember that, in introducing the backswing plane, we suggested that the golfer-reader imagine that at address his head is sticking out through a hole in an immense pane of glass that rests on his

To check if a golfer remains on his plane during his backswing, I stand behind him (facing down his line of flight) and slant my forearm and hand along the line of what would be his correct plane. When he swings back, I can then observe whether he stays on his plane, drops below it, or lifts his arms above the plane.

shoulders as it slants up from the ball. Now, on the downswing, as the body moves to the left and the right shoulder is automatically lowered, this causes the pane of glass to be shifted into a different position. Its lateral axis is no longer in line with the line of flight. It points slightly to the right of the target. (The pane is also tilted so that the leading edge is raised off the ground.) **When the golfer is on this correct downswing plane, he has to hit from the inside out.** When he hits from the inside out, he can get maximum strength into his swing and obtain maximum clubhead speed.

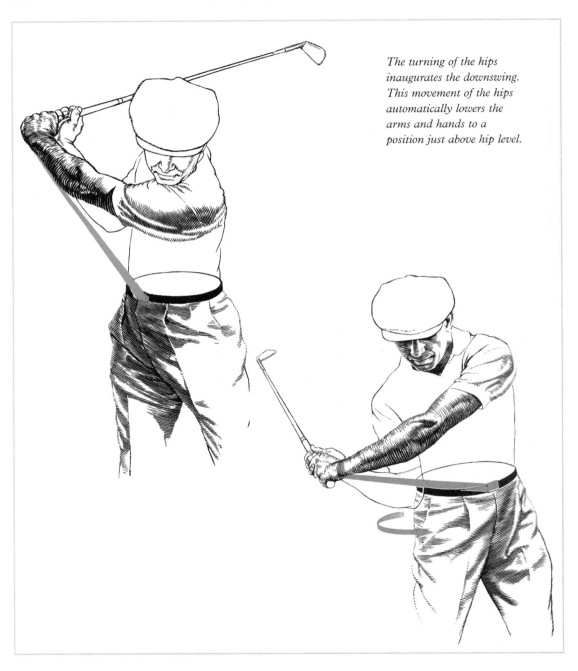

*The turning of the hips
inaugurates the downswing.
This movement of the hips
automatically lowers the
arms and hands to a
position just above hip level.*

The hips initiate the downswing.
They are the pivotal element in the chain
action. Starting them first and moving them
correctly—this one action practically *makes*
the downswing. It creates early speed. It
transfers the weight from the right foot to
the left foot. It takes the hips out of the way
and gives your arms plenty of room to pass.
It funnels your force forward toward your
objective. It puts you in a strong hitting
position where the big muscles in the back
and the muscles in the shoulders, arms and
hands are properly delayed so that they can
produce their maximum performance at
the right time and place.

To begin the downswing, **turn your
hips back to the left. There must be
enough lateral motion forward to transfer the weight to the left foot.**

This turning of the hips is activated by
several sets of muscles which work together.
**The contracted muscles of the left hip
and the muscles along the inside of
the left thigh start to spin the left hip
around to the left. At one and the same
time, the muscles of the right hip and
the muscles of the right thigh—both the
inside and the powerful outside thigh
muscles—start to move the right hip
forward.** In order for them to do this work,
these muscles must be stretched taut with
tension that is just waiting for the golfer's
signal to be released. This tension is built
up on the backswing by retarding the hips
but rotating the shoulders fully around.

The movement of the hips inaugurates
a whole chain of actions. The surest way to
wreck this remarkable machinery is to start
the downswing with the hands instead of
with the hips. If the average golfer will only
start his downswing with his hips, what a
world of difference this will make in his
swing and his shots, not to mention his score!

Let me put this even more strongly:
The main thing for the novice or the average
golfer is to keep any *conscious* hand action out
of his swing. The correct swing is founded on
chain action, and if you use the hands when
you shouldn't, you prevent this chain action.

After you have initiated the downswing
with the hips, you want to think of only one
thing: hitting the ball. On a full drive, I try to
hit the ball hard, sometimes as hard as I can.

Once a player reaches that phase of the
downswing where his hands are at about the
level of his hips—the start of the impact segment of the swing, we might term it-if he
has performed the swing correctly up to that
point, he is so set up that he instinctively hits
through the ball and follows through correctly. You can't keep from doing it right. It
helps a golfer, nonetheless, to have a clear
idea of what the arms and the hands actually
do during this climactic part of the swing.

What is the correct integrated motion
the two arms and hands make as they
approach the ball and hit through it? What
does it feel like as it is happening? Well, if
there is any motion in sports which it resembles, it is the old two-handed basketball pass,

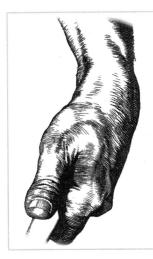

The left wrist begins to supinate at impact. The raised wristbone points to the target.

from the right side of the body . . . . As he shifts his weight from his right foot to his left to get all his power into his throw, the player flings the ball at the target just as hard as he can, whipping the ball with both arms and both hands, since he can throw it harder and more accurately that way.

The great value, as I see it, of thinking in terms of this joint two-hand action is that it keeps the left hand driving all the time. During this climactic part of the swing, the left wrist and the back of the left hand begin to supinate very slightly—that is, to turn from a position where the palm is down to a position where the palm is up.

In the sequence, there is one position of such signal importance that it warrants close-up study. This is the position of the left wrist and hand at the actual moment of impact. **At impact the back of the left hand faces toward your target. The wrist**

bone is definitely raised. It points to the target and, at the moment the ball is contacted, it is out in front, nearer to the target than any part of the hand.

Supinating sets up a number of extremely desirable actions. It helps the player to develop a properly wide forward arc. It puts him in a position where his arms are well extended at impact and will be fully extended just after impact as they swing out toward his objective. The wider his arc, the more room he has in which to build up clubhead speed, the prime factor behind distance.

There are a few other points related to the impact area and the follow-through that we should discuss now.

To start with, most golfers—whether or not they actually achieve it in their swings—have the mistaken idea that at the moment of impact both arms should be straightened out to their full length. This, of course, isn't right. **At impact the right arm is still bent slightly.**

At that point just beyond impact where both arms are straight and extended, the clubhead reaches its maximum speed—not at impact. This terrific speed carries the golfer right on around in that big high finish. At the completion of his swing, the player's belt buckle does not point directly at his target. It should point definitely to the left of his target.

As regards the legs, a great many golfers think that classical style prescribes that, at impact and throughout the follow-through,

In its general character, the correct motion of the right arm and hand in the impact area resembles the motion an infielder makes when he throws half sidearm, half underhand to first after fielding a ground ball. As the right arm swings forward, the right elbow is very close to the right hip and "leads" the arm— it is the part of the arm nearest the target.

the left leg should be as straight as a stick. Definitely not. If you keep your left leg straight, you prohibit your hips from making their full turn and restrict the whole free flow of your body to the left. When your weight doesn't get sufficiently transferred to the left, your arc is cramped, and your body, arms, and hands cannot release the full power they're capable of pouring into the shot.

When you're practicing this lesson, I suggest you spend some time reviewing the backswing plane and devote perhaps a half hour daily to the hip turn and the hit-through movements. Don't be afraid of swinging too hard.

I feel, and I have proved to myself, that I can hit a ball straighter if I hit it hard and full. As a matter of fact, when he is playing a long and testing course, a golfer who has a sound swing wouldn't mind at all having the physique of a giant. The more power he had at his command, the better he'd feel about it. He'd know how to use it. He'd be so long he'd be shooting back at the greens!

FROM *FIVE LESSONS: THE MODERN FUNDAMENTALS OF GOLF* BY BEN HOGAN

CHAPTER 16

CHUCK HOGAN

AUDIOTHERAPY

"The golfing establishment is only beginning to recognize that golf instruction may have done more harm than good."

"Voodoo doctor" is the term *GOLF Magazine* used to describe Chuck Hogan when he burst to teaching prominence back in 1986. At the time, Hogan was helping dozens of PGA and LPGA Tour pros play some of the most inspired golf of their lives.

His methods, while a bit unorthodox, included no impaled dolls, tribal dances, or bubbling cauldrons. Indeed, far from trading in shrunken heads, Hogan was all about mind expansion, specifically the creation and use of vivid images to enhance performance. Among his success stories was PGA Tour player Mike Reid, who improved his putting dramatically after Hogan got him to see each putt as a corridor through two rows of green singing worms. Seriously.

Nothing that happened in the first thirty or so years of Chuck Hogan's life hinted at the mind-bending path his career would take. Born and raised in Oregon, he attended the University of Oregon, where he played on the golf team. His education was interrupted by a hitch in Vietnam, but he finished his degree and began working at a string of local driving ranges in the Eugene area, teaching and playing the game with modest success. However, the more he played and taught, the more he became convinced

It's all about the why and how of imaging— why detailed, compelling images are the key to better golf.

that something was missing, that the "what" of learning golf—the instructional content— was less important than "how" people learn.

Hogan had begun to explore the mental and strategic aspects of the game when he met a scientist named Dale Van Dalsem in 1983. Van Dalsem had developed a device—

Chuck Hogan's "beta state" techniques have helped several PGA Tour players.

age forty-three, and breathlessly pronounced his time with Hogan "the greatest experience of my golfing career."

On the heels of that success in the mid-1980s, Hogan founded Sports Enhancement Associates, an enterprise that began as a series of golf schools and expanded to include seminars for teachers in a dozen different countries. He has produced three videos and written ten books, but it is his first effort—*Five Days to Golfing Excellence*—that sets forth the ideas that most distinguish him. It's all about the why and how of imaging—why detailed, compelling images are the key to better golf and how any player, without the aid of headphones and electronic tones, can reach the hypnotic state from which those images flow.

> THE SECRET:
>
> **G**et into a "beta state" and conjure vivid, engaging mental images related to your swing and shotmaking. They will strengthen your confidence and thus your performance.

essentially a pair of headphones hooked up to an amplifier that played a series of low-frequency tones—that induced in its subjects a tranquil "beta" state, sort of an instant Zen from which they conjured detailed, colorful images that helped them play better golf.

Peter Jacobsen was among the first to benefit from Hogan's methods. A fellow Oregonian, Jacobsen was in something of a slump when he visited Hogan in 1984. The following week he won the Colonial Invitational. Other players whose careers were revitalized by Hogan's headphonic therapy include Johnny Miller, D. A. Weibring, and John Cook. Ray Floyd completed a session not long before winning the U.S. Open at

The book is not illustrated except for a few stick-figure drawings and cartoons, and the narrative—as with many books on the mental side—is at times hard to follow, but the results Hogan achieved with the best players in the world cannot be denied.

CHUCK HOGAN'S SECRET

You would have to have a distaste for life to be the passenger in a car whose driver attempts to operate his car in the same mechanically oriented way he operates his golf clubs. Instead of responding to the road, he is talking his way down it with the deliberation of his intellect. If there are any unknowns presented or pressures introduced, he'll intellectualize the car into the ditch, the highway's equivalent of a sand trap!

The same is true of any activity that requires precise calculations for performance. You respond efficiently only when you remain receptive to information being provided by the target or the task at hand. If you shift your attention to yourself, you take attention off the target.

Golf instruction has become an institution of self-awareness rather than target-awareness! Golf lessons, golf publications, golf commentators, and your golfing partners continually tell you what is wrong with some piece of your swing. You are continually bombarded with the notion that somehow you will be more accurate in relation to the target by thinking of your arm, head, leg, or club position. Golf has been replaced by golf swing.

There are some dramatic differences between golf swing and golf:

Golf swing is focused on self. Golf is focused on ball to target.

Golf swing is and is being taught as an act. Golf is and ought to be taught as a reaction.

Mental Mechanics for Your Best Play

The most efficient practice is 70 percent mental and 30 percent physical. Mental mechanics practice is a technique that you can engage in on a regular, daily basis to heighten your skills at monitoring and shaping your thoughts or images, so that they are advantageous and appropriate from minute to minute and, more to the point, from shot to shot. As you learn to shape your thoughts, your confidence will improve and your game will improve. And that's what you want.

The very recognition that you may be playing extremely well is likely to destroy the state of mind that you need to continue playing well. Indeed, most athletes of all sports, and especially golf, would agree that *seeing* and *feeling* the accomplishment of the goal before acting is the essence of confidence and the key to success. You recognize these experiences when you say the putt was *already in* before the stroke was made because *I could see the line* or *I just knew I was going to make it!* On these days when performance is optimum, the fairway is a *mile wide* and greens *huge* and trouble areas are *smaller than the ball.*

You achieve what you conceive. A new look at the ideas of seeing and feeling will put a whole new perspective on the subject of confidence. **The image *is* confidence.**

Mental imagery is continuous and ongoing; without it, your body would malfunction. It forms the basis of your perception, your speech, and your actions. Your images are your perception and your perception is your reality. Your practice of mental mechanics helps you develop an active, conscious role in developing and maintaining images.

General Relaxation Exercise

To enable yourself to develop vivid images, you must first reach a profoundly relaxed state. Here is how to get there:

Lie down or sit in a comfortable position. Close your eyes. Turn your thoughts to your breath. Breathe deeply. Take air in through your nose and exhale through your mouth. Let your stomach move out freely, and completely fill your lungs with air. Synchronize your breathing with your heart-beats.

Try this now: Breathe in slowly through your nose for six heartbeats. Inhale the air deeply into the bottom of your lungs. Hold your breath for three beats. Keep your shoulders and neck relaxed. Exhale through your mouth for six beats.

Let your body relax deeply, deeper than ever before. Take note of images that appear: What colors do you see, what textures do you feel, what temperature changes do you notice, what do you taste?

> The very recognition that you may be playing extremely well is likely to destroy the state of mind that you need to continue playing well.

Mental mechanics fosters imaging and maintains perceptions that generate confidence. Even though mental mechanics is new to golf, the language of imaging has existed alongside that of physical mechanics and golf. Expressions like *bite, take a seat,* or *get legs* originated as verbal descriptions of a player's image of what he wanted his ball to do at a particular moment.

> **The image of the shot will need a beginning (the strike) a middle (the flight) and a destination (the hole or target). The image should be as exciting, detailed, and complete as possible.**

For the originator of the image, there is great meaning in these statements. But, for the rest of us, copying the image, there is little or no particular meaning beyond the comedy. There is no mental/physical engagement which is actually going to help us with the end result of the shot.

But even at a low-level image state, there is a corresponding physical response. You cannot say the word *choke* without your mind forming a picture which activates body reactions of restricted breathing, constricted blood supply, tense muscles, and hormonal changes.

Images can be kinesthetic (feel), auditory (hearing), olfactory (smell), and taste, as well as visual. Images precede internal or external dialogue and are far superior directors of motor skills than self talk. The verbal description of an experience falls miserably short of the actual image or experience itself. The impact of a verbal description of an orange being peeled is far less than the impact of actually imaging yourself peeling one.

If you want to play like a pro, you must do exactly that. If you want to play like a winner, you must be a winner. You must hold the image of swinging like a pro, and more importantly, you must think like a pro or a winner. This means that your images must be vivid, engaging, and individual. You need to practice, on and off the course, fresh and inspiring images which are totally your own.

To begin with, you can review the clichés used in the game, put real meaning to them, and reform these verbal impressions into a stimulating image as it applies to a particular shot. What do the following *really* mean to you?

Career shot

Hit the flag

A 40-foot snake

Big thunder

Fly ball, fly

Bullet

Pure

Go in!

What picture does each of these convey after you give it deep thought? Does it also have an associated sound, feel, taste, and/or smell? If it does, then adding these other senses will aid in your calculations and in your actual shot-making process.

You will ebb in and out of your image development. One day the feel of the forward swing will match exactly the brilliance of the image you choose to direct your body. Perhaps the next day it will be difficult to find a strong and vivid image for the shot at hand. Take these days of difficulty as a sign that you need more practice, and practice regularly.

A pitch shot might come down like a paratrooper, a deflated inner tube, or a dart. Perhaps the shot calls for the ball to take off like a race car or run like a rabbit. Whatever the shot, the image of the shot will need a beginning (the strike), a middle (the flight), and a destination (the hole or target). The image should be as exciting, detailed, and complete as possible. You can draw from the environment on and off the course.

Set aside a few minutes a day for imaging practice. Take one-half hour a day during your personal creative time. Sit comfortably or lie down. Play or practice your golf game in your mind. Hit shots with a variety of images. Keep the images fresh and interesting. Some images will be concrete and others may be abstract in both character and result. You may wish to listen to music while doing this, or you may prefer silence. The more you practice the easier, more spontaneous, orchestrated, and engaging the images will become, and the more pragmatic their use will be as you carry them onto the course. Practice, as always, is the key to success.

FROM *FIVE DAYS TO GOLFING EXCELLENCE* BY CHARLES HOGAN

> **If you want to play like a pro, you must do exactly that. If you want to play like a winner, you must be a winner. You must hold the image of swinging like a pro, and more importantly, you must think like a pro or a winner.**

CHUCK HOGAN'S SECRET

CHAPTER 17

KEEP YOUR EYE ON THE BALL

"The only purpose of the golf swing is to move the club through the ball square to the target at maximum speed. How this is done is of no significance at all, so long as the method employed enables it to be done repetitively."

In 1970 *Golf Digest* convened a panel of the best instructional minds in America. Sitting around the table were super-teachers Bob Toski, Jim Flick, Paul Runyan, Eddie Merrins, and Gary Wiren, not to mention Cary Middlecoff and Sam Snead. Each of them had come to that meeting with convictions about how the game should be played. Then all of them got their minds blown by an imposing British chap named John Jacobs.

Ken Bowden, then editor of the magazine—and soon to depart for a career as Jack Nicklaus's Boswell—recalled what happened when Jacobs got the floor.

"John ran into a lot of opposition—not jealousy, the American mind is too open for that—because he was teaching a different concept. He turned the panel around to his way of thinking as soon as they realized they could learn from him. They resisted him until, from the pure logic of his argument, they

THE SECRET:

Understand the geometry of impact—clubface angle, swing path, angle of attack, and clubhead speed—and you'll be able to read your own ball flight, analyze your own mistakes, and correct your own faults.

John Jacobs—Ryder cupper, founder of the European Tour, course architect, TV broadcaster, and teacher par excellence.

was a strong enough player to win two professional events and make the 1955 British Ryder Cup team, a respected enough leader to captain the first two European Ryder Cup Teams, a talented enough architect to have several course designs to his credit, an able enough administrator to become the founding father of the European Tour, an insightful enough commentator to work telecasts for the BBC, and a canny enough businessman to have his name on the largest and most successful golf school in the world. Jacobs's accolades include induction into the World Golf Teachers Hall of Fame, honorary membership in the Royal & Ancient Golf Club of St. Andrews, and an Order of the British Empire from Queen Elizabeth.

Above all, however, he was and remains a teacher—arguably the most influential golf teacher of the last half century—and all because he kept his eye on the ball. John Jacobs offered no magic moves or fool-proof methods. Instead he brought the world's attention to what he called "the geometry of impact," the irrefutable laws that apply when clubhead meets ball. The first ten pages of Jacobs's *Practical Golf,* reprised here, should be required reading for all new golfers.

accepted that he was right. If you follow it through, he changed the thinking of the *Golf Digest* panel and, thereby, he changed the mass of American thinking about the golf swing."

Such an accomplishment would be a fine epitaph for any teacher, but in Jacobs's case it is just one of several accomplishments. He

JACOBS'S SECRET

First, Understand What You Are Trying To Do.

The only purpose of the golf swing is to move the club through the ball square to the target at maximum speed. How this is done is of no significance at all, so long as the method employed enables it to be done repetitively.

That is my number-one credo. It is the basis on which I teach golf. It may sound elementary, but I am certain that the point it makes has been missed by most golfers. Ninety-five percent of the people who come to me for lessons don't really know what they are trying to do when they swing a golf club. Their prime concern is to get into certain "positions" during the swing. Therein, they believe, lies the elusive "secret" of golf. They have either never known or have long forgotten that the only reason such positions are necessary *is to get the club to swing correctly through the ball.*

There are four possible impact variations produced by the golf swing that, in concert, determine the behavior of the ball. They are:

1. The direction in which the clubface looks.
2. The direction of the swing.
3. The angle of the club's approach to the ball.
4. The speed of the club.

Of these four, the alignment of the clubface at impact is the most vital. If it is not reasonably correct, it will cause errors in the other three areas. For example, the clubface being open—pointing right of target—invariably leads at impact to an out-to-in swing path through the ball. This in turn forces the club into too steep an angle of approach to the ball. The clubface *cannot* meet the ball either squarely or solidly. Conversely, a closed clubface at impact generally leads to an in-to-out swing path. That causes too shallow an angle of approach—the club reaches the bottom of its arc before it reaches the ball. Again, the clubface *cannot* meet the ball either solidly or square.

Do one thing right in the golf swing and it will lead to another right. Do one thing wrong and it will produce another wrong. In this sense, golf is a *reaction* game. Never forget that fact.

The direction in which the clubface looks is the most important of the four impact elements that determine the behavior of every shot you hit.

If your clubface aims left or right of target during impact, instinctively you will make "matching" errors in the path of future swings.

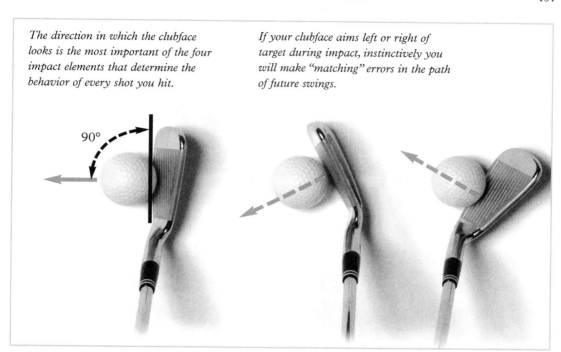

When your squared clubface produces on-target shots, instinctively you will swing the clubhead through the ball along the target line (A) on future attempts. If your clubface consistently points right at impact, you will swing from outside to inside (B), in an instinctive effort to prevent the ball from going to the right. If your clubface consistently points left of target at impact, you swing inside to outside the target line in an instinctive effort to stop the ball from going left (C).

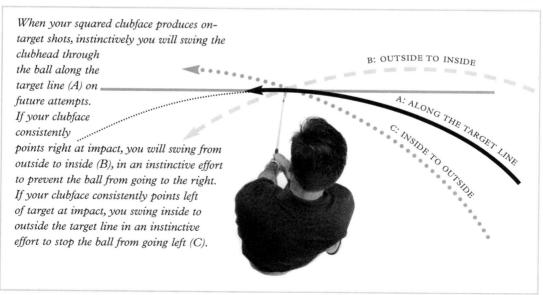

B: OUTSIDE TO INSIDE

A: ALONG THE TARGET LINE

C: INSIDE TO OUTSIDE

No

No

Yes

Swinging the clubhead across the target line from inside to outside to an excessive degree often causes it to contact the ground before it meets the ball. Swinging across the target line from outside to inside steepens the club's arc so that often it makes contact too high on the ball. Swinging the clubhead along the target line at impact creates a shallow approach arc that enables the clubface to meet the ball solidly.

Most of what you read about curing slicing tells you to do things like "slide the hips as the first movement of the downswing," "stay inside," "tuck the right elbow in," "hit late," "hold back your shoulders," and so on, ad nauseum. Unless you cure the *basic* fault—your open clubface at impact— you'll never do those things. You *can't,* because your *natural reactions* oppose them.

That is why the world is full of golfers who say "I know what to do but I can't do it." They can't do it because, whatever their conscious desires, their actual swing actions are reactions to basic major faults.

The thing we all react to most is the face of the club. You must realize—and never forget—that incorrect alignment of the clubface at impact on one shot affects the entire golf swing on the next. Any cure is not to be found in swing "positions." It lies in developing a grip and swing that brings the clubface square to your swing line at impact. Do this and all your reactions will be correct ones. Everything suddenly—and miraculously—falls into place. Now, if you swing from out-to-in, the ball will go to the left. You will immediately, *subconsciously,* make an effort to hit more from inside the target line. Your *natural* adjustment to help you do that will be to pull your body around so that you can swing that way. And—bingo!—suddenly you are set up square instead of open. Now you can swing the club so that it can approach the ball at the right level to hit it solidly in the back. Your shots start straight and fly straight. You've got the "secret"! Fantastic! And not one word about "hit late," "slide your hips," "keep your head down"!

Technically, golf is a much simpler game than most people realize. Here's another way to look at it simply. If you are consistently mishitting and misdirecting the ball, it should cheer you to know that there are only two basic causes. Either:

1. *You have an open clubface at impact,* which makes you swing across the target line from outside to inside, which in turn makes the club descend too steeply into the ball and thus not meet it solidly; or

2. *You have a closed clubface at impact,* which makes you swing across the target line from inside to outside, which makes the clubhead descend too shallowly into the ball, thus either catching the ground behind it or hitting the ball "thin" at the start of the upswing.

JACOBS'S SECRET

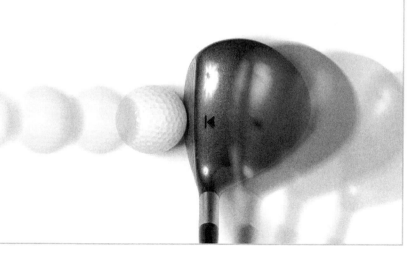

The distance your ball flies is governed not—as so many golfers think—by your clubhead speed alone, but by clubhead speed squarely applied. Thus long-hitting is as much a matter of achieving the correct "impact geometry" as using your muscles in a particular way.

The perfect impact occurs only when the clubhead at impact travels exactly along the target line and exactly faces the target. This is "square"—the only "square" in golf. This is your aim—the total objective of all you do with a golf club. What this book is all about.

There's just one more point I must make before we launch off into what I hope you will find an instructive and entertaining

Learning what I call the geometry of the game is a mental, not a practice-ground process. It isn't difficult but it involves sitting down and thinking for a few moments.

book. It is my number-two credo as a teacher of golf. It is this: "The art of competing is to know your limitations and to try on every shot."

What this really means is that the technique of striking the ball—the thing I personally deal in most of the time—is no more than 50 percent of the game. Temperament, intelligence, nerve, desire, and many other mental qualities make up the other 50 percent. So, when we are talking technique, as we are in the first part of this book, you might like to keep in mind that we are not dealing with the whole game. Unfortunately, even if you can learn to hit it like Jack Nicklaus, you still have to learn to play like him.

Learn—and Never Forget—golf's Basic "Geometry"

If what I said a moment ago makes sense, being able, *yourself*, to analyze errors in your clubface alignment and swing direction from the way your shots behave is obviously an absolute prerequisite to playing better golf.

Learning what I call the "geometry" of the game is a mental, not a practice-ground, process. It isn't difficult, but it involves sitting down and thinking for a few moments.

The behavior of every shot you hit is caused by a specific inter-relationship of the clubface angle and the swing direction at impact. Here is how:

Pull: Ball flies on a straight line but to the left of your target. The club's head is traveling across your intended target line from outside to inside that line at impact. The clubface is square to the *line of your swing,* but not to your *target line.* These shots often feel solid even though they fly in the

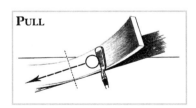

PULL

wrong direction. The direction the clubface was looking and clubhead was moving "matched," thus obviating a glancing blow.

Slice: Ball starts left of your target then bends to the right. The club is again traveling across the intended target line from out to in during impact, but this time the face is *open*—facing right—of your swing line. This creates a clockwise sidespin that bends the ball to the right as its forward impetus decreases. The more the clubface and swing path are in opposition, the more oblique the blow, the greater the sidespin and the bigger the slice. Also, the more your

BANANA SLICE

swing line is from outside your target line, the steeper will be the club's approach to the ball and the higher up—and thus more glancing—its contact on the ball.

Pulled Hook: Ball starts left of your target, then bends farther to the left.

Again, the club is traveling across your intended target line from out to in, but this time the face is

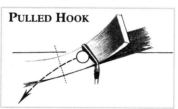

PULLED HOOK

closed to the line of swing. This combination of two faults in the same direction sends the ball disastrously to the left—the infamous "smothered hook."

Push: Ball flies straight but to the right of your target.

Again, the clubhead travel-

ing across your intended target line at impact, but this time from in to out. Your clubface is square to your line of swing, but *not* to your target line.

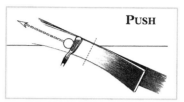

PUSH

Obviously the ball flies where both the clubface and swing path direct it—to the right. As with the pull, this shot often feels solid, because the blow is not of the glancing variety.

Hook: Ball starts right of your target, then bends to the left.

The club is again traveling across your intended line from in to out, but this time the face is *closed,* facing left of the line of your swing. This creates counterclockwise sidespin that bends the ball left once its forward impetus decreases. Unless the clubhead's angle of approach is so low that it hits the ground before it gets to the ball, a hooked shot feels much more solidly struck than a slice. This

QUICK HOOK

is because the club-face, by moving parallel to the ground

instead of sharply downward, contacts the back-center of the ball, not its top as in a slice.

Pushed Slice: Ball starts right of your target then bends more to the right.

Again, the club is traveling across your intended target line from in to out at impact,

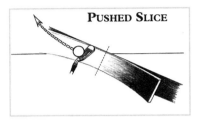

PUSHED SLICE

but this time the face is open to the line of your swing.

These two faults combining in the same direction send the ball devastatingly far right.

Straight Shot: Ball starts straight and flies straight along your target line.

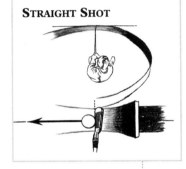

STRAIGHT SHOT

The clubface looks at the target and your swing line coincides with the target line at impact.

You are now able to analyze your own swing, and I hope you will at last appreciate what "analyze" really means in golfing terms. It doesn't mean standing in front of a mirror and trying to spot whether your left knee bends inwards or forwards, whether your left arm is straight or bent at the top, etc., etc. You can make a complete analysis of your swing while you shave, sit in a train, ride to the office, or lie in bed. *All you have*

to do is think about the way your golf ball reacts when you hit it.

It is obvious that, if you hook a lot, you'll probably also push the ball because these two shapes are in a *swing-path pair.* Both require a swing-path that is in-to-out during impact. Conversely, if you slice you will also pull, because these two shapes are the other *swing-path pair* (out-to-in).

Every golfer belongs to one of these categories. His offline shots will *start out* consistently left or right of the target line. A big bending of the shot, left or right, is dependent on the direction his clubface was looking, relative to his swing line during impact. A closed-clubface golfer will be a hooker who pushes the ball when he happens to return the clubface in the same direction he's swinging. An open-clubface golfer will be a slicer who pulls when he happens to return the clubface in the same direction *he* is swinging.

Want to be sure of your category? Here's how to find out.

First, take a driver to the practice ground and hit half a dozen shots. If they bend from left to right in the air, the clubface is open to your swing line at impact. If they curve the other way the clubface is closed. By using a club with very little loft, you will always get an honest picture of your clubface alignment at impact. Why? Because, since the club's loft is minimal, little backspin is created by a back-of-the-ball blow—too little, in fact, to override the sidespin imparted by the oblique contact of an open or shut clubface.

Next, take a 9-iron and hit a few more shots. Because of its greater loft, this club contacts the *bottom* back of the ball, imparting heavy backspin. Consequently, the influence of sidespin is reduced to the point where the direction in which the ball flies accurately reflects the path of your swing. For example, you will almost certainly hit the highly-lofted clubs straight, but left, if you are a slicer with the driver.

Before we leave golf's "geometry"—although it will be constantly referred to in this book—there are a couple more factors I'd like you to understand.

The first is that your club needs to swing *along* the target line only just before, during, and just after impact—a *matter* of a few inches. You *do not*, as some books suggest, have to swing it along the target line a number of feet in order to hit the ball straight. This leads directly to another point I'd like to clarify. You stand *inside* the arc you make with the club. The only way, therefore, that you can swing the club straight along the target line is to have it coming into the ball from *inside* the target line. Once the clubhead passes outside the target line in the downswing, it cannot swing along this line during impact, *but only back across it.*

By the same token, if your club is to follow a true arc, it will quickly move *inside* the target line again after you have struck the ball. Thus the clubhead path of a golf swing that hits the ball straight is not, as many people seem to believe, inside to out. *It is inside, to straight-through, to inside again.*

FROM *PRACTICAL GOLF* BY JOHN JACOBS

You can make a complete analysis of your swing while you shave, sit in a train, ride to the office, or lie in bed. *All you have to do is think about the way your golf ball reacts when you hit it.*

CHAPTER 18

ERNEST JONES

THE SWING'S THE THING

"There is more than one way of hitting. There is only one way to swing. The swing is everything. To strike the ball with power it is necessary to move the clubhead faster. But you cannot move the clubhead faster than you can swing it."

I n 1915 while fighting with the British Navy in World War I, Ernest Jones was badly injured. Sixteen pieces of shrapnel lodged in his right leg and the leg had to be amputated below the knee.

His loss was golf's gain. A fine player before the war, Jones was about to become the most influential instructor of his time. Born in Manchester in 1887, Jones had shown an early aptitude for golf, winning his local club's caddie prize three straight times before he was even a teenager. At eighteen, he became the club's assistant professional and the same year won the Kent Cup, the area's most important professional tournament. Jones

seemed on his way to a successful career as a playing pro.

Then he was called to war, and everything changed. Remarkably, however, only a week after leaving the military hospital, Jones was back on the golf course, and in his first round—walking with the aid of crutches and balancing on one leg as he swung—he stunned everyone by shooting 83—including a 38 on the front nine. A short time later, he shot 72 at his home course. Jones, through his misfortune, had learned something.

"The loss of my leg confirmed to me the fundamental truth that the stroke must be regarded as one complete action," he said. "You initiate it by swinging the club. Because I followed the

THE SECRET:

S wing the clubhead with your hands—the rest of the body will follow.

basic tenets of the swing, I discovered I could still play good golf, even on one leg. Playing on one leg disproved the emphasis which so many still place on body pivot."

Jones became fitted for an artificial leg and returned to his prewar form, winning the Kent Cup for

Jones tied a penknife to a handkerchief to demonstrate the proper pendulum swing.

a second time in 1920. But by then his thoughts of a playing career had been replaced by a determination to teach what he had learned to others. In 1924 he moved to America and began a career that would last for forty years, the last twenty of them in New York, where, from his office on the seventh floor of the A.G. Spalding Building on Fifth Avenue, he gave lessons to 36-handicappers and national champions.

Jones was something of a minimalist. "Perfection," he once said, "is achieved not when there is no longer anything to add but when there is no longer anything to take away. I try to eliminate all other considerations and to concentrate on one principle: the art of swinging the clubhead."

To convey his theory, Jones would attach a handkerchief to a penknife and show how,

when he held the handkerchief at the end and swung the knife back and forth like a pendulum, the handkerchief stayed taut. When he tried to move the knife through leverage action, the knife remained still.

Among Jones's prominent pupils were U.S. and British Amateur Champion Lawson Little, three-time Women's Amateur Champion Virginia Van Wie, and arguably the greatest woman golfer of all time, Babe Zaharias. But his lasting legacy is in the generation of instructors who followed in his footsteps. *GOLF Magazine* Top 100 Teachers Manuel de la Torre, John Jacobs, Bob Toski, Jim Flick, Eddie Merrins, and Dick Farley all are descendants of Ernest Jones, and although each has added a twist or tweak along the way, all have preached Jones's simple gospel: The swing's the thing.

JONES'S SECRET

Now we come to the meat of this discussion—the swing. It is the swing, and only that, which makes the golfer. Therefore, it follows that the golfer must understand what is a swing.

Quickly now, what is a swing? Can you answer correctly?

A swing is a definite form of motion. Webster devotes considerable space to defining the word. To swing is to have a regular to-and-fro motion, as of a pendulum; to oscillate. Swing, as a noun, is the arc or extent through which an object swings. It also is the force created by something swinging.

Carried over to golf, it is one continuous motion, to and fro, backward and forward, a definite form of motion which must be produced into the clubhead to create the greatest force of which your power is capable. It creates centrifugal force.

Unfortunately, those who have the best swings seem unable to pass on this information. They know how to swing, but not how to teach the swing. That is why so many fine golfers have been guilty of teaching doctrines which are false.

All golfers today talk about their swing. Unfortunately, to most of them it is nonexistent. But, in their misfortunes on the links, they'll ask:

"What is wrong with my swing?"

My answer is "nothing," because their swing is nonexistent.

No person can do more than one thing at a time. For that reason I insist that the golf swing can be but one continuous motion, and nothing else.

The form, the shape, of a swing is an arc or part of a circle. As I said before, to make a circle you draw one continuous line, not 360 because there are 360 degrees in a circle. Do you appreciate that? That one line, the golf swing, can be taught only through the use of the hands and fingers.

To be able to swing you must understand this fact. Since you feel the swing and since the hands are the only parts of your body which are in contact with the club, they must be the medium through which the swing becomes possible. You cannot feel the swing with your feet, your shoulders, your hips, or your arms.

When a good golfer swings he has, at all times, the feel of what he is doing with the clubhead. He does not see the myriad movements made by the many parts of the body when stroking. He never learned through a detailed analysis of the duties of each part of the body. He learned how to hold the club, how to stand, and he swung. He learned much as a child learns to swing the rope when skipping.

Thus, that good golfer, when addressing the ball, concentrates wholly on his hands, which are holding the club with which he must strike the ball. When he thinks only of hitting the ball with the clubhead through the medium of his hands, has eliminated all the other distractions, he finds that he does well, and that the remaining parts of his body have carried through their allotted duties, although he never gave them a thought.

You are trying to become a good golfer, not a contortionist. You must understand that the various members of the body are normally anxious to get busy too strenuously—and too soon. You must curb this instinct and, as I said before, the only way is to treat them as disastrous leaders, and as wholly admirable followers. Since the initiative is in the hands and fingers, the moment you properly move the club with the hands, everything else will be set into correct motion.

Try this test as an illustration. Place your hand on a table. Now draw an imaginary circle around your thumb, using your first finger. The thumb is the pivotal point.

When I have my pupils do this, I casually say:

"That wasn't hard. But tell me quickly, what did you do with your thumb?"

Three times out of four, the answer is: "Nothing. I kept the thumb perfectly still."

So I say: "Try it again."

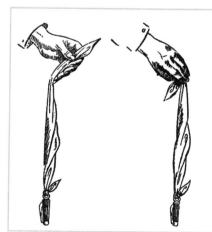

The best visual demonstration of a swinging action is the movement of a weight attached to the end of a string or handkerchief. The handkerchief, being flexible, cannot transmit power through leverage.

Immediately, the pupil realizes that the thumb has to move if it is to act as the pivot. It is impossible for it to remain still.

The same thing happens when you swing the clubhead around your body. Try it and you will see what I mean. Or try this, holding the club as you would a baseball bat. Swing it fast, horizontally, so that the force of the swing carries your body around in a pivot. Isn't the pivot the result of the swing, and not the cause?

I have another device with which I illustrate the swing, a pocket knife attached to a string. I swing the knife and the string is taut because a swinging action always is an expanding action with the weight exerting an outward pull.If you try this yourself, When you try it, you will notice how you guide the movement entirely through a feel of what is happening with the weight. So

long as the weight is swung, the string will be taut, regardless of whether the swing is short or long.

I also have a device known as the pro swing. It is built like a regular club, except that the bottom part of the shaft is a spring to which is attached a weight comparable to the clubhead. It is a most accurate check of whether or not you are swinging properly. Whether you swing the weight on the string or the pro swing, the moment you deviate from the proper action you will notice that everything goes wrong.

In golf, a swing is a positive, indivisible motion backward and forward. It has definite form or shape, which is an arc, or part of a circle.

A swing has perfect rhythm which can be put to waltz-time music. It is a measure of time, as is the pendulum of a clock. Like

You can practice by swinging a weight on the end of a string. When you start back properly, the string will be taut.

the pendulum, it takes the same measure of time to swing, irrespective of the length of the swing.

Thus, a short putt takes the same measure of time to complete as does a full drive, if the same club is used and held at the same place. The idea of swinging fast or slow is not possible in the same length of swing. Therefore, since a true swing takes the same measure of time, the longer the swing, the greater the force, or speed. The shorter the swing, the less the speed, or force.

Remember Galileo's law of falling bodies. Drop a solid, light weight and a heavy weight. Both take the same time to fall, irrespective of the difference in their weight. But the greater the weight, the more force in striking the object. So the more power you put into the swinging motion of the clubhead, the greater force you create. But if you overpower the swing, the force will die.

Swinging vs. Hacking

Although this chapter is entitled "Swinging vs. Hacking," it could as easily be called "Swinging vs. Hitting," or "Swinging vs. Jerking."

After listening in on countless locker-room discussions, perhaps I should have called the chapter "Swinging vs. Hitting." Remember: There is one categorical imperative in golf. **Hit the ball.** There are no minor absolutes.

Are there hitters as opposed to swingers?

You have heard golfers catalogued into groups of hitters and swingers. But such people do not know what they are talking about. All great golfers had to learn how to hit the ball. Because of their natural start they may not realize that. But, and I emphasize this for those who call themselves hitters, they cannot get the maximum force into the clubhead unless they swing.

Press, drag, push, snap, pull, etc.: None is a swing. Bobby Jones copied the action of a wonderful swinger, Stewart Maiden, when he was a boy. So, where great golfers are involved, you cannot say, "Swingers vs. Hitters." They are all swingers. Where the other kind are concerned, I think the best title becomes "Swingers vs. Hackers," or "Jerkers."

The first great difference between a swinger and a hacker is that the former gains better control over the clubhead. The swinger

If you continue to "swing the clubhead," the string will remain taut at impact and into the follow-through.

proves that you cannot move the clubhead faster than you can swing it. Thus, he is not guilty of the hacker's greatest failing, of trying to generate power with which to hit the ball by rushing the backswing, jerking the club from its position behind the ball, and then compounding his error by again rushing the downswing.

Were it possible to break down this noxious caricature of a golf swing, you would discover that the hacker, not knowing how to begin the swing back, tries to begin his downswing even before he has finished his upswing. This is not physically possible.

Unfortunately, in seeking instruction, the hacker frequently is told:

"Let the club do the work."

The teacher knows what he has in mind, and it is correct. But he uses the wrong words. What he means is that you cannot move the clubhead faster than you can swing it. So he should tell you to swing the clubhead. But he says: "Let the club do the work."

What sometimes happens is that the hacker transposes from one failing to another. He then tries to let the club do the work—without his participation. He does not use his hands, perhaps because he hasn't been told about the "feel" of the swing, lets the club fall against the ball. It is a fluffy stroke without any power or authority motivating the club's action.

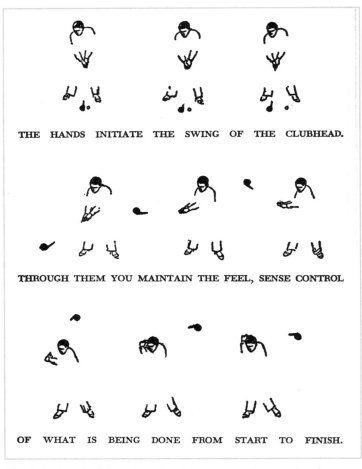

THE HANDS INITIATE THE SWING OF THE CLUBHEAD.

THROUGH THEM YOU MAINTAIN THE FEEL, SENSE CONTROL

OF WHAT IS BEING DONE FROM START TO FINISH.

The body is omitted from these drawings to prove that your hands control your swing and to enable you to sense the feel of the clubhead.

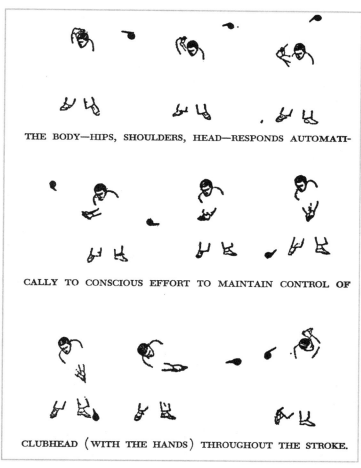

THE BODY—HIPS, SHOULDERS, HEAD—RESPONDS AUTOMATI-

CALLY TO CONSCIOUS EFFORT TO MAINTAIN CONTROL OF

CLUBHEAD (WITH THE HANDS) THROUGHOUT THE STROKE.

The other parts of your body simply respond to the movement of your hands. You do not consciously move your body while wielding the club.

This is a good time to distinguish between leverage and centrifugal force.

Leverage belongs on a golf course only when the greenskeeper uses a crowbar to uproot a deeply imbedded rock. In prying, he presses down hard, in order to force the object up. The power applied moves in one direction, while the object to which it is applied moves in the opposite direction.

This is what the hacker persists in attempting. He presses against the club with his fingers, as if to use it for levering. He creates pressure, which strains the arms. Try making a tight fist. Notice how it strains your fingers, the pain extending all the way up the arm. That is pressure.

You cannot create a swing by pressure. In a swing, everything is moving in the same direction around a center. That is centrifugal force. In the swing, you perform an action which is a joy. Thus, you can reduce to pain vs. joy the difference between exerting leverage, which is a painful process, as against swinging, which is exhilarating.

FROM *SWING THE CLUBHEAD* BY ERNEST JONES

There must be force in the swing. When the hacker learns that that force comes through controlling the clubhead with the hands and fingers, he is ready to move into the class of the swinger, where all good golfers belong.

CHAPTER 19

MASTER MECHANIC

"The body can duplicate a machine.
The trick is to understand the mechanics
and apply them until you have a 'machine feel.'"

Royal Troon Golf Club, July 16, 1982: Twenty-two-year-old Bobby Clampett sat before the microphones at the press tent of the 111th British Open Championship. He had just stunned the golf course; he was about to befuddle the world. For the second consecutive round, Clampett had shot the lowest score of the day, staking himself to a 5-stroke lead in his *first* British Open.

Virtually none of the two hundred members of the international press knew anything about him and they were full of questions.

"You're a wee lad and yet you hit the ball a long way," observed one Scottish scribe. "Have you any power secrets?"

"Yessir," said the polite young Californian. "I get my distance by snap-loading my power package while flat-loading my feet so that I can amplify my lag-and-drag pressure."

"Right . . ."

An intrepid Brit tried another tack. "You certainly played some splendid approach shots today. That one to 18 was stone dead. Is it true that accuracy with the irons is the strength of your game?"

"Yessir, I do consider myself extremely accurate, thanks to my ability to match my clubface alignment at impact-fix to the selected degree of horizontal hinge action."

> **THE SECRET:**
>
> Understand the physics and geometry of golf and you'll be able to develop a "machine feel" for the game.

"Yes, well, uh . . . thank you, Bobby."

Over the next two days, Clampett blew the tournament with rounds of 78 and 77. But he had made his mark. The British press that week brimmed with stories of Bobby's snap-loaded power package and of the book from which he had learned, Homer Kelley's *The Golfing Machine*.

Kelley was neither a writer nor a golfer by trade. He was an engineer's assistant at Boeing in

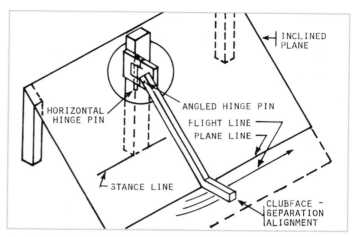

For Kelley, the golf swing was a matter of planes and hinges.

Seattle, who had spent over forty years mapping out the science of golf, analyzing and dissecting the swing until he'd identified why the ball goes where it does, how the club moves to make it fly long and straight or short and crooked, and what the human body must do to make the club cooperate. G.O.L.F., in Kelley's world, was a trademarked acronym that stood for Geometrically Oriented Linear Force. The best way to learn the game, in his view, was to learn the laws of geometry and physics and apply them on the fairways.

Ultimately, he "reduced" the swing to twenty-four components, three zones, twelve sections, and three functions. His findings allowed for approximately four hundred quadrillion different ways to hit a ball. Yes, that's four hundred quadrillion.

His book, written without the assistance of a co-author or editor, made golf sound like a game invented by Pythagoras for the diversion of Einstein. However, it did attract a loyal following, mostly teaching pros (among the most prominent was Ben Doyle, a Californian who became Bobby Clampett's mentor). Today *The Golfing Machine* lives on through a company of the same name whose mission is to promote Kelley's principles via a worldwide network of Authorized Instructors. These teachers must pass through a rigorous curriculum en route to obtaining the highest level of honors: the GSED (Golf Stroke Engineer Doctorate). Several of these graduates are among *GOLF Magazine's* Top 100 Teachers in America.

KELLEY'S SECRET

The relationships in the golf stroke can be explained scientifically only by geometry, because geometry is the science of relationships. So learn feel from mechanics rather than mechanics from feel.

There is much information herein that you won't need but there is none that someone won't need. This system ultimates in its own simplification. But without the supporting detail herein, that simplification could not have been conceived or supported. This book can support individual "MY Way" procedures but no "THE Way" theory.

The golf stroke involves two basic elements—the geometry of the circle and the physics of rotation. And only two basic strokes—hitting and swinging. The geometry is the same for both. And for all clubs and patterns. But, basically, the physics of hitting is muscular thrust, and of swinging, centrifugal force. Hitting and swinging seem equally efficient. The difference is in the players. If strong—hit. If quick—swing. If both—do either. Or both.

The geometry of golf has two aspects—the facts and the illusions, visual and sensory. When the facts are understood, the illusions not only cease to mislead but can be utilized. The physics of golf do not specify special "golf laws"—only the simple, universal laws of force and motion that you use every day because you cannot move yourself or anything else except in compliance with them. Physics merely takes the "seems as if" out of things. Including golf.

First use of this system might be to understand your present game before you abandon, replace, or scramble it. It may not be all that bad. At least it's familiar. Besides, habits can be harder to break than to reshuffle a little. This book may point up why you don't play better but also why you play as well as you do. At the very worst, it's the guided struggle versus the blind struggle. With this book you can do a lot of learning in your armchair.

The Machine Concept

It is soon apparent that the body can duplicate a machine. Grasp the parallel and escape limiting old concepts. Develop the "Machine Feel" to where you can just turn it loose and trust it. View the left shoulder as a hinge arrangement, not as a shoulder at all. The right arm becomes a piston—with steam or air hoses and the whole bit. The hands become adjustable clamps with two-way power actuators—for vertical and rotational manipulation. The left wrist is merely a hinge-pin allowing wrist cock but no wrist bend. The more of this translation a player can accomplish, the more understandable the procedures become.

This machine has three functions: to control A) the clubshaft, B) the clubhead, and C) the clubface. All other elements of the golf stroke design are concerned with facilitating and implementing these three activities. But if any of these other elements are unintentionally omitted (zeroed) or altered (different variation), the feel changes and the stroke becomes "ungrooved" and confusion sets in.

A mechanical device is simple and has few moving parts, but the human body as its counterpart has altogether too many. Every such part requires control by some pre-selected procedure.

> **Principles are simple—their applications get complicated. The Principle of golf is the "Line of Compression." The Mechanics of Golf is the production and manipulation of the "Line of Compression." Precision is recognizing and reconciling minute differentiations.**

Power and control are scientific and geometric and are proportionately and progressively dependable. Sheer determination or sheer muscular effort are helpless—except when directed at mastering the procedure which can bring acceptable results.

In every athletic activity, success seems to be unquestionably proportional to the player's sense of balance and force—whether innate or acquired. Off-balance force is notoriously erratic. The mechanical device has no balance problem but the human machine does, and mastery of the pivot is so essential for good golf.

FROM *THE GOLFING MACHINE* BY HOMER KELLEY

KELLEY'S SECRET

CHAPTER 20

DAVID LEE

THE FORCE BE WITH YOU

*"A golfer who learns to play using my system
does not have to rely on strength to make the swing.
A person who is getting older and losing strength or a female
player who never had strength to begin with need not worry.
Anyone over four feet tall can learn to hit the ball over 200 yards."*

The legend goes that in 1666 an apple fell from a tree and onto the head of Sir Isaac Newton, leading Newton to develop his Universal Law of Gravitation. Roughly 300 years later, a similar apple struck the noggin of David Lee.

A native of Hot Springs, Arkansas, Lee captained his golf team at the University of Arkansas, and in 1970, he made his way to the PGA Tour. Four difficult years later, he knew he was missing something: a proper golf swing.

From the beginning, he'd been an "upper-body" player, generating his power largely from a big turn of his shoulders and a vigorous swing of his arms. In the big boys on tour, he saw something different. "For hours I used to sit on the practice tee and watch Jack Nicklaus, Lee Trevino, and Tom Weiskopf hit balls," he said. "It didn't take a rocket scientist to figure out that their shots were not only better than mine but made with less effort. In their swings I sensed a different timing altogether."

Lee set about trying to imitate that swing, but made little progress. "I spent three months trying to hit one solid shot that didn't hook to some degree," he said. Then the apple fell. It was all a matter of timing his weight shift. "I'd always been taught that as the club swings back the weight moves to the right side, and as the club swings forward the weight moves back to the left side. The truth was that in an ideal swing the weight moved

David Lee helps one of his students get the feel of the Gravity Golf swing.

Exhilarated by his discovery, Lee was more determined than ever to become a great player. Then a wrist injury ended his career. So his mission became to develop a way of teaching this swing—this gravity swing—to the masses. A 1979 *GOLF Magazine* cover article brought him the attention he needed, and when both Nicklaus and Trevino publicly sang his praises, he was on his way. The Gravity Golf concept blossomed into a golf school, a book, two videos, and several appearances on the Golf Channel.

Lee's book is loaded with technical terms and reflects a stronger knowledge of physics than of English composition, but he at least recognizes this and occasionally disarms his readers with light-hearted advice (e.g., "Take a deep breath; this is going to be a long sentence."). Gravity Golf also involves drills that are best done in private—hitting shots from a cross-legged stance and from a one-legged stance, swinging back with only the left hand, swinging chicken-swing style, and swinging so that you literally topple forward through the ball. But all of them instill a feel for the powerful force of gravity.

> THE SECRET:
>
> Use gravity. Let the club "free fall" into the ball, with no applied force.

to the right and then began to return to the left *while the club was still going back.*" Essentially, the great players simply allowed their arms to fall downward to the ball. The weight of the clubhead, combined with the earth's gravitational pull, provided enough clubhead speed to produce an effortless yet powerful hit.

LEE'S SECRET

The proper origin of takeaway in the Gravity swing is the back and shoulders. After a proper grip is taken and the ball placed in the correct position relative to the feet for the type of shot desired, the arms and shoulders should extend downward and flex sufficiently to allow the **back and shoulders** to start the swing in *"one piece."*

As the swing begins, the shoulders, arms, and club should retain the same relative positions they had at the start. Initiating the takeaway with the arms and hands totally relaxed will set you in motion like a snake, with the shoulders getting ahead of the hands, which is not good.

Weight distribution should be comfortably balanced between the heels and the balls of the feet, with the hip muscles carrying most of the weight load. If too much flex in the knees occurs in the set-up, the quadriceps above the knees load, and proper rotary motion in the delivery is restricted. One should feel "light" on the feet with a sense of mobility. In a full swing, a rhythmical rocking motion from foot to foot during address will facilitate an easier start to the takeaway and will aid subsequent key elements in the swing. Being "frozen" at address creates tension problems and subsequent timing errors in the swing.

The tempo of the GRAVITY swing is in four beats. It is fast (powerful), slow, slow, fast. As we go along, I'll elaborate on each area.

The Heave

In order to achieve maximum clubhead speed and control, **it is critical to start the backswing with a back and shoulder movement that is powerful enough to allow all of the tension in the wrists, arms, and shoulders to fully release by**

the time the arms and club reach a point approximately at the seven-thirty position when the body is viewed like a clock from the facing position . . . long sentence, deep breath . . . **and yet for the arms and shoulders to be able to complete the backswing without any lift from the hands and arms beyond the seven-thirty point.** Read the last sentence at least twice more. If tension in the arms or shoulders remains beyond the seven-thirty point, timing in the swing is thrown off and the body will be pulled into a sway, or else the brain will sense the sway coming and freeze the weight transfer. Either way, trouble starts. My preference is to call the start of the takeaway a "heave," simply because the tension which allows the swing to start in one piece must be literally thrown out of the arms. It is a move made with the back, very akin to the way one would throw a "medicine" ball. None of my students like the word "heave," and frankly I don't either, but I have yet to come up with a more descriptive term for the way the takeaway begins.

Don't confuse yourself by thinking that a powerful start in the first movement (or heave) will make the backswing look fast. It is simply powerful. If you have ever tried to pick up a long board from one end and move it laterally, you know that because of the leverage resistance caused by weight and gravity, it is difficult to move. When the arms and club are "frozen" in one piece, and the torque to start them moving originates from one end of the system, it requires a brief but powerful move to set them into motion and complete the backswing *without* a lift from the hands and forearms, which we do not want to do. **Most amateurs trying to imitate Jack Nicklaus start the swing too deliberately and cannot release the tension from the arms and wrists at the proper time, because the**

The first move, or "heave," is powered mostly by the back—the feeling is similar to throwing a medicine ball.

The gravity swing in action: A heave, two releases, and a counterfall.

slow start creates a *need* to lift the arms and club in order to get them all the way back. The lift leaves tension in the arms at the change of direction, which inhibits an effortless start to the delivery and subsequently throws the swing-plane off. We'll talk more about the change of direction momentarily.

The Critical First Release

The point where the tension leaves the arms is what I call the "first release" and **its identification and definition may prove to be one of my most important contributions to golf.** The intensity of the heave and a properly timed point of first release are the major keys to maintaining timing and an ability to generate speed without effort. Incidentally, the first release is invisible both to the camera and the naked eye. Inability to see the first release, and the subtlety of feeling it, has created most of the puzzle around

swing mechanics for many, many years. Once you understand how the first release affects the rest of the swing, the entire picture of how the golf swing should work begins to take shape.

The reason that the first release is invisible is as follows. When the body is standing upright, with the arms hanging relaxed, the arms do not hang at total possible extension. Natural elasticity within the muscles causes the arms to hang about an inch or so above full extension. If you force the arms downward, and then allow them to relax, they will draw up slightly (about an inch). This you can see. However in the golf swing, when the arms are forced to full extension just prior to starting the club back and then put into motion by the back and shoulders, the point where the tension leaves the arms (approximately seven-thirty) becomes invisible. Because of the centrifugal momentum imparted to the arms and club by the heave or first movement, the arms remain

extended and do not draw up when the tension is released from them. The backswing continues beyond the seven-thirty point from the initial heave momentum alone, and requires NO additional muscle power. The heave, the first release, and the continuance of the backswing beyond the first release point, all appear smooth and deliberate even though a total tension change in the arms and wrists has occurred at the seven-thirty point. The arms, shoulders, and wrists, have totally relaxed and SHOULD NOT RE-TIGHTEN through the change of direction or the remainder of the swing. If tightening occurs during ANY part of the delivery, the speed of angular release between the club and arms coming into impact will be reduced and the efficiency of the swing diminished. Understanding the first release and how it affects everything that happens subsequently in the swing is a critical element in understanding the GRAVITY golf swing as a whole.

The Weight Transfer

In a full swing, by the time the arms have reached the first release point, the left leg should have completely relaxed and the weight already begun to shift to the right side. At the point of first release, the left leg could fully leave the ground. A total relaxation of the left leg must occur to allow proper weight transfer and to enable the body to correctly pivot against and around the right leg. Momentum from the heave should carry the body weight totally against a firm right leg, but not to a point where the right leg becomes vertical (that would be a sway). When the arms reach a point at approximately ten o'clock, they begin to stall or gently collapse. Up to this point, the arms and shoulders should remain comfortably extended due to centrifugal momentum, **not to forced extension.** When the arms begin to stall and the right elbow automatically starts to fold, the momentum from the heave (which has carried and held the body weight against the right leg) is released and gravity starts the weight transfer back to the left leg. The shoulders meanwhile, continue turning into the backswing as the weight falls back onto the left **heel,** and when the weight lands **fully** on that heel, they (the shoulders) are at maximum turn and the body is in a position called "full separation" or "coiled" (shoulders fully turned, weight back on left heel). By this time the right elbow has folded back into a tucked position and the forward body rotation of delivery is about to begin.

Be Careful of This

It is very important that the arch muscle in the left foot be relaxed as the weight shifts back to the left leg, otherwise the body weight cannot fall easily back to the left heel and the delivery will not start properly. Correct rotary motion for the delivery requires a fixed left axis position. Because the foot attaches to the leg in an "L" shape, the pivotal axis (left leg) and the swing-plane will not remain in their proper positions if the delivery rotation is made from the toe portion (or "ball") of the left foot. The entire axis leg will move backwards during delivery if the heel is not the pivot point. If delivery is made by turning on the front of the foot, unless compensations are made (too spooky and unreliable), the shot will go off line. The considerable strength of the left foot arch must not be used for balance dur-

ing the swing or it will cause problems with the swing flow and thus affect plane control. The arch muscles of the feet are so powerful, that unless the left arch is completely relaxed as the weight shifts back to the left leg, it will prevent the body weight from falling onto the heel. This will inhibit the next fundamental event from functioning properly. After the weight lands back on the left heel correctly, another critical (yet almost invisible) move must occur preceding delivery, and the necessity for that movement must be explained.

The All-Important Counterfall

When a golf swing of ANY size is made, the downward movement of the arms, hands, and club in the delivery prior to impact creates a centrifugal force pulling against the body, toward and approximately 20 degrees to the player's right of the golf ball. The forces that pull against the body during delivery have occurred to some degree in every golf swing that ever has been (or will be) made . . . the laws of physics say so. What this means to swing mechanics is as follows. In order to maintain perfect balance during the golf swing, a force MUST be present to offset the pull from the swinging hands, arms and club against the body during delivery. This is achieved by initiating, prior to the downswing, a backwards fall (counterfall) from the left heel, on a line 180 degrees (dead opposite) from the forward pull of the hands, arms and club. When this is done properly, these counteracting forces are exactly equal and opposite—the body remains off vertical through impact, and perfect equilibrium is achieved throughout. The body returns to vertical as the follow-through is completed. Without the counterfall we would be pulled off balance in the downswing and the swing-plane would leave its proper path. A correct counterfall causes the club path to move from inside the flightline to square at impact, and back to the inside on the follow-through.

The counterfall should begin on a vector approximately 70 degrees left of the intended flightline, or almost behind and over your left shoulder, and moves to the player's right as the club passes through the impact area.

The counterfall is a very subtle movement, yet an absolutely critical one. Any time you witness someone coming badly "over the top" during delivery, you know that they are not making an adequate counterfall preceding the downswing. The player will either pull, slice, or block the shot, or compensate for the plane change by clubface manipulation in order to hit the ball on line. The amount of counterfall required for each shot varies, depending on the speed of the delivery and the club selection. The harder the swing, the greater the centrifugal pull from the hands, arms and club against the body, and the greater the counterfall needed to offset those forces. If the correct degree of counterfall is utilized, exact equilibrium can

be maintained through impact to the finish of the swing, and the golfer will wind up in perfect balance upon completion of the follow through. Don't worry about having to calculate the proper degree of counterfall for each shot. When you train properly, you will teach yourself to do it automatically. Most professionals aren't even aware that they counterfall preceding delivery because of the subtlety of it. They know, if only subconsciously, that they will be off balance without it.

More About Weight Transfer

We need to digress for a moment and discuss weight transfer. It is not necessary to make any transfer of weight to hit a perfect golf shot. In fact, all shots of less than approximately 100 yards should be made from the left heel only and employ no transfer whatever, simply pivot back, proper degree of counterfall and pivot forward. The *only* time we need to transfer weight is when we are trying to hit a shot close to maximum distance. The use of weight transfer in the full swing adds approximately 5 to 10 percent additional club speed and equivalent percentage distance over a full swing that employs no transfer. A good rule to follow is that *unless you are making a full backswing, you do not want to make a weight shift.*

Follow me now: If you stand on your left foot only and pivot yourself into a counterfall, that counterfall will start **slowly,** as a tree begins to fall slowly when it is cut. The function of the weight transfer, when we want to hit the ball near maximum distance, is simply to add momentum to the start of the counterfall. This enables the pivotal movement of the delivery to begin *faster* **without an output of energy from the arms and shoulders or right leg, which would put the swing in conflict with the** third law of motion (action-reaction) and cause undesired swing-plane movement as well as an actual reduction in clubhead speed if the wrists tighten. This is exactly why a pitcher has a mound from which to pitch. The fall from the mound onto the front leg, creates greater momentum, a faster starting counterfall, and greater subsequent pivotal speed without increased effort. This allows the pitcher to whip his "rag-like" arm harder than he could from the flat ground, *without* throwing off his control. In the golf swing, when the weight shifts to the right leg and then falls back to the left leg, it (the weight) is moving laterally. When the weight lands back on the left leg, there should be *just enough* resistance from the left leg to deflect the lateral movement into the counterfall

> Without the counterfall we would be pulled off balance in the downswing and the swing-plane would leave its proper path.

which again, begins on a vector approximately 70 degrees left of the intended flightline. The weight transfer back to the left leg must be complete by the time the shoulders reach the completion of their backturn.

It is very important that on any shot where a weight transfer is employed, the transfer be 100 percent. A 100 percent transfer is defined as **approximately the farthest distance one can fall from the right foot to the left foot, and still clear the hip turn** *level*. If the feet are too far apart in the stance, the body will fall too much *against* the left leg in the second half of the transfer, and an upward level change in the hips will be necessary to complete the follow through. It requires an output of energy from either the right leg, or the shoulders and arms, to clear the turn from a "jammed" position. Swing efficiency is lessened and the integrity of the swing-plane is difficult to maintain when this happens. If the feet are placed *too close together at address*, there is *inadequate momentum in the fall from the right foot to the left foot* to start the counterfall with enough speed to achieve the desired rotational speed for the delivery. If that didn't immediately sink in, read it until it does. The reason for the importance of not having the feet too close together is this: If the brain senses an inadequate degree of fall momentum in the transfer, it will **involuntarily** trigger a flexing action in the body to achieve the desired and anticipated swing speed. Again the swing-plane is violated, and the player falls victim to the third law of motion. **As a general rule, whenever the brain senses an inadequacy of any kind in the golf swing, it will attempt, involuntarily, to make up for it with some type of applied force. Bad news! In order to achieve total efficiency and effortlessness in the swing, it is imperative that involuntary backlashes are avoided by correct set-up and proper movement from the very beginning of the swing.**

Delivery of the arms, club and body through the impact area should be all rotary on the left leg or pivotal axis. There should be no lateral movement during delivery. **All the lateral movement of the weight transfer, both to the right foot and back to the left, occurs during the takeaway.**

The Change of Direction

Let's go back for a moment and talk about the change of direction, since it is another critical part of the swing. It is very important that the origin (proper muscles) and intensity of the heave, which starts the backswing, be precisely correct, so that when coupled with a proper first release point, the arms and club will begin to stall exactly when they should. As previously mentioned, the desired amount of shoulder turn required to initiate the counterfall should be attainable without any lift from the hands and arms. It should be accomplished with heave momentum

alone. When the arms reach the stall point (between ten and eleven o'clock in a full swing), the folding of the right arm as it collapses should cantelever the club through twelve o'clock. From the twelve o'clock position, the club and arms should "free fall" into the beginning of the delivery as the shoulders continue turning back. By the time the club has fallen to between two and three o'clock, the shoulders have completed their turn, the right arm has fallen into a "tucked" position, the counterfall has occurred, and the forward rotation of the body on the left heel automatically begins and starts pulling the arms and club into the delivery. As centrifugal force begins to develop and increase during the downswing (assuming the wrists are tension free), it will effectively create the angular release (second release) of the wrists into impact, and the shoulders, arms, and club will be at full extension when the ball is struck. **If the momentum of the heave and the first release point are correct, the change of direction will occur by itself, with absolutely zero necessity to tighten the shoulders, arms or wrists.**

This raises another important point. Club speed is greatly affected by the degree of tension in the wrists at the point of angular (or second) release into and through impact. The speed at which the angles between the forearms and clubshaft are released is a measure of overall club-speed. **If the delivery is begun with an increase**

in tension in the shoulders, arms, wrists, and hands, resistance to the angular release of the wrists coming into impact occurs. In other words, the harder you try to hit the ball with tension, the more you slow the club down. It's sort of like pouring wet concrete, instead of oil, into the wrists while you are coming into impact. Although a flexing movement in the parts of the upper body will indeed bring the club down (Arnold Palmer), it simultaneously causes a *reduction* in release speed by creating tension in the wrists, which fights to inhibit the angular release. Because of his incredible strength, Arnold could literally "rake" or beat the ball with his shoulders and arms and hit it a long way. With better mechanics he might have easily outdriven

Good balance at the finish is the result of a properly executed swing.

Jack on a consistent basis, but because of technical imperfections it was difficult for him to do so (I still love him). Arnold didn't block that hook for nothing! He was terrified of it, although it stretches my imagination to envision Arnold being afraid of anything. However I can speak with authority on the frightening aspects of a pull hook. Maybe he wasn't as spooked as I was because he was strong enough to usually block it out. I wasn't. Arnold probably just viewed the hook as a malady of existence, and the "block" as something to give his swing individualism. Nevertheless, it is much easier to create club speed with relaxed wrists and rotary torque from the left leg and hip.

The Wrist Cock and Delivery

The cocking of the wrists in the swing should occur **naturally** as a result of heave momentum from the back and shoulders and the release of tension at the first release point. The cocking of the wrists should begin very subtly and continue throughout the takeaway and the change of direction. After the swing is started in one piece and the first release occurs at about seven-thirty, the momentum of the club (since it is lighter) will cause the club to start gaining on the heavier arms and cocking the now relaxed wrists. It is very important in the full swing that the wrists cock **subtly** throughout the change of direction and do **not** finish cocking until it is time for them to release into impact. **One of the most deadly sins in golf is to start the wrists cocking by lifting the club with the hands instead of allowing the momentum of the heave to cock them for you.** Doing this can cause the club to gain too quickly on the arms in the takeaway, ultimately causing an involuntary tension increase in the wrists in order to stop or slow the club down for the change of direction (trouble starts). This tension causes a **reduction** in delivery speed, as well as energy being turned back against the body and the swing-plane, causing plane movement. If the wrists are cocked as a result of the **proper** amount of heave momentum at the beginning of the takeaway, with tension-free wrists from the first release point on, **there will not be a need to hold a set or cocked position in the wrists during the downswing.** This is because the wrists will not finish cocking until it is time for them to "let go" at the second or angular release point. If the wrists are too cocked at the change of direction, there is tendency for the forward turn of the body to cause a "pitch-out" or early release coming into delivery and the hands will be behind the clubhead at impact (not good). Proper timing, created by correct origin of takeaway, proper heave momentum and first release, will allow total wrist freedom from the point of first release throughout the remainder of the swing. **NO manipulation**

to keep the arms and club "in plane" should be necessary** and maximum release speed into and through impact will occur.

Once the counterfall has begun and the arms have "free fallen" to the point where the wrists are ready to release into impact, muscular torsion from the gluteal muscles of the pivotal leg (left) can be blended **smoothly** into the rotational move to create maximum acceleration through impact. This should be the only muscular source of power within the swing and comes from within the axis and not from an extraneous source (arms, shoulders, or right leg). The hips should never be "thrown" through the ball, but simply blended into the turn with torque from the hip, which will not disrupt the balance.

As previously mentioned, impact in a correct golf swing should be **totally incidental** with no intent to strike or flex in the delivery. The follow through will occur naturally, assuming that nothing is done to restrict it. Balance at the finish of the swing is a *result* of everything having been done properly in the beginning. In the follow through, the right leg works like a *boat anchor* to keep the momentum of the swing from pulling the body off balance. The inside toe edge of the right shoe sole drags *after* impact and slows down the follow-through momentum.

FROM *GRAVITY GOLF* BY DAVID LEE

CHAPTER 21

BOBBY LOCKE

LOCKE IT UP ON THE GREEN

"From early in my career I realized that there was far more in putting than actually striking the ball, and I do not think any prominent golfer has devoted more time and thought and practice to this side of the game than I have."

In 1932 fifteen-year-old Bobby Locke missed a 4-foot putt and in a fit of teenage petulance, hurled his putter deep into the trees. His father, playing with him, walked off the course and that evening made it clear to young Bobby that if he ever threw another club it would mean the end of his golf career.

Locke never let go of that putter again. Indeed, so deftly did he wield the old hickory-shafted blade that he became, by general agreement, the greatest putter in the history of the game.

Locke was born in South Africa and was barely four years old when he took up golf. His only model was his father, a player whose handicap never got lower than 14. As a result, perhaps, Bobby adopted a less than orthodox stance and swing that caused him to play every shot with a pronounced right-to-left flight pattern. "His method," wrote Bernard Darwin, "is out of the common, but so most undeniably are the results."

He swung the putter into the ball from well inside the target line. Some say he actually hooked his putts.

How good was Bobby Locke? In 1950 he and Sam Snead played a series of sixteen challenge matches. Locke won twelve of them, tied two, and lost only two. The year he decided to try the U.S. Tour, he won five of the thirteen tournaments he entered. In his three years competing on American soil, he won fifteen times, one of those wins coming by a record 16 strokes. In all, Locke won more than eighty tournaments around the world, while amazing his opponents equally with his slinging-hook iron shots and his wizardry on the greens.

"That blankety-blank Locke was able to hole a putt over 60 feet of peanut brittle," said Lloyd Mangrum, while according to Locke's countryman Gary Player, "to compare anyone of his era to Locke as a putter is like comparing a donkey to a race horse."

Given Locke's success on the greens, one would think his putting style would have been widely adopted, but it never was, perhaps

Locke's putting prowess helped him win more than eighty tournaments.

because the mechanics of the method closely mirrored those of his full swing—he set up in a closed stance and swung the putter into the ball from well inside the target line. Some say he actually hooked his putts.

THE SECRET:

Hit your putts with topspin.

But there was more to it than that, and in *Bobby Locke on Golf,* a sort of instructional autobiography he wrote in 1953 after winning the third of his four British Opens, Locke shared all his thoughts on how to stroke the ball into the hole.

L O C K E ' S   S E C R E T

Among golfers, the putter is usually known as the pay-off club, and how right that is! Putting, in fact, is a game by itself.

Here you can see immediately how I change my grip for putting. First of all I grip the club in the left hand, and the grip is normal except that I position my thumb down the center of the shaft. The art of putting lies in the tips of the fingers. If you have a delicate touch, you are lucky. It helps a great deal. But remember, you must not grip tightly. You must grip loosely and do everything possible to acquire a delicate touch. The shaft of my putter is much longer than the standard men's length. I find that this gives me what I call "better head feel." By that I mean I can feel more clearly the weight of the clubhead as I swing. I grip my putter at the very end of the shaft and I use the same grip for all putts. Never change the position of the hands up or down the shaft whether it

My left thumb points straight down the center of the shaft . . .

is a long putt or a short putt, as that will cause inconsistency.

I have now placed the right hand to the club. I am using the overlapping grip as for all other clubs, but again the thumb is placed down the center of the shaft. Having the two thumbs in this position enables me to follow the clubhead through dead in line to the hole, and also helps to put topspin on the ball. It is so necessary to put topspin on the ball when putting, as it makes the ball run through on the line to the hole.

At one time, as an experiment, I tried the reverse overlapping grip with the index finger of the left hand lying on top of the little finger

. . . as does my right thumb.

of the right hand. I found it did not help my putting and it had a very bad effect on the rest of my game, making my grip for other shots feel most uncomfortable.

Having explained the grip, I will now describe my method of putting. First of all, I sum up the putt, and this is vital. Most putts are missed not because they are mis-hit but because they have been started on the wrong line and at the wrong speed. I examine the line of the putt, concentrating particularly on a radius of about three feet around the hole. This is where the ball completes its run, and what happens here is going to make or mar the putt. During this quick inspection, I remove any obstacles which might deflect the run of the ball, but, more important,

I always begin by carefully examining the line of the putt.

I check the pace of the green, determine how closely the grass has been cut, and whether the green is fast, slow, or medium-paced. Also I check the lie of the turf around the hole to see whether the ball will be going slightly uphill or downhill or dead level as it approaches the hole. It is at this stage that I determine how hard I am going to hit the ball, always, of course, taking into consideration the length of the putt.

I work to the rule that if the green appears to be fast, I will aim my putt at an imaginary hole 6 to 12 inches short of the hole. If the green appears to be slow, and particularly if during the last 2 or 3 feet to the hole the ground is uphill, I hit it firmly for the back of the hole.

Having made up my mind how hard I am going to hit the putt, I now get behind the ball to examine the contour of the part of the green my ball will have to cross. Chiefly I am concerned with slopes and any hills or hollows. According to the slope, I make up my mind on the direction of the putt, whether it shall be dead straight or whether I should aim for the right or left side of the hole. Once I have made up my mind as to the line of the putt and how hard I am going to hit it, I never change my mind. It is fatal to let second or third thoughts intrude as you are putting. You must make up your mind before you begin to address the ball, and never alter it.

So many putts are missed because at the last second the player thinks to himself, "Perhaps I had better hit it straight," or "I think it would pay to aim a little further left." Hitting a putt in doubt is fatal in most cases. Make up your mind what you are going to do, then go ahead and do it.

Now for the actual putt. In the first place, the weight is evenly distributed on both feet. I place the feet about 4 inches apart, with the right foot 3 inches behind the left in relation to a straight line from the hole to the left toe. This is known as a closed stance, and I adopt this to prevent myself from cutting across the ball and

I set up in a narrow, closed stance, with the ball directly opposite my left toe and my weight evenly distributed.

> **You must make up your mind before you begin to address the ball, and never alter it.**

imparting any sidespin. I position the ball directly opposite the left toe. This enables

me to hit the ball slightly on the upswing, whereas if the ball were farther back towards the right foot, there might be a tendency to chop or jab it. The actual putt I am making in this illustration is a 20-footer. I begin the address with the ball opposite the toe of the putter but actually strike the ball with the centre of the blade. I do this to avoid cutting the putt. If one addresses the ball with the center of the putter blade, there is a tendency to swing outside the line on the backswing resulting in a cut and the ball not running true. By addressing the ball near the toe of the putter blade, it is easier to take the

I start the club back to the inside, and keep the blade low. There is no wrist work at all and the blade stays square to the hole.

without opening the face. With a putter it is not impossible, and this is how I putt. I learned the method largely from Walter Hagen in 1937. The term he used for taking the club back and still keeping it square was that you "hooded" the face. He proved to me that this backswing applies true topspin to the ball and is in fact the only type of backswing with the putter that will apply true topspin. Hagen in his heyday was probably the world's greatest putter and I was happy to learn from him. It is essential in the method I am showing here that there should be no wrist work. Wrist work results in inconsistency—and missed putts. A point I stress in the backswing is that you must keep the putter low.

putter back "inside" the line of the putt, and in this way one is able to impart topspin at impact. Never hit a putt with the heel of the club. That puts check on the ball and it will not run as far as you expect.

I have now started the backswing, keeping the putter very low to the ground, almost brushing the turf. I am careful to take the putter back on the "inside," and notice there is no wrist work at all. Throughout the swing, the putter blade stays square to the hole. I want to emphasize that the blade does stay square to the hole. There are people who say it is impossible to take a club back "inside"

Watch these points, and with practice you will find that you can take the club back "inside" and still keep the blade square to the hole.

This is the completion of the backswing. The putter, left hand, and left arm to the elbow are in one

There are people who say it is impossible to take a club back "inside" without opening the face. With a putter it is not impossible, and this is how I putt.

At the completion of the backswing, the putter, left hand, and left arm to the elbow are in one piece.

At impact the left wrist is firm, the blade is square to the hole, and the head is down.

If a ball has true topspin, there are three entrances to the hole—the front door and two side doors.

piece. To make sure that the clubface does not open, the back of my left hand keeps pointing to the grass. I have now reached the "hooding" position. By "hooding" I mean keeping the putter face dead square, or if anything slightly closed, in the backswing. This will make sure of getting true topspin on the ball, provided the putter returns to the ball on the same line.

Here I am at impact. Notice that I keep the left wrist firm in relation to the forearm; the position of the left hand in relation to my putter is exactly the same. This means that the putter blade is kept square to the hole. My head is being kept well down until the ball has been struck.

Still no wrist work in the accepted sense. I am concentrating all the time on keeping that clubhead square to the hole and on keeping my head well down. It is only necessary to follow through as far as the club went back in the backswing.

The putt is now completed and you see the complete follow-through. My method of swinging the putter is the same as the swing

Into the through-swing, I concentrate on keeping my head down and keeping that blade square to the hole.

In the follow-through the club should go as far forward as it went backward in the backswing.

of the clock pendulum. The club goes as far through in the follow-through as it goes back in the backswing. Notice that though the head is turned to watch what is happening to the ball, it is still in the same position in relation to the body. It cannot be too much emphasized that the putting action must be slow and smooth, and above all the grip must be loose to maintain the most sensitive touch.

My putting is based on the fact that if a ball has a true topspin, there are three entrances into the hole—three chances, providing the speed is right. There is the front door and there are two side doors. Obviously it is safest to use the front door, but with my method, if the ball catches the left side of the hole it will fall, and if it catches the right side, it will also fall. By thinking of these three entrances, I always feel that I have three chances of sinking every putt.

FROM *BOBBY LOCKE ON GOLF*

CHAPTER 22

CARL LOHREN

LEAD WITH THE LEFT

"I'm going to give you one thought that will clear away the fog, one move that correctly done will give you an effective, repeating golf swing that will send you on your way to a lifetime of better golf."

It's not an exaggeration to say that Carl Lohren had an epiphany in his education as a golfer. Lohren, a graduate of the University of Maryland, had played golf there with Deane Beman, the two of them leading their team to a third-place finish behind perennial powerhouses Houston and Oklahoma in the 1958 NCAA Championship.

Beman, who would go on to modest success as a pro followed by major success as the Commissioner of the PGA Tour, was in his amateur days a superior player to Lohren, but not by much. During 1959–60, a period when Beman won both the British and U.S. Amateur Championships, Lohren took him to the fortieth hole of the final of the D.C. Amateur before losing and beat him in one-up in the thirty-six-hole final of the Mid-Atlantic Amateur. So Carl could play.

But like so many accomplished golfers, he was a tinkerer, never quite satisfied with his swing. He tried the pro ranks but only briefly. "I didn't have a method I trusted," he says, "and I'm not the kind to go out there and just try to make something work week after week." So he turned to teaching, all the while experimenting with his own golf swing.

At that time, most of the game's leading teachers were preaching a "small muscles game." Ernest Jones's notion of "swinging the clubhead," advanced a generation or so earlier, remained the method taught by most of the nation's professionals. Meanwhile, Bob Toski was into "the touch system," and Jim Flick was talking about the importance of feeling the clubhead in the hands during the swing. For a while, Lohren toyed with these ideas, but none of them brought him any sustained success.

Then, at the 1966 Carling World Open, he saw Ben Hogan hit a shot. From 150 yards, Hogan took a tiny swing on an 8-iron, taking his hands barely to belt high, but unleashed a powerful, low-flying shot that finished stiff to the pin. That started Lohren on the right road. The true epiphany, however, came a few weeks later, on a late summer evening at the driving range of the Nassau Country Club, just a mile or so from his home on Long Island. With one experimental golf swing he literally struck paydirt, and found a key that would change his life. His game improved immediately, bringing him a victory in the New York State PGA Championship, while at the same time, he became one of the game's most sought-after teachers.

Contrary to the touch-and-feel merchants of the time, Lohren advocated a golf swing initiated and dominated by the left shoulder, and his new approach caught on with golfers of every ilk, from the 36-handicap members of his club to his old teammate Deane Beman, who embraced the method emphatically, predicting it would become "the cornerstone of golf instruction for the foreseeable future."

Flushed with the success of his method, Lohren resolved to get it published in book form and sought advice from Beman. By then a canny veteran businessman, Beman told him "Your secret is too precious to share," but suggested they become partners in publishing. Beman took the idea to *GOLF Magazine*, *Golf Digest*, and book publisher Prentice-Hall, and they settled on *Golf Digest*.

In 1975 Carl Lohren's *One Move to Better Golf* appeared. The large-format edition of 125 pages was illustrated by Anthony Ravielli, best known for his work on Ben Hogan's *Five Lessons: The Modern Fundamentals of Golf*. The hardcover edition suffered from competition from books by Toski, Flick, Jack Nicklaus, and others, but in paperback, sales soared to twenty printings and half a million copies.

> **THE SECRET:**
>
> **I**nitiate your swing by turning your left shoulder forward—in the direction you're facing—rather than around.

> With one experimental golf swing he literally struck paydirt, and found a key that would change his life. His play improved immediately and he became one of the game's most sought-after teachers.

LOHREN'S SECRET

The purpose of a golf swing is to deliver a blow with an implement that will send a small ball flying far and in the desired direction.

Sounds simple enough, doesn't it? It isn't. To strike the ball far and straight, that implement—your golf club—must be swung with enough speed, at the proper angle of descent and on the proper path. Right away you've got yourself all kinds of complications.

There is nothing natural about the golf swing. If somebody says you are a natural golfer, he means you have excellent coordination. That helps, but it still doesn't get you halfway home. Ben Hogan once said that the first time you pick up a golf club, every instinct that comes to your mind is wrong. Watch a child the first time he or she is given a golf club and told to swing at a ball. The club is picked straight up and delivered with a strong right-sided blow as if the ball were a log waiting to be split with an ax.

Overcoming this instinct to hit at the ball with the dominant right side has been the curse of the golfer since the game was invented. Proposed solutions have filled countless pages of golf instruction through the years. Countless dollars have been poured into the pockets of countless teaching professionals by pupils searching desperately for the way. By the time the average player has been inundated with all the theories of arm movement, leg movement, weight shift to and fro, wrists cocking and uncocking, hand action, and other components of the complex golf swing, his mind is spinning so rapidly he has very little chance of understanding what a good swing is, let alone making one.

Right now I'm going to give you one thought that will clear away the fog, one move that correctly done will give you an effective, repeating golf swing that will send you on your way to a lifetime of better golf.

Start your swing with your left shoulder. At the moment of takeaway, the very beginning of the backswing, start your left shoulder

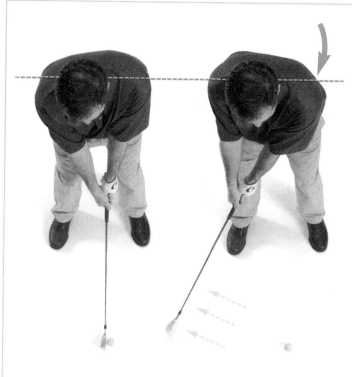

MOVE YOUR SHOULDER FORWARD TO START THE SWING

The correct starting move of the left shoulder must be forward. These two larger illustrations, viewed from a position that looks directly down at the top of the shoulders, show how this forward move immediately starts the shoulders swinging around the spine, which acts like a fixed axis for your backswing. Note that the hands and arms have not swung back sharply to the inside. This move extends the club back along a path that follows the shoulder line. Your thought should be only to start the swing. Once you have started it forward, let the rest of your swing happen naturally.

turning around your spine. One small area of the body . . . one move. I'm not asking you to change your swing. I just want you to give it *a new start.*

That probably sounds too simple to believe, but the whole secret of this system is here, at the start of your swing. To get the shoulders turning around correctly, you must think of starting the left shoulder *forward* in the direction you're facing, rather than around. This will start the shoulders turning around the spine on the right track.

Most golf instructors stress that a turn must occur, but they attach no significance to *when* it takes place.

I believe it must be the first thing that happens in your swing. The first and only action you need think about is to start the left shoulder forward. Since this one move is going to make you a better striker of the golf ball, I'm going to dwell on it at some length.

The important thing to understand about this move and the action that follows is that the shoulders turn rather than tilt in

START YOUR SHOULDER TOWARD THE HAND

An excellent guide to learning the correct starting move is to have a friend place his hand about an inch or two in front of your left shoulder in the position shown. Then just start your shoulder in the direction of that hand. It immediately will start forward and your shoulders will turn around your spine on the correct path.

relation to the spine. On the backswing, they revolve around your spine much as a searchlight sweeps around a lighthouse, at right angles to your spine.

When I discuss the left shoulder, I'm not talking about a spot. I'm talking about the entire left shoulder area, the upper left side of your trunk. I've never seen a player make a good, honest shoulder movement without having the shoulder, upper arm, back, and chest area move simultaneously.

When the left shoulder swings out, the right shoulder of course swings back. This movement, this swinging of the two shoulders around the

spine, is what maintains the axis for your swing. It also is a big factor in creating the windup of the back muscles, which results in that all-important windup.

Here is a drill that will help you identify the correct starting move. Stand perfectly

PRACTICE PIVOTING

Visualize your upper body being in a tube. Turn your left shoulder, and of course your right, in a perfect arc within that tube, without moving laterally at all.

erect and hold a club in a vertical position with your arms extended straight out in front of you. Be sure that you remain perfectly relaxed as you do the following. Start the left shoulder forward so that the shoulders turn in a perfect horizontal plane. This drill should help you capture the correct feeling. Remember that the upper body must start turning before the lower. You can gradually lower your arms and the club while practicing this drill until you are able to make the correct starting move from your normal address position. If you have trouble learning to move the upper left side correctly, here are two more key thoughts that may help you to make this move:

Here are two drills for people who have trouble learning to move the upper left side. They will help you get oriented to moving the left shoulder correctly. Think of starting to make a small U-turn with the left shoulder. Imagine it turning to where the right shoulder is. But only think of starting it there, not trying to turn it all the way. You can also visualize your upper body being in a tube. Turn your left shoulder, and of course your right, in a perfect arc within that tube, without moving laterally at all. These two drills will not, in and of themselves, result in the sound swing that the move creates. They are only aids for people who find it difficult to get the upper left side moving.

FROM *ONE MOVE TO BETTER GOLF*
BY CARL LOHREN

PRACTICE THE MOVE FROM AN ERECT STANCE

This drill will help you start correctly when you first try to make the move. Stand in a perfectly erect position (right), arms extended straight out, holding a club in a vertical position while remaining relaxed. Then make the move in a perfectly horizontal plane, simply by starting the left shoulder forward. Remember that the upper body must start turning before the lower. Remember this feeling and adapt it to a normal address position.

GEORGE LOW

PUTTING WAS HIS LIFE

"To putt well takes patience, study, care, and to my mind,
a lot more cunning and sheer nerve than it takes to haul off
and hit a ball as hard as you can with the longer clubs."

If you happen to be among the fortunate few who attended one or more Masters during the Palmer/Nicklaus era (roughly 1958–1986), then it's very possible you've rubbed shoulders with George Low.

He always stationed himself in the same place, alongside the large practice putting green that stretches between the ninth green and tenth tee. Not that you would have noticed him. George didn't attract much attention, just sat there grim-faced on his shooting stick, the sleeves of his alpaca cardigan rolled up in the manner of Julius Boros. He had Boros's physique, too, a burly build just shy of corpulence, acquired through decades of dedicated inactivity.

"George was born retired," said Hall-of-Famer Jimmy Demaret. A major hotelier dubbed him "America's Guest," a moniker that Low did little to dispel. "I never owned an overcoat," he boasted, referring to his summers lolling in the golf playgrounds of the north and winters of similar indolence in Florida.

Oh, for a while he had something resembling a job—he was a tour pro—and his game was strong enough that, in 1945, when Byron Nelson's streak of eleven straight victories finally came to an end in Memphis, it was George who was the low professional with a score of 275, 13 under par and one better than Nelson. (Freddie Haas, an amateur, won the event on a score of 270.) But the tour grind just didn't suit him, not when a living could be made more easily.

You see, George Low knew how to do two things very well—he knew how to ingratiate himself with people in high places and he knew how to putt—and he was able to parlay those two talents into a better-than-average lifestyle. "There ain't no point in loafing with a broke," he once told sportswriter Dan Jenkins, "because nothing falls off." So George loafed with the likes of Eisenhower, Sinatra, Palmer, and Nicklaus, along with captains of industry, royalty, and anyone with the willingness and wherewithal to keep him whole and happy. Some days he'd give them lessons; some days he'd just putt against them in high-stakes matches they had little chance of winning. Either way, he earned his keep.

> **He was born with touch and honed it ceaselessly his entire life while at the same time working hard to keep his putting method a secret.**

When Palmer won the Masters in 1960, he credited his victory to a putting lesson from Low. In 1962 at the Phoenix Open, Low approached Jack Nicklaus and asked him to try a putter he'd just designed. That putter—the George Low Wizard 600—would bring Nicklaus fifteen of his twenty major championships and seventy-eight of his one hundred career victories.

He had learned the game from his father, George Low, Sr., one of the first Scottish professionals to emigrate from Carnoustie to a club job in the United States. For twenty-five years he was the head professional at Baltusrol, then at similarly exclusive clubs in Vermont and Florida. Low, Sr., was a good enough player to finish second in the 1899 U.S. Open and a sufficiently prominent teacher to count Presidents Taft and Harding among his students.

So young George came by both his playing talent and networking ability naturally. As for his putting, he was born with touch and honed it ceaselessly his entire life while at the same time working hard to keep his putting method a secret. (That, after all, was the only thing George Low had to sell.) But in 1982—age seventy and perhaps running out of hosts—Low invited golf writer Al Barkow to collaborate with him on a book. *The Master of Putting* is a modest

> **THE SECRET:**
> Strike your putts with a descending blow, just above the equator of the ball.

little volume, just eighty-four digest-size pages illustrated with a few dozen black-and-white photos, but that's all Low needed to make his case.

Most of the other pundits of that time were preaching a straight-back/straight-through swing path to keep the blade square to the hole throughout the stroke, but Low would have none of that. His was a less contrived, less manipulated method, a little golf swing that had brought him a big life.

LOW'S SECRET

The Stroke—on the Downbeat

I won't beat around the bush about the putting stroke I use and believe is the best. The key feature is striking the ball with a slightly descending putter head—on the downbeat, as I like to say.

This is the opposite of what many people think, or are told to think, is the best way to putt: to hit the ball with a slightly ascending putter head—on the upbeat. The theory here is that an ascending strike imparts overspin to the ball, giving it a better roll. Conversely, therefore, people assume that a putter head hitting a ball on the downbeat will impart underspin, or that hitting the ball on a dead-level plane will put no spin on it at all.

The scientific fact is that *no* effective spin is imparted to a putted ball, no matter at what angle the putter strikes it. The ball first skids or slides along the ground for a short distance, then begins to roll. In terms of physics, the angle of the putter head contributes nothing to that rolling action, which always takes the form of overspin. The ratio of skid is generally about 20 percent of the full length of a putt.

However, it has also been shown scientifically that a ball can be made to roll sooner after the impact *if it is struck above its center.* Now, with my downbeat stroke—assuming the putter blade is of standard depth—the top half of the face will strike the ball *just above its center,* which means the ball gets into overspin—or true roll—almost as soon as it is struck.

The angle of descent (and ascent) of my stroke is about that of a very shallow saucer—the putter head is not coming down off a cliff to hit the ball. This produces a more positive, more emphatic blow than a rising hit, and those qualities are obtained without any artificial manipulation by the golfer. It is in the nature of a descending blow—be it with a hammer, a guillotine, a putter—to be not only more solid, more forceful, but more controlled: The putter head is not apt to change alignment at the crucial moment when it meets the ball.

Think of it this way: When you paint a flat surface going from top to bottom, you are emulating a putting stroke. Your best work is done—the most paint gets on with the least effort—with the first touch of the brush, which comes from a downward stroke. On the upward part of the sweep, there is a thinner application of paint. In short, the descending putting stroke at impact is the most efficient and effective.

From the Inside

There is a second important aspect to the

The key is to strike the ball with a slightly descending putter head.

path of the stroke—its angle in relation to the target line. That angle should always be to the inside of the target line on the back-stroke, with a return to square along the target line at impact. Actually, the full shape of a good putting stroke is a shallow crescent, with the follow-through the same length as the backstroke.

What's wrong with a straight-back, straight-through putting stroke? Nothing— for putts under 2 feet. Above that distance, there's nothing wrong with it, *if you can do it.* Unfortunately, that's tough, if only because it is an unnatural motion. A backstroke a foot long or longer will of its own accord want to go inside the target line, just as the club in a full golf swing will do so once it gets more than a few feet from the ball. To keep the clubhead from swinging inside requires manipulation by the golfer, and the golfer

who manipulates the club is setting himself up to err.

The most common tendency with a straight stroke is to take the club to the outside of the target line on the backswing. When you swing back on the same path, you will cut across the ball and pull it to the left of your target—although you could also push it to the right if the face is open. This is the classic slicer's action in full-swing golf.

The alternative would be to redirect the stroke, swinging it back on the outside, then, before the down-stroke begins, working the club back onto the target line or to the inside of it. The dangers in this kind of action should be obvious.

So, the club swings back to the inside pretty much of its own accord—especially if you set up with the hands relatively low, and the ball opposite the back half of the blade, then return to the ball on the same path, squaring to the target at the moment of impact. A good image to picture this action is that of a swinging door: The club is the door, which hangs on and swings around a hinge that is your hands.

Wristy But Not Flippy

As I said, the action of my stroke is comparatively wristy. However, while my wrists do break or cock a little on the backstroke, there is a *firmness* at all times. Mine is not a flippy stroke—loose or uncontrolled—

largely because of the pressure exerted on the handle by my thumbs and right forefinger. I believe that not letting the wrists cock would, once again, be unnatural in respect to the path of the backstroke. For the club to go back to the inside, *there has to be some wrist cock.*

I use a slight modification for putts over 30 feet, especially on slow greens. Then the overall action is not strictly from "the elbows down." Some upper arm and shoulder movement becomes necessary in order to achieve the necessary force and yet still maintain proper clubface alignment. The

The eyes are directly over the ball at address, and the open stance allows the best look at the line of putt. The open stance also lets the club move freely down that line, after impact.

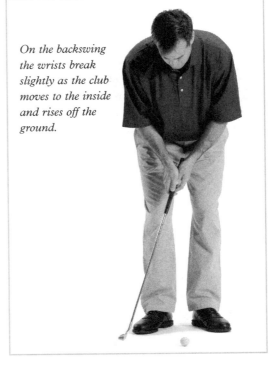

On the backswing the wrists break slightly as the club moves to the inside and rises off the ground.

stroke remains wristy, but it is now synchronized with some movement of the upper arms and shoulders.

An "Open" and "Shut" Case?

My right hand—specifically, my right thumb and forefinger—takes the club back and to the inside of the target line. The blade *appears* to open, and it *appears* to close on the forward stroke. Note I say *appears* to open and close. In fact, the putter face remains throughout in a square position *relative to the path on which the club is swinging.* In other words, if the tar-

get line could somehow be swung around with the movement of the putter face during the backstroke, as though attached to it, the two would remain in *an unchanging relationship* to each other.

A good way to get the feel of this is to make a putting stroke hitting, let's say, toward the north. Now stop the backstroke about half way, holding the blade in position, then turn your body to face east. If you now put the blade back on the ground, you will find it to be square to the target line. If the putter face truly opened, which would require a definite manipulation of the club with the

The top half of the putter strikes the ball just above its center.

With the descending stroke, the follow through is very short.

hands, you and an observer would see the toe of the club flare or fan out on the backstroke, then turn back on the forward stroke.

I stress these points because most golfers are accustomed to seeing that the putter face remains square *in relation to a target that remains stationary,* that is, the ball. There is nothing wrong with this in theory, but in practice it involves closing or shutting down the blade relative to the swing path—what we pros usually call "hooding." Most golfers who don't allow some wrist cock in their putting strokes are apt to hood the putter by rotating their left hand counterclockwise—moving it in such a way that its back faces more toward the ground. If you hood the putter going back, the inclination is to unhood or open it through impact—or even to close it yet more as you hit the ball. This either pushes putts to the right, or pulls them left of the target.

There have been a few good putters who have hooded the blade—Billy Casper, Bob Rosburg, and Horton Smith come to mind in this respect. However, all three were saved by the fact that they hit the ball with a *descending* blow, and thus reduced the risk of opening or shutting the blade at impact.

> **The best putters, with few exceptions, have had a very deliberate takeaway. Jack Nicklaus is the prime example. Jack says he stands over a putt as long as he does because he is waiting until he senses he is totally ready to move the club.**

Low on Low Backstrokes

Many golfers have been told that good putting comes from keeping the club low to the ground on the backstroke. Except for putts of 2 feet or less, I think this is an unnatural and hence a poor way to swing the club back because it produces a tendency to shove the club back rather than swing it. When you shove, you are apt to hood the blade and/or overinvolve the upper arms and shoulders in the stroke. In either case, you cannot develop the kind of repetitive action you need for correct speed and proper direction. With a pendulum-type stroke you can, and a pendulum-type stroke requires some *natural* raising of the club off the ground.

The amount the club raises depends on the length of the stroke, which in turn is dictated by the length of the putt. The longer the putt, of course, the higher the club will *naturally* raise off the ground.

With my descending putter head, however, the follow-through after impact is likely to be very short for putts under 15 feet. Indeed, sometimes the blade will pretty much stop or even meet the ground after impact, and there is nothing wrong with it.

On longer putts, the blade will raise up in the follow-through, naturally, without any special effort on your part.

The Tempo—Anything but Fast

A pendulum stroke, by definition, is a rhythmic stroke. Its opposite is the so-called pop stroke, which features a very short backswing and a quick, sharp, jabbing impact, with a follow-through usually much longer, proportionally, than the backswing. The pop stroke doesn't make music; it makes a bang. The pendulum stroke might be likened, in musical terms, to a fox trot. The tempo is relaxed and slow. In fact, I don't think a putter can be swung too slowly, *especially going back, which is where the tempo for the entire stroke is determined.*

The best putters in the game, with very few exceptions, have had a very *deliberate* takeaway. Jack Nicklaus is the prime example of this. Jack has said he stands over a putt as long as he does before stroking because he is waiting until he senses he is totally ready to move the club. I believe that this getting ready is tied up with his slow backstroke: He's waiting for the tension to drain from his arms and hands so he can take the club away smoothly and slowly. When you swing a putter back slowly, you have full control of the clubhead and that brings smoothness.

In a true pendulum stroke, the putter essentially just drops *down on the ball,* like an acorn free-falling from an oak tree. It may appear there is no acceleration at impact, but only to those not accustomed to seeing a truly evenly paced putting stroke. The majority of golfers, it seems to me, make too short a backstroke—I believe because they feel this is the best way to keep the blade on line. Then, understandably, they think they must give the ball a little extra hit to get it to the hole. The result is rarely smooth, and frequently the ball goes the wrong distance and well wide of the hole.

People tell me that better nerves are needed to putt my way than to pop putt. I think they are dead wrong. You need good (that is, calm) nerves to putt well any way you choose, but a short jab stroke can only get faster and jabbier the more nerves get into the act. If you *expect* to take the clubhead back a comfortable distance, allowing your instincts to determine how far, then the chances are pretty good that you'll make a slower, rhythmic pass at the ball. If you tell yourself to make an artificially short backstroke, then it will more than likely be a fast one. As far as I'm concerned, in putting, speed of stroke definitely kills.

FROM *THE MASTER OF PUTTING* BY GEORGE LOW

JIM McLEAN

THE X-FACTOR

"John Daly had the biggest gap—48.
Daly, of course, is the longest hitter in the game."

O f all the magic moves and miracle methods advanced over the past century or so, surely none has a more intriguing name than the X-Factor, a concept that captured the attention of the golf world in 1992 after an unlikely alliance between two teaching professionals.

The first of them was Jim McLean, by then established as one of America's leading instructors. A 1973 graduate of the University of Houston, McLean had played on NCAA Championship teams with the likes of Bruce Lietzke, John Mahaffey, and Bill Rogers, and had a more impressive golf swing than any of them. But he couldn't putt—at least not to pro standards—and so after a brief attempt at the Tour, he dedicated himself to a teaching career.

In his early years, McLean studied miles of swing videos and sought the wisdom of the top teachers, a list that included Jimmy Ballard, Jackie Burke, Harry Cooper, Manuel De La Torre, Gardner Dickinson, Ben Doyle, Jack Grout, Claude Harmon, Al Mengert, Johnny Revolta, Paul Runyan, Bob Toski, and Ken Venturi. Eventually, he distilled his knowledge into a teaching method that brought him jobs from three prestigious clubs in the New York area (Sunningdale, Quaker Ridge, and Sleepy Hollow), and then to the Doral Resort in Miami, where he started a highly successful golf school. Along the way he coached numerous top ama-

> **THE SECRET:**
>
> C reate a gap between your shoulder and hip turns— turn the shoulders a lot, the hips not so much.

McLean played on the University of Houston team with Bruce Lietzke, John Mahaffey, and Bill Rogers, and had the best swing of them all.

impressive than McLean's (Bel-Air, Riviera, and San Francisco). But McTeigue was also a Phi Beta Kappa psychology graduate from UCLA with an M.B.A. from Stanford, and had talents beyond lesson-giving. By the time he met McLean, he'd worked as a vice president of strategic planning for Taylor Made and had founded two companies.

One of those companies was SportsSense, a pioneer in applying high technology to the analysis and training of complex sports motions, notably the golf swing. To help launch the company, McTeigue had enlisted a group of consultants, including Jim McLean.

One of the devices developed by SportSense was something called the Swing Motion Trainer (SMT), a computer-tethered contraption that was strapped onto golfers to measure the precise movements of the swing. Together, McLean and McTeigue measured more than 150 professionals on the SMT, and when McLean saw the data, he realized it validated his long-held suspicion about how a powerful swing is made.

In December 1992 those findings became a best-selling cover for *GOLF Magazine,* and suddenly topic number one among golfers across the country was the X-Factor. A video followed, as did the book from which this excerpt is drawn.

teurs and professionals, gained exposure in the major golf publications, produced several instruction books and videos, appeared regularly on the Golf Channel and became arguably the most visible teaching pro in America.

Enter his unlikely collaborator, Michael McTeigue, a California-based professional with a list of club affiliations even more

McLEAN'S SECRET

The X-Factor

Whenever I teach amateur players, chat with them at the nineteenth hole about their games or a hot new ball, talk with them at tournaments, or fit them for a new titanium-headed driver, I'm reminded of the golfer's obsession with power. I'm also made aware of their misconceptions on how to produce longer tee shots.

Nine out of ten players think that they should turn their shoulders and hips more, and the harder they whale at the ball, the farther it will fly. It is possible they still haven't heard about the X-Factor discovery we made in 1992 with Mike McTeigue, and his SportSense Motion Trainer (SMT).

Our discovery: The generation of high clubhead speed and power in the golf swing has a direct relationship to the creation of a gap, or differential, between the shoulder and hip turn. In general, the bigger the differential, the farther you hit the ball.

What was even more interesting about the SMT data was that not one power hitter turned his shoulders precisely 90 degrees and his hips 45 degrees (previously thought

to be the ideal power-generating combination). For example, John Daly turned his shoulders 114 degrees, his hips 66 degrees; the gap being 48 degrees (114 minus 66 equals 48). Of all the pros tested, Daly had the highest "gap number." Daly is, of course, the PGA Tour's longest hitter.

In measuring the Tour pros' hip and shoulder rotation on the SMT, we found that all long hitters do not necessarily make big shoulder turns. Nor do all players who make big turns hit the ball a long way. However, every long hitter tested had a big differential—rotating his shoulders much more than his hips. More important, the big hitter's differential comes from a higher percentage of his upper body turn. What does this all mean? *Simple—it's how you turn, not how much you turn.*

The X-Factor Backswing: Creating the "Gap"

Think of your takeaway action as a miniature movement to the side, rather than as rotating around the center of your body. Golfers who immediately turn in their take-

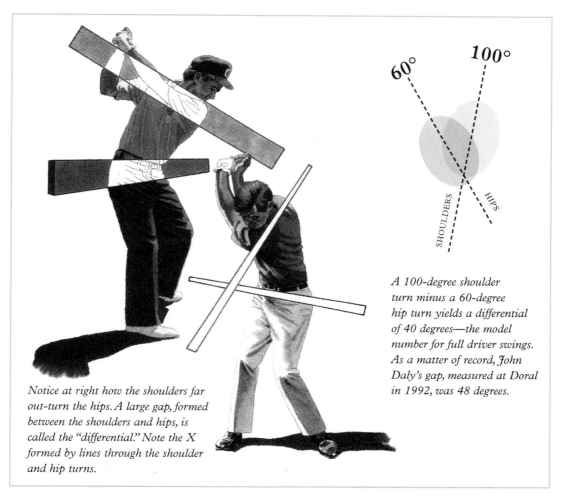

60° 100°

SHOULDERS HIPS

A 100-degree shoulder turn minus a 60-degree hip turn yields a differential of 40 degrees—the model number for full driver swings. As a matter of record, John Daly's gap, measured at Doral in 1992, was 48 degrees.

Notice at right how the shoulders far out-turn the hips. A large gap, formed between the shoulders and hips, is called the "differential." Note the X formed by lines through the shoulder and hip turns.

McLEAN'S SECRET

away tend to reverse pivot, shifting weight to the left (front) foot, rather than right, on the backswing.

It's important to understand that the hips make two moves: (1) lateral and (2) rotational. To properly load the right side, there must be a slight lateral move of the hips in the backswing; it keeps the right hip from reversing toward the target and is not a slide.

Hip action is tremendously important, because it allows the body's lower center to move slightly to the right, or away from the target on the backswing. When done correctly, the right side of your body will tend to line up; there will almost be a straight line,

As the shoulders and arms are still going back, the lower body reverses direction. At this point in the swing, many players feel weight being pushed downward into their right knee, as both knees start forward. As the shoulders turn, and the lower body reverses direction, the X-Factor differential, or gap, is increased.

are there only for feel. The arms, hands, and club move as a reaction to the turning of your shoulders and shifting of weight. You should feel the club and arms swinging away freely, the hands and arms tension-free. Don't worry about losing control; keeping grip pressure light allows the hands to feel the clubface. Let the clubhead follow the natural shape of the swing, rising gradually along an arc; don't push it down or pick it up quickly with your hands. The club will move naturally inside the target line in response to the hands and arms. It's not your job to take the club inside; it will go inside because you are standing to the side of the ball and there is shoulder turn. Don't pull the hands and arms behind your body. Rather, keep them in sync with the center. As long as the big muscles of the upper body control the takeaway, your swing won't become quick or jerky. Keep your rhythm smooth as swing speed gradually increases. Think smooth throughout the takeaway.

as opposed to having a "reverse C" from your right foot to your head.

For the advanced player, the arms and hands will move away in the backswing precisely with center. They are responding to center in a connected takeaway. The hands

As the hands reach the halfway point, you should feel that the axis of your swing has shifted to the inside of your right leg. That leg becomes the support post for the backswing, ensuring that you neither overturn the hips (and narrow your X-Factor gap), nor severely flatten the swing plane. Although I've barely mentioned the club in this book, you should understand that the clubshaft will seek the proper plane if you allow it to happen. The hands are now as far as they move away from the target, the result of moving the triangle away intact, keeping the wrists relaxed, and moving the club, arms, and shoulders together as a single unit: your backswing package.

> In measuring the Tour pros' hip and shoulder rotation on the SMT, we found that all long hitters do not necessarily make big shoulder turns. Nor do all players who make big turns hit the ball a long way.

The Letter "L" and Its Role in the X-Factor Backswing

As you coil the shoulders, the arms respond. In a natural arm swing, the left arm will remain straight (connected to the upper left side of your chest) due to centrifugal force and the weight of the club. At about waist high, the right elbow will naturally begin to fold. By the top of the backswing, the lower right arm and the upper right arm will form an "L," or approximately a 90-degree angle. In a model swing, the angle is 90 degrees, the perfect physics angle. Interestingly, the right elbow is around and behind the body (not to the side of the body). Many teachers think it should be pointing straight down, which is incorrect. Also, at the top of the backswing our research indicates the right forearm will be angled close to the player's spine angle. This is not exactly true with all players, but it is reasonably close (within a few degrees).

At the top of the backswing, I like to see the elbows nearly level. Again, it's not mandatory or an exact fundamental; just a very positive position to strive for.

The second "L" is made by the right wrist. When the right wrist is fully cocked back, the angle between the right hand and wrist joint forms nearly a 90-degree angle (or L position).

The third "L" is formed by the left arm and the clubshaft at the three-quarter position in the backswing, or shortly thereafter. These three Ls form a powerful package that will be part of your total release through the ball.

At the top, your chin should have rotated away from the target. Some players turn the chin as much as 45 degrees; the average is 20 to 25 degrees. Remember, the head moves slightly. Remember, too, power

Ideally, at the top of the backswing, the upper right arm and lower right arm will form an "L."

hitters on the PGA Tour shift their heads back between 1 and 4 inches, some even more. Please do not forget: Trying to freeze your head in position creates tension. Tension kills speed and you might even say, it destroys the swinging action.

Backswing Drills: For Creating the "Gap"

DRILL 1

Set up to a ball with a driver. Next, have a

friend place a clubshaft or towel on the ground, so that it extends outward from approximately your left heel, and runs perpendicular to the target line.

Now swing back a few times, trying to turn your shoulder area past the clubshaft.

The more you practice this drill, the stronger your shoulder turn will become. When you return to the course, you'll hit the ball much more powerfully.

DRILL 2

Practice your swing technique, using a wooden-handled broom. This is a drill I learned from renowned teacher Bob Toski. Because the broom is typically longer and heavier than a standard driver, it will encourage you to turn the big muscles of your shoulders—not make an overly handsy swing.

DRILL 3

In setting up to drive, drop your right foot back 12 inches farther away from the target line than your left. Hit a bucket of balls from this extra-closed stance, and you'll experience what it feels like to turn your shoulders powerfully on a flatter plane than your arms. Great for slicers with an overly steep shoulder tilt.

The X-Factor Downswing: Closing the "Gap"

As wide a gap as you create on the backswing, it will not amount to much unless you

The vital L positions, formed on the backswing, should be maintained as you make the critical first move in the X-Factor downswing.

way without conscious thought on your part. When you shift lower center first and/or lower the right shoulder, the arms and hands respond in the following ways:

The Ls in the Downswing

The three Ls you formed in the backswing will remain intact (or even increase) as you make the critical first move in the forward swing. This is the move that separates good ball strikers from poor ball strikers and it's done by the engine of the swing—your body—not the club, hands, or arms. The club, hands, and arms lower as the right shoulder and right elbow lower because of good body actions. As the swing continues, the left arm will fall down plane.

To keep the Ls together, you leave them alone. You do not pull down with the left arm. You do not pull the grip end of the club. Instead, you shift your lower center, or you re-center the body, which may well give you a pull feel. This can be done in several ways:

1. Shift the knees laterally.
2. Start the left knee toward the target.
3. Kick the right knee outward toward the target line (and in front of the ball).

release the power you build up. The Power Coil and creating the perfect X won't matter unless you make the correct sequence of moves to start down.

What's the secret to a powerful downswing? It is making the correct athletic moves, and starting down with lower center or your lower body. This shift will cause your right shoulder to work downward before it moves forward (a downward rocking motion). This initial lateral motion causes other things to happen in the correct

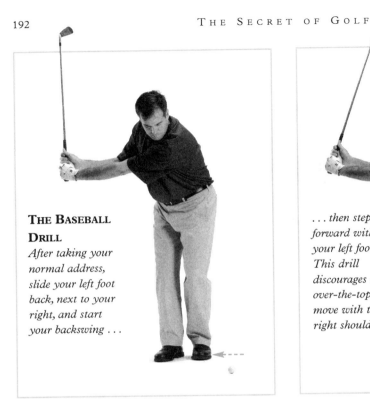

THE BASEBALL DRILL
After taking your normal address, slide your left foot back, next to your right, and start your backswing . . .

. . . then step forward with your left foot. This drill discourages an over-the-top move with the right shoulder.

4. Push off your right instep.

5. Bump the left hip toward the target.

6. Rock the right shoulder downward.

Do not:

1. Start with the hands (throw the clubhead from the top).

2. Rotate the shoulders (right shoulder moving out).

By simply lowering the Ls to the waist-high delivery position, you will have retained tremendous lag and saved the stored energy developed in the backswing coil described earlier.

Downswing Drills: For Closing the "Gap"

DRILL 1

Set up normally to a teed-up ball, using a mid-iron. Slide your left foot back toward the right, so that they practically touch each other, and the clubhead is about a foot behind the ball.

Start the backswing. When the club reaches waist level, step forward with your left foot, returning it to its original position, like a batter stepping into a pitch.

The clubhead will still be moving back as the lower body moves forward, which

Hitting shots with your right foot pointed outward 45 degrees gives you a feeling of freedom on the backswing . . .

. . . and keeps the lower body from either spinning out or sliding on the downswing.

automatically increases wrist work and prevents the right shoulder from leading the downswing.

DRILL 2

Practice moving the right shoulder downward at the start of the forward swing. This trigger encourages the hips to shift laterally toward the target. Also, it lowers the right elbow underneath the left arm, and drops the club into the hitting slot. Now you can hit from the inside, like all top Tour players.

DRILL 3

Assume your normal address position. Then widen your stance by placing your right foot well outside your right shoulder. Fan the right foot outward, so it points away from you at a 45-degree angle. Hitting practice shots from this position helps you eliminate any upper-body slide. It maintains a wide gap between your knees by dramatically slowing right leg action. It also keeps you from spinning the lower body too fast.

FROM *THE X-FACTOR SWING* BY JIM MCLEAN

MCLEAN'S SECRET

CHAPTER 25

EDDIE MERRINS

THE HANDLE'S MESSIAH

"While no teacher can completely eliminate human error, I have a system that will—if properly applied— do away with the mechanical errors that cause bad shots."

Thousand of golfers have taken lessons from Eddie Merrins—but it's a very elite group. His list of students includes everyone from Duffy Waldorf to Fred Astaire, Corey Pavin to Jack Nicholson, Arnold Palmer to Ringo Starr. Five-foot, seven-inch Merrins—the man known as "The Little Pro"— has had a big impact on golf.

Following an outstanding amateur career that included three Mississippi State Amateur titles and two Southeastern Conference championships while at Louisiana State, Merrins was primed for the pro ranks, and after a stint in the Air Force he joined the tour in 1957. But to help with his expenses, as many players did in those days, he simultaneously took a job as an assistant professional. He began teaching at the Merion Golf Club near Philadelphia, and the more he taught, the more he liked it.

Back then one of the other staff pros at Merion was Fred Austin, a disciple of Ernest Jones, whose exhortation to "swing the clubhead" had influenced a generation of golfers. But Merrins was an analytical fellow whose search for a better swing for both himself and his students told him the Jones method had flaws.

THE SECRET:

Control the handle. When you control the handle, you will control the club—and when you control the club, you will control the ball.

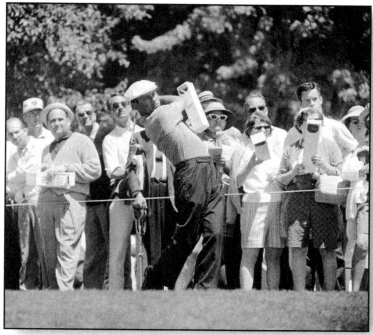

Merrins played the pro tour briefly but found that teaching the game was his true calling.

"When I taught golfers to 'swing the clubhead' as Jones said, I found the hands became too active, causing serious faults, such as 'hitting from the top,'" he said. "This in turn resulted in a loss of power and produced topped shots. The overactive hands also maneuvered the clubface closed, which resulted in hooks, or open, which produced slices.

"Another problem was that by accentuating the hands, the large muscles of the body didn't get into the act efficiently. In a good swing both ends of the club—the clubhead and the handle—as well as the body should be moving in the same direction at the same point in time in the swing. There had to be a better way."

That better way came to Merrins from a most unlikely source: tennis. The two-handed backhand, gaining in popularity at the time, struck him as exactly the same motion as a good golf stroke. He tried it, using his forearms to swing not the clubhead but the handle. Seeing immediate improvement in his own game, he began preaching the same to his students.

That was in 1960, and Eddie Merrins has been teaching golfers to swing the handle ever since. For most of that time he has been the head professional—and now professional emeritus—at the Bel-Air Country Club in Los Angeles, where he has spawned a procession of handle-swinging glitterati extending from Bing Crosby to Tom Cruise. Over that time, Merrins developed an entire teaching system, basing the development of power, accuracy, and shot-making around proper control of the handle. In 1973 he published his manifesto, *Swing the Handle—Not the Clubhead,* and in 2002, on his fortieth anniversary at Bel-Air, he issued his theories through a DVD that has sold over a million copies.

MERRINS'S SECRET

The Most Important Thought in Golf

Now I am going to give you what may be the single most important piece of golf instruction you will ever receive in your life. This is the key to my method, the one positive thought that will allow you to make a mechanically perfect golf swing. That thought is simply to: **Swing the Handle of the Club with Your Forearms.**

Please ponder that sentence a while. It represents the one overriding thought that you should have on every normal golf shot you make. I should state at this time that I do not believe it is possible to make a perfect golf swing every time. We are all human, and the human factor is bound to prevent us on occasion from producing machine-like perfection. However, I do believe that swinging your end of the club with your forearms represents the mechanical means for producing a perfect swing. The closer that you can come to executing this one simple thought, the closer you will come to enjoying perfection in your golf game.

Swinging the top of the club with your forearms can all but eliminate the worst shots in golf—the slice, the hook, the scuffed shot and the topped shot. This is true because all of these shots are caused by improperly influencing the clubhead with your hands and wrists. Slicing and hooking stem largely from opening and closing the clubface with your hands and wrists. Fat shots and topped shots result largely from throwing or flipping the clubhead into the ground behind the ball or over the top of it with your hands and wrists.

You see, your hands and your wrists directly influence the head end of your club for good or for bad—usually the latter. Your arms, and only your arms, directly affect the top portion of your club. Let's face it: You can turn your body back and forth all day, but you will not move the golf club until your arms also begin to swing. Or you can flip the club back and forth with your hands and wrists until the end of time, but this manipulation will only move the clubhead.

The point is simply that you can swing the handle end of your club only with your forearms. And only by swinging the handle end with your forearms can you eliminate the bad shots that result from misaligning and misdirecting the head end with your hands and wrists.

Also, as we go on we shall see that the *speed* at which you swing your forearms directly determines the *distance* you hit your shots. The faster you can swing your forearms, the more force you will impart to the ball. Thus, swinging the forearms not only gives you a way to keep your hands from misaligning and misdirecting the clubhead to the ball, but it also gives you a positive way to control the length of your shots.

How Your Arms Should Swing

First, it is important that you grip the club properly. That is, (1) hold the club with all eight fingers curling inward and upward toward your palms so that your elbows want to press inward to your side; (2) angle your thumbs across the top of the shaft to set

Swing this way . . .

. . . not this way.

In the ideal golf swing, your legs, lower body and arms and the entire club should all accelerate forward through impact. This forward movement will take place only if you accelerate the grip end—the handle—of the club. And only your arms—swinging freely—can accelerate the handle. Whenever you throw the clubhead forward with your hands and wrists, the top end of the clubshaft will tend to slow down. This, in turn, slows the forward movement of your legs, lower body and arms, and thus reduces the length of your shots. More important, throwing the clubhead forward with your hands causes mis-alignment of the clubface and distortion of the clubhead arc. Mis-hit shots result. The arms should swing the handle, not the hands and wrists the clubhead.

Point your right elbow down to swing your arms freely.

During the backswing your right arm should fold readily at the elbow so that it points more or less downward at the top of the backswing. From this position you can swing your arms freely through the ball in conjunction with the uncoiling of your body. If your right elbow flies outward and upward during your backswing, you will tend to lift the club and then shove or throw it back to the ball independently of your body turn, thus wasting much of your power. Properly curling your fingers inward and upward toward your palms when gripping helps force your elbows into proper position.

your hands in a palms-facing relationship, and (3) check to see that hinging your wrists at the base of your thumbs will cause the club to lift vertically.

Next, extend your arms and the clubshaft horizontally out in front of you and begin swinging the club back and forth around your body. You should be making more or less the same circular arc, first around to the right and then to the left, that a baseball batter would make in swinging his bat back and through.

Be sure that at all times you are swinging the grip end of the club with your forearms. There should be no flipping of the clubhead with your wrists.

You will note that as you swing the club around to the right on your backstroke, your left forearm tends to roll above your right. As you swing the grip end of the club back to the left, your right forearm gradually rolls above your left. You are swinging the club around your body in a semi-circular arc with your forearms rolling over each other as they swing the grip end of the club. This is the same basic arm motion that you will be using in your golf swing.

It might be helpful at this point to imagine that you are swinging a tennis racket instead of a golf club. Imagine that you are making a chest-high shot with both of your hands on the racket. As the ball approaches you would swing the handle of the racket away—back to the right—with your *forearms*. You would not flip the racket back with your wrists. Your left forearm would tend to roll slightly over as your right forearm tended to roll under.

As the ball came closer you would begin your forward stroke. Your forearms would reverse and start turning the handle of the racket to your left. As a result, your racket face would begin to turn into position to, as they say, "cover the ball." Your forearms would swing the handle of the racket through impact with the ball and beyond. At no time would your hands and wrists flip it. The ball compresses—flattens—on the strings of the racket and then recoils forward as your arms continue to swing the handle, just as the golf ball compresses on the clubface and then rebounds up and away.

Once you have mastered the feeling of swinging the grip end of the club around your body in a semi-circular arc with your forearms, you should make similar swings with the clubhead brushing the ground. Now you will be moving them on a plane that is somewhere between horizontal and vertical. This will put your semi-circular swinging motion into a somewhat upward-downward-upward pattern.

As you make this swing, you should find that your wrists are starting to hinge, but only at the base of your thumbs. This is the type of hinging and unhinging that allows you to connect the clubhead to the ball. It is the type of wrist action that gives height and leverage to your swing. It is not the type of wrist action that you would use to flip your clubhead back and forth. Remember, above all else, that you are still swinging the top end of the club with your forearms. There should be absolutely no tendency to influence the clubhead with your hands.

The best way to keep your hands from independently influencing the clubhead is to see that your arms accelerate as they swing down and through the impact area. So long as your arms accelerate—even on short chip shots and putts—you can swing the top end of your club. If your arms lag, your hands and wrists will take over and begin to flip the head end—the wrong end—of the club. You will begin to mis-hit your shots.

Swinging the top of the club with your forearms can all but eliminate the worst shots in golf—the slice, the hook, the scuffed shot, and the top shot—because all are caused by use of the hands and wrists.

In short, be sure that you not only swing the top of the club with your forearms, but that you accelerate them gradually in your downswing and through the impact area.

Not only is acceleration important, but so, too, is the positioning of your elbows during your swing. This is a highly neglected area of golf instruction. You'll recall that I asked you to curl your eight fingers in toward your palms in gripping so that your elbows would tend to work down and in toward your body, rather than up and out. While freedom of movement requires that your elbows move away from your side to some extent as you swing, they should never turn upward. They should always point more or less toward the ground instead of toward the sky.

> **The speed at which you swing your forearms directly determines the distance you hit your shots.**

The principle here is the same as that used by arm wrestlers, who bend at the elbow but always keep it pointing downward. These men use the elbow as a fulcrum and the forearm as a lever through which they transfer the power of their legs and body. In the golf swing, so long as your elbows are pointing more downward than upward, you can swing your forearms and turn your body *together* as a powerful compact unit. Once your elbows fly upward, this unit becomes separated. Your arms can't swing freely, and your body can't turn as a result of their swinging. Instead, your hands and wrists must take over, more or less apart from your body turn. You'll lose much of the power of your legs and body and deliver a weak, ineffective stroke.

If your elbows are working properly, your right arm will fold on the backswing as your left arm extends, and your left arm will fold on your throughswing as your right arm extends. This is the pattern of arm movement that allows you to use the power of both sides of your body. This pattern results from keeping your elbows facing properly downward so that your arms can swing the top of the club freely.

In folding the right elbow in the backswing, you will notice that the upper right arm (biceps muscle) contracts as the forearm swings the club around to the right of your body. This contraction adds an additional lift factor to the swing. In the downswing the upper arm gradually extends to lower the club to the ball. In the followthrough the left upper arm contracts as the forearms swing the club to the left of the body. This helps permit a high finish.

I regard the backswing as merely a preparatory movement for the forward swing. If a baseball player is going to toss the ball to a person 50 feet away, he doesn't think about how far he should cock his arm back. Instead he instinctively cocks it just far enough to throw the ball 50 feet. It's the same in the golf swing; if you are trying to hit a shot 50 feet, you should instinctively make just enough backswing to stroke the ball that distance.

Thus we have seen how your forearms should accelerate the handle of the club in a semi-circular arc around your body, with your wrists hinging only at the base of your thumbs and with your elbows pointing more or less downward throughout. This is the swing that I advocate in my method.

Full-Swing Practice Drills

Before your next practice session or round of play, swing your driver several times around your body on a horizontal plane, as if you were swinging a baseball bat. Make sure that your arms swing the handle of the club. This drill will not only help loosen tight muscles, but will also give you the correct golf swing feeling of turning the hub end of the club around your body in a semi-circular arc.

Practice hitting one-handed shots, first with just your right hand on the club, then just the left. Be sure in each case you swing the handle with your forearm. See that your right arm folds freely at the elbow during your backswing and then gradually extends during your forward swing. See that your left arm extends during your backswing and then gradually folds during your follow-through. Failure of either arm to fold when it should will produce a blocking action that inhibits free-swinging. This drill will not only build the correct feeling of the role that each arm plays in the swing, but it will also force you to swing your arms in proper rhythm. Only by doing so will you make solid contact with the ball.

In practicing to swing the handle, occasionally finish your swing and then return to your address position without re-gripping the club. Check to see if your hands are still gripping the club in their original position. If not, the club has slipped in your hands somewhere during your swing. This slippage indicates that you have used your hands and wrists to influence the clubhead, rather than your forearms to swing the handle.

FROM *SWING THE HANDLE—NOT THE CLUBHEAD* BY EDDIE MERRINS

MERRINS'S SECRET

CHAPTER 26

OBEY THE SIGNS

"I use a system that I think would be dynamite for any player. I call it the 'light system.'"

Never has the game seen a more astonishingly accurate iron player than Johnny Miller in his prime. During the mid-1970s, Miller struck his approach shots with such unrelenting precision that it was a rare round when his ball failed to clank into a flagstick.

The San Francisco native showed his brilliance early, qualifying for the 1966 U.S. Open at the Olympic Club (his home course) at the age of nineteen and then stunning the world by finishing in eighth place. Three years later, he graduated from Brigham Young University and immediately joined the PGA Tour. It was in the 1973 U.S. Open that he really made his mark, birdying the first four holes at Oakmont Country Club en route to victory on a championship-record final round of 63.

Over the next three years, Miller played golf at a level that few players in history have ever reached. In 1974 he won his first three events and eight out of the twenty he entered. A year later, he won six times around the world, including back-to-back victories at Phoenix and Tucson, where he shot 61 in each event, winning Phoenix by 14 strokes, Tucson by nine. In 1976 he added three more titles, including a 6-stroke victory in the British Open at Royal Birkdale. During those years, Miller was the best player in the

THE SECRET:

Read and follow the signs. Before you choose a shot or club for an approach, read the situation carefully and decide how much caution/aggressiveness it calls for.

Johnny Miller throws his golf ball to the crowd after winning the British Open Golf Championship at Royal Birkdale in 1976.

world—Jack Nicklaus included—and he knew it. "Right now I don't think there's anyone who can touch me," he said with a guileless candor that was to become his trademark.

Miller's explosive game, combined with his California surfer looks, made him an attractive spokesman for several major companies, including Sears, which began a Johnny Miller clothing line and sold so many white belts and powder-blue leisure suits that every Sears cash register was equipped with a "Johnny Miller" key.

A devout Mormon and the father of six, Miller began to spend more time at his family ranch. Just as suddenly as his star rose, it fell—from 1976 to 1980, he went without a victory. *GOLF Magazine* actually ran a contest in its pages ("What's Wrong with Johnny?") asking readers to offer advice. But to Miller's credit, he was as honest and unshrinking about his game during that period as he'd been at the height of his powers. "I can't break par," he said. "I can't break an egg."

Miller won sporadically during the 1980s but never recovered his full magic. His last hurrah came in 1994 ,when, as a forty-seven-year-old grandfather, he returned to his northern California roots to win the AT&T Pebble Beach National Pro-Am, his twenty-fourth career title. In 1998 he was inducted into the World Golf Hall of Fame.

Today's generation of golfers knows Johnny Miller as the straight-talking lead commentator for NBC's golf telecasts. His brutal frankness often rankles the Tour players, but he is always insightful and articulate, and his observations today are as piercingly accurate as his iron shots were three decades ago.

Only once did Miller publish his views on how to play the game, in *Pure Golf,* a book that appeared on the eve of his British Open victory and became an instant best-seller. Miller's frankness and willingness to depart from convention are evident throughout the book, as is his knack for conveying his ideas with vivid images, such as his "traffic-light system" for gauging aggressiveness on approach shots.

MILLER'S SECRET

In the same way that the type of shot you plan off the tee is influenced by the type of hole you're playing, so the shot into the green is governed by, first, your lie and, second, the situation at the green. I have a system that I use in evaluating these shots that I think would be dynamite for any player: I call it the "light" system.

If there's nothing to stop me hitting directly at the flag, I call this a "green light" situation. I've considered the pin placement, the trouble around the green, and all the other factors, and I have decided that there's no way I can get into trouble. The "green light" situation is purely when all systems say "go." If there are a couple of variables against me, then I call this a "yellow light" situation. Very probably I'll play a percentage shot to the middle of the green. The "yellow light"

situation is where your computer shows a couple of caution lights. Every once in a while you'll have a "red light" situation. As its name implies, this brings all normal plans to a halt. You just have to chip out of the trouble you're in the best way you can, even if it means conceding a stroke to the course.

To show you how the "light system" works out in practice, let's take a situation where I am 155 yards away from the pin and the hole is on the back of the green on the left. Right away, I know that I need a hook-spin 7-iron. My maximum for a straight shot with a 7-iron is 150 yards, but I'll get another 5 yards if I hook it a little. I look at the lie and it's perfect. I look at the trouble around the green; I can ignore the bunkers in front because the pin's at the back, and I'll be pitching the ball in the middle of the green, and I can forget about the bunker at the back because I know I can't hit the 7-iron more than 155 yards, even with a hook. Since there's nothing to prevent me shooting right at the pin, that's a "green light" situation.

Now let's assume the same general circumstances with these changes: The green is very shallow, the pin is tucked left with bunkers at the front on the left and at the

The seventeenth hole at Oakhill is a "green light" hole. Although it's a good par-4 463-yard hole, it's reachable and doesn't offer serious trouble. At worst, I may hit into a greenside bunker, which would mean I still have a chance at par.

The sixteenth hole at Firestone Country Club, in Akron, Ohio, where I won the World Series in 1974, could be described as a "yellow light" situation. You must use extreme caution. It's a reachable par-5 with two long wood shots (625 yards), but should your second shot stray to the right, it will catch the water. If there is ever any doubt in my mind on this hole, I'll always take an iron, play short, and then pitch in to the flag.

Third, let's assume that the shot is being played from the left rough. The lie is heavy and I've got to go under a tree to hit toward the green. If I punch a little 5-iron under and out, then I won't have enough loft on the ball to carry the bunker on the left and stop the ball on the green. If I play for the opening of the green, the ball could very well run through the green into the bunker on the right. Whichever way I look at it, I'm dead! This is strictly a "red light" situation. What I'd do is just punch the ball out short of the green and hope for a pitch and putt to save par.

There's one additional point that's worth making about this "red light" situation. Just because you're "dead" in the sense that you can't attempt to hit the green doesn't mean you should just

back of the green, and to top it off I have a skinny, tight lie. This lie favors a fade, not a hook, and this factor, added to the tough pin placement, means I've got several factors against me. So, it's a "yellow light" situation and I would play a percentage shot for the fat part of the green.

punch it out anywhere. Take the time to figure out the place from which it will be the easiest to get it up and down for your par, and try to hit the ball to that point. You should always try to set up your next shot—even from "red light" situations—if at all possible.

You can see, then, that my "light system" can readily be applied to your own game. It's just a matter of understanding your game and knowing your own capabilities. If, for example, you have a tendency to hit the ball reasonably straight but low all the time, and you're playing a course with a lot of elevated greens, then you're going to be playing a lot of "yellow light" golf that day. You're obviously not going to be able to go for a flag that is tucked behind a bunker because you don't have the height. You'll have to take one or two more clubs to clear the trouble. The main thing is to know your pluses and minuses when you're plotting your strategy and to always play your strongest suit.

Another vital element in deciding whether a situation is "green," "yellow," or "red" is how you are playing. If you're playing badly, then perhaps there will never be a "green light" that day. You'll just have to play on yellow all the time. However, "yellow light" golf isn't necessarily bad golf—I've played eighteen holes of "yellow light" golf and shot 68. Another time you might get too cocky and play "green light" golf all the way around and shoot a bad round. But this is all part of expe-

I consider the twelfth hole at Augusta National (Par 3, 155 yards) a "red light" situation. When the pin is tucked in the sliver of green on the left midway between the front and back bunkers, there is always danger. Especially in pressure situations, I'll play out to the right of the green.

rience. In my own game, I have learned the difference between how I'm hitting at the time and the variables that affect each shot. You, too, will have to learn that for yourself.

FROM *PURE GOLF* BY JOHNNY MILLER

CHAPTER 27

ALEX MORRISON

A LEFTY GAME FOR RIGHTIES

*"I have more than once made the wager
that I can teach any man, woman or child how to
make the correct swing in three minutes or less."*

Alex Morrison had chutzpah. When he gave his first golf lesson, he knew next to nothing about the game. In his own words, "I couldn't drive a golf ball 150 yards within 45 degrees of any given direction." He was sixteen years old, a shop boy at the Los Angeles Country Club, and his main athletic interest was tennis.

But on the morning when a new member mistook him for an assistant pro and asked for help, Alex obliged, winging his way through a series of instructional platitudes he'd overheard the head professional deliver to other pupils. The next day, the member returned to the club for another lesson, asking specifically for Alex. Then the member returned again and again for more lessons, bringing friends with him.

Fate had marked Alex Morrison, and so he decided he would teach himself to play golf, and then he would teach the world. Six feet tall but less than 130 pounds, he was told he had the wrong body for golf. "Physically, they told me, I was entirely unequal to the task of producing enough power and control in swinging a club to send a ball much farther than the end of the tee," he said. His first efforts bore little fruit, but the ever-confident Morrison reasoned that his failure was due not to his own shortcomings but to the weaknesses of the methods he'd tried. So he soldiered on, searching for a technique that would allow him to succeed—and eventually he found it.

His "new way" brought enlightenment not only to Alex but to his students as well, and before long he'd moved east and hung his teacher's shingle in the middle of New York

City. There, through aggressive networking and self-promotion, he enlarged his roster of pupils in both size and stature. He was particularly good at attracting celebrities of every stripe, from Babe Ruth to Rube Goldberg, Douglas Fairbanks to Henry Ford, not to mention two U.S. presidents. It was at Morrision's indoor range on 59th Street that Bob Hope and Bing Crosby forged their friendship during lunch breaks from their vaudeville rehearsals.

By that time Morrison had become something of a showman himself, combining entertainment and instruction in a revue at the Palace Theatre. He also toured the country giving golf lectures and shot-making exhibitions. One of his favorite stunts was to hit a ball off another man's head, a feat he claimed to have performed over 4,000 times without a fat or skulled shot (which in this case would have been the same thing).

Yes, Alex Morrison had chutzpah, but his greatest confidence was in the teaching method he espoused. One of the first proponents of a true swinging motion, he believed it could be achieved only when the muscles of the left side were allowed to lead. He called golf "a left-handed game for right-handed people," pointing to Bobby Jones and Ben Hogan (two natural lefties) as proof. And to lend ultimate credence, he converted Babe Ruth—baseball's most powerful left-handed hitter—into an accomplished right-handed golfer.

Morrison's method produced a more vertical and downward strike, which tended to get the ball up in the air faster, and it came at a propitious moment, as the golden era of golf architecture in America had produced a multitude of long and heavily bunkered courses, calling for high-flying approach shots rather than the bump-and-runs the game had always favored. But he wasn't one of those teachers who allowed his pupils to adapt his ideas selectively, and he did not offer quick fixes. Morrison demanded complete surrender. He also put his pupils in golf quarantine, forbidding them from setting foot on the course until they'd gotten the feel of the new swing and developed the confidence and control to put it into action.

Nonetheless, he insisted his teachings were not complicated, referring to the act of hitting a golf ball as "really a rather easy job." And for those he couldn't reach personally, he provided a manifesto. *A New Way to Better Golf* appeared in 1932 with a foreword by novelist Rex Beach and an introduction by Bernard Darwin. The first forty or so pages are thinly veiled self-promotion, but once Morrison sets forth his thinking, he does so in compelling style. Nearly 75 years after its publication it, remains one of the classics of golf instruction.

> **THE SECRET:**
>
> Point your chin in back of the ball and think of the swing as one full, smooth, flowing motion, controlled by the muscles of the left side.

MORRISON'S SECRET

In presenting a description of the correct swing, let us borrow a method of procedure from the movies. The reader undoubtedly has seen slow-motion pictures of athletic events—jumping, hurdling, diving, and the like. First the action is shown at normal speed, then repeated, but slowed down to a point that permits leisurely study of the muscular movements of the performer.

So with the golf swing. If we can get a picture of it as a whole, a general idea of it, we shall be better able to follow with understanding the "slow-motion" analysis of its various stages which we shall be seeing presently.

I have already given a few hints about the swing. I have said that its main object is to produce a whirling motion of the club through centrifugal force, thereby propelling the clubhead in a consistently true arc. I have said that the force of such a swing originates near the center of the body. Let's look a little deeper and see if we can discover the "why" of all this. To start things off, let's just fan a little about golf.

Every round of golf is made up of an almost endless variety of shots, few of them executed under precisely similar conditions. Our good friends the club manufacturers have given us some assistance in making those shots by putting at our disposal a large assortment of tools, with weight, and length, and loft scientifically graduated to take care of our problem of getting the ball from here to there. But we have all discovered that a great deal of the work is still left to us. We have noticed, for example, that improper movements of our hands or bodies sometimes nullify the efforts of the manufacturer to equip a club with a hitting surface that will consistently perform a specific job. Or when the ball rests on hard or rough surfaces, or lies in sand, or mud, or tough grass, we have found that we must do something besides pick the proper club out of the bag if we're to get the ball out where it belongs.

In short, we have made the interesting discovery that, if we play golf, we must learn not only how to execute a diversity of shots but how to repeat them consistently and at will. Permit me to offer a little observation of my own at this point, which is that we must also learn how to execute these shots in an easy and natural way; otherwise we shall find our skill forsaking us when confronted by the necessity of exercising it in the face of hazards either actual or imaginary.

Everything needed to supplement the work the club manufacturers already have done for us is found in the correct swing— an accurate, consistent, powerful, natural action, requiring for its successful perform- ance only that the player learn the proper positions and proper order of movement to be thoroughly relaxed and at ease.

Some years ago I worked out a defini- tion of the proper swing, one which, like the fundamentals of my own swing, I have found it unnecessary to change in any way. It is this: One full, smooth, flowing motion without mental or physical interruption.

Unless every item in this definition is satisfied, the correct swing cannot be made. It cannot be made when the player grabs the club as he would a baseball bat, pressing his thumbs against the shaft so that the muscles of his hands and forearms are tightly locked. It cannot be made when he grips the ground

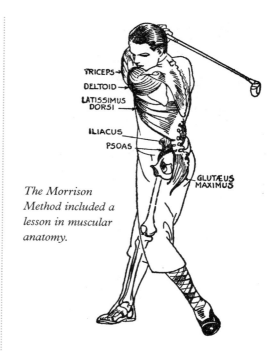

The Morrison Method included a lesson in muscular anatomy.

with his feet, thereby tightening the muscles of his legs; or, worse still, when he tries to keep his body in a fixed position and so con- trives to tighten up the muscles of his back. It cannot be made when he is doubtful about the outcome of his shot, or when the thought of hitting the ball hard enough is uppermost in his mind. Such mental distur- bances produce tension, and tension is fatal to the freedom of motion without which the necessary whirling motion of the club can- not be produced.

The most certain way of overcoming tension, and consequently insuring freedom, is through motion. From the moment the

The starting position favors the left side of the body, leaving the right side comparatively relaxed.

Starting the back swing. The weight shifts to the right.

The arms and hands move in response to the side motion of the hips.

hands are placed on the club until well after the ball has been hit, the entire body must be kept in motion. How much action there should be in the swing depends, of course, on the character of the shot, for obviously a drive requires more action than a putt. But an uninterrupted motion there must be, for no one anywhere ever made a good golf shot by holding a statuesque pose at the outset while he contemplated the crime he was about to commit, or by pausing part way through his swing to wonder whether he was on the right track.

In addition to freedom there must be power, properly generated and applied. A loose-jointed, flabby sweep of a golf club is not a swing, no matter how free and easy the maker may feel during the process. Power is obtained by the efficient employment of the bones, joints, muscles and tendons of the body to propel the club with maximum leverage.

The longer the lever, the greater the force produced. That is an elementary law of mechanics, demonstrated every time you use a crowbar or work the handle of an automobile jack. Consequently, the greater the "reach" in the swing, the more speed and power in the clubhead at the moment it strikes the ball.

You can demonstrate this point about leverage to your own satisfaction and at the

Most of the weight is placed on the right leg before any turning motion takes place.

The wind-up. The backward turning of the hips is followed by the backward turning of the shoulders and arms.

The final stages of the wind-up. The backward motion of the arms and bending of the wrists continue after the body turn is completed.

same time learn something about the origin of the force that works the lever, simply by wielding anything like a cane in much the same manner as a swordsman might execute a backhanded blow with his sword held in his left hand, palm facing downward.

Just stand erect and perfectly natural; grasp the cane, or whatever you use, firmly in the palm of your left hand. With this hand turned over so that only the back of it can be seen, draw your weapon well over to the right and then slash back again toward the left. You will note that an exceedingly powerful blow can be struck in this way. It is obvious, too, that extending your left arm to its full reach, and adding to the distance you draw the arm over to the right increases the radius or leverage and the power of your stroke.

Now shift your weight so that it is supported almost entirely on your right leg. Let your body turn around as far as it will go while you are drawing your left arm and the cane to the right. Slash out again toward the left. You will find a surprising amount of force added to the stroke by the turning of your body.

After you have gone through this motion a few times you will become aware that the main force propelling the cane comes, not from the arm itself, but from the twisting of your body; that this force seems to "flow"

Starting the downswing. While the arms and hands are completing the wind-up, the hips begin to shift toward the left.

Unwinding. As in the wind-up, the arms and hands move in response to the body action.

The moment of impact. The speed of the clubhead developed in the whirling motion assures plenty of power and accuracy in hitting.

from your lower back as you unwind, being transmitted through the muscles around your left shoulder, through your arm and hand to the weapon.

You can also see that this is a remarkably *free* movement; that your body performs it almost automatically, without strain, stress, or effort.

I shall let you in on a little secret. The motion just tested is, in many essential particulars, the identical motion by which power—maximum force and maximum leverage—is obtained in the correct swing. In no other way can it be obtained—so long as the requirements of a golf stroke remain what they are. Only by winding up the body

to its fullest, then releasing the accumulated force in an expanding motion like the uncoiling of a spring can a golf club be swung easily, naturally, accurately, and with maximum power.

I have already made the statement that golf is, in a way, a left-handed game for a right-handed player and a right-handed game for the left-handed player. This is rather an unfortunate way of stating the case, for the statement is inexact. Golf is really a two-handed game; yet it is still a left-handed game for the right-handed man to the extent that muscles on the left side of the body dominate those of the right side in every swing that is correctly made. *In the*

The left arm and hand dominate the action until after the ball has been hit.

After impact. The momentum of the clubhead swings the hands, arms and body.

The head does not turn until well after the ball has been hit.

correct swing conscious use is made of only one small group of muscles on the right side of the body.

I have studied the anatomy of golf as thoroughly as any layman could. I know the names and understand the action of all the principal muscles, bones, joints, and tendons used in swinging the club. There is no point, though, in airing my knowledge of anatomy in presenting this general description of the swing. Suffice it to say that practical experiment on myself and others, analysis of the swings of leading players by the slow-motion camera, discussion with surgeons and anatomists, and many hours with textbooks on anatomy have plainly proved that only when the swing is made somewhat in the manner of the little exercise we just tried, with the muscles of the left side of the body actively dominant during the action, can there be a free, natural, uninterrupted, powerful motion. When the muscles of the right side of the body are permitted to enter actively into the swing, there is conflict, constriction; muscles that should be expanding and unleashing their strength contract and hinder the action. One side of the body is fighting the other. The result? You have only to compare the heavy-handed, muscle-bound lunges of the average player with the easy, "professional" swing of the expert to know.

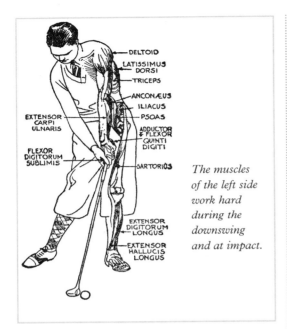

The muscles of the left side work hard during the downswing and at impact.

And so we can trace the force that propels the club as follows: It originates in the muscles of the lower back through body torsion such as tried just a little while ago. It is transmitted through those muscles around the *left shoulder* to the *left arm,* through this arm to the *left little finger,* and so through the shaft of the club to the clubhead. In addition, the hinge-like action of the *left* wrist helps to increase the power and speed of the clubhead. When properly carried out, each movement progresses into and harmonizes with the one following so that the swing truly is made one full, smooth, flowing motion without mental or physical interruption. Furthermore, as I believe we were able to demonstrate by swinging the cane, the use of the muscles on the left side of the body is perfectly natural, even though generally unfamiliar to most golfers.

Probably I do not need to say that there are certain mental as well as physical components included in the formula for the correct swing. The mental and physical processes involved, though, complement each other so closely that both may be included in the "feel" of the action. Psychology, concentration, the will to win, or anything similar you care to name will not help you perform the swing correctly if you do not acquire the feel. For this reason, when I show you the swing in slow motion, I shall try to describe its most vital stages in terms of what you should sense when executing the proper positions and order of movement.

The only way in which you can properly sense what you are doing with the various parts of your body during the swing, keep yourself "oriented," in other words, is by holding your chin entirely independent of the action. You must point your chin at a spot just back of

Some years ago I worked out a definition of the proper swing, one which I have found it unnecessary to change in any way. It is this: One full, smooth flowing motion without mental or physical interruption.

the ball and keep it pointed there until well after the ball has been hit. *No matter what method of swinging a club you may use, you cannot make a successful shot unless you do this.*

Lest there be any confusion, let me state here that I am not talking about the well-known maxims, "Keep your head down," or "Keep your eye on the ball." I mean exactly what I said; that the chin must be pointed back of the ball and kept entirely independent of the rest of the action until after the ball has been hit. It is the most important item in the performance of the correct swing, and I shall have a lot to say about it as I go along.

For the time being it is enough to say that, once the positions and movements of the correct swing are learned, pointing the chin in the way I have described permits the main action of the swing to be performed automatically. The player need not consciously direct any of the movements of his body or the club. I know of no other successful method of bringing this about.

Many of the statements I am making in this brief sketch of the swing, and those that I shall make as I proceed to a complete analysis and definite instructions for making it, I know will be considered erratic by those who have expressed their own opinions on the subject. However, the proof is simple, and, if at the end of my description the reader is still unconvinced, he may be sure that the fault lies in my exposition. I am endeavoring to make this outline as complete and as informative as I can. Consequently, I am including many details that the player need not think about once he has learned to make the swing properly. Indeed, once the player has caught the feel of the action, the only details he should be wholly conscious of are his starting position and the means of controlling the whirling motion of the club. And, as I have just said, the latter is taken care of automatically merely by the proper pointing of the chin.

> No one ever made a good golf shot by holding a statuesque pose at the outset while he contemplated the crime he was about to commit, or by pausing part way through his swing to wonder whether he was on the right track.

The method of playing which I advocate and which I am explaining in this book is basically sound. It is founded on nobody's personal opinions or idiosyncrasies but on the anatomical structure of the human body. Peculiarities of physique or temperament need be taken into account in successfully applying it no more than the length of your legs need be in walking.

FROM *A NEW WAY TO BETTER GOLF*
BY ALEX J. MORRISON

CHAPTER 28

ANDREW MULLIN

TAKE IT FROM THE TOP

"Think of the hours wasted by dedicated golfers trying to perfect a backswing that is really non-essential. It's frightening."

Andrew Mullin was sixteen years old, working at a driving range in Columbus, Georgia, when two gentlemen appeared on the tee.

"Anyone here give lessons?" one of them asked. "I'm a baseball player and I need some help." This was 1952, but the man bore a striking resemblance to a young Babe Ruth, and when he tossed up a practice ball and swatted it high and deep down the range with his driver, that resemblance only grew.

"I can help you, sir," said the enterprising young Mullin. (Although he was a fine high school player, he had never given a lesson in his life.) He spent a few moments with the stranger, correcting his grip and showing him how to make a proper swing. Then the man teed one up. On his first swing, he hit a soaring drive, string straight and nearly 300 yards.

"Wow," he said, turning to Mullin, "you're a great teacher!"

As the two men left, Mullin asked a coworker, "What's that guy's name?"

"Oh, that's Gay Brewer," was the reply. The same Gay Brewer who would go on to win the 1967 Masters and a dozen other PGA Tour titles. A college player at the time, he'd come to Columbus for the Southern Amateur.

Mullin didn't mind being hoodwinked. "I felt pretty good about my first lesson," he said, "but I'll never forget that baseball swing he made." It had planted a seed in his mind, a seed that would germinate when he moved to his second job—as a tennis pro.

When in 1956 the Columbus Country Club built a set of tennis courts, they hired tennis teacher Victor Ponce and Mullin became his assistant.

"'Get the racket back,' was Victor's mantra," recalled Mullin. "Over and over, he'd say 'get the racket back—I don't care how you do it, just get it back there so you're ready. Remember, the only stroke in tennis that counts is the forward stroke.' "

Now something had clicked—in tennis, it seemed, just as in baseball, there was no need for a backswing. You got yourself into a ready position, and swung at the ball from there.

Why, thought Mullin, couldn't the same apply to golf? At Georgia Tech, where he captained the golf team, he asked his engineering professors to weigh in. "They all told me the same thing," he said. "Motion in one direction cannot increase motion in the opposite direction. The backswing adds nothing to the power of a golf shot."

And so when Andrew Mullin began to teach golf, he chose the path not taken—he taught a golf swing without a backswing. At his Golf Fore Driving Range in Columbus he gave literally thousands of lessons—at first to youngsters and new golfers, then, as his results attracted notice, to players of all sizes and abilities. Word of Mullin's heterodoxy spread northward and in 1974, it reached the New York offices of *GOLF Magazine*. Desmond Tolhurst, the magazine's Senior Editor for Instruction, was dispatched to check Mullin out. Tolhurst, a tweed-jacketed Englishman, graduate of Cambridge and member of Royal St. Georges, had been with the magazine for two decades and had seen it all—but he'd never seen anything like Andrew Mullin.

"It was incredible, the results he was getting from students hitting essentially from a baseball player's stance," said Tolhurst, "and it all seemed so logical—eliminate the backswing

and you eliminate all that movement, all those bad takeaways, reverse pivots, and early hits. Over the two days I was there, I became convinced that this is the swing those shepherds on the links of Scotland should have had the sense to use 500 years ago. It would have made the game so much easier for the rest of us!"

THE SECRET:

Eliminate your backswing. Set up to the ball in a top-of-swing position, then pull down with your left side.

GOLF Magazine ran Andrew Mullin's bylined instruction story on the cover of its May 1975 issue. It generated more attention and publicity than the magazine had ever seen. For several months, Mullin's no-backswing swing became topic number one, from clubhouse grill rooms to the practice tees of the PGA Tour, where Johnny Miller, the game's hottest player at the time, was among those to verbally endorse the idea.

Thirty years later, Mullin still has people come up and ask him about that article. But his method never took hold. "It demands not only hard work but bravery," he says. "You need courage to walk out there and be the only golfer in town playing without a backswing. But I'm convinced that if just one of my young kids had somehow risen to national prominence—attracted attention and shown the world that great golf can be played by starting at the top—well, that might have opened the floodgates." The full text of his article follows.

MULLIN'S SECRET

The real importance of swinging without a backswing for me is that now I can teach the pupil to feel for himself the power and the consistency of a left-hand pulling action in the downswing without first having to perfect a backswing.

I first became aware of the vital importance of this pulling action of the left side a few years ago when I studied the teachings of Bill Strausbaugh and Jim Flick, who were then advocating what was called the "Square-to-Square" method. I was completely sold on their theory of the golf swing—that the top golfers pulled from the left side in the downswing, resulting in a late release, as opposed to the action of the majority of golfers, who throw with the right hand, resulting in too early a release. However, when I tried to teach their method, my problems multiplied.

It was too difficult for the average golfer to do, particularly the "curling under" action of the left hand early in the backswing to put the back of the left hand in line with the left forearm. This sets the blade in a square position. I was losing pupils because I couldn't get them to experience it.

The majority of golfers are right-handed and, as a result, their swings are dominated by the right side. A beginning golfer can feel his right-hand power and deliver a good lick with it. But he can't deliver a good lick with his left side. He therefore could never experience the power of the left-side pulling action in the downswing because of the right-hand takeover on the backswing. And he never got the club into the correct position at the top, except by accident.

Thus, defining the problem as an improper backswing and a faulty setup at the top, the only logical solution was to eliminate the backswing. In this way, you are assured of setting the club in the correct position *before* you start down.

Another point favoring the elimination of the backswing is that the most difficult movement for any athlete, of whatever degree of skill, is to change his motion from backward to forward. This change takes perfect timing, and any error in timing is disastrous. Having only a forward swing simplifies the action, making it similar to baseball batting and boxing actions.

> **The most difficult movement for any athlete, of whatever degree of skill, is to change his motion from backward to forward.**

Fishing is another sport besides golf that tries to incorporate a backward and forward motion. I'm referring to casting a rod. Anyone who has tried knows what causes a backlash. In my opinion, you can cast better with only a forward motion.

Having the left wrist in the correct position at the top is also important in that, if it is correct at the top, then it will be correct at the bottom of the swing, at impact.

All great golfers get their left wrist more or less in advance of the ball at impact. Yet they all use different methods to achieve this. Ben Hogan, for example, opened the blade slightly on the backswing, then turned his left hand counterclockwise in the downswing. Arnold Palmer takes the club back drastically to the inside, which sets his club in a closed position and his left wrist in a convex position at the top. (Lee Trevino incidentally has a similar action.) Palmer

gets his left wrist in the desired position at the top and does not have to manipulate the club coming down.

Still others "curl under" in the takeaway, or, like Johnny Miller, preset the club with an early wrist break. All these complications can be avoided by eliminating the backswing and by setting the left wrist in the correct position at the top.

When I began teaching what I call "The Swing of the Future," i.e., a forward motion from the top only, I found that I could get my pupils to feel the left-side pull very quickly. How much the pupil wants to develop his left arm to acquire the same distance and consistency depends on the pupil. You see, the right arm is more developed, more coordinated and stronger than the left arm. So it is necessary to make the left hand more dominant, more coordinated, and stronger so it will take over from the right. The only way I know to do this is to hit a lot of balls with the pulling motion of the left arm.

> **Fishing is another sport besides golf that tries to incorporate a backward and forward motion—the casting of the rod. In my opinion, you can cast better with only a forward motion.**

The "Swing of the Future" also helps the pupil feel his errors in pulling. You readily feel the right-hand takeover because of so many missed shots. The natural reaction to starting from the top is to cast with the right hand, but, because you can feel it and see the bad shots it produces, I can now sell you on the left-side, pulling downswing. If you had ever experienced the tremendous power with the least amount of effort that you get, you would tell me, like all my students tell me, "I can't believe it. I didn't know I had this kind of power in me."

About the most rapid way of convincing yourself that the "Swing of the Future" is valid is to try hitting some putts without a backswing. Just take the putter back, set the left wrist in front of the ball, and then lead through the ball with the back of the left hand. I think you will readily see how most missed putts are caused by a faulty backswing.

If I had you here for a lesson, I would then take you out on the practice tee. You would start off on the "Swing of the Future" with a 7-iron so that you could get the feel of the new action easily. Next, I would have you change clubs back and forth. I would

Top golfers pull with the left side, resulting in a late release of the hands in the downswing.

have you hit, say, a dozen shots with the 7-iron, then try about four shots with a 4-iron. Then back to the 7-iron for another dozen shots, then two or three shots with a 3-wood. I would keep returning you to the 7-iron so that you wouldn't lose the feeling.

I would have you go to your top-of-the-swing position and correct it, so that you had the back of the left wrist in line with the left forearm, a full shoulder turn, the club pointing at the target, a firm but not rigid left arm, the right elbow in to the side, your weight on the right side, a firm grip with the left hand, and a light grip with the right.

The exact position of the left wrist at the top is individual, depending on the golfer. Ideally, the left wrist should be slightly convex so that it will then be well ahead of the

Most golfers throw with the right hand and arm, resulting in too early a release of the hands.

ball at impact. However, I don't necessarily start out my pupils that way. I'll let them try several positions at the top, from convex to where the left wrist is in line with the left forearm. The position in which they have confidence is the one they should stay with. The extreme convex position of an Arnold Palmer is only possible for a very strong golfer. Most students settle for a square or only slightly convex position. Whatever the position, avoid a cupped or concave left wrist. This is the typical right-side-dominated position, which leads to an early release with the right hand and the club getting ahead of the hands at impact.

> Every so often a golfer comes to me and says he wants to shoot par or sub-par golf. If I think he has the necessary tenacity, I'll teach him the Swing of the Future.

There is a slight problem initially getting fully coiled—it is hard work. However, if anything has to "give" at the top, let it be the left heel. Raise it a little if you find it necessary.

Another problem is that golfers who have played for some years find it impossible initially to do without some backswing, even if it is only four or five inches. They find they have to give the club a "hitch," like a baseball batter. However, the desire to "hitch" the club can also be caused by the right hand taking over the swing. So, if you hitch it, make certain your left wrist remains straight and the left side stays in control. It's too easy to let the right hand put the left wrist into a cupped (concave) position, and that will defeat the purpose completely. However, you will find that. after a week or so of practice, you won't need to take a "hitch."

The overall key to executing the "Swing of the Future" is non-use of the right hand. To teach the left-side pulling action, I use various verbal keys, because how the correct action feels to the individual is personal. One pupil will respond to "pull with the left arm and hand," another to "pull with the left side," yet another to "hit it with the back of the left hand." Some feel the action starting in the legs; to them I'll say "drive with the knees." As long as the right move is made, how it feels to the individual doesn't really matter.

I tell all my pupils to have patience. You have to give up 20 yards of distance initially in order to gain 20 yards once you're proficient. And you're going to have bad rounds, at least to start with. You don't break a habit overnight. It's like smoking. Hitting with the right hand, which leads to an early release of the club, is a vice. You may break it on the practice tee, but initially you will revert to it under tension, when you're playing a round.

Largely because of the determination and practice that's required, I don't teach the "Swing of the Future" to every golfer who comes to me for a lesson. I have to decide whether to make him into a right-handed hitter or a left-handed puller. If the golfer is satisfied to shoot 85 to 90, without much practice, then I teach him to hit right-handed. He'll feel comfortable and get a lot more fun out of the game. But every so often a golfer comes to me and says he wants to shoot par or sub-par golf. If I think he has the necessary tenacity, I'll teach him the "Swing of the Future."

Actually, in my own teaching I've had the best success with high-school boys who have the drive to learn. I've kept several of the kids on the "Swing of the Future" for several weeks. But then they want to go out for their school golf team, and I know that I'll have to teach them a backswing. I know that they'll be laughed off the golf course if I send them out there without a backswing. I'm convinced that, in a few years, I won't have to teach these kids a backswing. Then they can spend all their practice time on a forward pull only. Think of the man hours wasted by dedicated golfers trying to perfect a backswing that is really non-essential. It's frightening.

However, even though I teach these kids the backswing, I encourage them to continue practice of the "Swing of the Future." It has considerable value in drilling the body in the correct top-of-the-swing position. They already are sold on the idea of pulling with the left side, so subsequently they concentrate on trying to find the "slot," as the pros on the Tour call the correct position at the top. Before, they weren't even conscious of the "slot."

> I tell all my pupils to have patience. You have to give up 20 yards in distance initially in order to gain 20 yards once you're proficient.

Summing up, in my opinion all it will take for the backswing to become as extinct as the dodo is just one "Johnny Miller" who uses no backswing. But I know that boy will have to have a lot of courage—it's tough to be first with a new idea.

FROM *GOLF MAGAZINE*, MAY 1975 ISSUE
BY ANDREW MULLIN

MULLIN'S SECRET

CHAPTER 29

NATURAL GOLF

THE METHOD
TO MOE'S MADNESS

*"With a scientifically simpler way to play,
we are aiming to become the game's newest revolution."*

Jack Kuykendall had a problem. He was forty-four years old, had aspirations to join the Senior PGA Tour—and his handicap was 12. But he reasoned that he had six years to get his game together, so in 1984 he quit his job as a laser physicist and threw himself into a ferocious regimen of lessons, practice, and play.

Two years later his handicap was 14. That's when he got mad. "There's got to be a better

way to hit a round object with a stick," he said. And so, with a scientist's controlled passion, he dissected the golf swing—tore it apart and put it back together again.

It was just forty-five days before he found a radical new way to strike the ball, a method that brought him remarkable results. On three consecutive days, Kuykendall, the 14 handicapper, shot scores lower than par— 4 under, 2 under, and 3 under. On the fourth day, he started a company that became known as Natural Golf.

In 1991 he was in California giving a Natural Golf demonstration, when one of his attendees, a Canadian teaching pro, said, "Hey, that looks just like Moe Norman's swing."

"Who the heck is Moe Norman?" asked Kuykendall.

Moe Norman was the Rain Man of golf. An eccentric and reclusive professional from

Ontario, Canada, Norman played extremely fast, wore mismatched outfits, said most things twice, and some days came to the course wearing as many as five wristwatches to be sure he had the correct time. More importantly, however, he was by general agreement the most astonishingly accurate ball striker the game has ever seen. He was the closest thing golf has ever seen to an "idiot savant."

Moe Norman stories abound—the day he hit three flagsticks in a row, the day he played fifty-four holes and in each eighteen-hole round scored a hole-in-one, the shortest with a 6-iron, the longest with a 3-wood. He held more than forty course records, three of them with scores of 59. One day he needed a birdie to break a course record. He'd never played the course and asked the professional accompanying him how to play the hole. When the pro said it was usually a driver and a 9-iron, Moe hit the 9-iron off the tee, struck a driver to within 10 feet, and sank the putt for a birdie.

Moe was a natural, totally self-taught, but somehow he'd adopted a method that was identical to the one Jack Kuykendall had developed through scientific trial and error— an abbreviated upper-body dominated move in which the arms and clubshaft flowed up and back on substantially the same plane.

When the two men met for the first time, it was a revelation for both of them. "All my life I've wondered why I was the best ball striker in golf," said Norman to Kuykendall, "and you are the first person who could explain it to me." Norman had found the man who could articulate his genius and Kuykendall had found the man who could lend credibility to his discovery. They became instant friends, Moe became the poster boy and spokesman for Natural Golf, and the two toured the country giving exhibitions that converted thousands of golfers.

Jack Kuykendall sold Natural Golf in 1995 and Moe Norman died in 2004, but the company and the concept live on. Today, the Chicago-based Natural Golf Corporation is a multi-media enterprise offering clinics, schools, books, videos, a magazine, a website, and a full line of Callaway-made equipment suited specifically to the Natural Golf method. Before he turned over the reins, Kuykendall wrote a book about his method. Although it has since been revised by Peter Fox and Ed Woronicz, for Natural Golf's disciples—currently 200,000 and growing—it remains the bible. The following excerpt covers the four key ingredients of the method.

> ## THE SECRET:
>
> Grip the club in your palms, line up the shaft with your forearm, widen your stance, and shorten your backswing.

THE SECRET OF NATURAL GOLF

Golf is a difficult game to play. Natural Golf simplifies it. The Natural Golf Swing System has fewer moving parts and angles than conventional golf.

Natural Golf's simplicity regularly produces strong, straight shots.

Natural Golf teaches its method in four simple fundamentals. They are:

Natural Palm Grip
Single plane setup
Wide stance
Face the ball at impact

How to Hold the Club

It is Natural Golf's first fundamental—the Natural Palm Grip—that makes playing golf so much easier for the Natural Golfer.

One note: The Natural Palm Grip works best with clubs with handles that are thicker than normal and non-tapered. When a Natural Golfer plays with conventional, narrow, tapered handles, he may feel as if the clubhead is twisting off square at contact. Inadvertently, he may also have a tendency to allow the handle to go back to being held in the fingers rather than keeping it in the palm.

> **The Natural Golf Palm Grip works best with clubs with handles that are thicker than normal and non-tapered.**

TRAIL HAND

Here is how you hold the club in your trail hand for the Natural Palm Grip:

The second knuckle of the index finger is underneath the handle, which runs through the palm and across the heel pad nearest the wrist. The "V" formed by the thumb and index finger is generally in line with the trail forearm. The end of the handle is away from the trail forearm and points at the lead shoulder.

LEAD HAND AND HANDS TOGETHER

Here is how you hold the club in your lead hand:

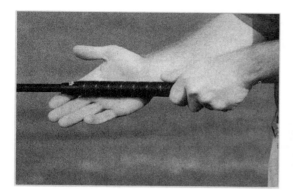

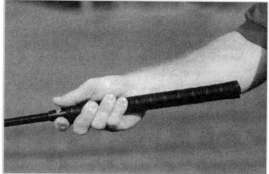

The second knuckle of the index finger is underneath the handle, which runs through the palm and across the part of the trail hand heel pad nearest the wrist (above).

The end of the handle is away from the trail forearm and points toward the lead shoulder. The trail hand thumb-forefinger "V" is in line with the trail forearm (left).

How the Natural Golfer sees his trail-hand grip (below).

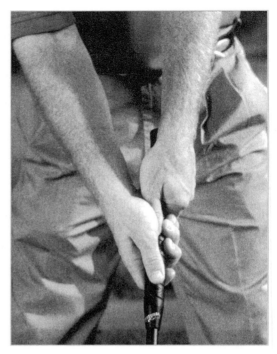

The lead thumb is on top of the handle and generally in line with the shaft of the club.

The full Natural Palm Grip

The second knuckle of the lead hand index finger is underneath the handle, which is held more in the fingers than in the palm hold of the trail hand. The handle is under—not on— the heel pad of the lead hand.

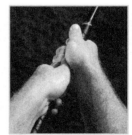

How the Natural Golfer sees his grip.

The second knuckle of the index finger is underneath the handle, which, in the lead hand, is held more in the fingers than in the palm hold of the trail hand. The golf club handle is under the heel pad—not on the heel pad—of the lead hand.

Together, the trail and lead hands on the club form the Natural Palm Grip.

A couple of notes of caution: First, the Natural Palm Grip is the way to hold a golf club. Do not mistake it for the way a baseball player holds a bat in the palms. Second, when you squeeze the handle of the club too tightly, you create muscle tension in the arms and shoulders. That tension interferes with well-coordinated golf swings. Natural Golf discourages you from gripping too tightly.

STRAIGHT-LINE RELATIONSHIP

In some ways, the Natural Palm Grip resembles its conventional counterparts, the different finger grips. The dramatic difference is hard to see from a face-on perspective, but when viewed from the perspective of looking down the target line, the Natural Golf Single-Plane Setup is easily differentiated from the two-plane conventional setup.

To repeat: The on-plane relationship between the handle of the golf club and the trail arm is the absolute foundation of the Natural Golf Swing System. It allows the golfer to start in the same position that he will end up in at impact, with fewer moving parts which means a more consistent repeatable swing.

The Straight-Line relationship between the handle and forearm is the foundation of the Natural Golf Swing System and produces Natural Golf's Square Tracking clubface swing path.

Bell ringers, tug-of-war contestants, fencers, painters, carpenters, javelin throwers, fishermen, marksmen, lecturers, lacrosse players, and lumberjacks all use the "tools of their trade" in the way a Natural Golfer holds a golf club.

The feet are slightly more narrow than the torso for short clubs, like wedges.

The Straight-Line Setup, made possible by the Natural Palm Grip, enables Natural Golf's Square Tracking of the clubface to occur.

The two-plane setup of conventional finger grips makes Square Tracking extremely difficult, if not impossible.

The Straight-Line grasping of the golf club's grip inspired Natural Golf's name.

Bell ringers, tug-of-war contestants, fencers, painters, carpenters, javelin throwers, fishermen, marksmen, lecturers, lacrosse players, and lumberjacks, to name a few, all quite naturally use the "tools of their trade" in the efficient Straight-Line way a Natural Golfer holds a golf club.

How to Set Up to the Ball: Feet

The Natural Golf stance is wide to encourage stability, balance, and reduced hip rotation. The insides of the feet are placed about torso-width apart when using a 5-iron.

They should be slightly farther apart for longer clubs and slightly closer together for shorter clubs. Your height, weight, and body proportions may influence slight stance adjustments from these guidelines. Taller, longer-legged Natural Golfers tend to have wider stances than Natural Golfers of average or shorter statures.

Natural Golf's Straight-Line Motion gives you confidence that you'll strike the ball squarely. As a result, your hands and arms tend to move through the hitting area strongly. The better balance of the wider

The insides of the feet are about as wide as the torso for a 5-iron.

The feet are slightly wider than the torso for long clubs like drivers.

stance provides stability for that strong striking motion.

As a Natural Golfer, you have the option of placing the feet so that the toes point either directly at the target line or are turned slightly off of it.

Posture

Once you get the feet placed properly, turn your attention to body posture. Tilt your upper torso and spine at an angle away from the target that encourages Natural Golf's

Straight-Line arm extension. This extension at address is key in allowing the club, arms, and body to return to this same position at impact.

The distance you stand from the ball will vary. It is affected by the length of the club. The shorter the club is, the closer you will be to the ball and the more upright the angle will be between the arms and the body.

Distribute your weight evenly between the heels and balls of the feet. Balance your weight evenly between your left foot and

THE SECRET OF NATURAL GOLF

right foot. Many successful Natural Golfers keep their "flat feet" very quiet and in full contact with the ground through the club's impact with the ball.

Hands, Clubhead, and Ball

How you position the hands in the Natural Golf Straight-Line Setup and how that affects the clubhead's relationship to the ball are unique to Natural Golf.

First, in the Natural Golf Swing System, you position the clubhead during setup so that the clubhead is generally body center. Why? The Natural Golf clubhead position

allows you to start the backswing on the proper path and ensures that the clubhead is behind the bottom of the swing's arc, as it should be.

With the Natural Palm Grip, this position is automatic because you point the handle of the club toward the lead shoulder. That creates another Natural Golf Straight Line extending from the clubhead, along the shaft, through the hands, up the lead arm toward the lead shoulder.

Successful Natural Golfers, including Moe Norman, achieve this position while assuming the Natural Palm Grip, which puts the handle of the golf club away from the

DRIVER

T H E   S E C R E T   O F   N A T U R A L   G O L F

In the Straight-Line Setup, only ball position and clubhead position behind the ball change from wedge to 5-iron to driver. For all clubs, the clubhead is at body center and there is a Straight-Line relationship between the clubhead and the lead shoulder.

For wedges and short irons, play the ball across from your body center. For the driver, fairway woods, and long irons, play the ball across from your lead hip or shoulder. For other clubs, play the ball between those ball position guidelines.

Now you know three of Natural Golf's four fundamentals:

1. The Natural Palm Grip
2. Natural Golf's Single-Plane relationship between the arms and shaft of the club
3. Natural Golf's slightly wider and more stable stance

You're almost Naturalized.

How to Move as You Swing

The fourth Natural Golf fundamental is the only one that relates to movement. We call it facing the ball at impact.

That is a significant departure from conventional golf.

Facing the ball at impact promotes Natural Golf's Square Tracking path of the clubface through the impact area. Square Tracking requires less leg, hip, torso, and arm rotation than conventional golf.

trail forearm with a very slight forward movement of the trail wrist.

Once again, the length of the shaft of the club affects the setup. With the end of the handle pointing toward the lead shoulder, the clubhead of a driver will set farther away from the ball than the clubhead of a wedge, and the lengths of the shafts of the other clubs will set their clubheads between those extremes.

Also affecting the distance between the ball and the clubhead is the position of the ball itself in relation to the golfer's body. In Natural Golf, you position the ball in relation to your body rather than your feet.

When you face the ball at impact using a Natural Golf swing, your body transfers energy to the ball in the direction you want the ball to fly. This contributes to a strong, straight Natural Golf ball flight.

The following pages provide you with a visual of the Natural Golf swing from two different "models." The first is a computer-generated model displaying ideal single-plane club mechanics. The second model is Moe Norman, the first Natural Golfer. While it is fun to study both sets of photos, it is important to note that you will develop your own unique Natural Golf swing, based on such variables as body shape, strength, flexibility, and balance.

BACKSWING

The Natural Golf full-swing movements that precede and follow the face-the-ball-at-impact position are economical, too.

Begin the backswing by extending the lead arm trailward as the trail arm folds. Keep your hands relaxed so they can "load energy" for the hitting action—by extending or cocking—without conscious effort. The hands don't move past shoulder height at the top of the Natural Golf backswing, this

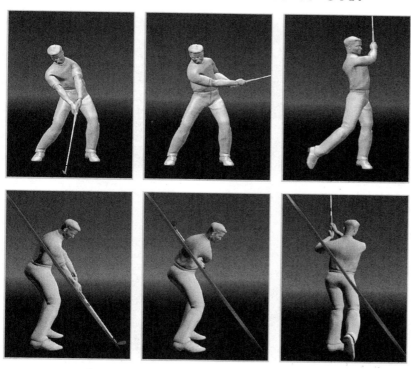

A computer-generated look at the Natural Golf swing. Notice how the club stays on a perfect single plane until well into the finish.

Check your position at the top of your backswing. The lead arm should not bend noticeably at the elbow and the lead shoulder should be under the chin.

FORWARD SWING

The forward swing is simply the arms moving the club toward the ball. It is achieved through a combination of lead arm acceleration and trail arm extension. Many successful Natural Golfers, including Moe Norman, accomplish this with a golf feeling that the lead arm is initiating the action, that the lead arm is pulling the trail hand and arm into the proper position in front of the trail hip.

"compact" backswing position will afford you better control while still creating a powerful swing.

The Natural Golf top-of-the-swing hitting position may be a familiar arm-hand position for you. The trail hand position resembles the "top-of-the-swing" position of activities such as hammering, throwing, and hitchhiking.

In Natural Golf, the lead and trail shoulders operate independently. The lead turns approximately 90 degrees from its starting position, while the trail shoulder only turns about 45 degrees.

Whether you accomplish this move with a "feeling" from the lead side or with a motion that originates from the trail side, it is important that the arms get in front of the trail hip prior to any substantial movement of that hip. It's what Natural Golfers call "independent arms" or a free arm swing.

Moe Norman demonstrates the swing that made him the most accurate ball striker the game has ever seen.

This arm freedom allows the golfer to face the ball at impact vs the conventional golfer who must twist and contort their bodies in an attempt to square the clubface.

IMPACT

During the forward swing, the weight of the clubhead will encourage a "loading" of energy in your trail hand. That loading creates an even greater angle at the trail wrist. Retain the angle until it straightens through the impact area. Your folded trail arm simply straightens through the impact area.

The release of the trail wrist angle during the instant of impact occurs naturally due to the free-swinging motion of the arms and clubhead, any conscious effort by you to affect the timing of that trail hand release will usually result in a poor shot.

The Natural Golf stance is wide to encourage stability, balance, and reduced hip rotation.

Those successful Natural Golfers who say they feel they are consciously pulling with the lead arm likely inhibit the brain's ability to consciously interfere with the natural release of the stored energy in the trail hand and arm.

During impact your hips stabilize on the desired square-to-the-ball flight line.

The hips are close to parallel to the desired line, as your weight shifts forward along it. The weight shift is coordinated with the momentum you've created by swinging your arms and club. Your head, at impact, is over the trail knee.

Having your trail heel remain on the ground allows your hips to stay nearly square until the ball has left the club and is well on its way toward its target. The way your trail heel remains in contact with the ground at impact is a distinct Natural Golf trait. It is virtually impossible for you to keep the trail heel in contact with the ground if your hips and shoulders are spinning in an attempt to square the clubface.

FINISH

Once the ball has left the clubface, the Natural Golf shot is technically over. As that occurs, you should find that both your arms are fully extended. The clubhead in a Natural Golf swing usually will extend farther along the target line than in a conventional swing.

An instant later, the lead arm folds, allowing the tension created by the momentum of your swing to release. The sensation is that the swinging motion of the club is pulling you into your finish. Following the swinging club to the finish, your arms and hips rotate, your weight transfers to the lead foot, pulling the trail foot off the ground as your torso turns toward the target and a balanced finish.

That's it. Those are the four fundamentals.

FROM *NATURAL GOLF* BY PETER FOX AND ED WORONICZ

BYRON NELSON

THE MAN OF STEEL

"All I was trying to do was find a better way to swing so I could make a living at the game. I found a way and as a result I've been credited by most experts with developing the modern way to play golf. But I sure wasn't thinking about that at the time."

Most casual golf fans recognize the name Byron Nelson, and closer students of the game know he holds a couple of records that will never be broken, namely the two marks he set in 1945: eleven consecutive victories and eighteen wins in a single season.

No one has ever played golf better than Nelson did that year, and few if any players have struck the ball with the purity and consistency Lord Byron exhibited throughout his career. Bobby Jones once said, "At my best, I never came close to the golf Nelson shoots."

A native of Fort Worth, Texas, Nelson was a contemporary of Ben Hogan. Indeed the two came out of the same caddie pen at the Glen Garden Country Club, where one year they tied for the caddie championship before Nelson won in a nine-hole playoff, 39 to Hogan's 40.

Nelson started playing the game in 1925, coincidentally the same year that the steel golf clubshaft was approved as legal for play by the United States Golf Association. For it was Nelson, as cerebral a golfer as he was naturally talented, who became the first player to adjust successfully from wood to metal by developing a different sort of golf swing.

Like most good golfers of the time, Nelson had what was called a caddie swing— a flat-planed, flat-footed, wristy backswing and an equally wristy flick through the ball. This was the method that had been used for centuries on the original links courses of

Great Britain, and had been brought across the Atlantic by the legions of young Scots who'd sought their fortunes as teaching professionals at American clubs. The caddie swing had evolved for two reasons: number one, it produced a low, driving shot that fit the windblown, fast running turf of the old links; and number two, it was the most effective way to wield hickory-shafted clubs.

"They had a lot of torque, or twist, in them," said Nelson, "so you had to roll the clubface open on the backswing and then roll it closed coming through the shot. If you didn't, the force of your swing would leave the face open when you struck the ball."

When Nelson got his first steel shafts—in his wooden-headed clubs only—he hooked them violently. "I could never figure out why," he said. "Then, about 1930, I got my first set of steel-shafted irons, and I began hooking with them as badly as I had my woods." At length, he realized the hooks came from the fact that he had continued to use his hand action to open and close the clubface, and that action was no longer needed. There was much less torque with steel shafts.

And so Byron Nelson came up with a new way to hit the golf ball: less hand action, more leg action, and a swing that kept the clubface square to the target for a much longer time.

In 1932, he turned pro at age twenty and finished third in his first event. There wasn't much money to be made on the Tour those days, so Nelson became a club professional, first in Texas and then in New Jersey, where in 1936 he won the prestigious Metropolitan Open. After that he was on his way. The next season Byron Nelson won The Masters and three other tournaments. Forty-eight more victories would follow.

It was not until 1976, however, that Nelson shared his thinking with the rest of the world, in *Shape Your Swing the Modern Way*, written in collaboration with *Golf Digest* Technical Editor Larry Dennis. Strangely—perhaps because Nelson's heyday was by that time well past—the book drew little attention, but ten years later it was re-released, with a foreword by Herbert Warren Wind, who called it "one of the best instruction books ever written." It is a slender volume, just over one hundred pages, but it brims with Nelson's vivid word pictures of the golf swing. The eras of Nicklaus and now Woods—with attendant advancements in equipment—have brought further refinements to the way a golf ball should be struck, but in truth they are only refinements. The big change came from Byron Nelson.

THE SECRET:

Make an an upright move into the backswing, use plenty of foot and leg action on the downswing, and keep the clubhead moving along the target line as long as possible.

NELSON'S SECRET

Posture: Be Balanced and Comfortable

Without proper posture, you have little chance of making a good swing. The proper posture puts you in good balance, with the weight evenly distributed and the knees flexed just enough to allow free footwork and leg action.

Your feet should be about shoulder-width apart at the inside of the heels for a driver shot, and you should be bent forward slightly from the hips. Your lower back should be straight and your arms should hang freely rather than reaching for the ball or crowding in too close to it. The left arm should be comfortably extended, the right arm and side relaxed. This places the left side in a slightly higher, leading position. The ball should be positioned in the center of the clubface and played just inside the left heel for iron shots. For drives, it should be placed off the instep or left toe.

Proper posture means good balance, with weight equally distributed and knees flexed slightly to allow free footwork and leg action. The feet are shoulder-width apart at the inside of the heels for a driver shot; the left arm is comfortably extended, the right arm and side are relaxed.

G. Ravielli

To reach the top of the backswing, turn the shoulders and swing the arms as far as possible without loosening the grip. Note that the wrists cock gradually until, at the top, they are set in the proper position.

The downswing is a chain reaction in which the left side pulls the left hand, arm, and clubhead down through the shot. But the feeling should be that the entire left side— foot, leg, hip, shoulder, and left arm—starts down together as a unit.

Starting the Swing: Take the Club Away with the Left Side

Although the swing actually starts when you take your first step in addressing the ball, the crucial moment comes just before the take-away on the backswing. It is here that you must make a vital movement called the *waggle*. The main thing to remember is that the waggle is just a little bitty swing that follows along the same path—for maybe a foot or so—that your full swing will travel. It's done mostly with the hands and arms and partly with your feet. You shouldn't be picking your feet up and moving them around unless you're out of position. But once you're properly lined up, you should still move around on your feet a little—almost within your shoes. The waggle sets the tempo for the whole swing, so if you're ever fidgety and jerky with this movement, it's going to be difficult for you to make a smooth swing.

As you complete your waggle and bring the club back to the ball, move smoothly into a *forward press,* which is just a slight movement of the weight to your left. Use your legs, being careful not to move your shoulders and the rest of your body too much. This will throw your clubface out of alignment. The forward press should simply be a slight transfer of weight to the left and then back to the right—a little rocking motion that gets your swing started.

Now take the club smoothly away from the ball on a straight line. How far back you take it depends on your type of swing. I once heard Arnold Palmer say that if he got started right during the first 14 inches of his swing he never had to think about anything else during the rest of it. That may be a slight exaggeration, particularly for a player who has less ability than Arnold, but it illustrates the importance good players place on the takeaway.

I believe that your takeaway should be in one piece. You should feel that you are starting the club back with your whole left side moving together with your left hand and arm. When I was playing my best, I definitely began my takeaway with my left side.

The Backswing: Wind Up Fully but Don't Overswing

The most important thing I can tell you about your backswing is: *Don't overswing.* It is absolute nonsense to think that a longer backswing will give you longer shots. Often just the reverse is true. The goal of the backswing is simply to wind up fully and put yourself and the club in position to strike the ball as squarely and forcefully as possible.

There is no standard backswing length that applies to everyone, because some players are more supple than others and can turn their bodies without moving off the ball. When I was younger, I could get my hands nice and high, and still not move off the ball. Now my swing arc is a foot and a half shorter.

To reach the top of your backswing, simply turn your shoulders and swing your arms back as far as you can. The length of your backswing depends on how fully you can turn your shoulders and how far you can swing your arms *without* doing any of these things: (1) loosening your grip; (2) moving your head; (3) relaxing and bending your left arm; (4) overcocking or cupping your wrists; (5) going up too far on your left toe. If you swing back as fully as you can without committing any of these errors, you will achieve the normal length of your backswing. These are checkpoints to be used in practice.

Here are some other *must-do's* in the successful backswing formula: Keep the head reasonably still and in position. Keep both hands firmly on the club. Keep the left arm straight—not rigid, but firm and straight. Keep the balance on both feet. Allow the legs to move, but have enough tautness in them to keep them from moving too far.

The wrists cock gradually during the backswing until, at the top, they are set in the proper position. It's important not to break your wrists too soon, or to drag the club back too far along the ground. Some players start too quickly with their hands and arms and leave their bodies behind. Others drag the clubhead, letting it lag a bit, because they're starting with their bodies.

When you're at the top of the swing, the club should be set at whatever stopping position is natural for you. Someone watching your swing should be unable to detect any particular point where your wrists start to cock. Those who do break their wrists too fast and pick the club up at the start tend to stop turning their shoulders. And those who go too far before the break either don't break at all or break too suddenly—causing a whiplash or bounce at the top.

The Downswing: Start Everything Down Together

I think of the downswing as a kind of chain reaction. The first link in the chain is the left side. It moves into and through the ball, pulling the hands down, into and through. The hands, in turn, pull the clubhead down, into and through the ball. The feeling should be that the entire left side—foot, leg, hip, shoulder, and arm—starts down together, as a unit. Any attempt to start either the legs or the arms first will result in mistiming that can ruin the swing.

The key to starting the downswing properly is the left knee. During the backswing it moves laterally to the right. Your downswing should begin with this knee, still flexed, returning laterally to the left. This movement will anchor your left heel and cause your legs and lower body to slide to your left, establishing that pulling pattern with your whole left-side arm-hand unit.

As the hips move to the left, the right knee moves toward the ball, allowing the right shoulder to come down and "under" properly. Your weight is moving from the inside of your right heel to the outside of your left heel, where it will be at the finish of your swing. Your left hand is still firmly in control of the club as your left side moves past the ball; your head remains steady in back of the ball; your body is beginning to bow into a reverse-C shape.

After the initial lateral movement, the left leg and hip start to turn out of the way—enough to allow the arms and hands to swing through on the intended target line. The lower left side stays down and through the shot, never coming up. The term "down and through" means that in the impact area the club is still moving on a slightly downward arc. If you are using an iron, strike the ball first and immediately afterward begin to take a divot. If you keep the left side leading and in control in the impact area, you will have no trouble staying down to the shot.

During the swing, I always try to imagine the back of my left hand, left arm, and the face of the club as being one piece, like a ramrod. That way I feel I'm not getting the face opened or closed. I just take this whole unit back and return it squarely to the ball. I might push the ball sometimes or maybe pull it slightly, but there is very little curvature of the ball in the air.

The finish of your swing is just a reflection of what you've done before. I will guarantee a nice, high, well-balanced finish if you have: (1) a firm grip; (2) a smooth, rhythmic swing; (3) a package backswing with everything moving as a unit; and (4) a chain-reaction downswing with the left side leading the hands and clubhead down, into, and through the ball.

FROM *SHAPE YOUR SWING THE MODERN WAY* BY BYRON NELSON

NELSON'S SECRET

JOE NORWOOD

OUT OF THE CLOSET

"If you have a golf swing,
you can play with hockey sticks."

During the summer of 1913, the world's best golfer, Englishman Harry Vardon, did a barnstorming tour of the United States, preparatory to what would be his epic battle (and upset loss to young Francis Ouimet) in the U.S. Open in Boston. One of Vardon's whistle stops was New York City where, at the famed Wanamaker department store, one of the young clerks made a golf swing that caught the master's eye.

The boy was just fifteen years old but he displayed a facility and fluidity of movement that so impressed Vardon that he invited the boy on the spot to become a golf professional and help spread the Vardon method. Thus began the sixty-five-year teaching career of Joe Norwood.

It was a career that would take him from New York to Massachusetts to Texas and ultimately to California and the Los Angeles Country Club, where he was the head professional for a quarter century. Norwood's star pupils included millionaires Howard Hughes and Jack Warner, actors Efrem Zimbalist, Jr., and Ruby Keeler, L.A. Dodgers Steve Garvey and Willie Davis, a long string of Tour pros from Harry Cooper to Ken Venturi,

> **THE SECRET:**
>
> Grip a golf ball between your thumb and forefinger, and do multiple practice takeaways to ingrain the proper backswing.

LPGA greats Babe Zaharias and Patty Berg, and even former President Gerald Ford who, it is alleged, learned at least briefly to hit tee shots without hitting spectators.

Norwood may have begun by preaching the Vardon gospel, and he surely absorbed a great deal from observing the likes of Vardon, Ouimet, Walter Hagen, Walter Travis, and other leading players of the time. But by the early 1920s he'd developed his own "blueprint for the golf swing," a unique meld of mechanics, psychiatry, and chiropractic. His conviction was that there were two ways to strike a golf ball—by pulling or pushing—and pushing was the only sane option. Essentially, he rejected the idea of a twisting, rotating torso and favored instead a true swinging action, controlled by the hands and arms.

At the center of Norwood's teaching, however, was the notion that golf could be

Joe Norwood with one of his coauthors, Marilynn Smith

learned in the closet—literally. The swing, he said, was a movement based on four basic positions, and anyone could instill those four positions in his or her muscle memory by following a daily five-minute regimen of indoor exercises. Golf-o-metrics, he called them.

In 1978 *Joe Norwood's Golf-O-Metrics* appeared under the triple byline of Norwood, LPGA Hall of Famer Marilynn Smith, and Stanley Blicker. Ms. Smith's role seems to have been simply as a model for a few of the book's illustrations, while Mr. Blicker,

although billed on the dust jacket as a professional writer, did little to clarify or codify the eighty-year-old teacher's thoughts. The text, written in the third person, can be tough going, its instructional nuggets often obscured in the miasma of "Joe believes" philosophizing. This is a book that must be read slowly, carefully, and more than once, to divine its full value. But Norwood and Blicker do reach clarity on the four key positions and the exercises necessary to ingrain them, the first and most important of which follows.

NORWOOD'S SECRET

Position One is the backswing that ends when the right forearm reaches a horizontal position. Anything higher than the parallel, or horizontal, is a lift, and there is no centrifugal force in a lift.

A simple way of making the backswing to Position One is to place the hands palm to palm and then lace the fingers together. Extend the left arm out of the shoulder and take the right forearm to a horizontal position that is about waist high. At no time does the forearm go beyond the horizontal position on the backswing. The elbow travels in a flat perimeter, and the flatter the elbow travels, the more the right shoulder gets into the swing, building up centrifugal force.

To practice Position One, take a golf ball and place the thumb and forefinger on it, set the wrist down, and take it back, making the elbow circle your rib cage. There is no limit as to how many times a day you can or should practice this exercise. The more you do it, the more supple your elbow will become. The more you perform this move, the easier it will be to make your thumb become your boss. It is impossible to make the circle around the rib cage too tight with the elbow, and the more you force the elbow around with the thumb and forefinger the more centrifugal force you will develop in the clubhead. The thumb chases the index finger, so this will give you the opportunity of squeezing the ball while going to Position One, thereby allowing you to practice two golf-o-metrics at the same time.

There are many ways to start the backswing, and Joe knows them all. The toe of the clubhead is the first thing that should start back, and the heel of the clubhead is the first thing that should start down. Straight back does not move the clubhead one iota. Watch it as it goes straight back; it is strictly a carry, then it goes into a lift, and by the time it is waist high, or higher, it hasn't gone into any part of an arc. Actually, it hasn't moved back in relation to the address position.

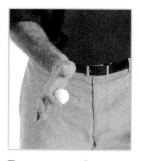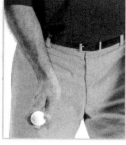

RIGHT-HAND CONTROL

Place the ball against the right forefinger. Then hook the forefinger against the straight line of the forefinger. Now place the right thumb by pushing downward against the ball. Practice for a perfect V position.

Joe's first move is 9 feet, and it goes into a half circle, developing pure centrifugal force, by contrast to the straight-back-and-lift action. Joe starts the backswing from a dead start. Those who need to waggle had better learn to waggle with the arms and not with the hands, since you will swing as you waggle. Learn to waggle with the arms and not with the hands, and learn to make a complete waggle by going to Position One; the forearm must be in a horizontal position—not partially there, but fully horizontal. The thumb and forefinger of the right hand will be in a vertical position. Most golfers will not crank the arm into the shoulder, and no benefits will be derived. The bad habit of lifting is hard to overcome.

One very important point to remember is that the thumb and forefinger must be put into Position One; it won't get there by itself.

The thumb and forefinger go back to get up, and not up to get back. Let the thumb chase the index finger; don't lift to get back.

The earmark of a Joe Norwood person is one who has a golf ball between the thumb and forefinger, squeezing and going to Position One, while in a courtroom, walking down the street, shopping in a supermarket, waiting for an elevator, *ad infinitum*. Practice, practice, practice.

Start each practice session with the following routine. Place both feet together, bend the knees, and have the knees and ankles touching. Now swing with the arms to and from Position One. Once you have developed a bit of rhythm from this stance, you will find that you will be able to fly the ball to about 90 percent of your potential. This will prove to you that a quiet body will enable you to make better and easier contact with the ball. It will also prove to your satisfaction that the gyrations of the legs and body won't add another 10 percent in distance to the shot. Once you realize how detrimental body movement and effort are in making a smooth swing, you will more readily develop tempo, rhythm, and control. This is how and where you will develop confidence. Be good to yourself, give yourself a chance to make a swing with fewer wavelengths: It will breed confidence only because you are getting to own your swing through control.

FROM *JOE NORWOOD'S GOLF-O-METRICS*

CHAPTER 32

JOHN NOVOSEL

A TIMELY DISCOVERY

"'No one ever swung a golf club too slowly,'
wrote the great Bobby Jones. Unfortunately, he was wrong."

Every once in a while, the gods of golf grant us dogged victims a "eureka," a moment of discovery by one of us that results in a breakthrough for all of us. Harry Vardon's overlapping grip, Ernest Jones's centrifugal force swing, and John Jacobs's ball-flight laws are examples as are the research-based findings of golf's patron scientist, Dave Pelz.

Golf's first twenty-first-century eureka occurred in the spring of 2000 when John Novosel discovered something he called tour tempo. Like Pelz, Novosel is neither a Tour player nor a teacher, just a golf-obsessed businessman with an inquisitive, inventive mind. A fine all-around athlete, he was a high school All-American football player and played center and linebacker for the Kansas State team. When two of his fraternity brothers introduced him to golf, he had no doubt he'd become a scratch player—but it didn't work out that way. "Just about everything I had learned about sports was refuted by golf," he said. "The more I practiced sometimes, the worse I got. I could hit it great on the range before a round and then play horribly. I could also do the reverse."

Novosel, like many beginning golfers, had read all the books and magazines, taken lessons, gone to golf camps—in short, tried everything—but none of it worked. Part of the problem was that so much of the advice was conflicting. One book would tell him to use his right side, another to use his left side, another to use his legs, another to use his arms, one to "hold the angle," another to "release the angle."

"The funny thing was that any of these ideas could work for a short period of time," he said. "But then I was searching again. It reminded me of the story about Bobby Jones—he was playing with a pro in New York and the pro asked Bobby what he thought about when he was swinging. Bobby's answer was 'whatever worked the last time.'"

That wasn't good enough for Novosel, and so he set out on his own to find a better way to play, a quest that turned him into an inventor of golf teaching devices. Today he owns four patents, including a swing training device called the XLR8R (pronounced "accelerator") that is endorsed by a number of top teachers and professionals.

One of those teachers is John Rhodes, a *GOLF Magazine* Top 100 Teacher from Fort Worth with a particular interest in the tempo of the swing. While with Novosel at the PGA Merchandise Show in Orlando in 2000, Rhodes talked of how he'd used a metronome to help his students time their swings correctly. Novosel gave the metronome a try and, like everything else, it did little to help him— but it did lead him in an important direction.

A few weeks later, while editing the videotape of an infomercial for his XLR8R, Novosel made the discovery of his life. He found—and later proved—that golf tempo is not an individual matter, as traditional instruction had held for decades, but is uni-versal and teachable. In other words, there is one ideal rhythm.

In fairness, Ernest Jones had suggested eighty years earlier that the ideal rhythm of the swing—from start to the top and back to impact—is a waltz-like *one*-two-three, *one*-two three, *one*-two-three, and that is what Novosel confirmed. But at the same time—and for the first time—he quantified precisely the cadence of that one-two-three and showed exactly how any golfer can ingrain it in his swing.

Unfortunately, that ingraining cannot be done through the printed word alone—sound is needed. That's why each copy of Novosel's book, *Tour Tempo*, comes with a CD bound inside its back cover. The CD plays a series of three pre-cisely timed tones, signifying the start of the swing, top of the backswing, and impact. Golfers, by matching their swings to those tones, can bring themselves relatively quickly into tour tempo. Clearly, we can't simulate those tones in print, so the following excerpt focuses not on instruction but on Novosel's discovery process. To get your own swing into tour sync, you'll need to get the CD, which comes in the book (see Appendix, page 388).

> **THE SECRET:**
>
> Get your swing in sync with the ideal tempo, a 3-1 ratio of backswing to forward swing.

NOVOSEL'S SECRET

Some of the world's greatest discoveries have been accidental. Henri Becquerel discovered radiation when he put uranium crystals in a drawer with some photographic plates. Archimedes gained his famous insight into the displacement of fluids while taking a bath. Isaac Newton, we are told, made an intuitive leap toward understanding gravity when an apple fell on his head.

The discovery of a mathematical constant in the golf swings of the touring pros may not be as important as those breakthroughs—to non-golfers, anyway—but it, too, was a product of serendipity.

The precipitating event took place one morning in the summer of 2000, when I was editing videotape for a golf infomercial at my home studio in Leawood, Kansas. The tape was a swing sequence of LPGA star Jan Stephenson, shot a few days before in Minneapolis on the practice range of the Rush Creek Golf Academy. Jan was hitting her driver and hitting it beautifully; the swing I was reviewing had sent the ball over 250 yards to the opposite end of the range. I ran the tape back and forth on our editing equipment, frame by frame, studying the positions Jan was in at various points in her swing.

For no particular reason, I looked at the digital frame counter, which appeared in a little box above and to the right of the image. (Broadcast video is composed of 30 images per second, so an individual frame occupies the screen for about 33 thousandths of a second. Each frame has a specific "address" measured in minutes, seconds, and frames.)

Clicking the mouse to advance Jan's driver swing frame by frame, I noticed that she took 27 frames to get from the start of her swing to the top of her backswing and another 9 frames elapsed before the club arrived at the ball.

A 3-to-1 ratio.

I may have yawned. The conventional wisdom on tempo in the golf swing was that each golfer has his or her own individual tempo. I made a mental note of Jan's numbers and continued working. A few hours later I began studying the swing of one Eldrick "Tiger" Woods. We had a tape of the 1997 Masters, which Tiger had won by a tournament-record 12 strokes. I found myself looking intently at Tiger hitting an 8-iron approach shot. Running the video frame by frame, as I had with Jan, I noticed something strange. Tiger's 8-iron swing took 1.2 seconds from takeaway to impact, the same as Jan's driver swing. And just like Jan, he took twenty-seven frames to get to the top of his backswing and another nine frames to get back down to the ball.

This time, I definitely did not yawn.

In the summer of 2000, I started taping the television coverage of PGA Tour events for analysis in my studio. After studying the swings of numerous players, I quickly discarded the idea that 1.2 seconds was a standard swing speed for the top golfers. Nick Price, an aggressive swinger, took only .93 seconds from takeaway to impact. Mark Calcavecchia took 1.06 seconds. Bernhard Langer, a notoriously slow player, swung at a surprisingly brisk .933 seconds—shattering the conventional wisdom that swing tempo follows temperament.

But while the total elapsed time of the pros' swings showed some variation, a very clear pattern emerged when I counted the frames. Darren Clarke and Jeff Maggert took 21 frames to reach the tops of their backswings and 7 frames to come down.

A 3-to-1 ratio.

Phil Mickelson was 24/8. In fact, when I allowed for a one-frame differential (due to operator error and the fact that the video equipment can't get closer than 33 thousandths of a second), virtually all the pros timed out at the same 3-to-1 ratio. Contrary to conventional wisdom, the world's best players—regardless of their overall swing speeds—swung to the same, consistent standard.

I spent the rest of the summer checking the swings of the great golfers from the past. Film from the 1961 U.S. Open at Denver's Cherry Hills Country Club revealed that Arnold Palmer made his famous charge to victory with a 20/7 swing. Film from the 1946 Masters showed Ben Hogan swinging at 21/7 and the great man himself, Bobby Jones, swinging at 26/9. I was particularly excited when I found a tape of Al Geiberger in the second round of the 1977 Danny Thomas Memphis Classic. That, of course, was the day Geiberger shot the first 59 in PGA Tour history. When we put Geiberger's swings on the computer and counted the frames, we discovered that his ratio for that day was 27/9. *Perfection.*

As we accumulated more and more data, it was impossible to escape the conclusion that for at least fifty years, the world's best golfers

ADDRESS

TOP OF BACKSWING

24

have been swinging to a standard, specific rhythm. I decided to call this standard "Tour Tempo," because better than 95 percent of the touring pros we timed fit the model. Tempo was a universal standard in the golf swing that the individual golfer must conform to.

The data also contradicted the conventional wisdom that the pros take the club back "low and slow." A lazy backswing, by tour standards, is 27 frames (.90 seconds), and most pros take the club back in only 24 frames (.80 seconds) or 21 frames (.70 seconds). A ball dropped from shoulder height, to make a comparison that struggling golfers will understand, hits the ground in approximately 16 frames. Furthermore, certain players are "stealthy fast"—that is, they somehow manage to camouflage the speed

of their swings with a fluid motion. I was stunned, for instance, when I compared the swings of Greg Norman and Ernie Els on the same tee during the 2000 International at Colorado's Castle Pines Golf Club. To the naked eye, Norman's swing is faster by a bunch. *Everybody,* in fact, looks faster than Els, who got his nickname "The Big Easy" because of his slow, effortless swing. But when I timed their swings on the computer, Ernie was a frame *faster* than Greg from takeaway to impact. Obviously the naked eye can be fooled about tempo and speed in the golf swing.

Fortunately, to understand tempo we no longer have to rely on the unaided eye of the observer or the subjective testimony of the golfer. By the end of the summer of 2000,

TOP OF BACKSWING

IMPACT

8

I had collected enough data to conclude that Tour Tempo in the golf swing consists of two aspects.

Aspect number one is the *ratio* of (A) the elapsed time it takes a player to get to the top of the backswing from the start of the swing compared with (B) the elapsed time that it takes to get back down to impact from the start of the forward swing. This universal ratio is 3-to-1. It takes three times as long for a player to get from the start of the backswing to the top of his backswing compared to the time it takes to get from the start of the forward swing to impact. This can be expressed in frames of video as 21/7, 24/8, and 27/9.

Aspect number two is the *amount* of elapsed time, measured in hundredths of

a second, that it takes the club to go from the start of the backswing to impact. Three different elapsed times correspond with the three different ratios. Ninety-three hundredths (.93) of a second corresponds to 21-to-7. One and six one-hundredths (1.06) corresponds to 24-to-8. One and twenty hundredths (1.20) corresponds to 27-to-9.

These findings, although unexpected, absolutely make good sense. To have a consistent swing like the touring pros, you have to have a consistent time frame in which that swing takes place. You also have to have a consistent time ratio between the backswing and the return to the ball.

FROM *TOUR TEMPO* BY JOHN NOVOSEL

CAPTAIN BRUCE W. OLLSTEIN

MILITARY MANEUVERS

*"Make no mistake about it, golf is war.
If you're not looking to win,
you probably shouldn't show up."*

At New York's posh Riverdale Country School, they'd never seen anyone quite like Bruce Ollstein. Following graduation, as his classmates packed off for Harvard, Princeton, Yale, and other bastions of the best and brightest, Ollstein, the son of a prominent Manhattan surgeon, headed straight for the only institution he'd ever aspired to, the place he'd aimed for since he was a boy of six or seven: the U.S. Military Academy at West Point.

"I had two uncles who served in the Pacific during World War II," he said, "and I always looked up to them as men who had made a meaningful and substantive contribution to their country. I wanted to do the same."

The usual hitch is four years followed by another four or five years of active duty and reserve status. Ollstein stayed much longer, as an infantryman officer, drill instructor, chopper pilot, and today as a military consultant to the defense department. "The army has been my life," he says.

But his passion has always been golf. Ollstein brought to West Point a polished game weaned on the fairways of Shinnecock and Winged Foot, but in his years as a soldier, he found something different.

> **THE SECRET:**
>
> Wage war on the course. Do not simply outplay your opponents; outwit them—and take no prisoners.

"I'd always viewed golf as a gentleman's game, a walk in the park where each player made his way toward the hole, happily engrossed in his own game. At the Army base courses, it was all about competition—beating the other guy or the other team in the match. What's more, they transferred the military attitude to their matches—everyone, from the generals down to the privates, was engaged in trench warfare, with gamesmanship galore. They loved getting into each other's heads. And when they spoke, it was always in Army metaphors. After slicing a tee shot, a guy would say 'looks like I'll be taking a flanking attack on this green.' Bunker shots became desert warfare, and when you lost, you didn't just toss away the scorecard, you shredded the document."

So struck was Ollstein by the parallels between military strategy and match-play golf that he wrote an article for *Assembly,* the West Point alumni magazine. The magazine's editor liked it so much, he suggested that Ollstein develop it into a series. Instead, Ollstein wrote an entire book.

Combat Golf was published in 1996 and one of the first to endorse it was former Green Beret Earl Woods, taskmaster father of Tiger. Almost instantly the book took off, hitting several best-seller lists. Over the next several years Ollstein parlayed his authorial fame into mini-celebrity status, doing numer-

Captain Bruce Ollstein, a career soldier and passionate golfer.

ous TV appearances as well as clinics with superteachers David Leadbetter and Jim McLean. He even gave a lesson to New York Mayor Rudy Giuliani.

Ollstein's tone is avowedly tongue in cheek, but for those craving some advice on competitive strategy, this is more than just light entertainment. It's a useful look at how Patton or Napoléon or Caesar would have handled their golf matches.

OLLSTEIN'S SECRET

I f the enemy shows an inclination to advance, lure him on to do so.

—Sun Tzu

Psyops

The U.S. Army calls them PSYOPS, psychological operations. Every military in the world has personnel devoted to this singular purpose. Their mission: damaging the enemy's will to fight and misleading enemy personnel with covert counterintelligence to affect their decision making and overall morale. Napoléon Bonaparte once said, "The greatest general is he who makes the fewest mistakes." PSYOPS causes your adversary to make mistakes. It goes beyond merely feeding the enemy misinformation. It penetrates the enemy's psyche and permanently alters his ability to think clearly and fight effectively. Properly employed, PSYOPS turns your opponent into a bumbling, babbling nitwit who is incapable of coherent

thought and makes one mistake after another. And the best part is, he won't even know you're doing it. Even if you are unwilling to subject your opponent to such a cruel fate, be advised, do not skip over this chapter. You may not have the stomach for this stuff, but you can rest assured, the enemy's been using plenty of these tricks on you. And until you learn to recognize them, your score will continue to suffer and your game will never reach its full potential. Prepare to copy.

Kill 'Em with Kindness

Always concede a few short putts early in the game, allowing your opponent to pick up his ball without holing out. This preemptive gesture of goodwill nets two independent, positive results. First, it disarms your opponent, establishing the false precedent that this is a friendly game, and making him far more vulnerable to the PSYOPS that follow. Second, it denies him the opportunity to establish an early rhythm with his putter. Sinking those first 3-footers is a tremendous confidence boost at the start of a round. By denying your opponent the chance visually to observe his ball dropping into the cup on the first few holes, you are prohibiting him from getting settled. This Trojan horse will come back to rattle him later in the round when you demand that he putt everything out.

On the flip side of this, never accept a gimme unless it seals a win. If you are out of the hole in match play, or someone else has already tied to protect the skin, insist on putting out. It's a great opportunity to groove your championship putting stroke or test a quick fix if you are starting to get the yips. And remember, if you mess up on this hole, it doesn't cost you anything except pride.

the trouble out there." If he slices it into the closest banana republic, offer him a friendly mulligan and explain that he just "let up on it." You might say, "Really go after it this time." In all likelihood he will simply repeat his swing fault even more dramatically.

If water hazards send shivers down a particular opponent's graphite shaft, be quick to warn your foursome of impending danger as you pull up to the tee box. "Don't want to get caught short here, boys," you could offer. Or just, "Damn, that's enough ocean to start a naval academy." These kind little seeds will sprout nicely in the mind of your opponent. Just plant them and add water.

Always Support Your Friends

When your opponent is ready to lead Pickett's Charge, always give him a kind word of encouragement. Let's say he is a big hitter, but his fairway accuracy leaves something to be desired. On the tighter par-4's, you might want to remind him that he possesses the kind of power that can "get past

Nature Can Be So Inconsistent

I remember playing golf once at MacDill Air Force Base in Tampa, Florida, with the four-star commander in chief (CINC) of Special Operations Command. He had hit a high shot into a Redan par-3 and came up short right, center of the big bunker. As he stepped back, he was quick to comment on the unexpected winds above the tree-tops, and how he had really gotten a piece of the ball. "I should have used more club," I heard him mumble to himself.

The rest of us went back to our bags hoping to capitalize on his mistake. We all returned with weapons at least one caliber larger. The second hitter, a retired full-bird colonel, launched his balata bomb 10 yards over the green. I smiled at the general's aide, a major standing behind me. He returned a quick grin. The four-star had merely hit his shot a little off center. The general's loss of distance, due to a miss hit that only the general could feel, not to wrong club selection as he had claimed, cost him a "closest to the pin" but allowed for an excellent field-training exercise in counterintelligence. From that moment on, I never took a player's casual comments at face value. Next time you

hear an opponent declare, "I killed that putt," and your eyes see a ball still 2 feet short of the hole, don't assume a uniquely slow green. Proceed with caution or you may find yourself staring at a 10-foot return with no gimme in sight.

Share to Show You Care

Sharing a good joke or an interesting tale can really brighten a person's day. What better place for such friendly bonding than out on the course? Try to start these tidbits on the way to your opponent's ball, then promise to continue the story after he takes his shot. Don't be afraid to discuss provocative topics. Not too many players can focus with all these interesting things messing up their minds, though most believe they can. You'll be surprised how often you can share kind words with the same opponent. Just don't lose your own focus. If he starts talking on the way to your ball, ignore him.

The Game Has Its Slow Moments

Like combat, golf has a lot of downtime. Soldiers and golfers both face periods of waiting and reflection between the short-lived but intense action. This allows time for the participants to ponder their uncertain fates. They can either get psyched or lose courage. The recurring breaks between the explosions of individual golf shots can help or hurt a player. If your opponent hits a bad shot, don't make small talk. Show a respectful silence for his Titleist lost in the line of duty. Allow him to dwell on his mistake and ponder the consequences. If he hits a good shot, drop a quick platitude and proceed to discuss Congress's new tax bill. Don't let him thrive on his transient immortality. He might find an inner strength he never knew he had.

You must keep the momentum as long as possible, because it can shift faster than a political alliance. Just when you think the game is in the bag, a momentary loss of intensity can create a vicious mudslide, causing you to lose the round. Keep the pressure on with ruthless intensity, and don't fall prey to an opponent of many faces.

Consistency Is a Crack-up

Nothing has a more devastating effect on an opponent than consistent play. If you can keep it in the fairway time after time, get it up and down when the greens won't hold, and avoid those nasty three-putts when you are on in regulation . . . well, that's what it's all about. Let the other guy have the day's longest drive, and let him go right at that well-guarded pin. He may experience an occasional moment of glory, but it will come at a price. And watching you press forward without a major mishap will start to take its toll on his psyche.

Beware of Schizophrenics

Nothing can be more rewarding or unsettling than a sudden personality change in your opponent. If you are finally starting to pull away in the stretch, do not pull back on the reins. Your opponent may be wearing a sour face or a look of uncharacteristic sadness, but it's only a feint. He's trying to take advantage of your sympathetic nature, hoping you'll rush a few putts as charity for one of your less fortunate brethren. Don't let up.

FROM *COMBAT GOLF* BY CAPTAIN BRUCE WARREN OLLSTEIN

CHAPTER 34

DAVE PELZ

REMEDIAL READING

*"Almost every putt that every golfer
makes is the result of a series of mistakes."*

Had you been a grey squirrel, perched in the branches of one of the oaks overlooking the ninth green of the Sleepy Hollow Country Club in Scarborough, New York, at approximately 4 P.M. on Tuesday, September 20, 1994, you would have witnessed one of the most astonishing demonstrations in the history of golf instruction.

The man in charge was Dave Pelz. He was joined that afternoon by a pair of editors from *GOLF Magazine*. A week earlier, Pelz had phoned the magazine from his home in Texas with news that he'd made an important dis-

covery. He'd offered no details, just the assurance that the editors would be stunned by what they'd see.

Such a phone call, coming from just about any other instructor in the world, would have been met with skepticism. But not from Pelz. Dave Pelz offers no breathless promises, no magic methods, or razzle-dazzle claims. He deals only in facts, data, and proof.

A 1961 graduate of Indiana University, where he majored in physics, minored in math, and played golf on a scholarship, Pelz briefly considered turning professional. But he was troubled by what he refers to as his "perfect record" against one of his peers in the Big Ten—Jack Nicklaus. Pelz was perfect in defeat, losing twenty-two consecutive times to Nicklaus in tournaments where they both competed. So he decided to pursue a career in science. He joined NASA and worked with the agency in its heyday of space flight development, focusing on atmospheric conditions and satellite research.

After fifteen years, however, the lure of golf began to tug at him once again—not as a player this time, but as a researcher. In 1975 Pelz took a leave of absence from NASA and started Preceptor Golf, a company formed to manufacture the Teacher Putter (the first of what would be several patents under his name). A year later he gave up rocket science altogether and began a comprehensive study of the short game.

Using caddies, Tour players, and amateur golfers, Pelz spent more than three years entering the data from thousands of rounds (shot distance, finish point in relation to target, etc.). As a result he learned two important things: 1) the short game is 60–65 percent of golf; and 2) the players with the best short games are the ones who win most often.

In the quarter century since, Pelz has continued his research, testing, and analysis and in the process has established himself as the world's undisputed expert on all aspects of wedge play, sand play, and putting. Indeed, no instructor alive or dead has added more irrefutable knowledge to the game's textbook. At the same time, he has become a major success. His immensely popular short-game schools are based at prominent resorts throughout the country, he is the author of two best-selling "Bibles" on the short game and putting, he appears monthly in *GOLF Magazine* and constantly on the Golf Channel, and he has helped to sharpen the short games of nearly 100 PGA Tour players,

including Phil Mickelson, Vijay Singh, Tom Kite, and Lee Janzen.

The gap wedge was popularized by Pelz and the two-ball putter was invented by him. So were Perfy the Putting Robot and the Pelzometer, a major improvement on the Stimpmeter traditionally used to measure green speed. Groundbreaking instructional concepts such as the four-wedge system and the notion of optimum putting speed also came from Dave Pelz. He's even proved conclusively that, if you leave the flagstick in the hole, you'll enhance your chances of holing a chip shot—by precisely 34 percent. It's no coincidence that he is the only man to warrant two chapters in this book.

So when Dave Pelz calls and says he's made an important discovery, the odds are, he has. The demonstration he staged on that September afternoon in 1994 led to a *GOLF Magazine* cover article and an instructional video, both entitled "The Amazing Truth About Putting," and became the basis for the excerpt that follows, from *Dave Pelz's Putting Bible.*

THE SECRET:

Play more break— much more— and thereby develop a "non-compensating" stroke.

PELZ'S PUTTING SECRET

In testing more than 1,500 golfers, including 50 PGA Tour professionals, I discovered an amazing truth about putting. Not one of these players was reading as much break as actually existed on any one of their putts. In fact, most didn't even come close to reading anywhere near the true break.

Is it any wonder that all the putts missed by amateur golfers, 80 to 90 percent miss below the hole? Even Tour pros miss 70 to 80 percent of their misses on the low side.

The Subconscious Knows Better

While golfers don't recognize the true amount of a putt's break in their conscious minds, their subconscious minds do better.

How do I know? After asking these 1,500 golfers how much break they were playing, I asked them to putt at the same holes. But before they hit any balls, I measured where they were aiming their bodies, putters, and strokes. Again, I was amazed at the results.

While they told me they were playing break values that were less than a third of the real value, they were aiming to play breaks much closer, to between 65 and 75 percent of the true break values. So if the true break was 40 inches, they said they were putting at a spot 12 inches above the hole, then actually *aimed* at a spot between 25 and 30 inches above.

Possibly the most incredible aspect of all this was that not one of the golfers was aware of doing this. They didn't realize they actually were playing far more break than they thought they were or would admit to playing. Test this yourself: Stand on a putting green with your friends and ask one of them how much break he is

> **They didn't realize they were actually playing far more break than they thought they were.**

allowing for; then watch as he tells you one thing but does something completely different. You don't need any sophisticated equipment to see it.

The Subconscious Fights

Now, playing 70 percent of the break is much better than playing 30 percent, but it still isn't enough. Yes, the subconscious compensation corrects for a major portion of most players' inability to read greens, but even correcting to 70 percent means most golfers still should miss their putts on the low side of the hole.

But again, this is not the end of the story.

The In-Stroke Correction

Now take a look at what happened when these golfers actually made their strokes. Remember, they professed to playing less than a third of the true-break, then stood over their putts and aimed for 65 to 75 percent of the true-break value. Then, believe it or not, as they swung their putters, they subconsciously made in-stroke compensations to pull or push their putts onto a starting line at between 85 and 95 percent of the true break.

It was amazing, but it happened almost every time, and still happens whenever I run the test. When I first started researching this behavior, I thought, "How could golfers not know they are doing this?" I've since learned a very important lesson: *In golf, the subconscious always wins.* Golfers do many things they are not aware of. They don't swing the way they think they swing (for proof, watch someone's face the first time he sees his swing on video), and they don't play anywhere near the same break they think they're playing when they putt.

It Is Amazing

Take a look at the in-stroke compensations. If you tried to think about them, consciously trying to turn or correct your putterface angle and path during your stroke, I don't think you could do it. Yet there's absolutely no question that your subconscious can and does do it all the time. And actually does it pretty well, all things considered, rerouting the putter so the starting line of your putt is almost (but not quite) on the 100 percent correct line.

Let's Ignore It

It sometimes amazes me that golfers make as many putts as they do. Even though most golfers see or read less than 30 percent of a putt's true break, they never miss by the other 70 percent. In fact, most golfers come pretty close to making most of their putts. Their compensations, therefore, are very good, and since they are subconsciously controlled, seem very easy.

Which explains the response I often get from the golfer who is beginning to understand the problem, which is "I don't want to deal with it." He says, "If I'm compensating so well, and my subconscious is doing such a good job, why not let it be?"

The answer is simple. If you learned to read the proper (true) amount of break, you'd make more putts. You could use the same non-compensating stroke for all your putts. And learning to repeat one stroke for the rest of your golf career is much simpler and easier than trying to execute a different stroke, with different in-stroke compensation, on every new putt. The truth is, the more you compensate—that is, the larger your compensations become—the less accurate your putting results will be.

> **Watch not only your own putts but everyone else's in your group. The more breaks you "see" this way, the more accurately you will be able to imagine them (read greens) in the future.**

Let me say it again: By under-reading putts, you are requiring your subconscious to compensate by a different amount on every putt. That means your body must make a different stroke on every putt on every green. And there is no way you (or any golfer) can learn to properly execute a different stroke with different compensations on every putt nearly as well as you can learn to groove and repeat one stroke (one with absolutely no compensations) for all of those putts.

Seeing True Break

In theory, once you know visible break is about a third of true break, it should be easy to see a putt's true break. However, I don't want to mislead you about the difficulty of seeing even the visible break when you first start looking.

You need to practice seeing visible break. Every time you see a putt curving to the hole, try to focus and lock your vision onto its ball track. Make a mental note of where the ball reached its apex, when it got to its highest point away from the ball-hole line (the straight line between the ball and the hole). That distance is the visible break.

Now take that visible break, imagine moving it out to the distance of the hole, multiply it by three, and you'll have the true-break point and Aimline for the putt (or at least something very near to it). The more you look at putts this way, with a sharp focus and awareness of visible break, and what that means in terms of how much true break the putt showed, the easier it will become to see them both. Watch not only your own putts, but also everyone else's in your group (and not just on the course, but when you are competing and doing putting

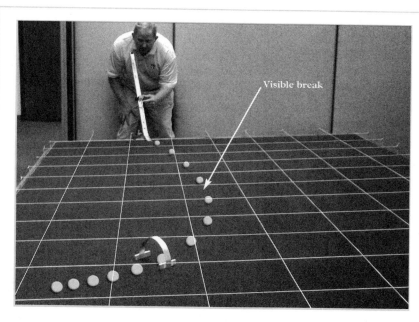

Visible break can be easily seen: It's the distance the apex of the ball track departs from the ball-hole line.

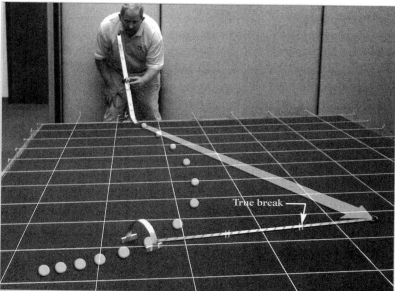

In your mind's eye, move the visible break out to the hole—multiply it by three—and you'll see the true-break point and Aimline.

drills on the practice green, too). The more breaks you "see" this way, the more accurately you will be able to imagine them (read greens) in the future.

Roll Putts with a True Roller

Another good way to see how much putts break is to roll balls with a True Roller, shown at left. It's the best device I've seen for providing true and accurate feedback on what the green is doing to putts.

I am not recommending for you to buy one (they're expensive and cumbersome), but believe me when I say that rolling and watching putts for just a few minutes from the True Roller will convince you that the true break in putts is much greater than what you used to think it was.

Eliminate In-Stroke Compensations

Golfers don't understand what line their putts start on, because they are looking down as they putt. They don't see their ball's starting direction, then when they do look up, they assume their ball is rolling on the line they aimed at and started it on. However, due to their in-stroke compensations and gravity (which always pulls putts downhill), neither assumption is correct. If you are ever to solve the problem of these unwanted compensations in your setup and your stroke (which you probably have on all

The True Roller starts balls rolling on the Aimline you choose, at the speed you select. If you don't play enough break at that speed, you miss the putt low every time. The True Roller provides immediate, accurate, and reliable feedback.

breaking putts), you must learn to practice without them.

How do you establish a "no compensations allowed" condition of practice? It's simple. Orient your stroke to start all your putts on an Elevated Aimline, and don't allow any compensations to take hold. You do this by practicing breaking putts with your Elevated Aimline marked and guarded on the high side.

1. Read your putt, which in this example you read to break 6 inches right to left.
2. Mark the spot from which you will practice this putt, because you will practice it repeatedly (and you must putt repeatedly from exactly the same spot each time).
3. Position one end of your Elevated Aimline 6 inches to the right of the hole (at the true break point where you read the putt to break from).
4. Stretch the Elevated Aimline exactly over the middle of (and 9 inches above) your ball, leaving enough room behind the ball to make a backswing.
5. Place a second ball directly under the Elevated Aimline, 17 inches in front of the ball to be putted. Place a blocking plate with a quarter-inch clearance from the second ball on the uphill side of the Aimline. Remove the second ball, and you are ready to putt.

The Elevated Aimline stakes are connected by elastic thread, which is suspended 9 inches above the Aimline of your putt. The blocking plate (a book, soda can, or almost anything else) is positioned just above your starting line (Aimline) to prevent your subconscious from pulling or pushing your putts uphill.

If you set up to putt as in the example above, your first few putts probably will hit the blocking plate. (I've seen thousands of golfers do this, so don't think you're the only one.) The subconscious of most golfers reverts to habit and pushes the first few putts a little uphill into the blocking plate. Then, when you finally get your first putt to roll past the blocking plate without hitting it, the ball will probably miss the hole on the low side of the cup if your speed was anywhere near the optimum (17 inches past the cup). The low miss happens because the Aimline most golfers choose initially is too low and doesn't allow for enough break once their normal compensation uphill is blocked.

If this happens to you, reset the Elevated Aimline higher, move the blocking plate to again guard the high side of the new Aimline, and putt again. Repeat this re-aiming, re-setting, and putting until you can make the putt by starting it along your Aimline, rolling at the optimum speed.

Yes, this is more trouble than your usual putting practice. But it is also the best way to learn to make breaking putts. I recommend you use Elevated Aimlines and blocking plates on all your breaking-putt practice for

Golfers don't understand what line their putts start on, because they are looking down as they putt. They don't see their ball's starting direction, then when they do look up, they assume their ball is rolling on the line they aimed at and started it on.

PELZ'S PUTTING SECRET

at least three to six months, all the while concentrating solely on making the ball start on the right line at the right speed (because that's what good putting is all about). Once you get the Elevated Aimline set for the true break, keep your blocking plate sitting just a quarter of an inch above a ball on that line, guarding against any subconscious compensations. After practicing this way for a while, your subconscious will begin to learn that the best way to hole breaking putts will be no compensations to your pure-in-line-square stroke, starting putts on the true-break Aimline.

> After practicing this way for a while, your subconscious will begin to learn that the best way to hole breaking putts will be with no compensations in your pure-in-line stroke.

Read Greens Better, Make More Putts

If you practice this way (without compensations), while simultaneously learning to read greens better, you are well on your way to becoming a great putter. This system works because you learn a noncompensating in-line stroke and learn to read greens better at the same time. This system works because when you do both correctly, you are rewarded by making more putts. This is in contrast to what has happened over the years to golfers who work hard to learn simple, noncompensating strokes, then found they didn't work (they missed too many putts) when they took them to the golf course and continued to underread the break in their putts. Of course they didn't realize that their poor green-reading was the cause of the problem.

By being open-minded, understanding about subconscious compensations, and learning how to putt on greens without them, you open the door for your conscious mind to feel free to read the proper (true) break. When you do both (read true break and use non-compensating strokes), you make putts. With accurate (true break) Aimlines, when you make better strokes—with no compensations and solid impact, a square face angle through impact, and better touch—your putts go into the hole. As you continue to practice making noncompensating strokes, and the better you read the true break of your putts, the more putts you will roll into the center of the hole.

> By being open-minded, understanding about subconscious compensations, you open the door for your conscious mind to read the proper (true) break.

My Five-Step Green-Reading Procedure

I have one more concept essential for improving your ability to read greens. It's basis is that the more consistent and repeatable you are at performing tasks, the more boring, simple, and habitual they become—the key word here being "habitual." The more of a habit you can make green-reading, the less effort and concentration you have to expend doing it. Therefore, since we all have only so much capacity and energy to perform, the less you extend yourself in the rudiments of reading greens, the more you have left to focus on the difficult part, the visualization of how much putts will actually break. After studying this for a few years, I have come to believe a five-step process for reading greens is about the best you can do in the time available on the golf course. I recommend you learn to do it quickly, the same every time, without leaving anything out.

1. Determine the pure downhill direction around (within six feet of) the hole.
2. Stand behind the hole on the extended ball-hole line and verify in your mind's eye that you believe the downhill direction seen in step 1.
3. Walk around and stand behind the ball on the ball-hole line and reverify your chosen downhill direction.
4. Move downhill (usually only a side step) until you can begin to imagine a perfect ball track rolling into the hole. Visualize the amount of visible break on that ball track.
5. Visually move this visible break distance out to the hole, multiply it by three, and move downhill until you are on the true-break Aimline and you can "see" the true-break ball track at the perfect "optimum-17-inches-past" speed in your mind's eye.

FROM *DAVE PELZ'S PUTTING BIBLE*

DAVE PELZ

ONE SYSTEM— TWELVE SHOTS

"Where you putt from is more important than how well you putt."

Short-game guru Dave Pelz has filmed literally miles of tape and video for his various instructional videos, DVDs, and appearances on the Golf Channel. However, the segment he most enjoys talking about concerns a shot demonstrated not by Pelz himself, but by one of his pupils.

The student addresses a 60-degree wedge shot, taking his stance less than 3 feet away from Pelz with the blade of the wedge facing directly at the big man. Then the student takes a full-out swing at the ball, barely miss-ing the big man's foot as the club moves through impact. Incredibly, the ball pops off the clubface almost vertically, climbs lazily up the length of Pelz's 6'2" frame, barely missing his nose, and plops down about 3 feet in back of him. A cut shot extraordinaire.

Pelz took part in that death-defying stunt because he had absolute trust in the student wielding the wedge: Phil Mickelson. Now, you might expect that Mickelson, pos-sessor of what is generally agreed to be the most artful short game in the world, would have little use for the mechanical methods of Dave Pelz, but the truth is quite otherwise. In fact, Mickelson credits Pelz for helping to build that short game. The two have worked together for several years, and it was Pelz who first convinced Lefty to carry four wedges, and then showed him how to get the most out of them. Mickelson also sought out Pelz in early 2004 for some fine-tuning on his wedge game, just before his dramatic victory in the Masters.

Pelz loves working individually with the game's best players (he's so busy these days that he confines himself to players ranked fiftieth in the world or higher), but he treats them essentially as he does 30-handicappers. No student gets his personal attention—whether the name is Mickelson, Kite, Singh, or Sorenstam—before first going through a full three-day short-game school. And regardless of the pupil's level of talent, Pelz does not allow much room for personal theories. His teaching is based strictly on research and data.

> **In fact, Mickelson credits Pelz for helping to build that short game. The two have worked together for several years, and it was Pelz who first convinced Lefty to carry four wedges, and then showed him how to get the most out of them.**

During the late 1980s, he spent hundreds of hours observing PGA and LPGA Tour players as they hit wedge shots of various distances. As a result, he developed an uncanny skill—by watching a player swing he could predict almost exactly how far the ball would go. He'd stand to the side of the player and, as the player made impact, whisper "51," "75," "93."

> **No student gets his personal attention—whether the name is Mickelson, Kite, Singh, or Sorenstam—before first going through a full three-day short-game school.**

Down the fairway, a spotter armed with a walkie-talkie would radio back the actual yardages, and they were always within a yard of Pelz's calls.

At first, not even Pelz knew exactly how he was able to do this. Then it dawned on him—his calls were based purely on watching the length of the players' backswings. From that realization grew one of his most important contributions to teaching—the 3 × 4 system—three lengths of backswing applied to each of four different wedges. Pelz unveiled his concept in a cover article for *GOLF Magazine* and then began incorporating it in his network of short-game schools. When *Dave Pelz's Short Game Bible* appeared in 1999, the 3 × 4 system was a key component, and it follows here, chapter and verse.

PELZ'S SHORT GAME SECRET

Timing the Wedge Swings

As I got to know more and more players, and watched more and more swings, I realized not only that there was a characteristic shot three-quarters of the length of their full-swing distance for each player, but that it was always the result of the same-length backswing—just about when the left arm was parallel to the ground and the left hand was as high as the left shoulder (they were all right-handed players).

There was also a ½-shot distance swing, with another repeatable backswing position that proved surprisingly consistent for the players: the left hand stopped at a position just below the hips.

As I continued working with various Tour players, we needed to refer to swings between the ½ and ¾ positions, but we had nothing to call them until one day it dawned on me that from a frontal view, the length of every player's backswing could be precisely correlated to the hour hand of a clock.

Imagine that his left shoulder is the center of the clock, and his left arm is the hour hand (forget the club). In these terms, the full swing, for the full-length wedge shot, is the result of making a synchronized turn to the maximum "zero-coil" position, where the left arm is at 10:30 on a clock face. So we called that his 10:30 swing. The same system described the previous ¾-length shot as a 9:00 o'clock swing, because the left arm is horizontal at the top of that backswing.

The third repeatable and often recurring swing, the ½-length swing, also could be accurately described as a 7:30 swing.

By using time descriptions of the three different backswing lengths, we created and named the three most commonly used finesse swings

By using time descriptions of the three different backswing lengths, we created and named the three most commonly used finesse swings as the 7:30, 9:00, and 10:30.

(and shots) as 7:30, 9:00, and 10:30. These three are the basic finesse swings, which every good player should "own" because they are easy to execute and they produce three known, repeatable, and controllable distances. It is the same as having three different clubs in the bag that produce those same distances. By "timing" the wedge swings, we also created an infinite array of swings and shot distances in between the three reference swings.

By practicing and grooving these three swing lengths, my players multiplied their easily reproducible distance shots with each wedge in their bag. They had the full-finesse-swing yardage (about 90 to 95 yards for their sand wedges), which they achieved by making a synchronized backswing that went back to the 10:30 position. (Note: The 10:30 finesse swing usually flies the ball about 10 yards shorter than a full coil-and-hit power swing for the same club.) They also had a shot at around 68 to 73 yards, the result of swinging back to the 9:00 position (75% of 90 yards); and a 45-yard shot (50% of 90 yards), which came from swinging back to 7:30.

While the exact yardages differed from player to player,

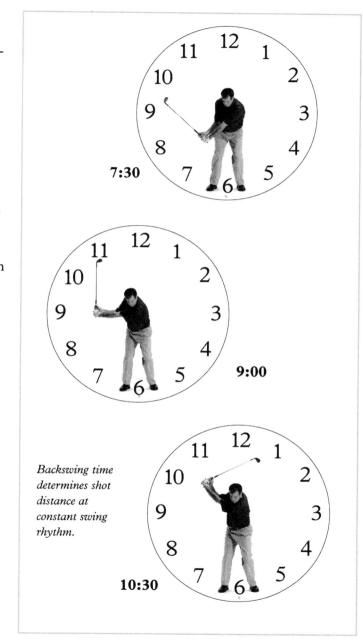

Backswing time determines shot distance at constant swing rhythm.

> **The rhythm of all the swings must be the same, and the backswing lengths for each of the three reference swings must be repeatable. If they're not, they won't produce repeatable distances.**

the 50%, 75% and 100% ratios remained almost constant. Having named the backswing lengths by the hour hand of a clock, the players now possessed the ability to produce a complete range of distances simply by thinking about the "time" of their backswing. If they wanted to hit the ball slightly farther than their 9:00 distance, they took their backswing to 9:15 or 9:30. A slightly shorter shot became an 8:30 swing.

Working with a System

There are a few practical recommendations I can make for learning to time your distance wedges. Begin each swing with a "slow-ish" one-piece takeaway to the top of the backswing (slow by your standards, not in comparison to anyone else). Come down and through the impact zone aggressively (not hard, but positive: Imagine "saaawish-swish" is your backswing-to-through-swing rhythm), and make a full, high, well-balanced finish. You should be able to hold your pose with your weight fully on your left side and only the right toe touching the ground.

One more time: *The rhythm of all the swings must be the same, and the backswing lengths for each of the three reference swings must be repeatable.* If they're not, they won't produce repeatable distances in practice or on the course. You can practice your 9:00 backswing at home in front of a full-length mirror (you won't believe what 10 or 20 swings every night for a few months will do for your ability to repeat these moves).

One last piece of advice. Cock your wrists continuously, gradually as you make your backswing, and have them fully cocked before you get to the right backswing "time." If you wait to cock your wrists until you've reached the right time, the swing will carry on as you cock and get too long for the distance you want. Also, keep your left arm extended throughout the swing, until it folds at the finish. Not only will this keep your swing radius constant, but it's the easy way to judge backswing time and length.

My "3 × 4 System"

With the 7:30, 9:00, and 10:30 finesse swings grooved into your game, you can add three more distances inside 100 yards to your repertoire simply by adding another wedge, different from your other two, to your bag. Many manufacturers make more lofted "L" or third wedges, with about five

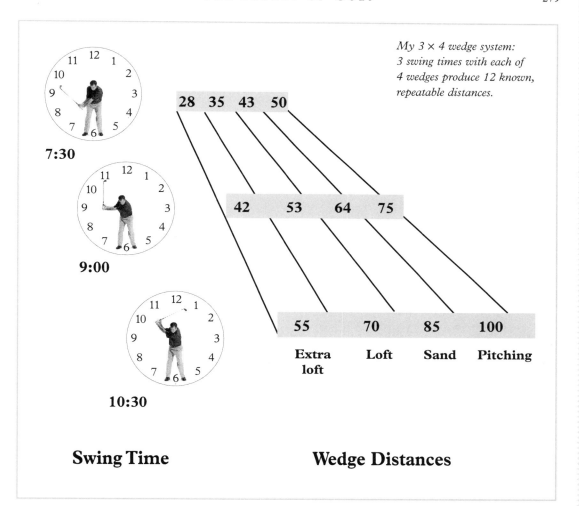

My 3 × 4 wedge system: 3 swing times with each of 4 wedges produce 12 known, repeatable distances.

7:30

9:00

10:30

28 35 43 50

42 53 64 75

55 70 85 100

Extra   Loft   Sand   Pitching
loft

Swing Time

Wedge Distances

degrees more loft than the standard sand wedge. Some even make the extra lofted "X wedges," with about 64 degrees of loft (4 or 5 degrees more than an L wedge).

A little reminder: No matter how many wedges you carry or what their lofts, they are not as important at this point in your

development as working on your ability to make quality finesse swings. This means how well you control the distances your short-game shots fly, and how well you deal with getting those shots into the "Golden Eight" feet around the hole. No matter how many wedges you have to choose from, if

The bad news: 1) You have to give up one or two of the irons you're used to playing with; and 2) You have to keep track of twelve new shot options inside 100 yards, shots you've never had before.

you can't make the proper finesse motions to the correct backswing times, then nothing else matters. So learn to make your finesse swings first, and then you are ready for my 3 × 4 wedge system.

Actually, you already know the basics of the system. It consists of learning to play three distinct shots with the three finesse swings of 7:30, 9:00, and 10:30 backswings, with each of four different wedges to produce twelve known and reproducible carry distances inside 100 yards.

The math is simple: three swings times four wedges equals twelve distances. But the philosophy calls for something more: You want to own these twelve shots.

To Control Your Shot Distance Accurately Enough to Make Your Next Shot (Putt) Imminently Holeable

---

Consider that the "mission statement" of your short game. And consider the implica-

tions. It would be like having eleven extra clubs in your bag when you're competing with someone of similar skill who has only one club and no idea how to control the distance for any shot inside 100 yards. Who do you think will win?

And remember: You can be as talented with all twelve finesse shots as you are with one, because the same swing works for them all. The only difference is the length (time) of your backswing, which you vary to match the length of your shot.

Good News–Bad News

First the good news. My 3 × 4 System is simple, easy to understand, easy to practice, and easy to execute. Every golfer I've ever seen use it has improved his short game and ability to score.

Now the two pieces of bad news: (1) You have to give up one or two of the eight irons (2 through 9) you're used to playing with; and (2) You have to keep track of twelve new shot options inside 100 yards, shots you've never had before.

Don't think that you're now suddenly able to master every up-and-down situation. No matter how many wedges you carry or how many finesse-swing lengths you learn, your scores won't go down until you get good enough with your short-game shots to stop them within the "Golden Eight" and make the next putt.

Is This Mission Impossible?

If you saw a set of golf clubs for the first time and were told how far each club carried the ball, it might be difficult to remember all those numbers. But having played for a while, you have no trouble remembering that your 7-iron carries the ball 140 yards. That knowledge is part of your game. I'll now show you how you can avoid having to remember any numbers while improving your game from 100 yards in.

Go to a practice range and hit between ten and twenty solid shots (which may require twenty-five to thirty swings) with your pitching wedge using your 9:00 finesse swing. Walk off (or, even better, "shoot" with a laser range finder) the carry distances of the solid shots, write down the yardages, then average the numbers to determine your 9:00 pitching-wedge distance for that day. Do this for a few days to find your best estimate for the average distance you can expect when you hit a shot with that club and swing.

Do the same with your 10:30 and 7:30 swings while you're there. This will give you three numbers: the average yardages for your 7:30, 9:00, and 10:30 swings with your pitching wedge. Write them on a little piece of paper or adhesive dot and stick it to the shaft of the pitching wedge. Put them upside down on the back of the shaft so you can read them when you are ready to hit without taking too much time. Cover the dot with a piece of clear tape, long enough to wrap around your shaft and stick on itself. This will protect the numbers from wear, tear, and weather. (If you're worried, it's perfectly legal by USGA rules to do this.)

Do the same thing—hit ten to twenty shots, average the distances, repeat over a few days, arrive at three averages—for your other wedges. Tape those numbers to the shafts. Now it will take you just a second or two to be confident of your yardage and club for the swing you want to make. You don't have to remember distances on the course: They'll be right at hand when you need them.

Whenever you have a shot inside 100 yards, guess which club has a shot distance closest to the distance you need and pick it out of the bag. Quickly check that you chose the right club, make a good, realistic practice swing to the right time on the backswing, and—if you feel good—fire at the pin.

> You can be as talented with all twelve finesse shots as you are with one, because the same swing works for them all. The only difference is the length (time) of your backswing, which you vary to match the length of your shot.

FROM *DAVE PELZ'S SHORT GAME BIBLE*

CHAPTER 36

CHI CHI RODRIGUEZ

WALL POWER

*"At 120 pounds I need all the power I can find,
because I have a big family to feed."*

In the 1940s, while Ben Hogan, Byron Nelson, and Sam Snead were famously dominating the world of golf, young Juan Rodriguez was swinging a club carved from the limb of a guava tree to swat balled-up tin cans around a dusty sand lot in Puerto Rico. From that humble beginning, Chi Chi Rodriguez went on to win thirty tournaments and more than $7 million in prize money, all while becoming the game's unmatched entertainer and philosopher.

One of six children, Chi Chi grew up in Rio Pedras, just outside San Juan. His father worked fourteen hours a day as a laborer, never earning more than $18 a week, and for a time, Chi Chi worked side by side with him in the sugarcane fields. Then one day he wandered past a golf course and his life changed forever. He first became a caddie and then took up the game, displaying an extraordinary eye-hand coordination and imagination for shot-making. By the age of twelve, he'd shot 67 and his career path was set.

THE SECRET:

Throw yourself against a wall. Hit hard against a braced left side.

On the PGA Tour, Chi Chi became known as much for his playfulness as his play. He dressed colorfully, favoring Day-Glo pink and turquoise shirts and a jaunty fedora (underneath which lived the game's worst-ever toupee). "I used to put my hat over the hole when I made a birdie or eagle," he said "because I felt the bird could fly out." When some of his fellow competitors complained, he changed his routine, delighting galleries with a brief sword dance after every significant putt.

What he lacked in physical presence, Chi Chi made up for with an intense will to succeed. "The expression 'the eye of the Tiger' is mine," he claimed in an interview at the end of his career. "Since I was a kid, I had a picture in my house of a tiger, and I'd look at his eyes for about thirty minutes without blinking. That was my goal every day. I'd look at that tiger and I wouldn't blink. I would just draw his eyes out. A tiger always gave me the strength because a tiger shows no hate, he doesn't show any fear, he just shows that he is in control. That's why I used to do that, and I would just say that I got the eyes of a tiger. The TV personalities use that phrase now. Well, that's created by me."

Chi Chi also followed a rigorous fitness regimen decades before it became popular among his Tour colleagues, and while on the senior circuit, in an attempt to stay youthful, he once traveled to Germany and had himself injected with lamb embryo cells. But the key moment in his career came in 1963, when he made a major change in his swing and suddenly began hitting the ball prodigious distances, regularly outdriving Nicklaus, Palmer, and the rest.

Chi Chi Rodriguez delighted galleries for 40 years with his celebratory sword dance.

Four years later, in a book of just seventy-four pages, Chi Chi shared his unorthodox key—"a perfectly solid left wall" against which he threw his entire body in the downswing. For a brief time, it became the bible for all golfers of small stature.

RODRIGUEZ'S SECRET

Always Experiment

My swing may not be picture-pretty, but it enables me to coil enormous power in my body, which I release when I hit the ball. It is a swing that confounds the purists because most of the things I do are wrong. But I still get results, my own way. This is why I have said repeatedly that experimentation is so important in determining what is most comfortable.

Backswing

Now, from the beginning, let me analyze my swing and the movements that make it smooth. At address, my left arm is extended and relatively relaxed. My right arm is completely relaxed and tucked in to the side. My right shoulder is lower than the left. My feet are positioned slightly farther apart than the shoulders.

I start my downswing with a tremendous pull of my left hand.

On the backswing, I use a slow turn. I don't particularly concentrate on taking the club back with the hands. I just think of a good turn of the shoulders and hips. My body, during the backswing, is moving laterally off the ball, to the right. Principally, this increases the distance the clubhead travels on the backswing and gives me the arc of a much bigger man. Because of this, I naturally get more club velocity.

> My swing may not be picture-perfect but it enables me to coil enormous power in my body, which I release when I hit the ball. It is a swing that confounds the purists because most of the things I do are wrong. But I get results.

I also take the club back very low to the ground so when I come back I flatten the path of the clubhead through the ball. I accomplish this by bending the knees and turning my legs during the backswing, more than is customary for the average golfer. When the club has reached the top of the backswing, I am in a semi-crouch.

By now, my left knee has moved well to the right of the ball and I eventually come off my left heel—much more so than a bigger man does. This additional leg turn is essential in my swing, however, allowing me to coil the muscles in my right thigh and reach for the fullest extension possible of the left arm and the muscles of the upper back. This, then, is where I generate the power in my downswing.

Downward Movement

The down movement is the most important part of my swing. When I have reached the desired height of the backswing, I pause slightly. With my backswing completed, I am braced and crouched. My shoulder turn is now about 90 degrees, but the hips turn much less. My left heel is higher off the ground than is usual for golfers. I then start the downswing with a tremendous pull of my left hand. It may appear that I am trying to hit the ball with the bottom part of the club held in the left hand.

But about halfway down, things change. I throw my right shoulder as hard and fast as possible into the shot, with a sweeping motion. Now it appears that I am trying to hit the ball with my right shoulder alone. This hard swing-through with my right shoulder is not just a fast, jerking motion. It is part of my complete, smooth downswing.

At this point I am also using my legs to the fullest extent. When I start back toward the ball, my left heel has been slammed back into the ground. Note also that I keep my wrists cocked as I start down. Then I drive laterally into the ball with a combination of the forceful movement of the left arm, the right shoulder, and the muscles in the right thigh.

The left foot serves as a brace—if it breaks, so does the swing.

These are the muscles I spoke of in the backswing, the muscles that were fully wound up at the top of my back movement. Now I use them for power, and the power pushes me forward. Halfway down, my knees are wider apart as I brace my lower body to withstand the impact shock. The wrists still are cocked, and the left arm is straight. My right elbow has returned to my side.

Impact

On impact, my right arm extends as I hit the ball. My left foot gives way to tremendous unwinding action. My left shoulder moves up rapidly, showing a very pronounced tilt and turn of the shoulders. By now, my weight has moved well off the right side, which is normal since the clubhead has moved through the ball and started up. My hips, shoulders, and knees are turning at their greatest momentum at this point. My head position shows that I don't let it restrict my swing. Although the clubhead has struck the ball only a second earlier, my head has turned so that I am looking down the fairway.

Extremely important now is that my left leg is still braced so it can absorb the force of the swing. The wall is strong. It has not crumpled. Whew! Even talking about it tires me out, and I am violating my philosophy on golf. I would not want the average golfer to think of all those things when he is swinging. He would probably wind up missing the ball.

Concentration on Shoulder and Hip Turn

What you should do is apply and try some of the rules. See if they work for you. Then practice. It is the only way to improve the swing and get the power you need. If you are going to keep one thing in mind when you start the backswing, concentrate on getting the good turn of the shoulders and hips.

Also keep in mind that you are inviting trouble by starting the downswing with a hard pull or thrust of the right arm only. Start the downswing with a tremendous pull of the left hand. By doing it with the right, you cause the wrists to break or uncock near the top of the downswing. This causes a loss of power by the time the clubhead reaches the ball. The initial right-arm pull also can cause you to lose your correct aim. The result is usually a drastic hook to the left or a bad slice to the right.

FROM *CHI CHI'S SECRETS OF POWER GOLF* BY JUAN (CHI CHI) RODRIGUEZ

DR. BOB ROTELLA

GET OUT OF YOUR OWN WAY

"If you argue that a goal is unattainable and say,
'I'm just being realistic,' what you're really doing is justifying
a negative attitude. I contend there are no limits,
and that you create your own reality."

Question: What do Davis Love, Padraig Harrington, John Daly, the New York Yankees the San Francisco 49ers, the U.S. Olympic Equestrian Team, and the Chrysler Corporation have in common?

Answer: Dr. Bob Rotella. All have been coached by the world's most famous sports psychologist. From the fairways to the playing fields to the boardrooms, Rotella has worked his wiles on the minds of successful people to make them more successful.

His prize student may be Tom Kite, who first met Rotella at the Doral Open in 1984 and wrote of the experience a decade later in a foreword for one of Rotella's books:

"I was in one of those phases where I just couldn't seem to do anything on the course, and my scores showed it. I hadn't had a top finish in months and winning seemed as far away as the moon. But after a couple of meetings early in the week, when Doc did no more than refresh my memory of those great thoughts I usually have when I am playing my best, I went out and actually won the tournament, beating none other than Jack Nicklaus down the stretch. My swing hadn't changed but I was a new person. All of a sudden I could hit shots I could not even imagine the week before. I had a new best friend, and it was me!

"In the first twelve years of my life on the PGA Tour, I had established myself as a pretty decent player but had won only five official tournaments. In the past ten years since meeting Doc, I have won fourteen tournaments, played on the Ryder Cup, and won my first major, the U.S. Open. To say that I think he has helped make me a better player would be an understatement."

Rotella doesn't see himself as a mental guru—more a coach, and that is in fact how he began his working life, as the assistant basketball coach at Mt. St. Joseph Academy in Rutland, Vermont, the same high school where he'd excelled at both basketball and lacrosse. As a coach, however, Rotella began to realize that victory came not to those with the best jump shots and free throws but to those with the best attitude—the players who had the lion's share of confidence and concentration. And the more he observed, the more fascinated he became with the mental side of athletics. So when the chance came to go to the University of Connecticut and coach lacrosse while simultaneously studying toward a graduate degree in psychology, he jumped at it.

In 1976, having earned his Ph.D., Rotella was hired by the University of Virginia as head of its department of sports psychology. Back then, his exposure to the game of golf had consisted largely of boyhood summers caddying at the Rutland Country Club. But one of the editors of *Golf Digest* had gotten word or Rotella and his ability to focus and motivate athletes, and so the doctor was invited to speak at the *Golf Digest* teaching summit, a gathering of the game's best teachers and players for the purpose of sharing wisdom and information.

Among those at the table was Sam Snead, probably the most naturally talented superstar the game has ever produced, and a fellow not given to heavy bouts of introspection. Before making his presentation, Rotella was cautioned to expect Snead to take issue with everything he had to say. He was not surprised, therefore, when the first hand up at the conclusion of his remarks was Sam's.

But Snead looked him in the eye and said, "I hate to think how many U.S. Opens I would have won if I had heard someone a long time ago say some of the things you just said."

Rotella had been anointed. From that moment forward, he became golf's leading mental guru. More than a quarter century later, he remains the man the Tour stars seek when they're in need of a mental boost.

THE SECRET:

Have fun. Shed your expectations on the first tee. Forgive, forget, and be compassionate with yourself.

What Rotella imparts to his clients is neither complex nor mysterious. Essentially, he tells them to aim high, think positively, and trust their skills. Moreover, he instills those ideas in a way that is simple and straightforward. His basic message is to choose to succeed—get out of your own way and unleash the superior golfer that lives inside you.

In his first and most important book, Rotella shared his philosophy through a series of anecdotes and aphorisms. The chapter that follows has the same title as the book: "Golf Is Not a Game of Perfect."

ROTELLA'S SECRET

A few years ago, Tom Kite and I were in Austin, and we played a round at Lakeway Country Club with a couple of members of the University of Texas golf team. It was a beautiful day and a great match. They all shot between 69 and 73. Afterward, we all sat down for a soda, and it was obvious they were dying to ask a question. So I said, "What's on your mind?"

One of the guys replied, "Tom, we basically hit it as good as you did today. When we missed and hit a bunker, our bunker shots were as good as yours. When we missed a green, we got it up and down like you did. We scored within a shot or two of one another. So how come you're the all-time leading money winner and we're the number three and four golfers at the University of Texas?"

Tom grinned at me and said, "Do you want to tell them?"

"No," I said. "They'll believe it more if it comes from you."

"The difference," Tom said, "is that when you guys get in tournaments, the likelihood is that you'll lose your concentration on four or five shots every round. Over a four-day tournament, even if every lapse costs you just one stroke, that's sixteen to twenty shots a week, and that's the difference between being the leading money winner and losing your card. If one of these lapses costs you two or three strokes, or you get upset and lose concentration on a second shot, you can be talking about twenty-five to thirty strokes a week, and you won't even make the college golf team. Over a career, losing concentration once in a while can mean lots of strokes."

I joined in. "Today, each of you hit a few balls off line, into the rough or the trees. But since it wasn't a tournament round, you didn't let it bother you. You just went over and found the ball, pitched out, wedged up to the green, saved your par, and went on. But in the Southwest Conference Tournament, you might hit the same shot and overreact to it. You start telling yourself, 'You're such a jerk,' and 'Why does this always happen in a big tournament?' Before you even hit your next shot, you're convinced you're going to make bogey or double-bogey. And you do."

One of the things Tom, or any successful pro, does best is to accept his bad shots, shrug them off, and concentrate completely on the next one. He has accepted the fact that, as he puts it, "Golf is not a game of perfect."

This does not mean that a pro doesn't strive to eliminate mistakes from his game. He does, unless he wants to savor the joy of Qualifying School once again. But he understands that while striving for perfection is essential, demanding perfection of himself on the golf course is deadly.

Of all the tournaments Tom Kite has won, one of the most impressive to me was at Bay Hill a few years ago. He and Davis Love both butchered the final hole. Tom hit his approach in the water and Davis flew his over the green. What impressed me was the way Tom responded to the shot that went in the water. He then had to play a long wedge shot over the same water to a

Rotella helps students to get out of their own way.

tight pin. He could have dwelled on the way he hit the last shot so badly. He could have tried for the middle of the green or even the bunker, just to make sure he didn't make two splashes in a row. Instead, he hit that second wedge stiff, made the putt, and went on to win the playoff.

The television announcers and the golf writers weren't impressed. They don't think a guy who hits his ball into the water on the last hole deserves to win the golf tournament. But I knew how brilliantly Tom had responded to one of the fundamental challenges of the game:

No matter what happens with any shot you hit, accept it. Acceptance is the last step in a sound routine.

Getting angry is one of your options. But if you choose to get angry, you are likely to get tighter. That's going to hurt your rhythm and your flow. It will upset you and distract you. It will switch on your analytical mind and your tendency to criticize and analyze anything you do that falls short of perfection. It will start you thinking about the mechanical flaws in your swing and trying to correct them.

You will very likely play worse.

Alternatively, you could train yourself to accept the fact that as a human being, you are prone to mistakes. Golf is a game played by human beings. Therefore, golf is a game of mistakes.

The best golfers strive to minimize mistakes, but they don't expect to eliminate them. And they understand that it's most important to respond well to the mistakes they inevitably make.

Golf is all about recovering from bad shots. It's about getting up and down from sand traps. It's about knowing when it's smart to pitch sideways out of the rough and do your best to save par or bogey with your wedge and putter. It's about the exhilaration that comes from spotting a narrow path through the trees and threading your ball through it to the green. Viewed this way, any round you play will be enjoyable.

> On the first tee, you should have two goals. One is to have fun. The other involves the process of playing, not the results. This goal is to get your mind where it is supposed to be on every shot.

But if you bring a smothering perfectionism to the golf course, you will probably leave with a higher handicap and a lousy disposition, because your game will never meet your expectations.

Expectations are great if you confine them to long-range considerations. It's fine, for example, to expect that if you work at your game intelligently for an extended period of time, you will improve. But expectations can hurt you if they are narrowly focused on the results of a particular stroke, hole, or round.

Golfers in American society, though, tend to be people who are used to getting what they want. Many were born into families of wealth and achievement. Many of those who were not are people who rose to positions of wealth and status because of ambition and hard work. They expect to master golf just as they've mastered everything else in life. If they are competing, they expect to win. If they swing at a golf ball, they expect to hit it well, every time. When their golf fails to meet their expectations, what happens? They begin to judge how well they are doing against how well they expected to do. They get angry at themselves. They tie themselves up in knots.

This is not to say you should not think about hitting every ball to the target and believe that every shot will do just that. You should. But there is a fine difference between believing that the ball will go where you want it to go and expecting that it will and being upset if it doesn't. You have to put expectations out of your mind by the time you get to the first tee.

On the first tee, you should have two immediate goals. One is to have fun. The other involves the process of playing, not the results. This goal is to get your mind where it's supposed to be on every shot. If you do that, you'll shoot the best score you're capable of shooting that day, whether it's 67 or 107.

Having fun shouldn't be so difficult. You are, after all, out in the fresh air. You are playing in what amounts to an emerald park. Clipped grasslands, according to one theorist, have been the most soothing and emotionally satisfying habitat for man since the first humans dropped out of the trees. You are, presumably, in good company, the company of other golfers. You have a chance to strike a little ball and send it flying straight and true against the sky, an act that seems to resonate pleasantly somewhere deep within the human brain. These are the reasons you initially liked golf even though you couldn't play it very well. Savor all of them as you play. Let the joy of the game come to you.

Shooting the best score you're capable of on a given day requires that, to paraphrase something that's become trite, you become your own best friend—or in this case, a good caddie and pro to yourself. Can you imagine someone paying a caddie to berate him after a bad shot in this fashion: "You left that putt short! You're a wimp! No guts!" Can you imagine someone paying a teaching pro to get apoplectic and tell him he's an idiot for slicing the ball? Or to visit his hotel room after a bad round and remind him of all the mistakes he made that day?

No one would do it. Yet, every time I play golf, I see people doing it to themselves.

You have to be nonjudgmental. You have to forgive and forget and be compassionate toward yourself. But in our culture, people, particularly high achievers, are taught to judge themselves harshly. They're taught that being compassionate toward oneself is weak

and indulgent. There is a kernel of truth in this. There is a time and place for tough self-evaluation, and you will not improve as a golfer unless you honestly examine your game and work on its weaknesses.

But don't do it on the golf course.

When a shot is done, it's done. The only constructive thing you can do about it is to hit the next shot as well as you can. That requires that you stay optimistic and enthusiastic.

If you must have expectations about results, expect to make some mistakes.

Acceptance allows a golfer to be patient, and patience is one of the necessary virtues in golf. Sometimes players tell me they are sick and tired of hearing me say that they must be patient and keep believing that if they do all the right things, the results they want will follow. That's just one more thing they have to learn to be patient about.

If you remember to have fun, it shouldn't be too hard. When was the last time you were impatient when you were having fun?

Remember, too, that golf is not a game of justice. A player can practice properly, think properly, and still hit a bad shot. Or he can hit a good shot and watch a bad hop or a gust of wind deposit the ball in a sand trap.

A golfer can't force results to happen. He can only do everything possible to give those results a chance to happen. As Tom Watson once put it, to become a really good golfer, you have to learn how to wait. But you have to learn to wait with confidence.

On the Tour, there are many factors conspiring to raise a player's expectations, to encourage him to demand perfection of himself. When this happens, the work ethic that brought a lot of players to the Tour can become a double-edged sword, driving an individual to grind himself down in a dogged, joyless attempt to meet those expectations. A successful player has to develop the ability to evaluate himself objectively, to work harder when he needs more practice, but to ease up when he's tempted to push too hard.

Scott Verplank won his first PGA tournament, the Western Open, while he was still an amateur. He expected that his golf could only get better once he finished school and could commit himself totally to golf, practicing as long as he wanted, playing all the time.

It didn't immediately work out that way for him. Performances that would have won or at least finished in the top ten in any amateur tournament didn't make the cut on the Tour. He perceived them as failures. He responded as most good athletes have been taught to do, by working harder. He practiced all the time. He practiced when he shouldn't have, when what he really needed and wanted to do was sit in his hotel room and read a book. And the hard work didn't show up in better results. Eventually, he found himself returning periodically to Oklahoma State and asking the football coach to let him help out with the running

backs. It was the only way he could take his mind off golf.

Talking with him before the Buick Open one year, I emphasized the need for him to take it easy on himself. I told him it would be all right to stay in his room and read a book for a few hours instead of going to the practice tee all day. And I asked him to promise me that he would try to have fun.

I returned to Charlottesville to teach. On Thursday evening, I got a call from Scott.

"Gosh, Doc," he said, "I did it! I had fun all day long. And I'm leading! But what was really great was that I missed a 5-footer on the first hole and I didn't let it get to me! Made a 35-footer on the second hole."

"I bet you were invited into the press tent afterward," I said.

"Yeah, I was," he replied.

"And I bet that they asked whether Scott Verplank could win his first tournament as a professional."

"Yeah, that's all they talked about."

"Well, if you're not careful, they're going to have you thinking about the results you get instead of having fun. You might go out there fixed on shooting a certain number and keeping the lead and getting in position to win. You have to remember to throw away expectations, to just have fun and see what's the lowest score you can shoot. You have to attend to the process, not concern yourself with the results."

Of course, I would not be telling this story if it didn't have a happy ending. Scott won the tournament, and he called me up on

Sunday evening. After telling me what happened, he said he was being interviewed by the golf writer for a newspaper in Dallas, and he was having trouble explaining to him why the idea of having fun had just helped him win a breakthrough golf tournament. Then he put the writer on.

I talked for a while about the necessity to relax, enjoy the game, and accept mistakes if a player wants to do his best. The writer still didn't see it. He couldn't understand why having fun could be difficult.

"Try this," I said. "Tomorrow in your paper, ask everyone in Dallas who plays golf to try a two-week experiment. During the first week, after every shot that's less than perfect, they should get disgusted and angry with themselves. And they should stay mad even after they leave the course and go home. I guarantee you every one of your readers will be able to do it.

"The second week, tell them that after every shot, no matter what happens to it, they are not going to be bothered. They are to have fun, stay decisive, and keep ripping the ball to the target. They are going to have a ball no matter what they shoot.

"You can offer a big cash prize to anyone who can do what you ask during the second week, because I guarantee you there won't be many people, if any, who will be honestly able to collect it."

Retirees sometimes have a problem analogous to Scott Verplank's. He expected his golf game to improve immediately once he finished school and could play all the time. Retirees often expect to get good after they stop working and don't have to confine their play to weekends.

If you must have expectations about results, expect to make some mistakes.

When it doesn't happen that way, it's often because they forget that golf remains a game. They practice more, but they also raise their expectations every time they step onto the course. They forget how to laugh off mistakes.

Players plagued by perfectionism and unforgiving expectations would do well to remember the common sense their mothers taught them, or would have taught them if they'd paid attention.

Here's what Adela Saraceni told her son, Gene Sarazen, about perfectionism and expectations, just after he lost the 1927 U.S. Open by a single shot:

"Son, everything that happens to you happens for the best. Don't ever forget that. You can't win all the time, son."

Gene Sarazen said this little bit of advice stuck with him and helped him to develop a certain fatalism about his golf that allowed him to accept whatever happened and make the best of it. If Mrs. Saraceni were around today, I might be out of business.

FROM *GOLF IS NOT A GAME OF PERFECT* BY DR. BOB ROTELLA

ROTELLA'S SECRET

PAUL RUNYAN

LITTLE POISON'S BIG IMPACT

"Through necessity, I had a lifelong devotion to the short game, the searching for shortcuts that would somehow let me compete, and hopefully excel, in a world of stronger players."

At the peak of his power, leaning into it with everything he had, Paul Runyan could drive a golf ball all of 230 yards. That put him 30 to 40 yards behind his peers on the pro tour of the 1930s. But it didn't stop the man nicknamed Little Poison. Runyan bunted his way to twenty-nine victories, two Ryder Cup teams, a pair of PGA Championships, and the World Golf Hall of Fame.

The son of a dairy farmer from Hot Springs, Arkansas, Runyan milked cows only until he discovered a nearby golf course where he became a caddie and taught himself how to play. At five-foot-seven and 125 pounds, he was never built for power, so it's not surprising that the swing he developed featured a sizable sway back and through the ball.

"I had to work for it," he said. "I was not a natural. All the kids in the caddie pen beat me, until I just dug it out and became better."

That Depression-bred toughness would serve him for many years to come.

Playing against the likes of Gene Sarazen and Walter Hagen in their primes, Runyan was the Tour's leading money winner in 1933,

> **THE SECRET:**
>
> Grip the putter with your palms facing upward and inward and your arms at a 90-degree angle to each other. Then make a wrist-free stroke.

Runyan beat Sam Snead decisively in the final of the 1938 PGA.

with nine victories, and again the next year with seven wins. In the same year he won the first of his two PGA Championships, beating Craig Wood on the thirty-eighth hole of the final match.

What Runyan lacked in distance, he made up for in precision, particularly with his fairway woods, which he hit with the same accuracy that longer hitters displayed with their middle and short irons. But his secret weapon, without question, was his chipping and putting.

Runyan's finest hour came in the 1938 PGA Championship. It was contested at match play back then, and in the thirty-six-hole final his opponent was Sam Snead. Just blossoming into a career that would bring him an all-time record eighty-one victories, Snead was already known as Slammin' Sammy, one of the longest hitters the game had ever seen.

The pundits predicted a wipe-out, and that's exactly what it was—a record 8-and-7 win. However, the victory went not to Snead but Runyan. As Snead outdrove him by 40 yards and more, Little Poison popped wood shot after wood shot onto the greens of the Shawnee Country Club, and once he got to those greens—or even near them—he was in complete command. On the par-5 holes that day, Runyan wielded his wedge and putter for six birdies. At one point during the match, Snead said, "This isn't golf; it's magic."

After a stint in the service during World War II, Runyan became primarily a teaching professional and worked at several clubs on the West Coast. Although he'd dropped out of school after the eighth grade, he had a good mind for math. During a teaching stint in California, many of his pupils were engineers from the aerospace business, and he picked their brains, all the while refining his thoughts on putting and chipping.

In 1979, he assembled those thoughts between two covers, collaborating with Dick Aultman on *The Short Way to Lower Scoring*. What follows are his views on how to putt. A cogent, well-reasoned combination of art and science, feel and mechanics, the Runyan putting method remains as good a blueprint as there is on how to develop a reliable, repeating stroke.

RUNYAN'S SECRET

The grip and address position I advocate for putting, and for chipping as well, are designed to create a firm-wristed stroke. In these areas of the short game, wrist action serves no useful purpose. It merely decreases your chances of making solid contact with the club moving on the correct path, at the right speed. If you can learn to hold the putter and address the putt exactly as I suggest, you will have automatically reduced to the barest minimum any chance of either misconnecting with the ball and/or stroking it off your chosen line.

Flipping with the wrists makes the putterhead lift too abruptly during the backstroke, descend too abruptly during the downstroke and then flip abruptly upward again on the follow-through. All this upward-downward-upward movement reduces the duration that the putterhead is actually moving parallel with the ground at ball level. It also minimizes the duration during which the club is carrying the proper amount of effective loft. It can reduce the duration in which your clubface is aligned square to its path. It can reduce the duration during which your putterhead is moving along the line you have chosen. Most certainly, any flipping of the wrist loosens your grip, thus reducing your control of the putter.

Moreover, flipping the wrists also adds another speed-producing element to the stroke, an element that is not needed on these shorter shots. This added element makes it more difficult to control distance.

If you now putt with a wristy stroke, you may find that the change to a firm-wristed stroke will temporarily reduce your ability to control distance on your putts. However, once you become familiar with using a firmer stroking action, your distance control

PUTT WITH YOUR ARMS . . .

NOT WITH YOUR WRISTS

The ideal putting stroke disallows any hinging of the wrists, but allows each forearm to do its equal share in moving the putter back and forward on the proper path. This firm-wristed stroke helps eliminate any undue change in grip pressure, any unnecessary speed-producing element and any flipping of the putterhead—either upward-downward or opened and closed—all of which are likely to occur whenever the wrists come into play.

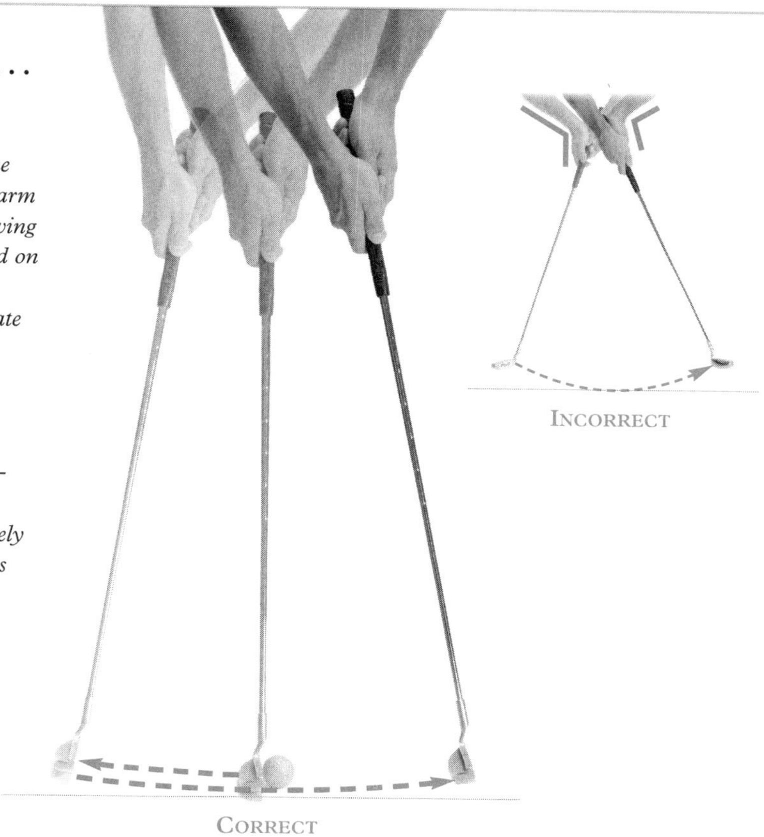

INCORRECT

CORRECT

will become better than ever. Not only will you have eliminated an unnecessary speed-producing variable, but your contact with the ball will be more consistent. Your ability to stroke putts in the right direction will also improve, because you will have eliminated a variable that can misalign the putterface and misdirect its path of movement.

With wristiness eliminated, the stroke you should arrive at is one in which the whole job of moving the putter back and forward is given over to your arms. Your hands will merely hold onto the club firmly, each with an equal amount of pressure that remains constant throughout the stroke.

It will be a stroke in which each forearm shares equally in moving the putter shaft back and forward, each pushing or pulling with an equal amount of effort and, most important, each directing that effort in the

MODEL ADDRESS POSITION FOR PUTTING

This is the ideal address position for putting. By adopting all aspects of pre-stroke positioning, you can preset yourself to putt the ball in the right direction automatically, without conscious mental effort. This frees your mind to focus solely on distance as you actually swing the putter.

same direction. If your arms work together equally, each directing its efforts in the same direction, and if your hands grip with equal and constant pressure, the club will move on a consistent path and the clubface will always be square to that path.

However, the path on which I think your putter should move back and forward is not a perfectly straight line. I'm sure you are aware that on full shots with longer clubs, the clubhead arcs around your body to some extent. It may start back away from the ball straight along your target line, but then it gradually moves more and more to your side of that line—the inside—as it swings back

and up. During the downswing it arcs back to the line before returning to the inside after contacting the ball.

It is natural that your putting stroke should follow this same pattern, but to a lesser degree. Though you do stand closer to the ball when putting than on full shots, you still must stand to the side of it. For this reason, it is natural that your putterhead move a bit to the inside during your back-stroke, then back to the line as it returns to the ball. The extent that it moves to the inside will depend on the length of your stroke. On short putts, where the stroke is relatively short, the putterhead may not leave your putting line a noticeable amount. On long putts, however, it might move an inch or more to the inside before your backstroke is completed.

On these longer putts, especially, attempting to move the putter back on a perfectly straight line requires an unnatural maneuvering of the arms and hands. This maneuvering must then be reversed perfectly—and, again, unnaturally—during the forward stroke to return the putter back to the ball on a similarly straight path.

It is also unnatural for you to try to keep your putter facing in the same direction throughout your stroke. This requires an abnormal counterclockwise turning of your arms and hands during the backstroke and a perfect reversal during your forward swing.

Instead, it is natural and logical that the putter face square to its path, not to the target line, throughout the stroke. As the path moves gradually to the inside during the backstroke, the putter should gradually face more and more to the right of the putting line. Then it should gradually return to its original facing as the putterhead itself returns from inside to along the putting line during the forward stroke.

Again, I believe that if you can adopt the positions I assume before putting, to the point that they feel natural to you, you will have accomplished all that is humanly possible to strike putts solidly in the right direction. You then will have created a situation that frees you to focus solely on the one

remaining element—distance—as you actually make your stroke.

Arms. In the firm-wristed stroke, the arms must do the job of moving the putter. Thus, their positioning at address is critical, both in relation to each other and in relation to the club itself.

If you are right-handed, your left forearm should be set directly in front of the putter shaft. Your right forearm should be directly behind it. If you were to add an extension to the top of the shaft so that it continued upward between your arms to your stomach, both forearms would parallel that extension. Neither would be above or below it. Put another way, if a spike were driven horizontally through your forearms, it would pass directly through this shaft extension.

When your forearms oppose each other in this way, directly in front of and behind the shaft, they are in perfect position for each to do its fair share in channeling power directly through the shaft to move it on a proper path with the putterface remaining square to that path.

There is one other aspect of arm positioning you should notice and, hopefully, adopt. Observe the angle at which my forearms join the club. An angle of about 90 degrees is formed between the arms. The shaft, if extended upward, would split this 90-degree angle. Thus each forearm approaches the shaft at an angle of about 45 degrees.

This angling of the arms to the shaft is important because it determines, in large part, your overall posture at address. If the angle between the shaft and the forearms is less than 45 degrees, because the arms are too close together, you will be forced to stand too upright. This puts you too far above your work, too far from your job of making solid contact. It makes your stroke too willowy, too lacking in crispness and control of the putterhead.

You could address putts with your arms angled to the club at less than 45 degrees, however, and still assume a proper posture. But to do so, you would need to grip too far down on your putter, perhaps below the leather. This would shorten the putter to the extent that, on long putts especially, you would need to make an inordinately long or forceful stroke to get the ball to reach the hole.

The opposite extreme, angling the arms to the shaft at more than 45 degrees, forces

POSITION OF ARMS

The goal is to set the forearms so each can direct an equal force directly through the puttershaft, pushing and pulling it back and forward on the correct path. They should be positioned directly in front of and behind the shaft so the shaft, if extended upward, would run directly between them (large illustration). You cannot direct equal force through the shaft in the right direction if this extension would run above or beneath the forearms, or if either arm is set above or below the extension (smaller illustrations).

you into an extremely crouched address posture. This is a lesser evil than standing too tall—at least it gets you closer to your work. Unfortunately, this wide angling of the arms to the shaft also weakens your hold on the club. It tears your hands away from the shaft and can lead to a willowy, uncontrolled stroke unless you greatly intensify your grip pressure. This, in turn, tightens your arm muscles and inhibits their ability to move freely back and forward,

especially on longer putts that require a relatively long stroke.

Increasing the arm angles to the shaft beyond 45 degrees also tends to force your upper arms away from your side, where I think they should rest gently as you address the putt.

I have given you quite a bit of information about the wheres and whys of arm positioning in this section. However, the main points to remember are that the forearms set

Not only should the forearms be directly in front of and behind the imaginary shaft extension, but each should angle down to the shaft at 45 degrees (large illustration). If this angling is less than 45 degrees, you will need to stand too tall—too far from your work (smaller illustration, top) or grip too far down on the shaft. If the angle formed between each arm and the shaft is more than 45 degrees (smaller illustration, bottom), your elbows will be forced outward so they inhibit free arm movement. You will be forced to rely on your hands and wrists instead, and you may be forced to grip the putter too tightly to retain control of it.

directly behind and in front of the club with neither being above or below the imaginary shaft extension, and that each approaches the shaft at a 45-degree angle.

Hands. The putting grip I advocate does more than merely encourage a firm-wristed stroke. It also allows you to position your arms correctly, as I have just described. You will find it unnatural, perhaps impossible, to position your arms correctly if you do not position your hands correctly. The reverse applies as well.

The ideal position for the hands when putting and chipping is for each palm to be facing inward and upward at a 45-degree angle. In other words, each palm should face midway between directly upward and directly inward toward the other.

The best way for you to see and feel the logic behind this putting-chipping grip is actually to set your hands on a putter. Hold the club about ¾ inch from the end of the shaft. Sole its head flat on the ground, just far enough away from your feet so that it is directly below the bridge of your nose when you bend comfortably from the knees and hips.

You should find that this grip naturally makes your

upper arms want to rest lightly against your rib cage, as they should. Your forearms will set directly in front of and behind the club. The shaft will be angled toward you so an extension of the grip runs straight up to your stomach, parallel with your forearms. Neither forearm will be above or below this extension. Each forearm will angle in toward the club at an angle of approximately 45 degrees.

Now, to appreciate why this is the ideal grip for putting, I would like you purposely to alter the position of your hands and note what happens.

First, turn your hands away from each other so they both face directly upward. As you do this, you will notice that your elbows want to press in too firmly against your rib cage. This would stifle free movement of

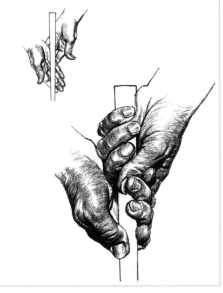

POSITION OF HANDS
Position each hand so that the palm, if opened, would face upward and inward at 45 degrees. Thus each should face midway between directly upward and directly inward to each other. This way each hand thwarts the other from opening or closing the putterface during the stroke. The grip pressure should be equally firm in each hand and should remain constant throughout the stroke.

your arms during the stroke. You will also notice that the club wants to come loose in your left hand, which would force you to grip too tightly and further impede free arm movement. You will notice, too, that the clubshaft wants to move outward away from you, so that the club begins to rest on its toe end. This sets the shaft above, not between, your forearms. The push-pull force of the arms during your stroke would no longer pass directly through it, as it should. It would be difficult to move the putter on a proper path. Hopefully this experiment will help you appreciate that facing the hands directly upward is less than ideal.

Next, I would like you to turn both hands inward. Turn them beyond the original 45 degrees until both palms actually face each other. Neither palm is now facing upward or downward. As you make this adjustment, you should find that the shaft gradually lowers to the extent that its imaginary extension would run below your forearms. This again would make it difficult to push-pull the club with your arms in the right direction. You should find that your upper arms want to move away from your rib cage. You may feel some tension in the muscles at the back of your upper arms, tension which would inhibit your arm movement during your stroke.

You will notice, too, that your elbows have spread farther apart, thus widening the angle between each forearm and the club well beyond the prescribed 45 degrees.

Finally, you will again notice that your hands tend to loosen their hold on the club.

Thus, you can see some of the ways in which the palms-facing grip thwarts your efforts to position your arms and club in what I consider to be the ideal relationship.

There is a way for you to grip the club with your palms facing without sacrificing this relationship. You will experience that solution by merely "standing taller," by bending less from the knees and hips. Try it.

Quite honestly, there are some excellent putters who do use the palms-facing grip. I feel it is less than ideal, however, for the reasons you have just experienced. To use this grip fairly effectively; you must stand too tall at address. I feel, again, that for most people this sets them too far above their work. It reduces their ability to control the business of solidly contacting the ball with a crisp, firm-wristed stroke.

Thus far, in each of the three grips I have asked you to try, you have set your hands on the club in what I consider to be a "neutral" position. That is, each palm was faced upward and/or inward an equal number of degrees. This neutrality of hand positioning is extremely important in putting and chipping because it helps you return the putter to the same facing at contact that it was in when you aimed it at address.

Facing the palms in a neutral position creates an equal amount of resistance in each hand and arm. Each thwarts the other from opening or closing the putterface prior to contact. Thus the neutral grip allows you to push and pull equally with each arm while maintaining an equal and constant amount of grip pressure in each hand throughout the stroke. To me this is natural and ideal.

Finally, I would like to stress that you hold the club with an equal amount of firmness in each hand—just enough to inhibit any wrist action—and that you maintain this same degree of firmness in each hand throughout your stroke.

Eyes. If you will pardon a quip, in putting the eyes should not be overlooked. Where you position your eyes at address can affect the direction in which you aim the putter before you stroke and where you direct it as you stroke.

You should position your eyes at address so that a line extended across them would be directly over your putting line. Setting your eyes over the line helps you see the correct line to the hole. Thus you improve your chances of aiming the putter in the right direction. Also, since we tend to adjust our stance and body alignment according to where the club is aimed, aiming correctly leads to proper stance and alignment. This, in turn, greatly simplifies your instinctive ability to stroke on line. In short, proper eye positioning helps tremendously in making the ball roll where you want it to roll.

Setting your eyes out beyond the ball, over an area outside the line, tends to make you see an incorrect putting line, one that appears to be to the hole but is actually to the left. Thus, you tend to aim and stroke to the left, at least on your first attempts. Thereafter, having seen the ball finish to the left, you will still aim in that direction—because of the mispositioning of the eyes—but you may compensate by pushing your stroke out to the right of where you had aimed, thus creating a glancing blow.

The reverse tends to happen when your eyes are set over an area that is on your side of the line, the inside. You will tend to misaim to the right and stroke in that direction initially. Then, seeing putts finish to the right, you

POSITION OF EYES

Setting the eyes directly over the putting line helps you aim the putter properly because you are better able to see the correct line. This helps your feet and body remain parallel to the line. It enables you to stroke on the proper path, from inside to along the line.

will adjust by pulling your stroke to the left of where you had misaimed. The result, again, is a glancing blow. The rightward-aimed putter is swung to the left.

Where you position your eyes not only affects where you aim the putter and direct your stroke, it also affects the overall shape of your stroke. You will recall my mentioning that, because we stand to the side of the ball, the putterhead moves slightly to the inside of the line during the backstroke, noticeably so on longer putts. Thereafter, it gradually returns to the line and moves along it during contact with the ball before returning once again to the inside. You will be more likely to stroke along such a path if your eyes are set directly over the line.

Periodically check to see that you are setting your eyes directly over the putting line you have chosen. Aside from looking in a full-length mirror at home, you can do this during your practice sessions as follows: Once you have assumed your address position, while keeping your posture intact, lift your putter at the grip end with a thumb and forefinger. Let it dangle from the bridge at your nose. Hold it so that the putterhead extends lengthwise in the direction you are putting. If your eyes are properly positioned, the putterhead will cover the part of the putting line that extends immediately behind the ball.

Feet and ball positions. Where you set your feet in relation to the ball helps determine whether you will contact your putts solidly with the putterhead moving in the right direction. Also, proper foot positioning helps you aim the putter correctly in the first place.

Since you want your putter to be moving down the line when it contacts the ball, it makes sense to set your feet parallel to that line from the start. Set them so that an imaginary line across your toes would run parallel with the line on which you wish your putt to start.

Since you want to aim the putter down that line, I think it is optically advantageous to point each of your feet straight out, so that they are perfectly square to your line. You should play the ball directly opposite your left big toe—not the toe of your shoe, rather the actual big toe in your shoe. If you play the ball opposite that part of your left shoe, and if your left foot is pointing straight out at 90 degrees to your line, the lace of your putter, if extended toward you, would run directly along the inner side of that shoe.

I know all this sounds rather precise, but we need to put our feet somewhere, so why not do so in a way that helps us aim the putter and ourselves correctly?

Playing the ball opposite your left toe is ideal, because there it is best positioned for contact with the putterhead as it moves level with the ground, after it has finished moving downward, just before it starts its upward movement. The level angle of approach is more likely to create solid contact and a true roll of the ball than would a downward approach, if the ball were played too far

RUNYAN'S SECRET

back to your right, or an upward approach, if it were played farther forward to your left.

I think that normally it is best to stand with the outer edges of your shoes closer together than your shoulders are wide. Stand a bit wider—feet about shoulder-width apart—when putting in a strong wind. (If you do widen your stance in the wind, also grip a bit farther down on the club, so as to retain the 45-degree angling of the arms to the shaft.)

These stance widths should give you both sufficient balance and a steady suspension point as you move your arms back and forward. A stance that is too wide can lead to back and forward movement of the suspension point—swaying—which can adversely alter the path and facing of the putter. A stance that is too narrow may hinder your balance and/or make you stand too tall, too far away from your work.

Distribute your weight evenly between your two feet. Too much weight on the left foot may tilt the top of your putter shaft to the left, which will make you tend to stroke the ball with a downward moving and downward facing putterhead. Too much weight on the right foot can cause you to contact the ball when the putterhead has already started moving upward, a major cause of topping.

I find that many golfers tend to stand too far away, or they stand the proper distance away, but too tall. In either case, they are too far from their work. You will automatically stand the correct distance from the ball if you bend at the knees and well for-

ward from the hips, and if you apply the other positions described in this chapter.

In summary, the positions you should assume when putting, so you can consider them as a whole address position, are:

Hands. Hold the club about three-fourths of an inch from its top end—a bit lower in a strong wind—with each palm facing inward and upward at a 45-degree angle. Hold the club firmly with identical pressure in each hand.

Arms. Upper arms rest lightly against rib cage. Forearms set directly in front of and behind an imaginary extension of the clubshaft. Neither forearm should set above or below this shaft extension. Each forearm angles downward to the shaft at a 45-degree angle.

Eyes. Directly over an extension of the putting line directly behind the ball.

Feet. Set parallel with your initial putting line, each toe straight forward at 90 degrees to that line. Outer edges of shoes slightly closer together than width of shoulders, but shoulder width in strong wind. Weight evenly distributed between feet, so that puttershaft tilts neither forward nor backward at address or at contact.

Ball. Positioned opposite where your left big toe is in your shoe.

Procedure

I have spelled out the various positions of address that I feel are ideal. You will need to fit yourself into these positions several times, each time checking to see that all are in order. After you have done this, you will begin to feel the overall sensation of what I consider to be the ideal pre-stroke positioning on putts and chip shots. In a short time, you will be able to assume these positions almost automatically, with little or no conscious effort.

I must point out, however, that while it is most important to arrive at these static positions on every putt, it is equally important that you follow a certain simple procedure in doing so. If you go about finding this ideal address position in helter-skelter fashion, it is unlikely you will find it at all.

Here then is the orderly procedure I recommend you follow in addressing every putt:

1. Set your hands correctly on the club.
2. Approach the ball from an angle that is 90 degrees to your chosen line—that is, step up to the ball with your feet pointing in the same direction they will be pointing at address.
3. Bend forward from the hips so that your eyes are over the line and set the putter lightly on the grass behind the ball, taking great care to aim it down your line.
4. Position your feet according to your line and the aim of your putter.
5. Recheck the aim of your putter and finalize your address position, making any adjustments needed to reach the ideal positioning of hands, arms, eyes, and feet.

It is imperative that you learn to follow the above procedure before every putt. Most important, be sure that you aim the putter down your line before you position your feet. The ball and the putter, once aimed, must determine where you set your feet. If you set your feet before aiming the club, as so many do, you will aim according to where your feet are set—for right or for wrong—rather than down your chosen line.

Stroke

The whole reason for being so precise in positioning yourself correctly before stroking is simply so that you can automatically create a good stroke that solidly sends the ball forward in the right direction. The goal is to eliminate any need to think about how to stroke as you stroke.

If you adopt what I have suggested up to this point, you will be quite likely to make a firm-wristed stroke with each arm pushing and pulling equally on the shaft of the putter. Thus, your stroking motion and its rhythm should result from simply swinging the arms from the shoulder joints with the hands remaining constantly firm throughout. It should be a crisp, concise motion of the arms with no slackness or aggressiveness occurring in the hands and wrists.

FROM *THE SHORT WAY TO LOWER SCORING* BY PAUL RUNYAN

RUNYAN'S SECRET

CHAPTER 39

JENNIFER SCOTT

THE CASE FOR HYPNOSIS

"Winning professionals prove it every weekend. To lower your scores and have consistency with each shot, you must learn to take control of your inner mind—the same way you trained it to type or drive a car. This same control will also take care of first-tee jitters, putting yips, and obsessive negative thoughts."

Jennifer Scott has at least two distinctions from the other forty-five authors in this book. Number one, she is the only woman. Number two, she is the only one who can point to a series of laudatory reviews in *New York* magazine—not for her golf instruction but for her singing.

Back in the 1980s, had you wandered into the cabaret at the New York Sheraton or the Hilton, or maybe Danny's Hideaway or A

Quiet Little Table in the Corner, the dulcet tones flowing from the stage might well have been those of Ms. Scott.

"I never really intended to become a performer," she says, "but by the time I reached my thirties I was still sort of aimless—no career, no idea who I was. All I knew was that singing made me feel alive. A friend of mine was playing piano and singing in New York clubs, and she told me I could do the same. 'A piece of cake,' she said."

It wasn't. Although Scott had sung in the all-state chorus in high school for two years,

> **THE SECRET:**
>
> Allow yourself to drift into the hypnotic state in which you can groove your swing mentally.

she had a lot to learn about singing professionally. But she was focused and she was persistent. Two years later, she had the first gig in a career that would thrive for over a decade.

Still, there was something missing in her life. She'd left college in her junior year and wanted to finish, so in 1991 she enrolled in Ottawa University near Phoenix, majoring in psychology. A couple of her fellow students turned her onto hypnotism and she was instantly hooked.

"As I began working with it, I realized how familiar it was," she says. "As a little girl, I'd learned about hypnosis without knowing it. I'd learned how to tune out my parents' nagging by escaping into a good book, a TV show, or simply by daydreaming. I'd vaguely hear Mom or Dad ask me to set the table or clean up my room. But my focus would be intently on what was in my mind. I didn't waiver. I could hold that focus for hours, even though it would seem like only minutes."

Jennifer made hypnosis the focus of her major term paper and after graduation, she became certified as a clinical hypnotherapist. Together with her new husband, she began a life and career that were miles away and worlds apart from the New York stage. Initially she focused on helping people quit smoking or lose weight or overcome phobias of various kinds. It was her husband Donn, an avid golfer, who made her turn to golf.

"He was frustrated with his game," she says. "He couldn't break out of his comfort rut, played mostly in the 90s. He'd worked with many golf pros—got excited at first, but then went right back to mediocrity. One day he came up to me and said 'Jennifer, you help people lose weight, stop smoking, and you even help women deliver babies without chemical anesthesia. The least you could do is help me break 90!' "

Donn became the guinea pig for a golf self-hypnosis program that would become known as Own the Zone. Within two years he'd gone from a 14 handicap to a 9.8 and Jennifer had established herself as the preeminent hypnotist in the golf field. In

Jennifer Scott helped her husband lower his handicap by four strokes.

2002 her two-CD program *Own the Zone* was hailed by *GOLF Magazine* as the best product of its kind. On the heels of that review, she joined the magazine's staff as a mental fitness coach and columnist for golfonline.com. She also teaches at the San Diego Golf Academy and travels the country giving seminars as well as one-on-one lessons. Her book *Get the Hole in Your Head—Own the Zone* is about to be published and will include the passages that follow.

SCOTT'S SECRET

L et me dispel the myths about hypnosis:

"Hypnosis is weird."

"Hypnosis makes people look stupid."

"I'll lose control under hypnosis."

"Hypnosis is dangerous."

These myths stem from seeing stage hypnosis in theaters and nightclubs, where people act strangely—almost as if they're asleep. But no one is "being controlled." Quite the opposite. Some people are just more suggestible than others and more willing to go along with the hypnotist. Just as they might be at a party when their guard is down. Remember, stage hypnosis is for entertainment. It's fun, but never harmful. Your subconscious mind would never allow you to do anything against your morality or well-being.

However, keep this in mind: Suggestion has power. If, on stage, you might believe that you were smelling rotten eggs when no eggs exist or the fragrance of beautiful roses when no roses are present, then why couldn't you train yourself through this same power to improve your golf game? You can.

Golfers, Ride That Wave

You have an extraordinary power that resides within you. It's a light that shines through you so powerfully that once lit, you can ride it like a mighty wave.

Let yourself imagine for a moment that you're a fearless child paddling out to deep, turbulent waters on your surfboard. You're confident because you know what's coming. You trust that as you let go and focus, you'll soon connect with the wave's movement. You'll ride that wave. Let it carry you. Feel its rhythm. Hit its sweet spot. You'll get a thrilling ride that will carry you safely and surely to its inevitable destination.

Both your conscious and subconscious mind are important but they have very different functions.

The rhythms of those waves never cease. They're endless. Waiting for us to ride again and again. They soothe our stress as we let ourselves connect with the primordial pulsing of these rhythms—the sounds and movements that echo everywhere in the universe. We feel at one and at peace with this knowing.

What a gift to know that we can quiet our mind chatter and settle into the natural rhythms of nature! Picture with me now that all the planets in our solar system are continually and rhythmically moving. Our beautiful planet Earth rotates around its own axis as well as moves with its sister planets around the sun. Nothing in our vast universe is at rest. Everything moves. There's a flow to this movement. An extraordinary harmonic movement that only could be generated by our creator.

When your mind chatter can be tuned out by tuning into this eternalness—this peaceful state of oneness—you're in hypnosis.

Isn't this state also "the zone"—that mystical place that all athletes seek yet can't master? Isn't this the feeling of effortless golf when time and space seem to disappear?

Now you can see the connections between the natural rhythms of nature, hypnosis, and the zone.

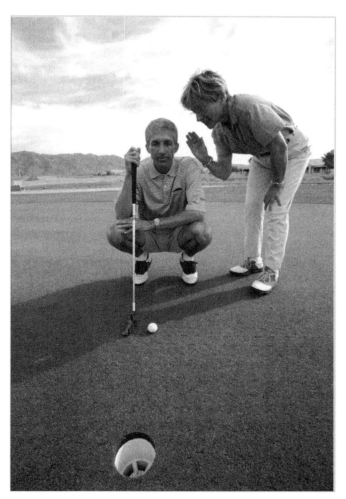

Create pleasurable images—good memories—to draw upon for each shot you face.

SCOTT'S SECRET

The Power of Hypnosis

Here's an exercise to help you experience the power of focused concentration on a target. First, make a pendulum by taking a piece of dental floss about a foot long and

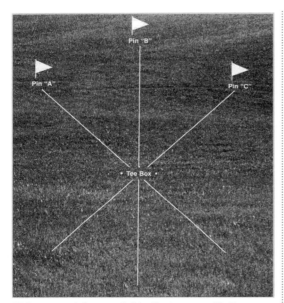

Using a pendulum and this diagram, you'll discover the power of the subconscious mind.

tying it to a large paper clip. Then set this book on a table, open to this page.

Sitting in a straight-backed chair, hold the pendulum with your thumb and forefinger and rest the elbow of that hand on the table and suspend the pendulum over the diagram with the three pins marked A, B, and C.

Now stare at that pendulum. Put all of your attention on it. Then visualize or imagine that it's moving from the tee box to pin B. Just let it happen. Soon you'll see the pendulum swinging as you envisioned. Now change the mental direction. Imagine or picture it swinging from the tee box to pin A. If you're like 95 percent of my clients and

seminar attendees, you're seeing the pendulum swinging as you envisioned. Now picture or imagine it swinging from the tee box to pin C. Watch it change, slowly.

If you're frustrated because it isn't moving, you're probably too tight. Thinking too much about it. If you're this tight and controlling with a pendulum, think of how tight and controlling you are with a driver. Do you really want that?

Here's another experiment. Read the following script to a friend: *Close your eyes and put your arms straight out in front of you. Now picture or imagine that I'm placing a very heavy book on top of your right hand. It's so big and so heavy that it's weighing down your whole arm. Don't fight the weight of this book. Allow in the imagery. Believe that book is there, weighing down your right arm. Now imagine that I'm tying strings around your left wrist. Those strings are attached to big red, white, and blue helium balloons which are lifting up your left arm. Your left arm is getting lighter and lighter as the balloons lift up that arm. Your right arm is heavier and heavier as the enormous weight of that book weighs it down.*

Now have your friend open his or her eyes to observe where the arms went. The more these suggestions were believed, the more the arms reacted. Switch roles: Have your friend read this script to you and see what happens. How open are you to suggestion?

What's most important for you to know is that if the arms moved, it's your subconscious mind that moved them. Not your conscious mind. And you did it with no discernible effort or control. It just happened.

Both your conscious and subconscious mind are important, but they have very different functions. You should understand this if you want to improve your golf game.

When I think of the mind, I see an iceberg. The tip of the iceberg is like your conscious mind—the part of your mind that tries to figure everything out. Tries too hard and gets you in trouble with all those swing thoughts. Worry thoughts. Sure you need that "thinking" mind for course management, but other than that, give it a rest!

What you want to do is activate the other part of your mind—the subconscious, which is just like that hidden, mysterious part of the iceberg. If you let in my suggestions about the book and balloons, you accomplished this.

Once you allow imagination to activate this part of your mind, you're automatically in hypnosis. It's as simple as that. You didn't have to "try." Trying never gets you there. Effort never gets you there. Try to hit a really long drive, and what happens? You tighten up your arms, your shoulders, your hands, and you lunge. Nothing good happens.

You see, hypnosis is a natural state of mind that you drift in and out of throughout the day without knowing it and without "trying" to get there. How many times have you been amazed that after driving your car and arriving at your destination you were oblivi-

ous of actually doing the driving? Who told your foot to step on the gas or brake? Not your conscious mind. It was listening to the radio!

You're in hypnosis when you're so engrossed in a book or movie that you forget where you are. The same thing might happen when you stare at a burning candle or watch the gentle movement of a stream. You're in hypnosis when fantasy begins. You stop judging. You allow. Imagination gets triggered. The more deeply your imagination gets triggered, the more deeply you're in hypnosis. You're in a heightened state of awareness when time and space seem to disappear. It's a state of effortlessness. A state of flow.

Does this sound like "the zone"? Because that's exactly what it is. On the golf course, you might have a few holes with this sense of effortlessness—maybe even most of a round. But, inevitably,

> You see, hypnosis is a natural state of mind that you drift in and out of throughout the day without knowing it and without "trying" to get there. How many times have you been amazed that after driving your car and arriving at your destination, you were oblivious of actually doing the driving?

You can learn to hypnotize yourself into a pre-shot bubble of confidence.

what happens? You start "thinking" about what you're doing. You become self-conscious. Instantly, the "flow" goes away. So do the birdies.

I call all of these situations random hypnosis. Random coming in, random going out.

There's another kind of hypnosis: purposeful hypnosis. You can trigger this when you step into your imaginary pre-shot bubble, like the one you see on page 316.

Once you've analyzed your next shot and selected your club, your trigger will be a deep breath. Hold it for a few seconds so you clear your mental palette. (Notice that your mind chatter stops when you hold your breath.) Then think the words *peace, harmony, relax, relax* as you slowly exhale. Just taking a

deep breath will relax tension, but adding these healing words will instantly put you in the zone.

Practice this exercise as often as possible off the course. The words *peace, harmony, relax, relax* will then become a soothing mantra that will penetrate deeply into your subconscious mind. (To be most effective, it's important to hold your breath for several seconds as you think these words.) With adequate practice, this exercise will work like a charm and will always trigger purposeful hypnosis and your pre-shot bubble.

How to Hypnotize Yourself and Develop Sensory Recall

Do the following exercise three times a day. Do it once before going to sleep, once before getting out of bed in the morning, and once during the day. If your real swing is inconsistent, groove it mentally.

Find a comfortable spot—either lying down or in a comfortable chair. Arms at your sides, legs uncrossed. Then take a long deep breath, filling your lungs to capacity. As you slowly exhale, feel a wave a relaxation going all the way down to the tips of your fingers and the tips of your toes. Take another signal breath—signaling to your subconscious mind that you are now ready for self-hypnosis.

Imagine yourself walking down a flight of ten steps. Take your time. As you slowly go down these steps, you find yourself walking through a foggy mist. You and the steps seem to disappear in the fog. Once you get down to the tenth step, you emerge from the mist—right onto your favorite golf course.

It's a beautiful day. The sky is a bright blue. You can barely look at the sun, it's such a brilliant bright yellow. Feel the warmth of that sun on your face and hands. Now feel your hands grip your club—firmly but relaxed. Your body is calm. Butt out. Knees bent just the right amount. Sense your position now . . . in direct alignment with your target. Take a deep breath, think *peace, harmony, relax, relax* and let your breath out slowly. See yourself begin the swing. Nice and easy. Feel your hands, arms, and hips rotate smoothly. Pause. Swing. Accelerate through the shot. Hear the whish of that acceleration as your clubface strikes the ball—right at the sweet spot. Click! Feel your perfect follow-through. See your ball take off and soar in the air. See the whiteness of it contrasted against that blue, blue sky.

You are so pleased with this perfect shot. You tell yourself repeatedly how confident you are, how much fun you have playing, how easy this game is.

Create these pleasurable images of each one of your shots. Ask for the good memories. They're all there and will pop up from their files in your subconscious mind.

Always use language in present tense: "I feel; I see," etc. The more vivid your colors, textures, sounds, and feelings are, the more your subconscious mind will believe your scenarios. Even if your real swing is inconsistent, self-hypnosis will help you groove it mentally. This will help your muscles re-create it on the golf course. You'll find yourself executing those good shots again and again.

FROM *GET THE HOLE IN YOUR HEAD— OWN THE ZONE* BY JENNIFER SCOTT

> You're in hypnosis when you're so engrossed in a book or movie that you forget where you are. You're in a heightened state of awareness when time and space seem to disappear. A state of effortlessness. A state of flow.

> Even if your real swing is inconsistent, self-hypnosis will help you groove it mentally. This will help your muscles re-create it on the golf course.

SCOTT'S SECRET

CHAPTER 40

FRED SHOEMAKER

THROW YOUR CARES AWAY

"Michelangelo supposedly looked at a block of marble and saw David inside. That's my experience as an instructor. The golfer exists, fully there, but he has stuff covering him up. The game, for me, is to let him out."

The more Fred Shoemaker played golf, the less he enjoyed it. The son of a naval officer, he was introduced to the game on the island of Guam while his father was stationed there.

"I had an ideal setup," Shoemaker said. "A convenient course, time to learn and experiment, and the support of family and friends without any pressure or competition." He blossomed quickly and by age twelve was a certified prodigy. When the family returned stateside, he became the number-one player on his high school team.

But that brought a different kind of golf, full of competition and scorekeeping, and although Shoemaker won his share of matches, he found himself losing interest in the game. A love-hate situation had evolved and it continued throughout his college years at the University of California at Santa Barbara and beyond. He had the skills to be a Tour player but none of the desire.

"The whole experience had become very narrow to me, consisting only of practicing, playing, and talking about golf," he wrote in his book. "I found myself wondering why anybody would want to do this for a living."

So he didn't. Instead he joined the Peace Corps and got far away from the game, in West Africa. Even there, however, he couldn't shake the bug and so, during his Christmas break, he made his way to the Ghana Golf Club where a chance eighteen-hole match changed his life.

Shoemaker's opponent was a local man, a handsome cheerful fellow about his own age and height, who came to the first tee in shorts, a T-shirt, and bare feet. The fellow was clearly an inferior player to Shoemaker but he defeated his American visitor 2 & 1, and Shoemaker had an epiphany.

"My game that day was filled with anxiety and self-doubt, which made me play worse than I was able to play," he said. "By contrast, he played with a joy and a sense of freedom, and, as a result his game allowed him to play closer to his potential."

The problem, he realized, was that people invariably overthink the game. "When you ask people what percentage of the game is mental, most will tell you it's pretty high. But the truth is, it's not mental at all—you have a physical ball, a physical club, a physical body. And when people can finally let go of these crazy things they have in their heads, it's amazing what can happen."

With that premise—freeing people up to play their best—Shoemaker returned from Africa and developed a highly successful teaching practice in Northern California. While there he met a kindred spirit, *Golf in the Kingdom* author Michael Murphy, and Shoemaker began to teach a "Golf in the Kingdom" workshop at Murphy's Esalen Institute in Big Sur. Two years later he founded the School for Extraordinary Golf in Carmel.

The premise of Extraordinary Golf is to clear the mind, to purge all the lessons, swing thoughts, fears, concerns, prejudices, and just let golf happen. Extraordinary golf, he says, is inside all of us—it's just a matter of letting it out.

The key, he says, is to stay in the present—to be aware of the swing you're making but not to judge it. Past golf swings are irrelevant. Future golf swings haven't happened yet, and therefore are equally meaningless. "The fellow who makes a million dollars on the pro tour, when he steps up to the first tee, has the same crazy things going through his head that are going through yours," he said. "But he has learned to let it go, and be present at the task at hand."

When Shoemaker's book appeared in 1996, it offered little in the way of hard advice, just a few New Age–type exercises. One of those exercises, however, took the golf world by storm, as much for its outrageousness as its effectiveness. On a whim during a lesson, Shoemaker asked his pupil to let go of the golf club as he swung though—essentially, to throw it down the range. What he found is that when people throw their clubs, their movements are much more free and natural than when they swing. From that point on, club-throwing became an integral part of Fred Shoemaker's extraordinary school.

> **THE SECRET:**
>
> Throw your club. Fling it fearlessly down the fairway and see how your body performs with compete freedom. Transfer that freedom to your swing.

SHOEMAKER'S SECRET

Technique and Power

In the thousands of golf lessons that I have given over the years, there have been three things that almost all students have told me they wanted: consistency, proper technique, and power. We'll talk about consistency later, so now let's look at technique and power. Everyone wants to hit the ball farther, even if they can already hit it a mile. And why not? It's a great feeling!

Even though most golfers know that increased distance doesn't automatically lead to better scores, watching that ball fly a long way is a big part of the experience and enjoyment of the game.

There have been innumerable books written on power—I've read many and you probably have, too—and they all have their special approach, their special secret. Over the years I've tried many different methods, with mixed results. But through a combination of chance, persistence, and plain good fortune, my students and I have discovered a way to teach power and technique from a new point of view that has yielded remarkable results. Not only has it produced a dramatic increase in students' power, it has also led to insights that have opened up a whole new way of looking at the swing. Directing students in this particular exercise and seeing the amazement, delight, and transformation it produces in them and their swings has been a constant source of enjoyment for me and for the coaches I work with. Let me tell you how it all came about.

Serendipity

One afternoon I was hitting a few balls at the range while waiting for my next lesson to begin. As I often do at times like this, I started fooling around with the club, just having fun and seeing what might happen. By chance I found that if I hit the ball and immediately let go of the club, the club would fly straight ahead about 20 yards. I did this a few times and it intrigued me, so I decided to try it with my next student, a man who had about a 25 handicap.

I asked him to hit the ball and release the club immediately after impact. He did so and the club flew almost directly to the left—the "hook" direction, since he was a right-handed golfer. Luckily, there were few other people on the range and it didn't interfere with anyone. As I retrieved the club, I wondered why it had landed where it did. I asked him to try the exercise again and the same thing happened—directly left. I then tried to simplify things by saying, "Just throw the club straight after you hit the ball," but it didn't help. No matter how many times he tried, he couldn't get the club to go straight, yet I could, every time.

> **In the thousands of lessons I've given over the years, there have been three things that almost all students have told me they wanted: consistency, proper technique, and power.**

I realized that something interesting was going on here. My student was getting frustrated, so I told him not to put a ball on the tee, but simply to take a golf swing and throw the club straight ahead. This time the club went straight, and I noticed a change in his swing. It happened that I had a video camera sitting on a tripod, filming the whole thing. We rewound the tape and took a look at it.

When he was hitting the ball, his position through impact was that of a typical golfer: His body almost stopped, the club completely released. He sort of "snapped" at the ball, with the club moving hard to the left after impact. But when the ball was not there and he simply threw the club, a remarkable change took place. A remarkable and instantaneous change. Watching it on tape, I was amazed and exhilarated—something special was going on here. From that point on, the club-throwing exercise became a part of my teaching process.

Scene of Transformation

I will illustrate the wonderful things that happen during this exercise by describing one of my favorite workshop scenes—one that has been repeated many times but which I continue to find fascinating. It takes place in the late afternoon on the first day. Earlier in the day, the students have done the club-throwing exercise with some old clubs I keep for this purpose. The other coaches and I have videotaped each student taking two swings. The first is their normal golf swing, and they hit a ball. The second—immediately after—is a swing with no ball present, and they simply throw the club straight ahead.

We gather in the meeting room to watch and discuss the videos, all twenty or so of us—typically about fifteen students and five coaches. The first person we take a look at is Richard—a forty-eight-year-old with a 10 handicap. Richard has played golf for thirty years—longer than any student in the group—and has tried everything he could think of to achieve a consistent golf game. Yet by his own admission, his game is erratic and often frustrating.

Club-throwing will instill a freedom of movement . . .

First I cue up his regular golf swing, and we play it a couple of times. Richard has a slightly better swing than the average golfer, but even he can see why it's not efficient or powerful: reverse weight pivot, club "thrown" from the top of the backswing, body stalling and a release of power before impact, clubhead "scooping" the ball. There he is on tape for all the world to see, and he's surprised (he wasn't aware of much of what he was doing), dismayed, and uncomfortable.

I go through Richard's swing point by point in front of the group, and it's an upsetting time for him. We talk about what it would take for him to improve, and I ask him what he would do first. He says, "I'd get my weight back." I ask him if he's tried that before. He says yes, but obviously it's had little effect. I ask what he would do next, and he says, "Delay the lag." I ask if he's tried that before, and he says yes, but to no avail. This pattern continues for a few more areas of his swing.

. . . that you can transfer to your actual golf swing.

By chance I found that if I hit the ball and immediately let go of the club, the club would fly straight ahead about 20 yards.

I finally look right at him and say: "If you've tried everything before and it hasn't worked, why should you expect anything to change at all? By your own admission, there are many things that are awkward and inefficient about your swing. Fixing all of them looks like a long and really difficult process." Richard now feels like he's stuck and sees nothing that can make any real difference in his game. He's really disheartened. He says, "I thought this was supposed to be a positive golf school. I feel really discouraged." He's at the point of breakdown, ready to give up on all the methods he's tried before. Cruel as it may seem, bringing him to this point is a necessary part of the process. This is a crucial moment in the exercise.

I then cue up the video of Richard throwing the club. I ask him: "Could you ever imagine yourself swinging like a golf pro?" His answer—"not really"—is typical of most golfers. I have found that very few people are capable of even imagining themselves doing extraordinary things, and thus resign themselves to mediocrity. I then ask Richard what position he would like to have at the top of his backswing.

> I stop the tape at the impact frame, and there it is. Richard, Mr. 10-Handicap-Slightly-Better-Than-Average-Golfer, looks like he belongs on the cover of a golf magazine.

As he describes his ideal position, I pause the club-throwing video at the backswing frame. His weight is set differently—instead of leaning toward the target, his body is coiled behind the ball. I say, "Something like that?" The light of amazement and enthusiasm comes into his eyes. "Yeah!" he says. "Like that!" Next I ask him what position he'd like to have at impact, and he says, "I'd really like to retain my wrist angle, and have my body moving with the club, not ahead of it or behind it." I stop the tape at the impact frame, and there it is. Richard, Mr.-10-Handicap-Slightly-Better-Than-Average-Golfer, looks like he belongs on the cover of a golf magazine.

Magic Moment

Richard just sits there, stunned, looking at his video. There's the swing he's always wanted, the one he never really thought he'd be able to do. He doesn't know what to say. The other students are equally surprised and amazed. A feeling—a spark—goes through the room. People realize that something extraordinary is happening, and they don't quite know how to react. They smile, shake their heads, chuckle—there's almost a giddy feeling in the air. It's a marvelous moment and a delight for me to be a part of. I play the tape a few more times to let it sink in.

Then I turn to Richard and ask him a question that is at the core of the whole learning process: "If you're already able to swing the way you want, what do we need to teach you?" From here we introduce the themes that will guide us over the next few days.

The first two themes are these: 1) Your instincts are extraordinary, and basically you've gone against them from the time you first started golfing. 2) When Michelangelo created *David*, he went to a block of marble and removed everything that wasn't *David*—he added nothing; great golf is likewise a process of removing the interference you've put on yourself, almost from the very first day.

We all instinctively know how to propel an object in the most efficient way possible. If given time to experiment—without preconceived ideas of right and wrong-we will feel our way toward the motion that provides us with our maximum power. Great golfers are people whose natural (club-throwing) swings are very similar to their regular swings. It is entirely possible that these excellent golfers play closer to their instincts than others. They don't constantly think, juggle, and adjust as much when they swing. They are much better able to step up to their shot and just let it go.

Instinctive Knowledge

This is the club-throwing exercise, so let me give you some words of caution. A thrown club can be a dangerous object. It is possible in these exercises to throw the club a lot farther and a lot more off line than you expect. The area all around you should be clear, even in back (I have seen clubs go backward), and when you are doing the full swing, you should have at least 50 yards of space in front of you. Pay particular attention to the "hook" direction (left for a right-handed golfer, right for a left-handed one) because clubs are very likely to go that way, and travel a fair distance. Please be careful, and use old clubs.

The purpose of these exercises is to establish a connection between the ball, the club, your body, and the target. In the concentration exercises, the aim was to maintain focus on a single, real thing throughout the two seconds of the swing. The golf ball, the club, and the body were used as objects of focus. But since the target is the ultimate objective in golf, the question arises: How can I focus all my attention on something like the golf ball and still be aware of the target? From studying concentration for the last twenty years, I have found that it is not exclusive: You can include both the ball and the target in your focus. This is clear from the way you drive a car. Your immediate attention is on the traffic and the road conditions, but you are also aware of where you are going. Your destination—your target—guides you. It's your goal, and you never lose awareness of it. Knowing where you're going is the key, as these exercises will show.

The first part concerns chipping. Find an open grassy area that's at least 50 feet long. Grab an iron—it doesn't matter which one—and take a chipping stance, with your target a spot about 25 feet ahead. With your eyes on the target, take a normal chipping stroke and release the club toward the target. Repeat with the other irons. Get a feeling for the action of tossing and how it relates to the target: how far the hands go back, the hand position when the

> **We all instinctively know how to propel an object in the most efficient way possible. If given time to experiment—without preconceived ideas of right and wrong—we will feel our way toward the motion that provides us with maximum power.**

club head passes through the middle point, how the body moves. Toss about twenty or thirty clubs.

Next, do the same thing, but close your eyes when the club starts back. Toss the club toward the target you have in your mind's eye. Again, toss twenty or thirty clubs this way, just getting the feel of it. Remember, no evaluations, no judgments, only awareness. Then, take your normal chipping club, keep your eyes on the target, and take the same tossing swing, but this time don't let the club go. Keep taking swings and see if you can feel what happens.

As in all the exercises, understanding what's going on is the lowest rung on the ladder of development. It's not what you understand but what you experience that's the important thing.

> Great golfers are people whose natural (club-throwing) swings are very similar to their regular swings. They don't constantly think, juggle, and adjust. They are much better able to step up to their shot and just let it go.

Now chip some balls about the same distance you were tossing the club. See if you experience any difference between the throwing motion and the chipping motion. That's the whole game-feeling difference. Experiencing what's possible (club-throwing swing) and experiencing what you do (regular swing) make you aware of the gap between them. In sensing these differences, you'll actually feel the position that's necessary to produce excellent chipping. Learning in golf is the ability to sense the differences between the two motions.

In the second part of this exercise, repeat the four activities: 1) throw clubs looking at the target; 2) throw clubs with eyes closed; 3) look at the target and take the throwing motion, but hold onto the club; 4) chip some balls about the same distance as the throw—but this time change the focus. Focus now on distinguishing your natural timing—that of the club-throwing swing—from the timing when you actually hit the golf ball. Are they the same or not?

Pay attention to the club rising, the movements of the body, and the time the swing takes. How long does it take for the body to move back and forth? Where is the acceleration and how soon after you start the downswing does it begin? How does this change in the different swings? The moment you try to fix your swing, you'll be unable to sense the timing, and the exercise won't have much value. Be patient and stay with the awareness, and you will begin to discover the timing that you naturally have.

The first part of this exercise was to notice the technique of how things happen. The second part was to notice the timing of how things happen. Now this third part is to notice the balance. Repeat the sequence, but this time take a new focus. How is the body centered when you throw a club? Where does your weight move? Where do you feel on balance and where off balance? Feel for any difference between the balance when you throw a club and the balance when you chip a ball.

When you begin to make some distinctions from these exercises, you're ready to go further. Take it into pitching. Do the same steps as above, but this time hit 30- to 50-yard shots. (Remember the warnings I mentioned at the beginning of the chapter, and make sure there is enough room.) You won't be able to throw the clubs as far as you hit the shots, but that doesn't matter—just toss the clubs as far toward the target as the pitching swing will allow. Become aware of the technique, the timing, and the balance. When you begin to develop distinc-

The main purpose of this whole exercise is to become aware of the relationship between the ball, the club, your body, and the target. Golf is never about just one part, it is about the relationship of all the parts.

tions here, then you're ready take it to the full swing. But don't rush yourself. Don't think quick fix; think mastery. A good principle to go by is to swing the club only as fast as you can feel it without major blind spots. In the pitching swing and the full swing, you may not be able to toss the clubs straight at first—you will likely hold on too long and throw toward your "hook" direction. But keep your focus on the target and soon the clubs will go reasonably straight.

This exercise also works for putting (though of course you shouldn't toss clubs on the green, only on the grassy areas nearby). As I said earlier in the book, the timing and the blind spots are similar for all swings.

The main purpose of this whole exercise is to become aware of the relationship between the ball, the club, your body, and the target. Golf is never about just one part, it is about the relationship of all the parts. The cornerstone of this relationship is the target; that will dictate how much body and club are used. From many years of coaching, I've noticed that the most important part of the relationship—target awareness—is the one that's most often missing. Changing the point of view from the ball as goal to the target as goal is the key to this exercise.

FROM *EXTRAORDINARY GOLF: THE ART OF THE POSSIBLE* BY FRED SHOEMAKER

CHAPTER 41

BOB TOSKI

FEELINGS, NOTHING MORE THAN FEELINGS

"Deer-like strength is ten times more important than hippopotamus strength. An ounce of touch is worth a ton of brawn."

During the 1960s and '70s, the predominant source of inside information for American golfers was *Golf Digest,* the monthly magazine founded in 1950 by two Chicago entrepreneurs.

With twice the circulation and clout of any other golf publication, it not only reported on the game but influenced the trends, theories, and opinions of the day, most notably in the area of instruction through its advisory panel of leading players and teachers.

Hall-of-Famers Sam Snead, Byron Nelson, and Cary Middlecoff all were mem-bers, along with "Little Poison" Paul Runyan on the short game, while the teaching contingent included Jim Flick, Davis Love, Jr., and Dr. Gary Wiren. But one member of that panel stood out from them all: Bob Toski. So often did he appear on the cover, and so forceful were his articles, that for a time it seemed Toski was *Golf Digest* and *Golf Digest* was Toski.

The eighth of nine children raised by Polish immigrants Mary and Walenty Algustoski, Bob was born in Haydenville, Massachusetts. His mother died when he was six, and by age ten he was spending his summers caddying at the Northampton Golf Club. After graduating from high school, he did a wartime stint in the armed forces before turning pro in 1948. He struggled at first but improved gradually and in 1954 had his breakthrough—four victories, including the

Bob Toski reacquaints himself with the feel of a true swinging motion.

videos, a signature line of golf equipment, the lead instructor role for the Golf Digest Schools, and a TV contract with NBC, where he dispensed his tips to millions. His most inspired book was *The Touch System for Better Golf,* co-authored in 1971 with Dick Aultman and the editors of *Golf Digest.* Back then, *Golf Digest* tightly controlled the design and typography of all its publications to reflect the magazine's pages, so this is a large-format book with bold type and numerous full-page illustrations. Also typical of the *Golf Digest* of that era, the cover billed it imperiously as "the first book to tell you how your swing should feel."

Toski gets to his point quickly and intriguingly, asking the reader on page one to find a pen and sign his name four times as quickly as possible. His point is that golf is a game of agility more than strength, that the club should be moved with a swinging motion created by the hands, wrists, and arms. The body simply turns and shifts to support the swinging of the hands and arms. Fundamentally, however, *The Touch System* presents not so much a method as a collection of like-minded tips and images. Some of the best of them follow.

THE SECRET:

Feel your way. Use images and sensations from the non-golf world to improve your game.

Tam O'Shanter Invitational with its whopping first prize of $50,000. Three years later at age thirty, Toski quit the Tour to spend more time with his young family and to begin the most successful teaching career the game had ever seen.

Spikes on and wallet full, Toski was just 5'5" and 135 pounds (Snead nicknamed him the Mouse), but he brought to his teaching an animated, dynamic style with a healthy dose of showmanship. In 1960 *Golf Digest* gave him an ideal stage and he parlayed his prominence into a string of successful books and

TOSKI'S SECRET

Building Feel Off the Green

Too many golfers fail on clip shots from just off the green because they choose the wrong club. The best club is the *least-lofted* you can use to carry the ball just onto the smooth surface of the green, without its rolling far past the hole, as the illustration below demonstrates. The least-lofted club will roll the ball the farthest. Thus you won't need to strike it so hard. You can take a shorter swing with less leg and body movement. With this *simpler* swing, you'll find it much easier to control the movement of the club-head back and forward through the ball.

Most people have better success rolling an object to a target than they do lofting it. Thus most golfers have better success chipping short shots just onto the smooth putting surface, and letting the ball bounce and run to the hole, than they do lofting it most of the way with a pitch shot. The chip shot is also safer because the less-lofted chipping clubs require a shorter, simpler, and less forceful stroke than do the more-lofted pitching irons. Ideally you should use the least amount of loft

When chipping, use the least-lofted club possible—this will allow you to make a short, controlled swing.

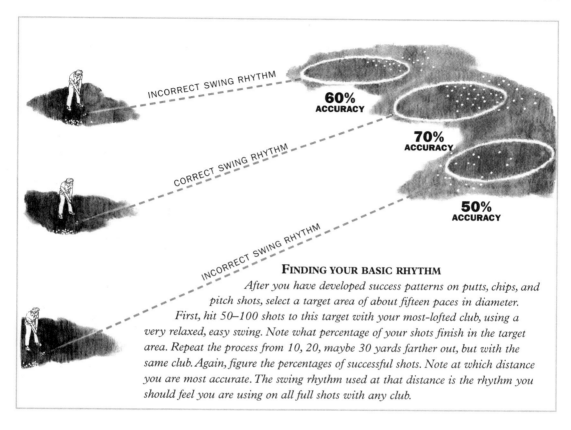

INCORRECT SWING RHYTHM

60% ACCURACY

70% ACCURACY

CORRECT SWING RHYTHM

50% ACCURACY

INCORRECT SWING RHYTHM

FINDING YOUR BASIC RHYTHM

After you have developed success patterns on putts, chips, and pitch shots, select a target area of about fifteen paces in diameter. First, hit 50–100 shots to this target with your most-lofted club, using a very relaxed, easy swing. Note what percentage of your shots finish in the target area. Repeat the process from 10, 20, maybe 30 yards farther out, but with the same club. Again, figure the percentages of successful shots. Note at which distance you are most accurate. The swing rhythm used at that distance is the rhythm you should feel you are using on all full shots with any club.

T O S K I ' S   S E C R E T

required to land the ball just onto the smooth putting surface without its running far past the hole.

Find Your Full Swing Rhythm

Something you'll notice when you try longer shots is the temptation to hit the ball "hard." You may find yourself, almost subconsciously, beginning to swing with more force than you really need. You must avoid this temptation at all costs. Everyone has a basic rhythm or pace

to his swing. It is very difficult to increase the pace of your swing without sacrificing control of the club. Swing too hard and you'll mis-hit the shot. You won't get the full mass of the clubhead into the ball.

Also, forcing your swing ruins your timing, the coordination of your moving parts. Poor timing causes a loss of clubhead speed before it reaches the ball. You'll waste your kinetic power. Also, you'll overuse your arms and neglect the big muscles of your back and legs.

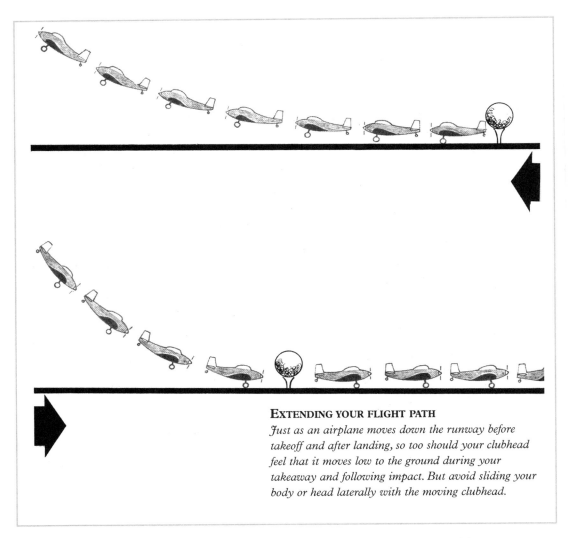

EXTENDING YOUR FLIGHT PATH
Just as an airplane moves down the runway before takeoff and after landing, so too should your clubhead feel that it moves low to the ground during your takeaway and following impact. But avoid sliding your body or head laterally with the moving clubhead.

You will know when you're losing control. Your shots won't feel squarely struck. Your shots won't finish near the target. They won't fly on a relatively consistent trajectory. Swinging the club will feel like hard work.

Put your priority on making square contact with an accelerating clubhead that's moving through the ball. *The best way to develop distance in golf is to first develop a basic rhythm that allows you to make square contact with a well-timed swing.*

How Your Swing Should Look

You might assume that the bottom of the clubhead's path is identical to that of the ball swinging on the end of the chain. This isn't quite so, and it isn't the image that you should have of the shape of the swing, except on putts. The modern player does certain things in his swing that extend the length of the clubhead's movement at ball level before it begins to move upward. For one thing, by maintaining a slight flex in his left knee *through* impact he avoids stiffening and raising his left side. He "stays down" with the shot—and so does his clubhead.

Thus the path of the clubhead through the ball, as you should imagine it, is more level just after impact than just before impact. Imagine that the clubhead is an airplane coming down for a landing, as illustrated at left. It gradually flies lower until it reaches the runway—ball level. Then it rolls forward along the runway—at ball level.

The path of the clubhead going back, away from the ball during the takeaway, takes on just the opposite pattern. At this stage you want to establish width in your swing. You want a nice, full extension of your left arm. The clubhead should move back fairly level and low to the ground for a few inches. Imagine an airplane taking off in the opposite direction, rolling down the runway and then gradually swinging into the air.

One danger in visualizing such clubhead paths going away from and back to the ball is that you might be tempted to level out your clubhead path by swaying your body laterally in the direction the club is moving. While it's fine to imagine the clubhead going back low and swinging through low, it's also necessary to imagine your head as the "hub" of your swing. Always keep it centered in its original place and you will not sway.

How Your Swing Should Feel

I'd like you to imagine that you are sitting in a canoe in the middle of a small lake. Since one end of the lake is lower than the other, gravity pulls you in that direction, toward a small waterfall.

You sit in the canoe and you can feel it being pulled slowly toward the waterfall. It's a smooth pull—no jerks. But as you get closer, the pull gradually becomes stronger and stronger. The boat moves faster and faster. You can't stop it. Suddenly you're over the waterfall, swoosh . . . splash . . . and you're hurtling down the stream.

This is just one of many images I use to relate the feel of the proper downswing to my pupils. Your clubhead is just like that canoe. It starts from an almost static position. Then it begins to move slowly, then gradually faster, but always smoothly. It's being pulled down and forward toward the ball, faster, faster, and then, "pow," and it's gone, lashing through the ball and beyond.

Many pupils react favorably to this analogy. They begin to start their downswing

Imagine that your hands blend together throughout your swing like a good dance team. The left hand controls the right, gently and smoothly, just as the male dancer leads the female. The two partners never separate.

slowly and smoothly instead of with one big jerk. They begin *swinging* the clubhead instead of pushing and shoving it. They start whipping the clubhead *through* the ball and beyond, rather than merely swinging at it.

Your hold on the club should feel consistently *light*—not loose or tight—throughout your swing. Also, the pressure of *one hand against the other* should remain constant.

As you swing, imagine that your hands are like a good dance team. They're close against each other, moving together. There's never any separation between the two. The man—your left hand—is the leader. Your right hand responds to your left, but they never move apart or squeeze together tightly.

FROM *THE TOUCH SYSTEM FOR BETTER GOLF* BY BOB TOSKI

TIMING YOUR DOWNSWING
The feel of the proper downswing is similar to what you would experience if you were sitting in a canoe being gradually drawn toward a waterfall. You should feel that your legs and left arm are pulling the clubhead toward the ball, slowly at first, then faster and faster until it "swooshes" through. This feeling of gradual acceleration will occur only if your shoulders follow, rather than lead, your legs.

CHAPTER 42

MISSING IMPOSSIBLE

*"At first I found it hard to believe that every
4-foot putt would drop, but as the days passed,
I learned to accept my invincibility."*

During the latter half of the twentieth century, Paul Trevillion became well known throughout the European sports world, but not for his ability to play or teach golf. Trevillion was, and remains today, one of the most acclaimed sports illustrators Great Britain has ever produced. His work—on a range of games including basketball, football, rugby, soccer, and tennis—has appeared in numerous books, magazines, and newspapers.

But Trevillion's passion was always golf, where he not only illustrated books but occasionally wrote them as well, including an instruction title co-authored with Peter Alliss, and a definitive account of the 1969 Ryder Cup Matches entitled *Dead Heat*.

That Ryder Cup is best remembered for the way it ended, with Jack Nicklaus graciously conceding a putt to Tony Jacklin at the final hole that not only tied their match but allowed Great Britain and Ireland to gain a halve with the United States for the overall competition with fourteen points apiece. The putt has been variously estimated by those

THE SECRET:

Use a very short putter and bend steeply over the ball, using a split-handed grip— the shorter the putt, the lower your right-hand should be on the putter shaft.

present at between 2 and 5 feet, and Nicklaus's gesture is regarded in golf circles as the game's supreme act of sportsmanship. "I knew Tony would make that putt," he said, "but I didn't want to see him have to do so under all that pressure."

Trevillion's interest in that match might well have stemmed from a nasty experience he'd had at about that same time involving a short putt. Playing a casual round at the Enfield Golf Club near London, he'd come to the fifteenth hole, a par 5, and struck two straight and mighty blows, the second of which had taken his ball not simply to the green but to within 4 feet of the cup. It was the first time in his life he'd reached the hole, and he was understandably a bit shaky as he addressed his putt for eagle.

Using this stroke, Trevillion made 1,000 straight four-foot putts.

It never reached the hole. So convulsively ham-fisted was Trevillion's stab, and so infuriated was he in the wake of his failure, that his artistic temperament took over—he knocked his ball off the green into the woods, stomped off the golf course, and gave up the game, never to play a serious round again.

But although Paul Trevillion stopped playing golf, he never stopped thinking about that putt—about the absurdity of having struck two grand shots, only to miss the hole from inside a club length. And so he began observing and experimenting with putting techniques—most notably the split-handed grip then advocated by two-time PGA Champion Paul Runyan. Then he started tweaking, adding some ideas of his own.

The result was one of the strangest-looking strokes ever to occupy a green—sort of a combination of golf and snooker—but a stroke with which Trevillion became so adept that he sank (or at least claimed to have sunk) 1,000 consecutive 4-foot putts. Indeed, so confident was he that his method was *the* method that he challenged the entire world to a putting contest. In the January 22, 1970, edition of Britain's *Golf Illustrated*, Trevillion crowed "I Am the World's Best Putter" and put up £1,000 of his own money against all comers.

Several tried, but no one ever beat him. The following year, Trevillion's *The Perfect Putting Method* appeared in the United States. Today, it is still available in the United Kingdom, as both a book and a DVD, under the title *Missing Impossible*.

TREVILLION'S SECRET

I discovered my putting secret from watching Joe Davis, Walter Donaldson, and other top world snooker players in action. I was impressed that they never attempted to lag up when 10 feet from the pocket. Every time they lined up, it was with a positive attitude—ball-to-pocket. At all times they split their hands on the cue and saw to it that they had one hand (depending on whether they were right- or left-handed) as near to the ball as possible. It is this which gives them the precision control.

Also, they get their heads right down behind the ball. This, of course, is one of the major reasons why Sam Snead's putting helped him to conquer the "yips." He had his hand right down the shaft giving maximum control and his eyes positioned as near to the ball as possible. Being right down there close to the ball, helped give Snead a feeling of confidence.

Ask a friend to throw a dart at a 3-foot disc on a wall. Start him at ten paces and then watch how his confidence grows as you reduce the distance from the target. Place him 4 feet from the disc and he never misses.

Being an artist, I am well aware of this when drawing, for really detailed work my fingers move down the pencil as near to the point as possible.

Take the experiment a stage further, stand on a table (2'6"—standard height) and look down—a jump from that height looks fairly formidable. Now lie flat on the table and look down—it looks so easy you could roll off with confidence.

This brings us back to Paul Runyan, who, over thirty years ago, split his hands on the shaft but made the mistake of using a longer putter. Runyan, in seeking a method to stabilize himself in a heavy wind, anchored the butt end of his shaft against his waist with his left hand and extended the right hand down the shaft, with good results. At that moment in time, Runyan was one step from solving the mystery of putting. With his split-handed grip, Runyan, from a distance of 2 feet, knocked in 400 putts without missing as against 143 with his old method. Then Runyan embarked on a false trail—he believed the style to be at a disadvantage on longer putts; the swing arc was limited by the anchored left hand. So Runyan turned to using a longer putter and this was his big mistake. He should have allowed his left wrist to act as a **hinge**.

I have practically half the problem facing Runyan when sinking a 4-foot putt. By using a longer shaft, Runyan pushed his eyes up too far from the ball and in doing so increased his problem of distance.

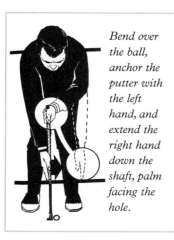

Bend over the ball, anchor the putter with the left hand, and extend the right hand down the shaft, palm facing the hole.

Like the person lying on top of the table, when I get my eyes right down there over the ball, a 4-foot putt is unmissable. And 4-foot putts are missed—just watch the professionals.

How to Address the Putt

Having bent from the waist, check that both your right and left hands are at the same level, for this will ensure that your shoulders are also level. Now bend your left arm to anchor the club at the top with the hand. Check now that the palm of your right hand faces the hole. You can now, with no restrictions from your left hand, produce the ultimate in putting—an unhindered right-handed stroke.

Why We Bend Over the Ball

The center of the putting swing is the top of the spine between the shoulder blades. By bending well over the ball, the axis on which the shoulders and arms rotate is parallel to the green. You now have the perfect set-up for the pendulum putting stroke.

The orthodox putting method tends to raise the left shoulder and lower the right. When in this position, if there is any shoulder movement during the putt, the left shoulder will tend to turn away from the line causing the putt to be cut.

Soleing the Club

The orthodox putting method encourages the golfer to stand too erect at address, resulting in too much weight placed on the heel of the putter, so causing the toe-end to rise above the level of the green. Such an

For putts of four feet and under the putter must be taken straight back and straight through.

The Trevillion Method

With my split-handed putting method, the left hand serves but one purpose: It anchors the club position. Now the right hand is free to do its job—**unhindered** by the left. The stroke now becomes one of simplicity; the right hand, with all fingers on the club, assumes complete authority over the striking action. The left wrist breaks naturally, allowing the stroke to be completed in a positive manner.

I can think of no other sport except golf where fellow professionals check each other's grip—which, to my way of thinking, leads me to believe that over-emphasis on the Vardon grip has **hindered** as much as it has helped golf, especially **putting**.

The Pencil Putt Test

When putting, the secret is to take the putter straight back and through—an extremely difficult thing to do if you adopt the Vardon overlap grip. You can prove this for yourself by holding a pencil in your normal putting grip and then drawing a line. It will, I assure you, be far from straight. Now hold the pencil in just your right hand (providing you are right-handed) and draw another line under the one which you have just completed. You will, I promise, be surprised just how much straighter the second line is.

action destroys the balance of the putter. Furthermore when the putt is struck the ball will be hit high up which results in that dull sound that usually means, even if the putt is on line, it will not reach the hole.

By splitting the hands and bending over the ball as in my method, the golfer soles the club correctly without any mental adjustment on his part. This means when he strikes the ball the blade of the putter is directly parallel with the green so producing the sweet sound of a well-struck putt.

The correct soleing of the club is one of the most neglected parts of putting and if you doubt me, adopt your normal putting stance (side-on) in front of a mirror and check for yourself. I promise, many of you will be surprised by your image.

The Right-Hand Position for All Length of Putts

During its early days, the most queried aspect of my split-hand putting method was the position of my right hand on the shaft for different lengths of putts. As you can see, for putts of 12 feet and over. there is a 6-inch gap between the anchor-hinged left hand at the top of the shaft and the right hand, which strikes the ball. For putts under 12 feet but over 4, my right hand is approximately halfway down the shaft. For short putts of 4 feet and under, the right hand drops as close to the blade as possible, in my case approximately 8 inches.

The shorter the putt, the lower the right-hand position.

The reason I raise the right hand up the shaft for the longer putts is simply because success depends on a longer swing-line, which can best be obtained with the hands high up the shaft.

But I insist, for those really short tricky putts where feel is all-important, you must get your right hand well down. I, personally, can feel the blade strike the ball, almost as if I had struck it with my hand alone.

Memory-check: Always ensure that the thumbs of both hands are kept on top of the shaft.

The Perfect Putting Stroke

For putts of 4 feet and under, the putter must be taken straight back and straight through. The path of the clubhead on the forward swing simply retraces the path it took on the backswing.

The reason it is a mistake to swing the club back inside the line for putts of 4 feet and under is this: When a golfer swings the putter blade back inside the line, he opens the face, and having opened it going back, he now has to close it coming into the ball to ensure a square hit at impact. The problem now is whether he closes it enough. If he does not, he will push the ball right of the hole; conversely, if he closes it too much, he will knock the ball to the left. With only a one in three chance of a square face at impact, putts are missed.

The only way you can ensure that the putter blade remains square to the hole throughout the stroke is to swing it straight back and straight through, and you can do this easily enough if you keep your **right palm** facing the hole throughout the stroke.

For putts that exceed 4 feet in length, the putter blade should be taken back just slightly inside the line with your left wrist acting as a hinge. A word of warning on the follow-through: Ensure that your right palm goes straight through to the hole.

FROM *THE PERFECT PUTTING METHOD* BY PAUL TREVILLION

CHAPTER 43

HARRY VARDON

THE GRIP
THAT SEIZED MILLIONS

"It differs materially from most others, and if I am asked to offer any excuse for it, I shall say that I adopted it only after a careful trial of all the other grips of which I had ever heard."

They don't go there anymore, but maybe they should. For decades, each time the American Ryder Cup Team traveled to British shores, they would begin their stay with a pilgrimage to the English town of Totteridge, to place a wreath on the grave of Harry Vardon.

He was the greatest player of his era, and his era lasted a long time. From 1896, when he won the first of his record six British Opens, until 1920, when he came within a stroke of winning the U.S. Open at the improbable age of fifty, Harry Vardon was the man to beat.

He dominated golf just as long and just as certainly as Jack Nicklaus would half a century later.

But he was also the Arnold Palmer of his time. Vardon made three barnstorming tours of the states—in 1900, 1913, and 1920—and the way his travels energized golf in the United States made him a hero not only in his native land but in America as well.

An unlikely one, too. Born in 1870, the son of a gardener on the Channel Island of Jersey, Vardon seemed destined to follow in his father's footsteps until greens of another sort exerted their pull. When a rudimentary golf course

THE SECRET:

Grip the club with the pinky finger of your right hand overlapping the second finger of your left hand.

took shape on the island, Harry and his brother Tom both took to the game. Tom became good enough to land a professional's job at St. Anne's by the Sea and in short time Harry followed in a position at Ripon, just before his twentieth birthday.

Vardon was self-taught, largely because there was no one on the island of Jersey who knew how to play the game, let alone teach it. But this turned out to be a blessing, as the method he developed on his own was superior to the one that had been *de rigueur* for decades. Until that time, golfers knew only the "St. Andrews swing," a flat-planed, sweeping stroke intended to keep the ball under the stiff links land breezes. Vardon took the club back more vertically and hit down on it a bit. As a result, his ball flew on an elegantly high trajectory and even his longer shots landed softly on the green. His technique would make him the most accurate approach player the game had ever seen.

"He was so accurate with those high-floating, quick-stopping brassie shots that he would put the ball as near the hole in two as his toiling, sweating adversaries would put their third, the chip," wrote Bernard Darwin. "What hope was there against such a man? In his great years, nobody had any real hope."

Vardon won more than sixty tournaments around the world (including fourteen straight in one season) in an era when only a few bona fide events were staged each year. "The more triumphant Vardon became," said Darwin, "the more utterly he routed his

Harry Vardon combined the dominant game of Jack Nicklaus with the fan appeal of Arnold Palmer.

rivals, the more his style became admired. And when he was making victorious progresses up and down the country, 'Have you tried the Vardon grip?' was almost as common a greeting amongst golfers as 'Good morning.'"

There is some question as to whether Vardon was the first to use the grip that was named after him, but what is beyond doubt is that he was the man to popularize it. Today nearly three quarters of the world's 50 million golfers hold the club as Harry did a century ago. He first discussed his grip in his book, *The Complete Golfer*, from which the following is excerpted.

VARDON'S SECRET

Now comes the all-important consideration of the grip. This is another matter in which the practice of golfers differs greatly, and upon which there has been much controversy. My grip is one of my own invention. It differs materially from most others, and if I am asked to offer any excuse for it, I shall say that I adopted it only after a careful trial of all the other grips of which I had ever heard, that in theory and practice I find it admirable—more so than any other—and that in my opinion it has contributed materially to the attainment of such skill as I possess.

The favor which I accord to my method might be viewed with suspicion if it had been my natural or original grip, which came naturally or accidentally to me when I first began to play as a boy, so many habits that are bad being contracted at this stage and clinging to the player for the rest of his life. But this was not the case, for when I first began to play golf, I grasped my club in what is generally regarded as the orthodox manner, that is to say, across the palms of both hands separately, with both thumbs right around the shaft (on the left one, at all events), and with the joins between the thumbs and first fingers showing like two V's over the top of the shaft. This is usually described as the two-V grip, and it is the one which is taught by the majority of professionals to whom the beginner appeals for first instruction in the game. Of course it is beyond question that some players achieve very fine results with this grip, but I abandoned it many years ago in favor of one that I consider to be better.

My contention is that this grip of mine is sounder in theory and easier in practice, tends to make a better stroke and to secure a straighter ball, and that players who adopt it from the beginning will stand a much better chance of driving well at an early stage than if they went in for the old-fashioned two-V.

My grip is an overlapping, but not an interlocking one. Modifications of it are used by many fine players, and it is coming into more general practice as its merits are understood and appreciated. I use it for all my strokes, and it is always when putting that I vary it in the least, and then the change is so slight as to be scarcely noticeable. The photographs illustrating the grip of the left hand singly, and of the two together from different points of view, should now be closely examined.

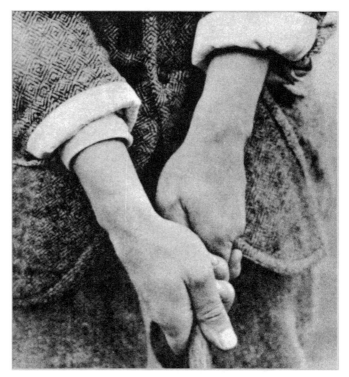

The Vardon grip, in the hands of the man himself.

It will be seen at once that I do not grasp the club across the palm of either hand. The club being taken in the left hand first, the shaft passes from the knuckle joint of the first finger across the ball of the second. The left thumb lies straight down the shaft—that is to say, it is just to the right of the center of the shaft. But the following are the significant features of the grip. The right hand is brought up so high that the palm of it covers over the left thumb, leaving very little of the latter to be seen. The first and second fingers of the right hand just reach round to the thumb of the left, and the third finger completes the overlapping process, so that the club is held in the grip as if it were in a vice. The little finger of the right hand rides on the first finger of the left. The great advantage of this grip is that both hands feel and act like one, and if, even while sitting in his chair, a player who has never tried it before will take a stick in his hands in the manner I have described, he must at once be convinced that there is a great deal in what I say for it, although, of course, if he has been accustomed to the two V's, the success of my grip cannot be guaranteed at the first trial. It needs some time to become thoroughly happy with it.

We must now consider the degree of tightness of the grip by either hand, for this is an important matter. Some teachers of golf and various books of instruction inform us that we should grasp the club firmly with the left hand and only lightly with the right, leaving the former to do the bulk of the work and the other merely to guide the operations. It is astonishing with what persistency this error has been repeated, for error I truly believe it is.

Ask any really first-class player with what comparative tightness he holds the

A century later, the Vardon overlap remains the most commonly used grip in golf.

club in his right and left hands, and I am confident that in nearly every case he will declare that he holds it nearly if not quite as tightly with the right hand as with the left. Personally I grip quite as firmly with the right hand as with the other one. When the other way is adopted, the left hand being tight and the right hand simply watching it, as it were, there is an irresistible tendency for the latter to tighten up suddenly at some part of the upward or downward swing, and, as surely as there is a ball on the tee, when it does so there will be mischief. Depend upon it, the instinct of activity will prevent the right hand from going through with the swing in that indefinite state of looseness. Perhaps a yard from the ball in the upward swing, or a yard from it when coming down, there will be a convulsive grip of the right hand which, with an immediate acknowledgement of guilt, will relax again. Such a happening is usually fatal; it certainly deserves to be. Slicing, pulling, sclaffing, and the foundering of the innocent globe— all these tragedies may at times be traced to this determination of the right hand not to be ignored but to have its part to play in the making of the drive. Therefore in all respects my right hand is a joint partner with the left.

The grip with the first finger and thumb of my right hand is exceedingly firm, and the pressure of the little finger on the knuckle of the left hand is very decided. In the same way, it is the thumb and first finger of the left hand that have most of the gripping work to do. Again, the palm of the right hand presses hard against the thumb of the left. In the upward swing this pressure is gradually decreased, until when the club reaches the turning-point there is no longer any such pressure; indeed, at this point the palm and the thumb are barely in contact. This release is a natural one, and will or should come naturally to the player for the purpose of allowing the head of the club to swing well and freely back. But the grip of the thumb and first finger of the right hand, as well as that of the little finger upon the knuckle of the first finger of the left hand, is still as firm as at the beginning.

As the clubhead is swung back again towards the ball, the palm of the right hand and the thumb of the left gradually come together again. Both the relaxing and the re-tightening are done with the most perfect graduation, so that there shall be no jerk to take the club off the straight line. The easing begins when the hands are about shoulder high and the clubshaft is perpendicular, because it is at this time that the club begins to pull, and if it were not let out in the manner explained, the result would certainly be a half shot or very little more than that, for a full and perfect swing would be an impossibility. This relaxation of the palm also serves to give more freedom to the wrist at the top of the swing just when that freedom is desirable.

I have the strongest belief in the soundness of the grip that I have thus explained,

for when it is employed both hands are acting in unison and to the utmost advantage, whereas it often happens in the two-V grip, even when practiced by the most skillful players, that in the downward swing there is a sense of the left hand doing its utmost to get through and of the right hand holding it back.

There is only one other small matter to mention in connection with the question of grip. Some golfers imagine that if they

> **The great advantage of this grip is that both hands feel and act like one.**

rest the left thumb down the shaft and let the right hand press upon it there will be a considerable danger of breaking the thumb, so severe is the pressure when the stroke is being made. As a matter of fact, I have quite satisfied myself that if the thumb is kept in the same place there is not the slightest risk of anything of the kind. Also if the thumb remains immovable, as it should, there is no possibility of the club turning in the hands as so often happens in the case of the two-V grip when the ground is hit rather hard, a pull or a slice being the usual consequence. I must be excused for treating upon these matters at such length. They are often neglected, but they are of extreme importance in laying the foundations of a good game of golf.

FROM *THE COMPLETE GOLFER* BY HARRY VARDON

VARDON'S SECRET

CHAPTER 44

PAUL WILSON

THE BYRONIC MAN

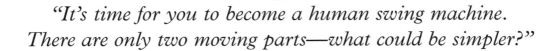

"It's time for you to become a human swing machine.
There are only two moving parts—what could be simpler?"

Canadian teaching professional Paul Wilson was born in 1966. That makes him the same age as the owner of golf's only perfect swing. In 1996, when the two of them were both thirty years old, they got together, and the result was a new way to teach the game.

Wilson, a fine player as a youth, had turned professional with hopes of playing the Tour, but was unable to play with the consistency needed at the top level. "I tried everything," he said. "I hit a thousand balls a day (I counted them), I went to some of the best teachers and schools in the world, but no one could tell me what I needed to do. It was a very depressing and disappointing time of my life."

Ultimately, he became a teaching professional but continued his quest for a reliable, repeating swing. It was nearly a decade before he found it—in a magazine.

It was a photograph of Iron Byron, the mechanical golfer used by the USGA to test golf equipment. "I'd seen it before," said Wilson, "but this time I saw not a machine but a golfer—a golfer with an ideal swing that made contact on the sweet spot every time." Wilson got on the Internet and found video of Iron Byron in action. Then he got in touch with the robot's inventor. The more he studied his subject, the more he became convinced that the hitting machine's simple, compact move could be copied effectively by mere mortals.

> "I'd seen it before," said Wilson, "but this time I saw not a machine but a golfer—a golfer with an ideal swing that made contact on the sweet spot every time."

He tried it on his own game and got immediate results. "Instead of missing half the fairways, I began to hit the ball 300 yards down the middle, dead straight. Nine years later I haven't lost it, and I never practice. Too bad Iron Byron and I didn't meet when I was younger."

Wilson isolated three keys to the robot's swing and, after watching numerous videos of the game's top players, found those same three elements in every swing. These keys became the basis of his teaching method, a method that won him recognition as Ontario's Teacher of the Year in 1997, made him a regular on Canada's *Score Golf* TV show, and brought him two appearances on the Golf Channel. Ken Steven, a writer and book publisher, saw one of those Golf Channel appearances, scheduled himself a

Ken Steven and Paul Wilson pose with Iron Byron, the original swing machine, and its inventor, George Manning.

> **THE SECRET:**
>
> Copy the swing of ball-hitting machine Iron Byron.

lesson with Wilson, and became a big believer in Wilson's methods. Together they produced *Swing Machine Golf,* one of the most handsome and compelling books of recent years. Were it not an instruction manual, this lavish 210-page volume could pass for a coffee table book, with 400 color photographs, many of them juxtaposing Wilson's swing dramatically with that of his mechanical cohort. In keeping with its high-tech inception, *Swing Machine Golf* is not available at bookstores—only through the Internet.

WILSON'S SECRET

Setup

You can see that my setup is very similar to that of Iron Byron. The machine is resting on a solid base that keeps it stable during the swing. My legs are also spread far enough apart to create a solid base. The machine is positioned parallel to the target

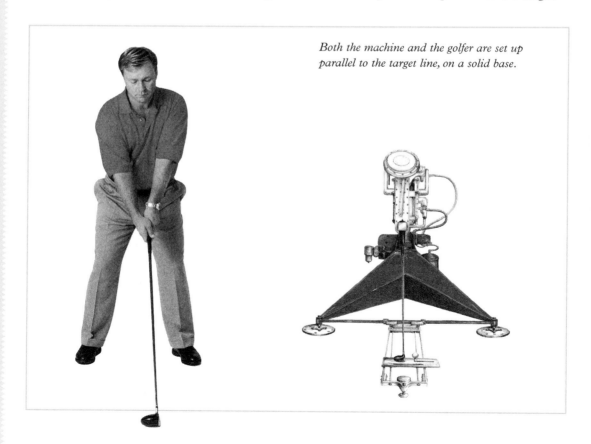

Both the machine and the golfer are set up parallel to the target line, on a solid base.

line. I take care to ensure that my feet, hips, and shoulders are also aligned parallel to the target line.

The machine's drive cylinder tilts toward the ground so the club can reach the ball. My spine tilts from the waist in a similar manner. Because Iron Byron has a straight arm, I copy this by extending both of my arms as much as possible without locking the elbows. Finally, I check to ensure that my grip is correct and that my arms are free of tension, so my wrists can hinge freely, just like the machine's, once the swing begins.

Iron Byron sets up exactly the same way every time. You need to do this, too, because a consistent swing starts with a consistent setup. I'm going to show you how to do this in two of the upcoming lessons.

A consistent swing starts with a consistent setup.

Both machine and golfer tilt toward the ground from the upper body.

At the Top

If you don't have the elements that are seen in the Iron Byron at the top of your backswing, you'll never hit the ball consistently. That's why I care more about how you look in this position than in any other.

The machine's drive cylinder fully rotates to the right in order to get the club to the top, and I achieve the same thing by rotating my shoulders. Because the machine can't bend its arm, I copy this by keeping my left arm straight throughout the backswing. Just like the Iron Byron, my wrists fully hinge at the top to set the club into position. Notice that the machine has not

Like the machine, I make a full rotation to the right side.

changed the angle of its drive cylinder; it's exactly the same as it was at setup. My spine angle also remains constant.

When you watch the pros swing, you'll notice a variety of backswing styles; Jim Furyk, Ray Floyd, or Lee Trevino come to mind. They may look a little unusual taking the club back, but that's just personal flair.

The important thing is this—by the time they've reached the top of their backswing, each of them has done exactly the same things: completely coiled the torso, hinged the wrists rather than the left elbow, and maintained the spine angle that was assumed during the setup.

The wrists hinge, the left arm remains straight.

Impact

Impact is the moment of truth. The whole idea is to get the clubface to return to a position that is square to the ball in order to hit a straight and solid shot. The three key swing elements of the Iron Byron automatically make this happen. They

each add consistency to your swing in a different way.

First, consider the effect of body rotation. If you coil your torso then simply let it uncoil, it will naturally return to its starting position, the same way a spring would react if you tightened its coil and then let it go. Next, if you keep your wrists

At impact, both machine and golfer return the clubface squarely to the ball.

loose, they'll unhinge in an unrestricted manner to return the clubface squarely at impact. Finally, there's the effect of body tilt. If you don't lift up or dip down, chances are excellent that your clubface is going to end up pretty much where it started by the time it reaches impact.

Impact is the moment of truth. The whole idea is to get the clubface to return to a position that is square to the ball in order to hit a straight and solid shot.

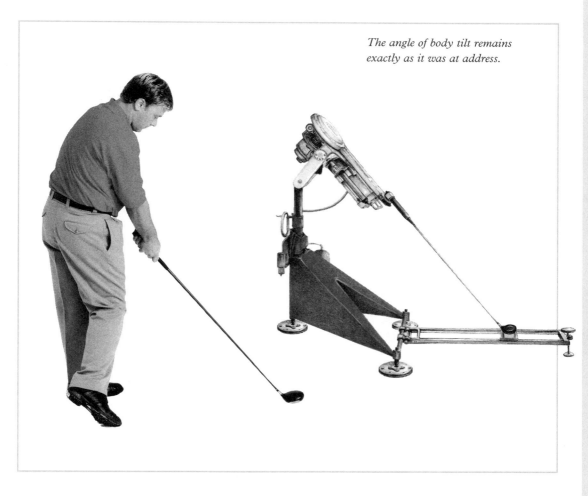

The angle of body tilt remains exactly as it was at address.

Follow-Through

The Iron Byron continues to rotate its drive cylinder past impact, all the way to the finish position. You should also continue to uncoil your torso all the way to the finish, as I am showing here. The pivot point for this uncoiling is your left leg. Virtually all of your weight will, therefore, be on your left leg by the time you get to the finish position. Remember, the machine doesn't have to turn itself to look where the ball goes, but I do. That's why my finish position looks different from the front view. If you keep the camera facing me as I turn my upper body, you can see that, just like the machine, I've maintained a forward tilt in my torso, and my wrists have fully re-hinged.

If you're in the same position as me and Iron Byron at the finish of the follow-through, chances are good that you've hit a solid shot. That's because this finish position is the natural result of doing all the right things to hit the ball correctly.

FROM *SWING MACHINE GOLF*
BY PAUL WILSON

In the follow-through, both Iron Byron and golfer have fully uncoiled. The only difference is that the golfer faces the target while Iron Byron is able to remain facing the ball.

CHAPTER 45

A CARTOONIST DRAWS NEW INSIGHT

"All golf theory until now has been founded on a false premise—that both arms swing to the ball at the same rate of speed."

O ver the one hundred years or so that people have contemplated the mysteries of the golf swing, most of the breakthrough discoveries have come, as one might expect, from teaching professionals.

Occasionally, a top player—a Harry Vardon or Ben Hogan or Henry Cotton—has had something substantive to contribute, and even more rarely the source of inspired thought has been an inventor (Mindy Blake), a psychologist (Tim Gallwey), or a scientist (Dave Pelz). It's safe to say, however, that until recently, the teaching of golf had never benefited from the insights of a cartoonist.

Enter Michael Witte. An English major at Princeton, Witte was art editor of *The Tiger,* the campus humor magazine. He parlayed that passion for comic drawing into a thirty-year freelance career as an illustrator for numerous leading magazines, including *The New Yorker, Time, Money, Town and Country, Sports Illustrated,* and *GOLFMagazine.*

Beginning in 1978, Witte and his psychologist wife Sally were blessed with three athletic sons. Witte began a second career as a Little League coach, which eventually grew into a personal quest for the mechanical secret

In 2002, while studying the action of Cardinals Slugger Mark McGwire, Witte noted a movement that gave him insight into the golf swing.

of hitting a baseball. He began by immersing himself in instructional books and videos but found them lacking and launched an obsessive search of his own, spending thousands of hours freeze-framing videos. What he found was that his artist's understanding of anatomy allowed him to see things that others missed.

So insightful were Witte's findings that both the Kansas City Royals and the St. Louis Cardinals brought him on as a hitting consultant. In 2002, while studying the action of Cardinals slugger Mark McGwire, Witte noted a movement that gave him insight into the golf swing: the pinch.

"It's a subtle move—it travels no more than an eighth of an inch," he said. "And it's paradoxical—a small backward motion concealed in the middle of a simultaneous large forward move, occurring faster than the eye can see. But that minute

Witte's distinctive cartoons have appeared in numerous national magazines.

movement has enormous effect."

Essentially, it's a pinching backward of the leading upper arm against the torso, just at the moment of impact. Having studied miles of videotape of the game's greats past and present, Witte found that this pinch contributed mightily to both clubhead speed and directional control. Following an illustration assignment for *GOLF Magazine,* he hooked up with Top 100 Teacher David Glenz, whose own thoughts on the swing confirmed Witte's theories. They are now coauthoring a book tentatively entitled *The Pinch: The Historically Overlooked Magic Move That Will Change Your Game.* The following is from the manuscript.

THE SECRET:

Pinch your left arm against your body as you move through impact.

WITTE'S SECRET

Extension and how to achieve it have been completely misunderstood by conventional golf gurus. Lacking awareness of front arm "Pinch" deceleration, they typically describe it as a "release" of both arms occurring immediately after impact. No theoretical model could be more harmful to the swing.

If you're trying to swing rapidly down and through, "releasing" your front arm into extension, that arm will be separating from, not linking backward to, the torso during and after impact. Inevitable velocity and power leakage will result. Worse, you're likely to wind up being a "clucker." You'll have a "chicken wing," the most dreaded swing flaw in golf. Here's why.

Every golfer attempting extension confronts an anatomical dilemma. How it's solved largely determines how good the golfer will be. To appreciate it, stand as if you are addressing the ball (without a club) and fully extend your front arm away from your torso in the direction of the target. This is an approximation of the position you will arrive at if you achieve your objective of "releasing" your front arm into full extension. Now, without changing your address position, slide your back hand along your front arm as far as you can reach. Unless you are blessed with a front arm that is dramatically shorter than your back arm or a back arm longer than your front, or both, you should find that your back hand extends only to the middle of your front forearm.

> **Every golfer attempting extension confronts an anatomical dilemma. How it's solved largely determines how good the golfer will be.**

The Pinch

GOLF THEORY HAS
HISTORICALLY BEEN
MESMERIZED BY THE
LARGER FORWARD
MOVE AND OVERLOOKED
THE SMALLER BACKWARD
MOVE.

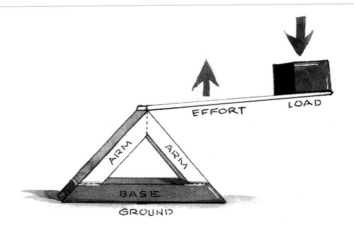

THIS IS A THIRD-CLASS LEVER WITH A ROD WHICH RESTS ON A PIVOT CALLED A FULCRUM (A FIRST-CLASS LEVER LIKE A SEESAW LOCATES THE FULCRUM IN THE CENTER OF THE ROD WITH EFFORT AND LOAD ON OPPOSITE ENDS). FOR OUR PURPOSES, WE HAVE HOLLOWED OUT THE FULCRUM, GIVING IT TWO ARMS RESTING ON A BASE...

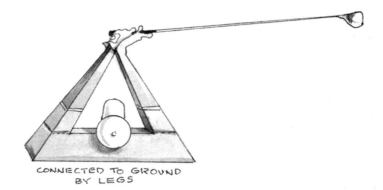

CONNECTED TO GROUND BY LEGS

..., SO THAT IT LOOKS LIKE A GOLFER VIEWED FROM ABOVE.

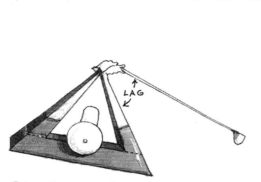

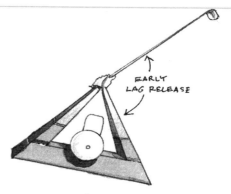

GREAT GOLFERS LAG THEIR WRISTS
UNTIL THE LAST MOMENT AND
RELEASE THEM EXPLOSIVELY,
ARRIVING AT IMPACT JUST IN TIME.

AVERAGE GOLFERS HAVE SLOW,
INEFFICIENT WRIST LEVERS.
TO GET TO THE BALL ON TIME,
THEY HAVE TO RELEASE THEIR
WRISTS EARLY...

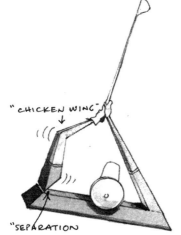

INEFFICIENT WRIST LEVERS
ARE INEVITABLE WITH A DIS-
TORTED FULCRUM LIKE THIS.
BUT TRYING TO <u>ACCELERATE</u> THE
FRONT ARM <u>SEPARATES</u> IT FROM
THE BASE AND THE "CHICKEN
WING" IS THE ONLY WAY THE DUFFER
CAN SLOW DOWN THE FRONT HAND
SO THE BACK HAND CAN CATCH UP.

GREAT GOLFERS <u>DECELERATE</u>
THE FRONT ARM WITH THE BACK-
WARD "PINCH." IT <u>ANCHORS</u> THE
FRONT ARM TO THE TORSO BASE.

FULCRUM INTEGRITY AND WRIST
LEVER EFFICIENCY ARE
ASSURED.

The dilemma? At full extension, your back hand must end up in front of the front arm hand even though it's attached to the arm attached to the back shoulder. How do you get the back hand in front?

"Pinch" extension is the only theory to account for the ability of great golfers to arrive at extension with two elongated arms converging on a clubshaft pointed directly at the target.

Not by swinging your front arm down and through. Halfway through your downswing, you'll inevitably experience an unconscious awareness that should you achieve your objective, your front hand will be moving too fast for the back hand to catch up and extending too far for the back hand to move in front. Your instinctive solution is to decelerate the front arm by pulling the front hand back. The front arm then bends and "shortens" allowing the back hand to pass the front hand.

Problem solved—except that a "chicken wing" is a flawed solution to the anatomical dilemma. It clucks. Because the front arm is denied full extension, the swing is "cut off"—decelerated prematurely—destroying any hope of power. Worse, the bent front arm exerts horizontal pull on the club, sabotaging linear directional control.

Great golfers solve the anatomical dilemma differently. They use the "Pinch." "Pinch" golfers are not "releasing" the front arm into extension. As their hands approach the back hip during the downswing, "Pinch"-braking at the front armpit establishes a backward link that they use for leverage to aggressively lift the front shoulder upward just before and at impact and pull it backward immediately after impact. The front arm goes with it, "shortening" in order to permit the back hand to pass the front hand, both arms fully elongated. It's another "Pinch" paradox—extension by retraction of the front arm.

"Pinch" extension is the only theory to account for the ability of great golfers to arrive at extension with two elongated arms converging on a clubshaft pointed directly at the target. Linear directional control is assured. Clubhead velocity is uncompromised.

Move out of the coop, cluckers. Adopt the "Pinch" and you'll soon be golfing in the upscale neighborhood at the corner of "Extension" and "Retraction"!

FROM *THE PINCH* BY MICHAEL WITTE

WHEN A SPEEDING CAR HITS A BRICK WALL, ITS MOMENTUM IS TRANSFERRED TO THE UNBUCKLED DRIVER, WHO CATAPULTS THROUGH THE WINDSHIELD.

IN CHAMPIONSHIP GOLF, THE UPPER FRONT ARM IS THE BRICK WALL. IT "PINCHES" BACKWARD, COLLIDING WITH THE FORWARD MOVING AND ROTATING TORSO. MOMENTUM IS TRANSFERRED TO THE DRIVER, WHICH CATAPULTS THROUGH THE BALL.

CHAPTER 46

MR. X

AN ANONYMOUS BENEFACTOR

*"No one, so far as I know, seems to have appreciated
the two basic fundamentals that are missing from orthodox
instruction, namely posture and the shape of the hands.
These are the masters' built-in secrets."*

During the last half century, most of the breakthroughs in golf instruction have come from American sources. With just a very few exceptions, Great Britain, where the game was born and nurtured, has been silent since the days of Harry Vardon and his overlapping grip. Indeed, it's arguable that the last big splash came nearly forty years ago, and from a most unlikely source.

In the late 1960s, readers of England's venerable *Golf Monthly* were served a series of eye-catching instruction articles under the byline of Mr. X. Who was this mysterious teacher? Was it three-time British Open Champion Henry Cotton? British PGA founder and instructor to the pros John Jacobs? The new star on the European tour, Tony Jacklin? No, in fact it was not even a professional golfer. Mr. X turned out to be a seventy-year-old retired London businessman, later revealed as Robert Russell. And not only was he not a professional, he hadn't taken up the game until he was forty-three years old.

> **THE SECRET:**
>
> Adjust for your "thumb yield." Then address the ball so that your body forms a reverse "K."

Like most of us, Russell struggled as a beginner. One week, he'd make progress, the next week he'd lose ground. When the irons worked, the woods failed him. And he never seemed to be able to generate the power he knew was within him.

After six years of hard practice, he'd reached a single-digit handicap, but he was still not satisfied. Then, through an intense study of photos of the game's best players he began to notice certain similarities of physique and comportment—assets that

Gary Player greets Mr. X.

few weekend golfers shared. And these distinctions were not confined to the golf swing. Mr. X began to notice marked differences simply in the way great golfers stood at the side of the tee, waiting to play.

When a physiotherapist confirmed his findings, Mr. X reasoned that, if he could simulate those assets, he would be able to improve his game. So he thrust himself into an intense conditioning program—two hours a day for eight weeks (this in an era when few athletes—and no golfers—did physical training). The result: He created a golf-specific body, with golf-specific strengths and flexibilities, and thereby lowered his handicap to scratch. Two decades later, well into his seventies, he was shooting his age regularly, a feat that less than one percent of all golfers ever accomplish.

Russell's articles for *Golf Monthly* generated more reader mail than the magazine had ever seen. In 1968, the series was made into a book—*Golf Lessons with Mr. X,* which was published by *Golf Monthly* in the U.K. and *Golf Digest* in the U.S. It sold so many copies that another book followed—entitled, not surprisingly, *More Golf Lessons with Mr. X.* On both sides of the Atlantic—and a generation before the era of fitness centers and personal trainers—anonymous Robert Russell got thousands of golfers to drill their bodies into playing shape.

The following excerpt, from *Golf Lessons with Mr. X,* focuses on two of Russell's key notions—the value of "thumb yield" and the virtues of the reverse "K" address position.

MR. X'S SECRET

Hands

The set of the **thumbs,** especially the left thumb, is of great importance to the golfer. Golfers like Snead, Nicklaus, Townsend, and many other leading players have thumbs that yield back well beyond a right angle, whereas the majority of club golfers have thumbs that will barely yield beyond 70 degrees.

Let me explain why such a thumb yield is necessary, assuming we use the Vardon overlapping grip. At the top of a master golfer's swing, there is an acute angle between the left arm and the clubshaft; also, their left wrist is more or less **in line with their left forearm,** and not buckled in and under the shaft as is the case with most club golfers.

The fact that masters reach the top with their left wrist in this desirable position, is proof that their left thumb has yielded well beyond the right angle, and has not acted like a wedge, or, even worse, like a recoil

> **Golfers like Snead and Nicklaus have thumbs that yield back well beyond a right angle.**

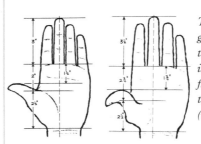

Martin Roesink, a tour professional of the 1960s, was blessed with a super-flexible thumb.

The average golfer's thumb (left) is not as flexible as the master's (right).

A Simple (Mechanical) Line-Up Drill

If your thumb is not as flexible as that of Dave Thomas, an outstanding British professional, you'll have to make adjustments to compensate.

The average handicap golfer has very little idea about the way to line up correctly. This is partly because he is more conscious of the ball than of the target. He also allows his head to hang down when talking aim. So his eye-line, when he does look at the target, is some inches away from his shoulder line. As he usually already has his clubhead placed at the ball, this action will almost certainly set his shoulders, hips, and feet **open.**

spring, upon the clubshaft. If, therefore, you are a golfer with an inadequate thumb yield—which you cannot alter—you have to find a means of overcoming this handicap. There are two methods open to you. One is to shorten the length of your backswing (if you use the Vardon grip) to prevent the left thumb buckling the left wrist in and under the shaft. The other is to change from the Vardon grip to the Whitcombe interlocking grip and to use thickened grips under the left hand—your professional can show you this grip, and thicken the grip on one of your clubs to test it out.

There is a simple mechanical line-up drill which does the trick, and which can be understood by everyone. It is based on the fact that the left shoulder socket **must be exactly opposite the lowest point in the golf swing.** For the ordinary drive, in which the clubhead should meet the ball at the

The average handicap golfer has very little idea about the way to line up correctly. This is partly because he is more conscious of the ball than of the target. He also allows his head to hang down when taking aim.

In the proper address position, the head is raised and the body bends from the hips.

lowest point of the swing, or very slightly beyond that point, the left shoulder socket should be opposite the center or front edge of the ball.

For shots with iron clubs, the left shoulder socket should be opposite the deepest part of the divot that you expect to take after impact with the ball. For a 7-iron, this will be about **3½** inches in front of the ball.

Now consider the other factor that helps you to benefit from the mechanical line-up drill. If you measure from your left eye to a point opposite your left shoulder socket, you will find that the distance is approximately 5 inches for a man and 4 inches for a woman. The tip of the nose is about 1 inch farther away from the shoulder socket.

From this you will readily appreciate that, when you are standing upright, a line through the center of your face, shoulders, hips, and feet will be about 6 inches to the right of a line through what is to be the low-

est point of the swing, i.e., a line through the left shoulder socket. So we arrive at this important point—that, for all shots, the line through the center of your head is going to be six inches behind the lowest swing point on all full shots.

Once this point is appreciated it becomes very simple to take up your stance correctly.

This is the simple drill for doing so with the driver. Place the clubhead with the face 6 inches to the **right** of the **front** of the ball (i.e., about 4½ inches to the right of the **back** of the ball). With the clubhead in this

If you measure from your left eye to a point opposite your left shoulder socket, you will find that the distance is approximately 5 inches for a man and 4 inches for a woman.

position and the shaft exactly squared to the intended line of flight, bring your feet together exactly beneath the shaft line, making sure that the shaft line follows a line through the center of the hips and shoulders. When you are standing in this position, the ball will be opposite your left shoulder socket. Use a mirror as a check.

> **There are many golfers who have realized the importance of the "K" address and who assume it more or less subconsciously.**

Now move your left foot to the left, parallel to the line through ball and target, so that the ball is opposite the left heel. Next move the right foot exactly the same distance to the right. (This adjustment must be deliberately and carefully executed, otherwise the feet will not be evenly spaced on both sides of the shaft line.)

The fourth, and final stage, in this line-up drill is to move the hips, hands, and clubhead leftward until the club is grounded behind the ball. You are now in a mathematically correct position for hitting your drive. This movement is made by an "all-in-one-piece" lateral slide of the right knee, hips and hands, accompanied by a slight tilting of the shoulders.

There are one or two ancillary adjustments that can be made. One is to slew the left foot around on the heel so that the left toe is pointing slightly outwards. Another is to move your feet a little bit back from the target line through the ball to give you your correct distance from the ball.

When all this has been done, your hands should be directly on the line from your eyes to your left toe cap.

Now apply this principle to lining-up with a 7-iron. Remember that in this shot the lowest part of the divot should be about 3½ inches in front of the ball. This means that the back of the ball, at address, will be about 6 inches to the right of the lowest point of the swing (i.e., what should be the lowest part in the divot).

Accordingly, when you apply the drill that I have recommended for the driver to the 7-iron, you will start with the clubhead 1 inch behind the ball (and not 4½ inches behind as was the case for the driver). You will then continue the drill, except that you will not widen your stance as much as you did for the driver, and you will turn your left toe out more. You will also move the hands forward slightly, but without moving the clubhead, so that your hands will blot out your left ankle or the bottom of your trouser leg. The shaft of your 7-iron will then be correctly tilted, with the hands slightly in advance of the ball, to produce the correct divot after impact.

For clubs between the driver and the 7–iron, you will make appropriate adjustments of the relationship of the ball to the lowest point of the swing. With a long iron— a 2 or 3—the divot is going to be shorter

MR. X'S SECRET

and shallower, so the back of the ball will be about 3–4 inches to the RIGHT of the lowest point of the swing.

Now for the Professional Method. Here it is for comparison with the Mechanical Method.

The Professional Method in Four Stages, with Concentration on the Target Instead of the Ball

There are many golfers who have realized the importance of the "K" address and who assume it more or less subconsciously. For such players there is another stance drill which embodies a more natural approach to the business of setting yourself up for the shot. When you read the details of this drill, you may well realize that it seems to be a description of the way that many of the top tournament players take their stance.

Here it is:

a) Take stock of the shot from behind the ball, looking in the direction of the target. At the same time take your grip, bedding the shaft well into the **roots** of the fingers of the left hand. This is best accomplished when you are holding the club in a vertical position.

b) Place the clubhead on the ground behind the ball with the hands immediately above the spot you intend to be the **lowest** point of the swing. If you are using a driver, then the hands should be immediately above the front of the ball. If you are using a short pitching iron (with which it must be your intention to hit down on the ball and take a divot after impact), then you should lay your hands above a spot five or six inches in front of the ball.

When you assume the address position correctly your body takes the shape of a reverse "K." A common error is to set up in the shape of a "Y."

Having done this, you **keep your hands in the same position relative to the ball throughout the rest of the drill.**

c) Now slew the body, hips, and feet round—like a ship at anchor. With your

The "K" Position.

eyes in the target, **not on the ball,** aim your shoulders at the target, or a trifle to the right of it. (N.B.: Never aim to the left of the target with your shoulders except for very short approach shots.)

Shift your feet to suit the alignment of your shoulders, and to get them at the right distance from the shot line.

When you are correctly in position your hands, for a drive, should blot out the left toe cap from view. For a short iron shot, your hands should blot out the left ankle.

d) Turn the head to the front. Focus the eyes on the **back** of the ball. Have the chin point to a spot about 6 inches behind the ball. Now arch your back in the way I have already described and you are set to play.

Many teachers of golf recommend having the ball opposite the left heel for the drive. There is nothing wrong with this. It is good advice.

Unfortunately thousands of handicap golfers, in trying to carry it out, contrive in the process to get themselves lined up incorrectly. Then they wonder why they hit a poor shot.

The explanation is simple. Subconsciously they want to look straight down the line of the shaft to the ball. The only way they can do this, if the ball is opposite the left heel, is by adopting an open stance. They open the shoulders. They open the hips, sometimes excessively. They open their feet.

In this position they fondly imagine that they still have the ball opposite the left heel. In point of fact, they actually have it well towards the center of the stance and are **aiming with the body well to the left of their target.** However, the face of the club is still being held to aim directly at the target. So it is little wonder that, when they play, the ball goes off-line.

The prime fault is that they feel they must look straight down the shaft at the ball. This is a common error.

In the correct address position (for any normal shot), the line from

In the correct address position, the line from the left eye to the ball should pass behind the hands, not through them. It should also pass behind the shaft of the club, only intersecting it just above the ball.

the left eye to ball should pass **behind** the hands, not through them. It should also pass behind the shaft of the club, only intersecting it just above the ball.

I can put it another way. When you are lined up correctly, the shaft of your club should appear to be tilted to the left. This is an illusion. You can check this for yourself quite simply in your own living room or bedroom. Take your driver and address a ball on the carpet so the shaft is vertical (i.e., not tilted either towards the target or away from it).

Keeping the clubshaft in that position, adjust your address with the ball opposite your left heel, until it appears to your eyes that the shaft is tilted quite appreciably towards the target. You may even get the illusion (and it is an illusion) that the clubshaft is pointing outside your left shoulder.

Now check your head position in relation to the ball. You will find, or should find, that you are looking directly down **not at the ball,** but at a point about 6 inches **behind the ball.**

Moreover you will almost certainly find that your shoulders are parallel to the target line. Indeed you may have the illusion of the shoulder line being slightly shut, i.e., pointing to the right of your target. But this is an illusion, as you can easily check by having someone place a club across your shoulders.

You are now in a correct position for playing the shot. Your hips will, or should be, slightly open, and the line joining your heels,

With the drive, in which you wish to sweep the ball away, you should meet the ball at the lowest point of the swing. So you should have the ball immediately opposite your left armpit at the address. This very often coincides with having it also opposite the left heel.

will, or should be, parallel to the target line.

The lowest point of the swing, for all shots, should be immediately opposite the left armpit.

With the drive, in which you wish to sweep the ball away, you should meet the ball at the lowest point of the swing. So you should have the ball immediately opposite your left armpit at the address. This very often coincides with having it also opposite the left heel.

I have previously explained the adjustments that have to be made for playing shots with other clubs. So I will not touch on them at the moment. I'll merely remind you that, with fairway shots, you will normally be hitting down on the ball at impact. This means you will set your hands slightly in front of the ball at address.

The shaft will be slightly tilted towards the target. When you do this, and are lined up correctly, then the clubshaft will appear to be even more tilted towards the target than it did for the drive.

This apparent tilt of the clubshaft will give you the feeling that you are going to hit the ball out to the right. You should have this feeling (or illusion). The ball will not go to the right. It will go straight. Once you have gained confidence in the results you can achieve from this position, you will cease to be distracted by the illusion.

One thing you must avoid. You must not try to achieve the illusion I have described (of the clubshaft appearing to tilt towards the target) by standing with your head opposite the ball and pushing your hands towards the target so that the shaft is indeed tilted. This will **not** work.

The important thing is to line up so that the shoulders are parallel to the target line and your chin pointing down at a spot about six inches behind the ball. If you also have the ball opposite your left heel and the shaft not tilted (or only slightly tilted), you will then be in the ideal "K" position.

FROM *GOLF MONTHLY'S LESSONS WITH MR. X*

MR. X'S SECRET

CHAPTER 47

COUNT YOGI

THE BEST PLAYER YOU'VE NEVER SEEN

"No matter how I play, I'm never off my system. I more than likely will be the only consistent golfer that ever lived."

He could break 70 playing either right-handed or left-handed. He had fifty-five holes-in-one, and in the 1934 Chicago Open, he made two of them back to back, the first on a par-3, the second on a par-4. Three times, in Open competition, he shot scores in the 50s. One day he played eighteen holes in 57 minutes and shot 69.

Another time, he played seven rounds in a single day, shooting in the 60s all seven times. He once hit a golf ball 435 yards. And those feats don't begin to tell the story of the mysterious and colorful Count Yogi.

No one—not even he—knew where he was born. It was either Montana or India. His father was of Bavarian descent (Yogi's given name was Harry Hilary Xavier Von Frankenberg), but his mother is thought to have been a Native American. One report lists him as a direct descendant of Chief Sitting Bull.

All that is certain is that when Yogi was a young boy his family settled on the outskirts of Chicago where his abusive alcoholic father

THE SECRET:

Set up with your hands behind the ball and your left arm slightly bent. Take the club back to the inside, use little weight shift, and pick the ball cleanly off the turf—feel as if you're hitting up on the ball.

Much of Count Yogi's life is shrouded in mystery, but there was never any doubt about his ability to play the game.

Part prodigy, part promotional genius, Yogi parlayed his talents from the mean streets of Chicago all the way to Hollywood.

ness, street smarts, and entrepreneurial flair.

However, what brought Count Yogi fame and success was his ability to play golf, an ability that he claimed was literally delivered to him by God. He'd discovered the game at age six, peering through the fence of a golf course near his home, and had taught himself to hit a ball by picking up a stick and imitating the swings of the club members. One day, a year or so later, he was in a cornfield stroking homemade golf balls made of mud, straw, and cornhusk over the tops of the corn when he experienced a divine encounter. A voice, he said, spoke to him from above and gave him the knowledge and understanding of how a golf swing should be made. The voice assured him that if he were to swing that way, he would have a lifetime of health and happiness and would bring the same to others.

Thus inspired, the enlightened boy began to play golf like few mortals before or since. By age twelve he was shooting consistently in the 60s. By fourteen he'd turned pro, and over the next two decades, he set scores of course records and won dozens of tourna-

ran a small farm. At age eight, he ran away from home and ended up in the mean streets of Chicago's South Side, where he became entangled with the likes of Al and Frank Capone. There was more than one occasion when "Blackie" (as he was known then for his great shock of jet-black, wavy hair) came close to losing his life, but he survived through a combination of intelligence, tough-

ments in the Chicago area. Because of his ethnic looks and unorthodox method, however, he was shunned by the PGA of America and never got a chance to display his skill on the national stage. Despite the admiration and support of his peers—Hogan, Snead, Nelson, and Palmer among them—Yogi never gained the legitimacy he so wanted.

And so at the peak of his playing talents, he left Chicago for California and became a teaching pro. Although he arrived in Los Angeles nearly broke, and had to begin as a caddie, his reputation grew quickly, and within a short time he was teaching at Bob Hope's Toluca Fairways Driving Range in Hollywood, where his students would include Hope, Dean Martin, Mickey Rooney, Howard Hughes, Senator John F. Kennedy, and President Dwight D. Eisenhower. It was another of his pupils, songwriter Hoagy Carmichael, who christened Harry Frankenberg with the moniker Count Yogi. For a while he wrote golf columns for Fox and RKO and made numerous radio and television appearances, including the variety shows hosted by Steve Allen and Groucho Marx.

In 1950 he entered the prestigious Western Open and led the field of qualifiers with a course-record 66, two strokes lower than Lloyd Mangrum and eventual winner Sam Snead, but when the PGA got wind of his presence, they sent him a telegram forbidding him from teeing up in the tournament.

So for the last thirty or so years of his life, Count Yogi took his show on the road, as a trick-shot artist, traveling over 3 million miles and doing over 7,000 exhibitions, all the while preaching his method as infinitely superior to the traditional teachings of the PGA.

Lessons with Yogi rarely lasted more than fifteen minutes—he claimed that was as long as he needed to instill his Yogi system, a combination of swing mechanics, mental coaching, and Eastern mysticism. He did his best to explain it all in a book that was almost as curious and inscrutable as he—*Five Simple Steps to Perfect Golf*—from which the following is drawn.

> In 1950, he entered the Western Open and led the field of qualifiers with a 66, two lower than Lloyd Mangrum and Sam Snead, but when the PGA got wind of his presence, they sent him a telegram forbidding him from teeing up in the tournament.

COUNT YOGI'S SECRET

Articles on the golf swing appear endless. Thousands of words have been written in magazines, newspapers, and books about the golf swing—revealing a tip or two by a professional. The full swing has been broken down into several segments and photographed with high-speed, stop-action cameras. One article will play up the importance of the hands, another the legs. Some stress the wrists. Others cite the importance of the shoulders or hips.

So much is said that a beginner or handicap golfer easily becomes confused. It's a case of "paralysis by analysis," as the saying goes.

Probably the biggest problem in the past two decades of golf has been the emphasis on power. Smooth, graceful swingers seem to be disappearing in favor of hard-hitting, fast-swinging power swingers. Some college players, inspired by tour pros, are becoming power swingers. It used to be that you would see some of the best swings on college campuses. The quest for power in the swing has been ruining golf. Golfers are being afflicted with physical problems, mostly back or hip strains and tendonitis from swinging so hard.

> **The quest for power in the swing has been ruining golf. Golfers are being afflicted with physical problems, mostly back or hip strains and tendonitis, from swinging so hard.**

Country club and public course players give up the game in disgust when they fail to achieve the power they seem to think they need to enjoy the game and score well.

The simple answer to a good golf swing is rhythm and smoothness. Be relaxed. Be graceful. Your rhythm will be better. Your clubhead speed will be faster. Your distance automatically will improve and, most important, your accuracy will be good. You don't have to be blessed with a muscular physique, strong hands and wrists or forearms or powerful shoulders or athletic legs to hit a golf ball far and straight. I'm 5'8" and usually weigh the average for my frame and height. I am not muscular and never have been.

My hands are not strong. My legs are fairly thin (enough so that I don't like to show them off). Yet I have always hit a golf ball straight and far. I'm just one example. Even better examples are the small golfers on the Ladies Professional Golf Association tour in the decade of the 1970s, such players as Betty Burfeindt (5'4", 115 lbs.), Marlene Bauer Hagge (5'2", 120 lbs.), Sandra Palmer (5' 1/2", 117 lbs.), Clifford Ann Creed (5'4", 105 lbs.), Judy Rankin (5'3 1/2", 110 lbs.), and Laura Baugh (5'5", 118 lbs.), to name just a few. They can all hit the ball far and straight.

A lot has been written on various theories of the swing that has been referred to as "inside-out," "outside-in," and "square to square." I won't go into the details of explaining those because I'm afraid I, too, might confuse you.

How, then, does one swing correctly? Here's how I swing— and have been swinging for more than fifty years:

Downward straight back inside and then

The simple answer to a good swing is rhythm and smoothness.

Yogi always held his right hand on top of his club and teed his ball with his left hand.

Standing with feet together, look at loft-line of clubface as you prepare to take your stance.

Take a step with right foot, placing clubface's loft-line down behind ball as your lineup guide.

Step with your left foot turned outward just behind the right foot after addressing the ball.

back under the ball straight up the proverbial arrow line of flight.

I swing that way under all conditions:
Regardless of the club.
Regardless of the lie of the ball.
Regardless of the slope of the ground.
Regardless of the texture of the grass, rough, sand, or even hard ground, asphalt, or cement, I always address the ball on an up-arc angle of the clubface's loft-line and in the center of the clubface. My hands are always behind the ball—never ahead, on any shot, any time. I never open the clubface, never close it, never holding it to punch it into the ground or the sand. This theory applies to all swings—even short shots and putts. All shots.

I never "swing the handle," never swing the clubhead, never concentrate on swinging the V's of my arms and elbows, and never use firmness or power at any time. I stress that a golfer cannot ever be too boneless or too loose, nor too muscleless. Be relaxed. Be graceful. Don't attempt to concentrate on the so-called various phases of the swing. Once your teaching professional teaches you correct conception of the swing, you are on your own. You don't need continual lessons all your life. Players who are always seeking, experimenting, thinking and analyzing their game only end up getting confused. Only repetition

> **I stress that a golfer cannot ever be too boneless or too loose nor too muscleless. Be relaxed. Be graceful.**

Move right foot back to square up stance parallel to line of flight. Stand tall and loose.

Take clubhead straight back loosely, down and inside, as far as you can go. Stay flatfooted.

Your finish should be with knees even, left foot turned out, and on the tip of your right toe.

After finishing, lower the club by your thigh, letting the shaft slide and hang loosely in your hand.

is improvement. You must establish an infallible mental routine.

Let me explain as simply as possible how to swing a golf club. It's the way I have done it for over fifty years and it's the way I have taught some 20,000 pupils. My pupils were able to do it after a few lessons. So can you. Unlike all other stalemated ways of playing this wonderful mistreated game, you'll find peace and happiness with this way.

Keep your head down loosely over the ball; put your chin out because your shoulder will be passing under your chin. As you mentally drag your clubhead straight back low to the ground, delicately and effortlessly, straight back away from you and slightly inside, your clubhead will always be arced the same in the backswing, different for everybody—no two people have the same backswing. It should be a full backswing without any pronation of the hands and without any wrist cocking. Because you are swinging relaxed and graceful and not attempting to be powerful (and awkward), you'll find that your front knee goes downward toward the ball as your back knee bends all the way back. In other words, as you drag your clubhead straight back downward away from you on an inside line, your body will also twist downward loosely as your shoulder turns under your chin and both feet remain entirely on

Unlike all other stalemated ways of playing this wonderful mistreated game, you'll find peace and happiness with this way.

Finish the swing standing tall and loose, always standing on the extreme tip of your right toe.

the ground—flatfooted. The right elbow is not bent into the body on full swings.

Mentally return your clubhead under the ball from your inside straight-back backswing to straight up the arrow of the loft-line line of flight, finishing with your club around your neck and above your shoulder. You should look up the instant the clubface makes contact under the ball. You should

> I have eliminated virtually every idea suggested in instruction articles in books, magazines, and newspapers. I keep the swing simple and think only of being relaxed, graceful, and smooth.

finish the swing standing tall and loose, always ending on the extreme tip of your right toe. Your front knee will be entirely flexed back as was your back leg's knee on the backswing. The weight at the finish has gone against the outer aspect of the front foot (left foot). It is important that your left foot be turned outward in the address or you can pull muscles and incur all types of aches and pains. Your stance is too wide if your back foot (right foot) is too far back. Your stance is too narrow when the back knee protrudes beyond the front knee. The width of your stance is not governed by the width of your shoulders, but rather by the length of your legs from the arches to the knees.

After your swing, you must do something with the club to avoid looking awkward, as many golfers appear—even Tour pros. The deltoid and pectoral muscles have expanded from the swing, so now you must draw your hands down with your elbows alongside your waistline to relax with a good posture as you watch where your ball goes. (Your playing partner probably won't be looking at your ball's flight that closely, and the shortage of caddies today makes it essential that you keep an eye on it as it rolls along the ground.) As you watch your ball, slide the clubshaft gracefully through your hands and balance it with your fingers gently—the way you should carry your club at all times. Mentally mark the location of your ball before leaving this position.

I have always been a consistently straight golf-ball hitter because I have eliminated virtually every idea suggested in numerous instruction articles in books, magazines and newspapers. I keep the swing simple and think only of being relaxed, graceful, and smooth.

FROM *FIVE SIMPLE STEPS TO PERFECT GOLF* BY COUNT YOGI

COUNT YOGI'S SECRET

WHERE TO FIND MORE INFORMATION ON THE SECRETS

Many of the excerpted books are now out of print in their original editions, but some are available in later editions, British editions, or in paperback. If you can't find a copy of a book in your local bookstore try a retail Internet site such as amazon.com, barnesandnoble.com, or ebay.com; an antiquarian book dealer such as abe.com, or a golf book collector such as rhodmcewan.com.

Chapter 1 **Tommy Armour**
How to Play Your Best Golf All the Time
Simon & Schuster (New York), 1953.

Chapter 2 **Dick Aultman**
The Square-to-Square Golf Swing: Model Method for the Modern Player.
Golf Digest (Norwalk, CT), 1971.

Chapter 3 **Jimmy Ballard**
How to Perfect Your Golf Swing Using "Connection" and the Seven Common Denominators
Golf Digest (Norwalk, CT), 1981.
Videos and golf school also available.
Web site: www.golfspan.com/instructors/jballard/3dayschool.asp

Chapter 4 **Peter Beames**
Walk-Thru to Par
Jefferson International (Los Angeles), 1984.
Video also available.

Chapter 5 **Paul Bertholy**
Golf Swing Construction 101-The Bertholy Method Revisited
(written by Doug Ferreri)
Privately printed (Loxahatchee, FL), 2002.
Golf school also available.
Web site: www.paulbertholy.com

Chapter 6   Mindy Blake
The Golf Swing of the Future
Norton (New York), 1973.
Videos and golf school also available.
Web site: www.reflexswing.com

Chapter 7   Percy Boomer
On Learning Golf
Alfred A. Knopf (New York), 1946.

Chapter 8   Julius Boros
Swing Easy, Hit Hard
Harper & Row (New York), 1965.

Chapter 9   Henry Cotton
Thanks for the Game
Sidgwick & Jackson (London), 1980.

Chapter 10   Joe Dante
The Four Magic Moves to Winning Golf
McGraw-Hill (New York), 1962.

Chapter 11   J. Douglas Edgar
The Gate to Golf
Privately printed (Washington, D.C.), 1920.

Chapter 12   W. Timothy Gallwey
The Inner Game of Golf
Random House (New York), 1981.

Chapter 13   Phil Galvano
Secrets of Accurate Putting and Chipping
Prentice-Hall (Englewood Cliffs, NJ), 1957.
Golf school also available.
Web site: www.galvanogolf.com

Chapter 14   Darrin Gee
*One Shot at a Time: Seven Principles for
Transforming Your Golf Game and Your Life*
Book in progress. Golf school available.
Web site: www.spiritofgolfhawaii.com/

Chapter 15   Ben Hogan
*Five Lessons: The Modern Fundamentals
of Golf;* A.S. Barnes (New York), 1957.

Chapter 16   Chuck Hogan
Five Days to Golfing Excellence
ISBS (Portland, OR), 1986.
Web site: www.chuckhogan.com/

Chapter 17   John Jacobs
Practical Golf
Quadrangle (New York), 1972.
Web site: www.jacobsgolf.com/

Chapter 18   Ernest Jones
Swing the Clubhead
Dodd, Mead (New York), 1952.

Chapter 19   Homer Kelley
The Golfing Machine
Star System Press (Seattle),
1969; revised 1983.
Web site: www.thegolfingmachine.com

Chapter 20   David Lee
Gravity Golf
Gravity Golf, Inc. (Royal, AR), 1994.
Video and golf school also available.
Web site: www.gravitygolf.net

APPENDIX 1

Chapter 21   Arthur d'Arcy Locke
(Bobby Locke)
Bobby Locke on Golf
Simon & Schuster (New York), 1954.

Chapter 22   Carl Lohren
One Move to Better Golf
Golf Digest (Norwalk, CT), 1975.
Video also available.

Chapter 23   George Low
The Master of Putting
Atheneum (New York), 1983.

Chapter 24   Jim McLean
The X-Factor Swing
HarperCollins (New York), 1997.
Video also available.

Chapter 25   Eddie Merrins
Swing the Handle, Not the Clubhead
Golf Digest (Norwalk, CT), 1973.
Video also available.
Web site: www.swingthehandle.com

Chapter 26   Johnny Miller
Pure Golf
Doubleday (Garden City, NY), 1976.

Chapter 27   Alex Morrison
A New Way to Better Golf
Simon & Schuster (New York), 1932.

Chapter 28   Andrew Mullin
"It Makes Sense to Start from the Top"
GOLF Magazine (New York),
May 1975 issue

Chapter 29   Natural Golf
(written by Peter Fox and Ed Woronicz)
Natural Golf
McGraw-Hill (New York), 1997.
Video and golf school also available.
Web site: www.naturalgolf.com

Chapter 30   Byron Nelson
Shape Your Swing the Modern Way
Golf Digest (Norwalk, CT), 1976.

Chapter 31   Joe Norwood
Joe Norwood's Golf-O-Metrics
Doubleday (Garden City, NY), 1978.

Chapter 32   John Novosel
Tour Tempo
Doubleday (New York), 2004

Chapter 33   Captain Bruce W. Ollstein
Combat Golf
Viking (New York), 1996.
Email: capt.p@att.net

Chapter 34   Dave Pelz
Dave Pelz's Putting Bible
Broadway (New York), 2000.
Video and golf school also available.
Web site: www.pelzgolf.com

APPENDIX 1

Chapter 35 **Dave Pelz**
Dave Pelz's Short Game Bible
Broadway (New York), 1999.
Video and golf school also available.
Web site: www.pelzgolf.com

Chapter 36 **Chi Chi Rodriguez**
Chi Chi's Secrets of Power Golf
Viking (New York), 1967.

Chapter 37 **Dr. Bob Rotella**
Golf Is Not a Game of Perfect
Simon & Schuster (New York), 1996.

Chapter 38 **Paul Runyan**
The Short Way to Lower Scoring
Golf Digest (Norwalk, CT), 1979.

Chapter 39 **Jennifer Scott**
Get the Hole in Your Head—Own the Zone
(Book in progress)
Audio CD and golf school available.
Web site: www.ownthezonegolf.com

Chapter 40 **Fred Shoemaker**
Extraordinary Golf: The Art of the Possible
Putnam (New York), 1996.
Web site: www.extraordinarygolf.com

Chapter 41 **Bob Toski**
The Touch System for Better Golf
Golf Digest (Norwalk, CT), 1971.

Chapter 42 **Paul Trevillion**
The Perfect Putting Method
Winchester Press (New York), 1971.
Video also available.

Chapter 43 **Harry Vardon**
The Complete Golfer
Methuen (London), 1905.

Chapter 44 **Paul Wilson**
Swing Machine Golf
StoryTrend Publishing (Thornhill, Ontario),
2004. Golf school also available.
Web site: www.swingmachinegolf.com

Chapter 45 **Michael Witte**
*The Pinch: The Historically Overlooked
Magic Move That Will Change Your Game*
(Book in progress)

Chapter 46 **Mr. X**
Golf Monthly's Lessons with Mr. X
Golf Digest (Norwalk, CT), 1969.

Chapter 47 **Count Yogi**
Five Simple Steps to Perfect Golf
Nash (Los Angeles), 1973.
Video and golf school also available.
Web site: www.countyogigolf.com

APPENDIX 1

APPENDIX 2

SECRETS BY CATEGORY

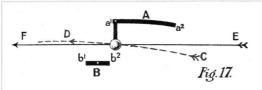

The Square-to-Square Method took the golf world by storm (page 10).

Julius Boros shows how to swing easy and hit hard (page 60).

Ben Hogan's advice for the downswing: Turn your hips (page 114).

A. Long arm of Gate.
B. Small arm.
C.D. Line to be taken by the club-head.
E.F. Line of direction.

Fig. 17.

The Gate to Golf banished slices (page 84).

Natural Golf breaks all the rules (page 236).

Ernest Jones makes his point with a pen knife (page 138).

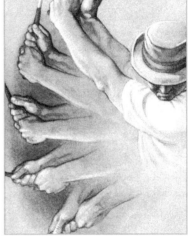

Byron Nelson's secret was less hand action and more leg action (page 240).

APPENDIX 2

Alex Morrison believed the muscles of the left side of the body controlled the swing (page 208).

Bob Toski's teaches the touch system (page 328).

Paul Wilson, *page 348*
The Byronic Man

Michael Witte, *page 358*
A Cartoonist Draws
New Insight

Mr. X, *page 366*
An Anonymous Benefactor

Do the pinch at impact (page 358).

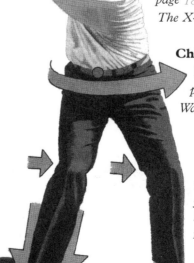

Fred Shoemaker, *page 318*
Throw Your Cares Away

Bob Toski, *page 328*
Feelings, Nothing More Than Feelings

Harry Vardon, *page 342*
The Grip That Seized Millions

Count Yogi, *page 376*
The Best Player You've
Never Seen

POWER

Jim McLean,
page 184
The X-Factor

Chi Chi Rodriguez,
page 282
Wall Power

The gap between your shoulders and hips determines power (page 184).

Count Yogi preached grace and elegance (page 376).

Use topspin to putt like Bobby Locke (page 162).

How to sink 1,000 straight four-footers (page 336).

Miller lights (page 202).

Golf as warfare (page 258).

Darrin Gee's advice transforms your game and your life (page 106).

APPENDIX 2

ACKNOWLEDGMENTS

This was a book with numerous moving parts, and it could never have come together without the help and kindness of many people. Foremost among them is my friend, co-author, and business partner Mary Tiegreen. Mary is not only an award-winning publication designer, she is the author, along with her husband Hubert Pedroli, of several previous books, including three on golf. Even more important, she's one of the world's great "idea people." A quick chat with Mary usually produces concepts for three or four books. *The Secret of Golf* came to life during one of our first conversations, and at the same time we formed a company called Arran House Press. This is the first of what we hope will be many books under that imprimatur.

Arran House is the name of the building in which my wife and I now live, an old stone townhouse that sits alongside the 18th hole of the Old Course at St. Andrews, Scotland. When we moved here in the fall of 2003, I feared that a transatlantic collaboration with Mary—who lives where we used to, in suburban New York—was a prescription for chaos. But Mary, thank goodness, is technologically several gigabytes ahead of me and her Mac computer seems to be capable of everything except slow-cooking a rib roast. She even has a webcam attached to her monitor, and once she showed me how to rig one up to my own laptop, the two of us, along with our respective spouses and dogs, were happily chatting back and forth, all for way less than the price of a phone call.

The co-star on Mary's side of the camera was her tireless assistant, Angela Escalante, a one-woman production department whose scanning, transcribing, photocopying, and collating kept me, Mary, and our forty-six authors somehow in sync and moving forward. Thank you, Angela, not just for your good work but for your perpetual smile.

Since most of the secrets had appeared in previous books, the procurement of reprint rights was a major task. Help came from numerous quarters but perhaps none more unlikely than Jerry Tarde. For two decades Jerry and I were direct competitors—he as the editor of *Golf Digest* and I the editor of *GOLF Magazine*. Happily, however, we've always managed to remain friends, and when I approached him for help on rights to several of the *Golf Digest* books, he was generously cooperative, as were his colleagues Bob Carney and Julie DiMarco.

Another Julie, my friend and former colleague at *GOLF Magazine* Julie Hansen, came to the rescue with rights assistance.

My thanks go to Mrs. Paul Bertholy, Eddie Boros, Mrs. Joe Dante, Phil Galvano, Jr., Darien Gee, Mrs. Homer Kelley, and Eddie Pelz for the kind of help only a family member can provide; to Lorin Anderson, Steve Foehl,

Jim Frank, Cheryl Leb, Rhod McEwan, Carl Mickelson, Dr. Glennis Rickert for their assistance with research; to Joe Daniels (The Golfing Machine), Doug Fererri (The Bertholy Method) Tim Nichols (Count Yogi Golf), Ken Steven (Swing machine Golf), and Ed Woronicz (Natural Golf); and to authors Darrin Gee, Chuck Hogan, David Lee, Carl Lohren, Andrew Mullin, Bruce Ollstein, Jennifer Scott, and Mike Witte for chatting expansively about their secrets.

I am indebted to Lorin Anderson, Steve Foehl, Rhod McEwan, and Tom Secrest for helping me track down various books and authors and to the USGA and the Royal & Ancient Golf Club of St. Andrews for the use of their splendid libraries.

The crisply detailed photos that illustrate most of the chapters are the work of Leonard Kamsler, the finest photographer in the history of golf, and I'm indebted to another *GOLF Magazine* colleague and friend, Greg Midland, for coordinating the photo shoot. As for the model in the photos, PGA Professional Brian Crowell, I can't decide whether he more closely resembles Jim Nantz or Jim Carrey—what's important, however, is his grace and accuracy in mimicking the many different address positions and swings on the preceding pages.

At Workman Publishing I'm grateful to Peter Workman for immediately recognizing a good idea when we presented it to him and for his uncanny ability to tweak, fiddle, refine, and enhance our concept—indeed, just about any book concept—so that the finished product is immeasurably more compelling than it was as originally proposed. Jennifer Griffin deserves a medal—and a raise—for her contributions as the book's general editor. If the timing of her phone calls to me was any indication, she worked on this book around the clock, seven days a week, and her attention to detail—and quality—were remarkable. Thanks to Paul Hanson and Patrick Borelli for their design guidance, and to Barbara Peragine for her impeccable work and grace under pressure.

Finally, my eternal thanks go to the two ladies in my life—to my wife, Libby, who has now suffered with patience and good humor through the gestation of a dozen books, all of them on a subject in which she has zero interest, and to my  West Highland White Terrier, Millie, who was not only there—sitting on my lap, at my feet, or behind my head—for every word of this book, but also kindly posed for our corporate logo.

CREDITS

Text credits: Pages 5-9, reprinted with permission of Simon & Schuster Adult Publishing Group from *How To Play Your Best Golf All The Time* by Tommy Armour, Copyright © 1953, by Thomas D. Armour. Copyright renewed © 1981 by John Armour and Benjamin Andrews; pages 12-17, courtesy of Golf Digest, Inc., from *The Square-to-Square Golf Swing* by Dick Aultman, Copyright © 1970 by Golf Digest, Inc; Pages 20-27, courtesy of Golf Digest, Inc., from *How To Perfect Your Golf Swing Using 'Connection' And The Seven Common Denominators* by Jimmy Ballard, Copyright © 1981 by Jimmy Ballard, published by Golf Digest/Tennis, Inc.; Pages 30-33, from *Walk-Thru To Par: Improve Your Golf in 10 Easy Steps* by Peter Beames with Frederic Swan, Copyright © 1985 by Peter Beames, published by Jefferson International Publishing; Pages 36-43, courtesy of Doug Ferreri, from *Golf Swing Construction 101: The Bertholy Method Revisited* by Doug Ferreri, Copyright © 2003 by Doug Ferreri, published by OTW Publishing, West Palm Beach, FL; Pages 46-53, reprinted with permission of Souvenir Press Ltd., from *The Golf Swing Of The Future* by Mindy Blake, Copyright © 1972 by Minden Blake, D.S.O., D.F.C., M.Sc., published by Souvenir Press Ltd.; Pages 56-59, reprinted with permission of Random House, from *On Learning Golf* by Percy Boomer, Copyright © 1946 by Percy Boomer, published by Alfred A. Knopf, Inc.; Pages 62-67, from *Swing Easy, Hit Hard* by Julius Boros, Copyright © 1965 by Julius Boros and Lealand R. Gustavson, published by Harper & Row, Publishers; Pages 70-71, courtesy of Golf Digest, Inc., from *Thanks for the Game*, by Henry Cotton, Copyright © 1980 by Henry Cotton, published by Sidgwick & Jackson Ltd.; Pages 74-83, reprinted with permission of Random House, Inc., from *The Four Magic Moves To Winning Golf*, by Joe Dante with Len Elliott, Copyright © 1962 by McGraw-Hill Book Company, Inc., published by McGraw-Hill Companies; Pages 86-91, from *The Gate To Golf* by J. Douglas Edgar, Copyright © 1920, published by Edgar & Co.; Pages 94-99, reprinted with permission of Random House, Inc. from *The Inner Game Of Golf* by W. Timothy Gallwey, Copyright © 1979, 1981 by W. Timothy Gallwey; Pages 102-105, from *Secrets of Accurate Putting and Chipping* by Phil Galvano, Copyright © 1957 by Prentice Hall, Inc.; Pages 108-113, courtesy of Darrin Gee, from *One Shot at a Time: Seven Principles for Transforming Your Golf Game and Your Life* by Darrin Gee, Copyright © 2004 by Darrin Gee; Pages 116-121, courtesy of Golf Digest, Inc., from *Five Lessons The Modern Fundamentals Of Golf*, by Ben Hogan, Copyright © 1957 by Ben Hogan, published by Golf Digest, Inc.; Pages 124-127, courtesy of Charles Hogan, from *5 Days To Golfing Excellence*, by Charles Hogan, Copyright © 1986 by Charles N. Hogan; Pages 130-137, from *Practical Golf* by John Jacobs with Ken Bowden, Copyright © 1972 by John Jacobs and Ken Bowden, published by Quadrangle Books, Inc.; Pages 140-145, from *Swing The Clubhead And Cut Your Golf Score* by Ernest Jones and David Eisenberg, Copyright © 1952 by Ernest Jones and David Eisenberg, published by The Cornwall Press, Inc.; Pages 148-149, courtesy of The Golfing Machine, from *The Golfing Machine*, by Homer Kelley, Copyright © 1986, published by Star System Press; Pages 152-161, courtesy of David Lee, from *Gravity Golf*, by David Lee, Copyright © 1994 by David Carson Lee, published by Gravity Sports Concepts Inc.; Pages 164-169, from *Bobby Locke on Golf*, by Arthur d'Arcy Locke (Bobby Locke), Copyright © 1953 by Country Life Limited; Pages 172-175, courtesy of Golf Digest, Inc., from *One Move To Better Golf* by Carl Lohren with Larry Dennis, Copyright © 1975 by Golf Digest, Inc.; Pages 178-183, reprinted with permission of Scribner, an imprint of Simon & Schuster Adult Publishing Group, from *The Master Of Putting*, by George Low and Al Barkow. Copyright © 1983, by George Low and Al Barkow; Pages 186-193, reprinted with permission of Harper Collins Publishers, from *The X-Factor Swing*, by Jim McLean with John Andrisani. Copyright © 1996 by Jim McLean; Pages 196-201, courtesy of Golf Digest, Inc., from *Swing The Handle Not The Clubhead*, by Eddie Merrins with Dick Aultman, Copyright © 1973 by Golf Digest, Inc.; Pages 204-207, reprinted with permission of Johnny Miller Enterprises, from *Pure Golf* by Johnny Miller and Dale Shankland. Copyright © 1976 by Johnny Miller, published by Doubleday and Company, Inc., New York; Pages 210-217, from *A New Way to Better Golf* by Alex J. Morrison, Copyright © 1935 by Alex J. Morrison, published by Simon & Schuster, Inc.; Pages 220-225, courtesy of Golf Magazine, May 1975, from *It Makes Sense to Start From The Top* by Andrew Mullin, Copyright © 1975 by Times Mirror Magazines, Inc.; Pages 228-239, courtesy of Jim McNaney, from *Natural Golf: 7 Minutes to Better Golf* by Peter Fox and Ed Woronicz, Copyright © 2002 by Natural Golf Corporation; Pages 242-247, courtesy of Golf Digest, Inc., from *Shape Your Swing The Modern Way*, by Byron Nelson with Larry Dennis, Copyright © 1976 by Golf Digest, Inc.; Pages 250-251, from *Joe Norwood's Golf-O-Metrics* with Marilynn Smith and Stanley Blicker, Copyright © 1978 by Joseph Norwood,

Marilynn Louise Smith and Stanley Blicker, published by Doubleday & Company, Inc., New York; Pages 254-257, reprinted with permission Random House, from *Tour Tempo* by John Novosel with John Garrity, Copyright © 2004 by John Novosel with John Garrity, published by Doubleday & Company, Inc., New York; Pages 260-263, courtesy of Bruce Warren Ollstein from *Combat Golf* by Bruce Warren Ollstein. Copyright © 1996 by Bruce Warren Ollstein; Pages 266-273, reprinted with permission of Random House, Inc., from *Dave Pelz's Putting Bible* by Dave Pelz with James A. Frank, Copyright © 2000 by David T. Pelz, published by Broadway Books, a division of Random House, Inc.; Pages 276-281, reprinted with permission of Random House, Inc., from *Dave Pelz's Short Game Bible* by Dave Pelz with James A. Frank, Copyright © 1999 by David T. Pelz, published by Doubleday & Company, Inc., New York; Pages 284-287, courtesy of Juan (Chi Chi) Rodriguez from *Chi Chi's Secrets of Power Golf* by Juan (Chi Chi) Rodriguez. Copyright © 1967 by Juan Rodriguez, published by The Viking Press, Inc., New York; Pages 290-295, reprinted with permission of Simon & Schuster Adult Publishing Group from *Golf is Not a Game of Perfect* by Robert Rotella. Copyright © 1995 by Robert Rotella; Pages 298-309, courtesy of Golf Digest, Inc., from *The Short Way to Lower Scoring* by Paul Runyan with Dick Aultman, Copyright © 1979 by Golf Digest, Inc.; Pages 312-317, courtesy of Jennifer Scott, from *Get The Hole in Your Head-Own The Zone* by Jennifer Scott; Pages 320-327, reprinted with permission of G.P. Putnam's Sons, a division of Penguin Group from *Extraordinary Golf – The Art of The Possible* by Fred Shoemaker and Pete Shoemaker. Copyright © 1996 by Fred Shoemaker and Pete Shoemaker; Pages 330-335, courtesy of Golf Digest, Inc., from *The Touch System For Better Golf* by Bob Toski with Dick Aultman, Copyright © 1971 by Golf Digest, Inc.; Pages 338-341, from *The Perfect Putting Method* by Paul Trevillion, Copyright © 1978, published by Winchester Press, New York; Pages 344-347, from *The Complete Golfer* by Harry Vardon. Copyright © 1905 by Harry Vardon, published by McClure/Phillips; Pages 350-357, courtesy of Paul Wilson, from *Swing Machine Golf* by Paul Wilson with Ken Steven, Copyright © 2002 by Paul Wilson, published by Storytrend Publishing, a division of Growth-Trend Marketing, Inc.; pages 360-365, courtesy of Michael Witte, Inc., from *The Pinch* by Michael Witte, Copyright © 2004 by Michael Witte; Pages 368-375, from *Golf Monthly's Lessons with Mr. X*. Copyright © 1968 by Mr. X and 'Golf Monthly', published by Pelham Books Ltd.; Pages 380-385, courtesy of Tim Nicholls, Count Yogi Golf Co., from *Five Simple Steps To Perfect Golf* by Count Yogi, Copyright © 1973 by Count Hillary Yogi, published by Nash Publishing Corporation. IMAGE CREDITS: Pages 3, 61, 115, 195, 203, 283, 297 courtesy of AP Wide World Photos; page 19 courtesy of Jimmy Ballard; pages 377, 378, 381-384 courtesy of Tim Nicholls, Count Yogi Golf Co.; page 73 courtesy of Eleanor Dante; pages 37, 38, 40-43 photographs by Randall Cheney, courtesy of Doug Ferreri; page 101 courtesy of Phil Galvano II; pages 14-16, 26, 116-118, 120-121, 197-198, 242-244, 291, 304, 329-332, 334-335 courtesy of Golf Digest, Inc; pages 116-118, 120-121 courtesy of Golf Digest and the Estate of Valerie Fox Hogan; pages 151, 154, 155 courtesy of David Lee/Gravity Sports Concepts Inc; pages 187-188 reproduced with permission of Harper Collins Publishers; page 123 courtesy of Chuck Hogan; page 107 photographs by Michael Darden, courtesy of Darrin and Darien Gee; page 110 photograph by Toby Hoogs, courtesy of Darrin and Darien Gee; page 185, 269, 270, 284, 286 photographs © Leonard Kamsler; pages 205-207 courtesy of Johnny Miller Enterprises; pages 232-239 courtesy of Ed Woronicz and Jim McNaney/Natural Golf Corporation; pages 311, 313, 314, 316 courtesy of Jennifer Scott; pages 69, 129 courtesy of Phil Sheldon © Phil Sheldon Golf Picture Library; pages 349-357 illustrations © Geral Billinghurst, photographs © Liam Sharp, courtesy of Ken Steven/Storytrend Publishing; page 147 courtesy of Joe Daniels/The Golfing Machine; page 343 courtesy of The Tiegreen Collection; page 359 photograph by Tim Parker; pages 361-363, 365 illustrations © Michael Witte. All the photographs our golf model, PGA Professional Brian Crowell, were shot by Leonard Kamsler.

ABOUT THE AUTHOR

George Peper was for twenty-five years the Editor-in-Chief of *GOLF Magazine*. Under his leadership the magazine became the most widely read publication in the game and was nominated for four National Magazine Awards.

Today Peper is Editor-at-Large of *Links Magazine*, where his column appears in each issue. He is the author of fifteen previous books, including the bestselling *Golf Courses of the PGA Tour* (over 400,000 copies in print) and *Cinderella Story*, in collaboration with actor Bill Murray.

For twenty years Peper wrote and produced the Masters Annual, the official chronicle of the Masters Tournament. In addition, he has written the scripts for over a dozen videos and TV specials. His 1999 script for *The Story of Golf*, a two-hour documentary for PBS, brought him an Emmy nomination.

Peper earned a B.A. from Princeton and studied toward a PhD in comparative literature at Yale before joining *GOLF Magazine*. A five-handicap golfer, he is a member of Sleepy Hollow Country Club (NY), Ballybunion in Ireland, and five clubs in Scotland, including the Royal & Ancient, where he recently became the first American member of the Club Committee.

Peper's wife, Libby, is a freelance illustrator whose vivid paintings of golf holes have appeared in numerous publications and on all three major television networks. In the fall of 2003, when the younger of their sons headed off to college, the Pepers sold their home in New York and moved to an apartment they have long owned, alongside the 18th hole of the Old Course at St. Andrews. George's experiences there will form the basis of his next book.

ARRAN HOUSE PRESS

INDEX

INDEX